THE TRUMP INDICTMENTS

THE
TRUMP
INDICTMENTS

*The Historic Charging Documents
with Commentary*

Introduced, Annotated,
and with Supporting Materials by

MELISSA MURRAY *AND*
ANDREW WEISSMANN

W. W. NORTON & COMPANY
Independent Publishers Since 1923

For information about permission to reproduce selections from this book, write to
Permissions, W. W. Norton & Company, Inc., 500 Fifth Avenue, New York, NY 10110

For information about special discounts for bulk purchases, please contact
W. W. Norton Special Sales at specialsales@wwnorton.com or 800-233-4830

Manufacturing by Lakeside Book Company
Book design by Lovedog Studio
Production manager: Julia Druskin

ISBN 978-1-324-07920-0 (pbk)

W. W. Norton & Company, Inc., 500 Fifth Avenue, New York, N.Y. 10110
www.wwnorton.com

W. W. Norton & Company Ltd., 15 Carlisle Street, London W1D 3BS

2 3 4 5 6 7 8 9 0

CONTENTS

THE PEOPLE OF THE STATE OF NEW YORK V. DONALD J. TRUMP
(NEW YORK INDICTMENT)

Preface

THE PURPOSE OF THIS BOOK

T HE PURPOSE OF THIS BOOK IS TO OFFER YOU AN OPPOR-
tunity to engage with, understand, and form your own conclusions about the four historic indictments against a former president.
Our commentary is meant to assist in that process. In the main introduction to the book we describe the broader context for these four
historic documents. Specifically, we provide a comparative perspective
that sheds light on how other legal systems have handled the shared
goal of ensuring accountability and a commitment to the rule of law for
misdeeds by senior political leaders. We then assess if Trump is being
treated comparably to others who are similarly situated—a hallmark
of a judicial system committed to the Aristotelian principle of treating
likes alike.

In addition to the main introduction, each of the four indictments is
preceded by short introductory remarks, which give some useful background. Finally, and significantly, each indictment includes generous
annotations from us, providing explanations and more granular detail.
In these asides, we account for prosecutorial decisions, consider various
decisions to be made at trial, and present "insider notes."

We hope you will find these materials useful for cultivating a deeper
understanding of the indictments. In the end, the book is intended as a
guide that readers may reference throughout the impending trials in the
four cases, and that will continue to inform discussion of and inquiry
into these historic prosecutions for years to come.

———

THE BOOK IS ORGANIZED by the four indictments, ordered according to our view of their significance: District of Columbia, Georgia,

Florida, and New York. Each of the four sections contains the brief indictment introduction, a cast of characters for that indictment, and the indictment itself. A brief timeline of key events follows the book's main introduction; an all-encompassing cast of characters appears at the end of the book.

INTRODUCTION

I could stand in the middle of Fifth Avenue and
shoot somebody, and I wouldn't lose any voters,
OK? It's, like, incredible.
                    —DONALD TRUMP

FROM THE START, DONALD TRUMP'S PRESIDENCY WAS unorthodox. Trump rose to fame in the crucible of 1980s New York City as a brash and flamboyant real estate developer. In a series of books and interviews, he touted himself as one of the country's most successful—and wealthy—businessmen. But even as he courted fame, Trump also courted controversy. Critics insisted that his real estate prowess was overstated—and that his empire was built on an uneven foundation, routinely teetering on the brink of bankruptcy.

No matter. For Trump, image was everything. On his telling, simply projecting an image of success, fame, and wealth was enough to manifest it as reality. And he was mostly right. Despite New York's oscillating real estate market, Trump reinvented himself in the 2000s as a television star who played a successful and wealthy businessman. The reality television hit *The Apprentice* featured a cast of wannabe moguls all vying for the chance to be Trump's right-hand man—to help the professed real estate titan oversee and run his vast empire.

Arguably, the show did very little to advance the careers of its various contestants. But it succeeded in introducing Donald Trump to much of America. Trump's fame had been concentrated in the New York press and in the city's real estate market. *The Apprentice* made Trump a household name—and gave Middle America the impression of Trump as a decisive, successful corporate titan who capably managed a sprawling business empire. Trump rode *The Apprentice* and his newfound national profile all the way to the bank—and, improbably, to 1600 Pennsylvania Avenue.

Despite his shifting political affiliations (he has alternately identified as a Republican, an Independent, and a Democrat) and high-profile friendships with Democrats (Bill and Hillary Clinton attended his 2005 wedding to Slovenian model Melania Knauss), Trump hitched his wagon to the Republican Party during President Barack Obama's first term. Indeed, Obama's two terms in the White House appeared to animate Trump's political ambitions, at which he had hinted at various points in his life. He routinely took to conservative television and radio outlets to deride President Obama—and his signature domestic policy initiative, the Affordable Care Act—as "big" government. He also was a leading promoter of the "birther" conspiracy theory, which posited that Obama, the first African American to be elected president, was not born on American soil, rendering his presidency invalid. On more than one occasion, Trump called upon the president to produce his birth certificate for inspection.

Although the birther theory was widely debunked, Trump nonetheless continued to voice claims that the Obama administration was both illegitimate and an utter failure. Specifically, Trump maintained that Obama was a "disaster" as a president, leaving the country weak and vulnerable to foreign threats and terrorism. And Trump saw himself as the antidote to all that Obama had wrought. For a time, Trump flirted with a possible 2012 presidential run against the incumbent Obama. He eventually abandoned the idea during the Republican primary in order to film another season of *The Apprentice*. Notably, in his statement withdrawing from the primary, Trump insisted, without evidence, that his "potential candidacy continues to be validated by ranking at the top of the Republican contenders in polls across the country."

As Obama handily defeated the Republican nominee, former Massachusetts governor Mitt Romney, cruising into a second term, Trump's criticism of the Obama administration grew louder. But notably, his critiques also focused on leading Republicans, whom he denounced for refusing to stand up to Obama. Over time, the tenor of Trump's broadsides—against Obama and against the Republican establishment—intensified. On Trump's telling, Obama had stoked racial resentment, opened the borders to Central American immigrants, bound the United States to the United Nations and multilateralism, and fueled the rise of the Islamic State.

Trump's critiques quickly took root in the fertile soil tilled by the nascent Tea Party movement, which touted fiscal conservatism and smaller government, but also soon gave rise to a populist strain of nationalistic conservatism that resisted globalism, immigration, and Beltway elitism in favor of supposedly more homespun values. And in a stunning marriage of Trump's political ambitions and this ascendant populism, on June 16, 2015, Trump descended a golden escalator at Trump Tower in New York City to formally declare his candidacy for the presidency.

To be sure, Trump was an imperfect vessel for the hopes of the rising populist tide. After all, he was an Ivy League–educated, twice-divorced city slicker who rose to fame as the scion of a real estate mogul. He bridged the divide between himself and his supporters with shared nostalgia for an America that they believed was disappearing from view—or had already been lost. Undergirding this nostalgia was economic anxiety leavened with an unhealthy dose of racism and xenophobia. Despite his elite background, Trump intuited that he could unite a portion of the working class and the middle and upper classes by tapping into widespread fears that they were losing ground. It was not hard to stoke these anxieties. By the 2010s, the demands of globalization had led to the outsourcing of factory jobs to overseas workers, while spawning an information economy that prioritized higher education and elite expertise. For some, these shifts, coupled with the growing wave of immigration from the Global South and demands for racial justice in the United States, concretized the sinking feeling that "ordinary"—i.e., white—Americans were losing ground, and losing their country. Trump would "Make America Great Again."

On the campaign trail, he was plain-spoken, delighting crowds by refusing to be "politically correct." He said the quiet parts out loud, mocking his critics, including a disabled journalist. Ripping a page from the 1968 Nixon campaign, he hammered on the need for "law and order," raising fears of increasing urban crime and anti-American terrorism. In particular, he singled out Muslims, insisting that they "hate" America, and thus posed an existential threat to the nation and its citizens. If elected, he vowed to secure the nation's borders, deal harshly with criminals, and improve the economy. In short, he would abandon Obama's vision of global communitarianism in favor of a more insular commitment to America and Americans. He would put "America first," allegedly restoring the nation to its earlier greatness, at home and abroad. After all, he was a "winner." And under his leadership, America would once again be a nation of winners.

For many, the Trump campaign, steeped in bombast and nativism, seemed doomed to failure. Hillary Clinton, the Democratic nominee and a former senator and secretary of state, seemed poised to make history as the first woman to be elected president. Clinton herself was no stranger to controversy. Deeply unpopular to many during her husband's first presidential term (1993–1997), she won the admiration of large swaths of Americans—and remade her image—in the wake of his cheating scandal and impeachment. After Bill Clinton's presidency, she had served in Washington, DC, as a hard-working junior senator and on the world stage as Obama's first secretary of state. Many expected that she would overcome the headwinds against the first woman as a major party candidate to run for president and handily beat Trump, whose own candidacy was, for many, a national joke. Clinton's email server scandal—and Trump's insistence that she should be "locked . . . up"—undermined her appeal. But by October 2016, after the release of a 2005 *Access Hollywood* interview between Billy Bush and Donald Trump in which Trump bragged that his celebrity allowed him to grab women "by the pussy," Clinton seemed headed for victory—and a reprise of Obama-style wonky governance. FBI director James Comey's late October surprise announcement that he was reopening the Hillary Clinton email investigation, in tandem with Russia's leak of hacked Clinton campaign emails, blunted the front-runner's momentum.

As the election returns rolled in on November 8, 2016, it seemed clear that, although Trump had not won the popular vote, the Electoral College would give him the victory. Trump cobbled together a coalition of voters that spanned the socioeconomic spectrum, including social conservatives and Christian evangelicals energized by his promise to appoint Supreme Court justices who would overrule *Roe v. Wade*. Winning by the slimmest margins in midwestern battleground states, Trump took the presidency, shocking many, including Trump himself.

WE HAVE RECAPITULATED this well-known recent history—seared into the memory of many Americans, regardless of where they are on the political spectrum—because it introduces leitmotifs that recurred throughout the Trump presidency, and indeed, are evident in the conduct that undergirds the criminal allegations in the four indictments presented in this volume. This history suggests an ongoing habit of promoting overblown and false claims—whether about birtherism, his wealth, his status in the 2012 field of Republican hopefuls, or even the height of Trump Tower in New York City. More troublingly, his penchant for ignoring hard facts would include promoting the ingestion of bleach as a remedy for the coronavirus. It also signaled a strategy of breaking norms and rules that would open a vein of distrust and grievance, and in turn, allow Trump to widen the Overton window of acceptable presidential conduct. His "brand" was transgression—an id with no super ego.

Trump's willingness to transgress norms contributed to his ability to command the attention—and imagination—of his supporters. His P. T. Barnum–esque approach to governing commanded the news cycle and snuffed out interest in Republican and Democratic rivals. With scant evidence of his ability to actually govern, Trump convinced a considerable portion of American voters of the need to "drain the swamp" and install in the White House a total outsider, a remarkable feat given his limited experience managing a largely unregulated family business.

Trump's unorthodox—and untested—approach to governing gave rise to a spate of legal challenges during his presidency, well before these four indictments were handed down. One cannot fully understand the genesis of the four indictments without examining the many legal skirmishes that punctuated the Trump presidency and the transition between the Trump and Biden administrations.

From the start, Trump's inner circle of advisors was unusual—to say the least. Several of them, including Steve Bannon, Michael Flynn, Richard Gates, Paul Manafort, Peter Navarro, George Papadopoulos, and Roger Stone, later would face criminal liability. And Trump's own conduct was similarly atypical. The first six months of his presidency were shadowed by claims that he had improperly fired James Comey. Comey became nationally known when, as FBI director, he took the controversial step, in the run-up to the 2016 election, of alerting Congress that he was reopening an investigation into then-candidate Hillary Clinton's maintenance of a personal email server during her tenure as secretary of state.

In January 2017, as the presidential transition was underway, Comey testified to Congress confirming Russian interference in the 2016 US elections, as well as an ongoing investigation into that interference. In March 2017, Comey confirmed that the FBI was investigating links between Trump associates and Russian officials and spies. In May 2017, after grand jury subpoenas had been issued to secure the testimony and records of Trump associates in conjunction with the Russia investigation, Trump unceremoniously dismissed Comey—only the second time an FBI director has been sacked since the bureau's founding. Comey's firing raised concerns that Trump's actions were self-serving and politically motivated. Indeed, Comey's firing prompted the Department of Justice ("DOJ") to appoint Robert S. Mueller III as special counsel to investigate the prospect of election interference. As the indictments collected here suggest, similar concerns regarding Trump's alleged efforts to protect himself from political or legal liabilities have shadowed Trump's other actions as president and his response to the 2020 election, which Joe Biden won.

The Comey firing is emblematic of another leitmotif in Trump's public life: the avoidance of meaningful accountability. As a candidate in the Republican primary, Trump boasted that he could shoot someone on Fifth Avenue in New York City and get away with it. So far, he has been proven effectively correct. He faced no meaningful consequences for his firing of Comey. And while Special Counsel Robert Mueller's investigation laid out numerous factual circumstances involving Trump that strongly suggested the obstruction of justice, Trump's status as a sitting president shielded him, per Justice Department policy, from any federal criminal indictment. As Special Counsel Mueller observed in congressional testimony, the mechanism for holding a sitting president accountable must be a constitutional one—namely, impeachment. Here too, however, Trump managed to elude ultimate accountability.

Not just once, but twice. Donald Trump achieved the ignominious distinction of being the only president in American history to be impeached twice. The first Trump impeachment, in January 2020, arose from a phone call. According to sources within the State Department, while on a phone call with Ukrainian president Volodymyr Zelenskyy,

Trump allegedly threatened to withhold congressionally appropriated military aid to Ukraine unless Zelenskyy agreed to say that the Ukrainian government was opening an investigation into Joe Biden and his son Hunter. At the time, Biden, the former vice president, was a candidate for the Democratic nomination. Trump insisted that the investigation need not be real—it just needed to give the appearance, ostensibly for prospective voters in the United States, that a foreign country was investigating Biden and his son for wrongdoing. In hindsight, the Russian invasion of Ukraine in February 2022, and the ongoing (as of this writing) war between the two countries, make clear why Trump's alleged threat was so compelling—American military aid was a vital part of Ukraine's ability to defend against its bellicose neighbor.

And critically, in the allegations about the Zelenskyy phone call, we can see the classic Trump tools at work—tools that would be redeployed in the conduct alleged in these indictments. During the phone call, Trump allegedly threatened Zelenskyy with the withdrawal of congressionally appropriated aid in order to induce the Ukrainian government to acquiesce to his demands for an investigation that would undermine a political rival's standing with the voting public. As the indictments maintain, in different circumstances, Trump routinely threatened retribution or political or legal consequences in order to persuade others to yield to his will and take improper actions to deceive the electorate.

Although a majority of the House of Representatives impeached Trump for his alleged conduct in the Ukrainian phone call—admitting Trump to the small fraternity of impeached presidents—there was not the requisite Senate supermajority to convict on the articles of impeachment. Trump remained in office, secure in the knowledge that he could not be criminally prosecuted and that impeachment was a paper tiger.

The second impeachment was animated by events that were even more alarming than the Ukrainian phone call. Following the January 6, 2021, assault by tens of thousands of Trump supporters on the United States Capitol, a majority of the House of Representatives again impeached the now lame-duck president. But even though millions of Americans watched in horror as the Capitol's defenses were breached on January 6, Trump would again avoid accountability. Some argued that impeachment was an improper remedy, because Trump would no longer be in office at the time of the Senate trial. To this end, the chief justice of the United States, who ordinarily would be required to preside over the impeachment trial of a sitting president, declined to preside over the second Trump impeachment. Instead, Vermont senator Patrick Leahy, as President Pro Tempore of the Senate, served as the presiding officer. And once again, there was no Senate supermajority to convict Trump of the impeachment charges. Enough Republican senators voted to protect Trump rather than their own lives or American democracy. Senator Mitt Romney has reported that some senators feared that a vote to convict would imperil the safety of their families and thus was not worth it—again suggesting the efficacy of Trump's strategy of using threats of political retribution or worse.

Yet the desire for greater clarity and accountability regarding the events that preceded and occurred during the Capitol riot led to new legal developments. In 2021, a bipartisan congressional committee was established to investigate the events of January 6. After a series of widely watched hearings that revealed the scope of the plot to overturn American democracy, in December 2022, the committee released its final report, which included sworn testimony from many Trump allies as to efforts to manipulate the 2020 election. The committee thereafter made most of its witness interview transcripts and exhibits public. In addition, the committee referred certain individuals to the DOJ for criminal charges, including the forty-fifth president of the United States, Donald Trump.

THE UNITED STATES IS venturing into uncharted territory with not one, but four, criminal indictments of a former president for crimes alleged to have been committed before, during, and after his presidency. But we are not the first country to have faced the challenge of how to deal with corruption by its most senior elected officials. This challenge has arisen often in other countries, including allies that we consider to be, and refer to as, "Western"-style democracies.

International comparisons offer at least two lessons. First, there is precedent for holding even former presidents to the rule of law without a country descending into what has been derogatorily referred to as a "banana republic." The recent examples of such righteous prosecutions are thus instructive that what we are currently engaged in here in the United States is a difficult, but normal, part of being a nation of laws.

Second, international precedents delineate what distinguishes a righteous prosecution of a political leader from a "show trial" of a political adversary selected precisely because of the political threat the person posed to the regime launching the prosecution. We can compare the four Trump indictments—in DC, Georgia, Florida, and New York—to determine which category they might fall into, that is, a righteous indictment or a "show trial" undertaken for political purposes.

In short: the DC January 6 trial, the Georgia election interference case, and the Florida documents case all reflect charges that have a long precedent of being charged against nonpolitical actors and people who appear far less culpable than Trump. The New York case is the only one where there is a dearth of cases in which similar charges were brought against nonpolitical actors, as we will discuss.

INTERNATIONAL PRECEDENTS

As Jack Smith knows well from his time as a lead prosecutor for the International Criminal Court (ICC), many countries have had to address alleged corruption and crimes by political leaders or former political leaders. The situation is not unusual, even though it poses unique and serious challenges.

Consider some recent examples. France has prosecuted not just one former president, but two presidents and one prime minister. Most recently, Nicolas Sarkozy (French president from 2007 to 2012) was charged with and convicted of illegally financing his presidential campaign as well as bribing a judge. He is awaiting yet another trial for more corruption and campaign financing crimes related to allegations that his campaign received illegal funds from Libya, among other charges. And, in a common playbook we may soon see in the United States, Sarkozy has been able to delay serving time in jail by appealing his criminal convictions.

In bringing those charges, French prosecutors could draw on their country's experiences having prosecuted successfully former French president Jacques Chirac (1995–2007) for illegal diversion of public funds, and French prime minister François Fillon (2007–2012), who was sentenced to four years in prison for embezzlement.

Lest one think France unique among European Union countries, turn to the East. German president Christian Wulff (2010–2012) was charged with corruption, and was acquitted in 2014; but that victory was cold comfort for him, as he had resigned in 2012 as a result of allegations that he accepted various financial gifts when he was governor of one of the German states.

And many readers will recall the criminal case brought against Italian prime minister Silvio Berlusconi (who served from 1994 to 1995, 2001 to 2006, and 2008 to 2011). He was convicted in 2012 of tax fraud, false accounting, and embezzlement. And like Fillon, he was sentenced to four years in prison. At the time of his death, Berlusconi was awaiting trial for inducing people to lie while he was prime minister.

European nations are not alone in the criminal prosecution of political leaders. Israel has seen Prime Minister Ehud Olmert (2006–2009) charged, convicted, and imprisoned for fraud, corruption, and obstruction of justice. And, of course, the current prime minister, Benjamin Netanyahu (1996–1999, 2009–2021, 2022–present) is, as of this writing, facing charges of bribery and fraud in three cases.

In the prosecution of Argentinian leader Cristina Fernández de Kirchner (president 2007–2015, vice president 2019–present), she was not simply convicted in December 2022 (of corruption for awarding of public works during her presidency) and sentenced to six years in jail.; she was also disqualified from holding further public office—a question the United States now faces.

We could go on: presidents or prime ministers in Brazil, South Korea, and Taiwan have all been recently and successfully prosecuted for a host of crimes. A chart should be illuminating:

COUNTRY/NAME/OFFICE

BRAZIL
Luiz Inácio Lula da Silva
President, 2003–2010
President, 2023–present

- Convicted in 2018 of taking bribes from engineering firms in return for public contracts.
- Spent a year and a half in prison.
- Convictions were annulled in March 2021 for lack of jurisdiction.
- In April 2021, the Brazil high court confirmed the annulments, paving the way for a new presidential run.
- Reelected president in 2023.

JAPAN
KAKUEI TANAKA
Prime Minister, 1972–1974

- Convicted in 1983 of accepting a $1.8 million bribe from the Lockheed Aircraft Corporation during his 1972–1974 term in office.
- Sentenced to four years in jail and a fine of 500 million yen.
- In July 1987, the Tokyo High Court upheld the conviction.

SOUTH KOREA
PARK GEUN-HYE
President, 2013–2017

- In 2017, Park became South Korea's first democratically elected president to be impeached and removed from office.
- Convicted of abuse of power and coercion in 2018 on the view that she used her office to pressure conglomerates to give millions to foundations run by a friend.
- Sentenced to twenty-two years in prison.
- Also found guilty of leaking confidential presidential documents to her longtime friend.
- Pardoned because of poor health in 2021 by Moon Jae-in, outgoing president of the opposing political party.

SOUTH KOREA
LEE MYUNG-BAK
President, 2008–2013

- Sentenced in 2020 to a seventeen-year term on bribery and embezzlement charges.
- Pardoned in 2022 by President Yoon Suk Yeol.
- Fine nullified (unpaid 8.2 billion South Korean won of the fine of 13 billion won imposed).

. . . .

SOUTH KOREA
LEE WAN-KOO
Prime Minister, 2015

- Imposition in 2016 of a suspended eight-month sentence for receiving illegal political funds.

. . . .

TAIWAN
CHEN SHUI-BIAN
President, 2000–2008

- Convicted in 2009 for money laundering and accepting bribes.
- Initially sentenced to life in prison—on appeal, the sentence was reduced to a nineteen-year prison term.
- Granted medical parole in 2015.

THE INTERNATIONAL CRIMINAL COURT

The International Criminal Court is another particularly apt and useful model. Useful because the court, which is in The Hague, Netherlands, owes its very existence to international support for the prosecution of senior political and military leaders. The very first lead prosecutor was Luis Moreno Ocampo (2003–2012), who made his name spearheading a series of criminal cases against Argentine generals. The United States, as of late, has been supportive of the court; indeed, recently it shared with the ICC evidence of Russian war crimes in Ukraine.

Special Counsel Jack Smith is well aware of these international examples of political leaders being brought to account for criminal misdeeds. Smith was an investigator for the ICC from 2008 to 2010, working on investigations into foreign government officials and militias for war crimes, crimes against humanity, and genocide. And from 2018 to 2022—that is, just before his current special counsel appointment, Smith was the Kosovo chief prosecutor. In that role he investigated and charged former Kosovo president Hashim Thaçi and commanders of the Kosovo Liberation Army.

Smith's time at the ICC came after he had served for decades as a state and federal prosecutor in New York (in the Manhattan District

Attorney's Office that brought the first Trump indictment, and the United States Attorney's Office for the Eastern District of New York). From 2010 to 2015, he served as the head of the DOJ's Public Integrity Section, which oversees national cases against politicians, regardless of political affiliation.

The state prosecutors who are overseeing the Manhattan and Georgia cases are also career prosecutors, with long and distinguished state or federal experience (or both), but Smith is uniquely aware of the importance of such prosecutions in the effort to support a global commitment to the rule of law. His experience has alerted him to the dire need for leaders who have committed serious crimes to be held to account, without caving to over-hyped fears that such prosecutions would render a country a so-called banana republic. Indeed, one might argue that by *failing* to hold corrupt leaders to account, a nation is transformed into a "banana republic."

SHOW TRIALS

There is an important caveat to the use of international prosecutions as models for the prosecutions of Donald Trump: the reality that some of these examples are mere "show trials" animated by political considerations—precisely what we do not want to emulate. That is the claim made by Trump himself, who decries the prosecutions as witch hunts by political operatives bent on defeating him in the courts since they cannot do so at the polls.

Setting aside Trump's particular style of invective, differentiating a "show trial" from a righteous prosecution is not actually that difficult. Examples of the former are certainly legion and from them we can glean two features that can be used to separate the two.

We could take as an example of a show trial almost any Russian criminal case against a political dissident (consider, for example, Alexei Navalny or Aleksandr Solzhenitsyn). These involve trumped-up charges, meaning charges without the requisite proof or proof that was manufactured by the state.

But there is a slightly more complicated type of show trial: a case that may be supported by legitimate proof, but is brought by a political opponent of the defendant for a crime that is not normally charged. An example is the prosecution of Yulia Tymoshenko in Ukraine. The criminal trial occurred under President Viktor Yanukovych, a Russian crony who had risen to power with the assistance of his American campaign manager Paul Manafort. (Manafort's right-hand man in Kiev was the Russian Konstantin Kilimnik, who is under indictment in the United States in a case brought by Special Counsel Robert Mueller. Kilimnik was identified in a bipartisan Senate Intelligence report into Russian election interference as a Russian spy.)

One of Manafort's jobs for President Yanukovych was overseeing a multi-million-dollar campaign to whitewash the criminal trial as being legitimate, after it was widely condemned in the United States and the European Union as an example of selective prosecution. Manafort's effort failed, and for good reason.

Tymoshenko was the prime minister of Ukraine in 2005 and from 2007 to 2010. She was the first and remains the only woman to hold that position. In 2010 she ran against Yanukovych for president and lost by several percentage points. Notably, Yanukovych, with Manafort at his side, ran on a campaign to lock up his female rival. (It was thus unsettling to see Manafort work for Trump in 2016, when the Republican candidate repeatedly called for *his* female political rival, Hillary Clinton, to be locked up.)

When Tymoshenko lost, Yanukovych actually carried out his campaign slogan, and Tymoshenko was tried for abuse of power for negotiations she undertook, as prime minister, for gas from Russia (prior trumped-up charges against her for misuse of funds had been thrown out or suspended). The problem with the charge was not that Tymoshenko was necessarily not guilty of acting without the authority of the legislature when she signed the contract (although that was questionable at best, and the proof suspect), but that the charge was hardly ever enforced and could surely have been lodged against many other Ukrainian politicians who were not particularly well known for their scrupulous adherence to the law.

Tymoshenko was convicted by the judge overseeing the case, after a trial in which Yanukovych himself testified. She was sentenced to seven years in prison and could not run for office during that term. She also was ordered to repay the astronomical sum of $188 million.

Numerous US officials—Republicans and Democrats alike, including John McCain and Hillary Clinton—protested Tymoshenko's incarceration as a product of selective prosecution. Indeed, Congress passed two bipartisan resolutions calling for her release. So did numerous EU countries and human rights organizations. Tellingly, when Yanukovych fled to Russia after the Maidan Uprising in 2014, the Ukrainian parliament voted to release Tymoshenko and decriminalized the conduct charged. Ukraine subsequently agreed in the European Court of Human Rights that the prosecution had been politically motivated and had violated Tymoshenko's rights.

What can we learn from this case and other show trials? First, in examining the validity of a prosecution it is necessary to fully understand the proof gathered by the government and any ways in which that proof might be tainted. For example: Was it illegally manufactured? This determination must normally await the trial in the case—and no definitive conclusion can or should be made until such a time—but one can sometimes glean some revealing information about the proof before a trial, such as from hearings in Congress or in court or from court filings, among other sources.

Second, even in a case in which there appears to be adequate and legitimate evidence, it should be asked if the charge is one that is routinely brought by the government and, if not, whether there is a good reason the charge is being pursued here. In other words, it is not enough that a criminal case *can* be brought. The rule of law requires more to demonstrate that the case is not merely politically targeting an adversary with a charge that is seldom if ever used or that is so mundane that everyone or anyone could be charged with it (for example, a traffic violation). In the United States, the legal standard for "selective prosecution" requires showing, in addition, an invidious purpose, such as targeting someone based on race or religion. If we are to avoid becoming Ukraine under the corrupt Yanukovych presidency, such an inquiry must be made and satisfied.

THE TRUMP INDICTMENTS

Three of the four Trump indictments—those in DC, Georgia, and Florida—readily pass the test for adherence to the rule of law. Why? Because there is ample, documented proof that the charges that have been lodged against the former US president have been brought many times before against others for similar—or in some cases, less egregious—conduct. And the known proof—from the January 6 committee hearing and subsequent release of its report and the underlying evidence it had collected during its investigation, and from court filings—gives every indication that the criminal cases are supported by evidence that is unusually strong. Does that mean a jury will unanimously find proof beyond a reasonable doubt in each case and on each charge? No. But it makes it considerably less than likely that a jury would find unanimously that Trump is not guilty of all the charges. (In the federal system and in New York and Georgia, a jury must be unanimous to convict *or* acquit.)

Reasonable minds may differ about the New York "hush money" case. The issue is not the strength of the case, which appears quite solid, but whether such charges are routinely filed against others in comparable situations. The New York charges are felony counts, and therein lies the rub. The indictment charges Trump with falsifying business records in the first degree, which is a class E felony. But simply falsifying business records is chargeable only as a class A *misdemeanor* in New York, and is criminalized as falsifying business records *in the second degree*. However, if the falsification of the records is undertaken with the intent to commit another crime or to aid or conceal the commission of another crime—whether that other crime is a felony or a misdemeanor—then the legislature considers the falsification offense more serious and permits the conduct to be charged as a "first-degree" felony. Accordingly, to render this a felony, the district attorney had to tie the falsification to some other contemplated offense. That is, charging falsifying business records as a felony requires the DA to prove beyond a reasonable doubt that the falsification of business records was undertaken as part of a broader effort to commit another crime or to conceal the commission of another crime.

To justify bringing the charges, the experienced DA Alvin Bragg gave a press conference where he addressed the issue central to the rule of law: Would a defendant who was not Donald Trump be treated the same way? Bragg insisted that the prosecution was not an effort to selectively target Trump, pointing to the fact that the office routinely (and recently) prosecuted falsification of business records charges as felonies and noting other prosecutions for the same crime.

While this is correct, this case is notable in that the *only* felony charge to be prosecuted is the crime of falsification of business records. Typically, a falsification of business records felony charge accompanies another, more serious felony. For instance, an employee who engages in embezzlement from her employer and creates a fake invoice to cover up the crime would be charged with both embezzlement and a business record felony.

The case raises other questions, as well. The DA has (commendably) filed in court a notice that enumerates for Trump and his counsel the other crimes upon which the DA intends to rely to support enhancing the falsification of business records charge to a felony—that is, the predicate crimes that, if found by the jury, would render the falsification of the records a felony, not a misdemeanor. Those crimes include federal and state election law crimes, tax crimes, and other misdemeanors. The legal strength of those predicates vary, as it is not entirely certain that all of these crimes can serve as predicate crimes in this context. For example, it is not clear that the New York falsification of business records statute contemplates the prospect of a federal crime—any federal crime—as a predicate crime to render a state misdemeanor charge a felony. Nor is it clear whether the New York legislature intended for only New York State offenses to serve as predicate crimes to enhance state-level misdemeanors to state-level felonies. These are open legal questions that are likely to be pursued during the trial and, if Trump is convicted, the appellate process.

To be very clear, none of this means that the New York charges against Trump were improperly pursued. It does mean, however, that Bragg will face calls to explain the decision to pursue this approach in this case. Such an explanation, in tandem with references to other cases that were comparably charged, would go far to mute claims of selective prosecution.

Fortunately, none of the other three Trump indictments come close to raising this issue. This is not based on our conjecture or opinion; it is a demonstrable fact.

Let's take the two cases—one in DC and one in Georgia—that arise from the January 6 attack on the Capitol and the events leading up to it. To date, prosecutors have brought hundreds of cases against those who attacked the Capitol on that day. As of this writing, the DOJ has reported statistics based on public court filings that reveal the following with respect to state and federal charges, across the country.

MORE THAN **1,146** defendants have been charged in nearly all **50** states and the District of Columbia.

- Approximately **398** defendants have been charged with assaulting, resisting, or impeding officers or employees, including approximately **113** individuals who have been charged with using a deadly or dangerous weapon or causing serious bodily injury to an officer.
    - Approximately **140** police officers were assaulted on January 6 at the Capitol, including about **80** from the US Capitol Police and about **60** from the DC Metropolitan Police Department.
- Approximately **11** individuals have been arrested on a series of charges that relate to assaulting a member of the media, or destroying their equipment, on January 6.
- Approximately **1,061** defendants have been charged with entering or remaining in a restricted federal building or grounds. Of those, **111** defendants have been charged with entering a restricted area with a dangerous or deadly weapon.
- Approximately **66** defendants have been charged with destruction of government property, and approximately **54** defendants have been charged with theft of government property.
- More than **317** defendants have been charged with corruptly obstructing, influencing, or impeding an official proceeding, or attempting to do so.
- Approximately **42** defendants have been charged with conspiracy, either: (a) conspiracy to obstruct a congressional proceeding; (b) conspiracy to obstruct law enforcement during a civil disorder; (c) conspiracy to injure an officer; or (d) some combination of the three.

These figures unquestionably demonstrate that if prosecutors developed a strong case (which all public evidence suggests they have, and then some), it would have been selective *non-prosecution* not to seek charges against Trump. Even if you omit all the trespass and assault cases from the above statistics, there remain 317 defendants who have been charged with crimes akin to those with which Trump is charged, namely obstructing an official proceeding or the like.

Nor can Trump rely on his absence from the Capitol as a distinguishing fact—indeed, it is not a particularly exculpatory fact, particularly given the evidence that he *wanted* to be there. But even leaving that aside, not all who have been charged and convicted were present at the Capitol on January 6. Enrique Tarrio, the leader of the Proud Boys, was not at the Capitol on January 6, 2021, but he was charged and convicted by a jury and sentenced to the highest sentence to date: twenty-two years in prison. That Trump has continued to align himself with the Proud Boys and another domestic terrorist group, the Oath Keepers, before and after January 6, hardly supports any argument that his charged conduct is dissimilar in degree or kind. To the contrary, the scheme laid out in the DC and Georgia indictments is far more egregious and far-reaching than anything that has been charged to date.

Trump's alleged scheme to reject the results of the 2020 presidential election involved: pressuring state legislators in battleground states, through threats and lies, to alter the vote tallies; enlisting slates of fake electors, including through fraud, in battleground states; filing false lawsuits; breaking into state election machines; plotting to seize voting machines; lying about Georgia election workers and pressuring them to lie about election fraud; enlisting the DOJ to say that it was investigating serious allegations of fraud when it was not and had in fact reported it had found no material fraud; and pressuring Vice President Mike Pence to violate his oath of office on January 6 and lying about his supposed assent that he had the power to reject the counting of the votes, when he told Trump he did not.

In short, nothing that has been charged in DC or Georgia against lower-level participants in the scheme compares in culpability to what Trump is charged with doing. Further, Trump was the leader of the free world, sworn to uphold the laws and United States Constitution—he was in a position that should be held to a higher, not lower, standard.

The Florida documents case is also unavailing if one is claiming a selective prosecution. The government routinely has charged illegal handling of classified documents in cases far less egregious than Trump's. Even cases that involve the improper retention of classified documents—without further dissemination of those documents by the defendant—are routinely charged. In the Florida case, Trump is not only charged with improperly retaining classified documents, but also with disseminating them to staff and visitors alike.

Just Security, a legal forum affiliated with New York University, has compiled a helpful chart of over two dozen relatively recent DOJ criminal prosecutions of "simple" retention cases—cases in which dissemination was not alleged. (See Model Prosecution Memo for Trump Classified Documents, Appendix A.) The DOJ precedent indicates that to decline to bring a case against Trump would be treating him significantly more favorably than other defendants, which would be antithetical to the rule of law and the principles of the DOJ Justice Manual. It would be a case of selective *non*-prosecution.

To evaluate the DOJ precedent, consider the salient known facts about Trump's conduct in connection with the illegal retention of documents and his obstruction of the National Archives recovery efforts and the DOJ investigation. Trump, who as president was the head of the intelligence community and law enforcement agencies, is now charged with—and all known evidence clearly supports the charge—illegally retaining thousands of government documents, hundreds of which are classified, including at the highest possible levels. "Top Secret" material, by definition, means its "unauthorized disclosure could reasonably be expected to cause exceptionally grave damage to the national security." Compartmented "Top Secret" information is even more sensitive, as even those people with a "Top Secret" clearance need special authorization to access such information.

Trump's retention of illegal documents persisted for more than eighteen months, in spite of direct communications with him or his counsel seeking the return of such documents and despite his knowledge that he was required to do so. This intransigence connotes a particularly hardened commitment to flouting the law. For instance, Trump did not return the first tranche of documents for a year, and then returned only some of the documents. Even after he knew of the interests of the National Archives, the DOJ, and the intelligence community in the return of all the documents, he returned only a second, incomplete tranche in response to the legal process. Finally, more than one hundred classified documents and thousands of government records were recovered involuntarily pursuant to a search warrant in August 2022, after eighteen months of seeking full compliance.

COMPARE TRUMP'S CASE WITH two of the cases from the twenty-five recent examples of criminal prosecutions for illegal retention of classified documents.

- In 2021, Asia Lavarello was charged with violating 18 U.S.C. § 1924. Lavarello was a Department of Defense employee who removed classified information and brought the documents home. Later, she took notes of classified information at the "Confidential" and "Secret" levels and kept those notes improperly at her desk. She also emailed the notes to herself. She claimed she was using the documents for a thesis, and admitted she removed the classification markings. She pleaded guilty to one count of unauthorized removal and retention of classified documents or material under § 1924. The government agreed that no "Top Secret" documents were involved and that Lavarello's false statements did not significantly impede the investigation. She was sentenced to three months' imprisonment.
- Kenneth Wayne Ford served as an NSA computer specialist between 2001 and 2003, holding a top secret security clearance. He was charged under 18 U.S.C. § 793(e), unlawful retention of documents and with making a false statement to a potential employer to hide the allegations from them. An FBI search of Ford's residence found sensitive classified information throughout his house, including numerous "Top Secret" documents in two boxes in his kitchen and bedroom closet. Evidence indicates Ford took home the classified information on his last day of employment at the NSA in December 2003. During the search, Ford admitted (and wrote a statement to the effect) that he sought to use the documents as reference points for his new job. Ford was arrested in January 2004. He went to trial and claimed he had been framed by the NSA and that his confession was coerced. Ford was convicted on December 15, 2005, and received a six-year prison sentence.

Now, we should point to one factor in these examples that works in Trump's favor. While these examples do not counsel in favor of non-prosecution—quite the contrary—there is precedent from which Trump can argue for a lenient sentence if he were to plead guilty and accept responsibility. Senior officials who have been charged and plead guilty are afforded considerable leniency; far more than people at more junior ranks of the government—the precise opposite of what one would or should expect. Thus, for example, John Deutch, the former CIA director, stored highly classified information on his unsecure home computer, but was allowed to plead to a misdemeanor (and then was pardoned before he could be sentenced). And David Petraeus, another CIA director, took classified documents home and showed them repeatedly to his biographer, and then lied about it to the FBI when interviewed. He pled to a felony but was given an agreed-upon term of probation and paid a fine.

In short, three of the four indictments present straightforward cases where the rule of law demanded prosecution. And to be sure, the charges in the fourth indictment (the New York case) are also arguably warranted—if not as felony charges then as misdemeanors, even as the indictment presents open legal challenges. Taken together, the indictments are testament to the fact that nonpartisan public servants still exist, and are still doing their jobs, despite the former president's attempt to politicize and corrupt not only our elections, but American governance and the rule of law.

CHRONOLOGY OF KEY DATES

The notations [DC], [GA], [FL], and [NY] indicate dates that are particularly pertinent to one of the four indictments.

2017

- *January 20*—Donald J. Trump sworn in as the forty-fifth president of the United States
- **[NY]**
    - *February*—Check signed by Trump Organization Chief Financial Officer Alan Weisselberg and Donald Trump Jr.
    - *March*—same
    - *April*—Check signed by President Donald Trump
    - *May*—same
    - *June*—same
    - *July*—same
    - *August*—same
    - *September*—same
    - *October*—same
    - *November*—same
    - *December*—same

2018

- **[NY]** *August 21*—Michael Cohen pleads guilty in federal court in New York to five counts of willful tax evasion, one count of making false statements to a bank, one count of causing an unlawful campaign contribution, and one count of making an excessive campaign contribution

2021

- **[DC & GA]** *January 6*—Attack on the United States Capitol
- *January 13*—House of Representatives impeaches Donald Trump, citing the events of January 6; this is the second time that Trump has been impeached
- *January 20*—Joseph R. Biden sworn in as the forty-sixth president of the United States
- *July 27*—January 6 committee conducts preliminary hearing

2022

- **[FL]** *January 17*—Trump returns fifteen boxes to the National Archives
- **[FL]** *May 11*—Grand jury issues a subpoena for the production of all documents bearing classification markings
- **[FL]** *June 3*—Trump attorney Evan Corcoran returns a Redweld of documents to federal prosecutors
- January 6 Committee Hearings
  - *June 9*—January 6 committee conducts first hearing, featuring never-before-seen attack footage and providing viewers with an overarching narrative of the alleged scheme to overturn the 2020 election
  - *June 13*—January 6 committee conducts second hearing, exploring the promotion and spread of false claims of voter fraud in conjunction with the effort to overturn the 2020 election
  - *June 16*—January 6 committee conducts third hearing, discussing the effort to pressure Vice President Mike Pence to intervene in the certification of the Electoral College votes
  - *June 21*—January 6 committee conducts fourth hearing, explaining the scheme to advance slates of fake electors
  - *June 23*—January 6 committee conducts fifth hearing, exploring the election fraud conspiracy theories promoted in the wake of the 2020 election
  - *June 28*—January 6 committee conducts sixth hearing, at which Cassidy Hutchinson, a former aide to White House Chief of Staff Mark Meadows, testifies
  - *July 12*—January 6 committee conducts seventh hearing,

> discussing Trump's link to the militia groups that helped coordinate the January 6 attack on the Capitol.
>
> ○ *July 21*—January 6 committee conducts eighth hearing, discussing Trump's actions on January 6

- **[FL]** *August 8*—FBI executes a court-authorized search of Mar-a-Lago
- *October 13*—January 6 committee conducts ninth hearing, at which it announces a unanimous vote to subpoena Donald Trump
- *November 15*—Trump declares that he will run for president in 2024
- **[DC & FL]** *November 18*—Attorney General Merrick Garland appoints Jack Smith as special counsel
- **[GA]** *December 15*—Fulton County Special Grand Jury issues its report and recommendation (a redacted version of this report was released to the public on September 8, 2023)
- *December 19*—January 6 committee conducts tenth hearing, at which it reviews its findings and announces a series of criminal referrals, including one for Donald Trump, to the Department of Justice and congressional ethics committees
- *December 22*—January 6 committee releases its final report

2023

- *January 2*—January 6 committee publicly releases the evidence it has obtained in the course of its investigation
- **[NY]** *March 30*—A state-level grand jury in Manhattan indicts Donald J. Trump
- **[FL]** *June 8*—A federal grand jury in Florida indicts Donald J. Trump
- **[FL]** *July 27*—A federal grand jury in Florida issues a superseding indictment, filing additional charges and indicting a new defendant, Carlos de Oliveira
- **[DC]** *August 1*—A federal grand jury in the District of Columbia indicts Donald J. Trump
- **[GA]** *August 14*—A state-level grand jury in Fulton County indicts Donald J. Trump, along with eighteen other co-defendants
- **[GA]** *September 29*—Scott Hall becomes the first defendant to plead guilty in the Fulton County, Georgia, criminal case

- **[GA]** *October 19*—Sidney Powell pleads guilty in the Fulton County, Georgia, criminal case
- **[GA]** *October 20*—Kenneth Chesebro pleads guilty in the Fulton County, Georgia, criminal case
- **[GA]** *October 24*—Jenna Ellis pleads guilty in the Fulton County, Georgia, criminal case

2024

- **[DC]** *March 4*—Trial scheduled in the DC January 6 case
- **[NY]** *March 25*—Trial tentatively scheduled in the Manhattan DA hush money case[*]
- **[FL]** *May 20*—Trial scheduled in the Mar-a-Lago documents case[†]
- **[GA]**—As of this writing, no trial date has been scheduled

---

[*] The New York Judge overseeing this case has told the parties that the date may well be changed to accommodate the March 4 federal trial of the DC indictment.

[†] On November 10, 2023, the federal judge overseeing this case denied a defense request to put off the May trial date, but did so without prejudice to renewing the application later. However, the court's order set new and extended deadlines for pretrial filings, which strongly suggest that the court may be receptive to granting a later defense motion to delay the May trial date.

UNITED STATES OF AMERICA V. DONALD J. TRUMP

(DC JANUARY 6 INDICTMENT)

INTRODUCTION

ALL OF THE FOUR INDICTMENTS PRESENTED IN THIS
volume allege serious crimes with meaningful potential penalties. But of the four, the DC January 6 indictment is the one that focuses
exclusively on holding Trump—and only Trump—accountable for the
effort to overturn the 2020 presidential election. Put differently, the DC
January 6 indictment is an attempt to hold to the rule of law a political leader who allegedly sought to disenfranchise 80 million people
in order to remain in power illegally. The Union has not faced such
an existential threat since the southern states seceded, launching the
Civil War.

An interesting side note to this indictment involves its timing. From
the moment of the January 6 insurrection, it was not clear whether the
Department of Justice would investigate this case, bring these charges,
and go to trial before the Republican National Convention or the general election in 2024.

Prior to the filing of this indictment, the DOJ spearheaded a voluminous number of significant criminal cases against hundreds of January
6 defendants. But most of these prosecutions focused on the attempted
uprising's foot soldiers. What about the leaders in the White House
or those colluding with them? For well over a year, there was scant
movement on any of the higher-ups. The DOJ's mantra was that it was
pursuing a "bottom-up" investigation, focusing first on the people
who actually stormed the Capitol and then seeing where those efforts
would lead.

But reports revealed that the prosecutors in charge of the January
6 foot soldier cases could not mention "the 'T' word" in their weekly
meetings with senior supervisors at DOJ. And when Cassidy Hutchinson (Mark Meadows's senior aide) testified at the January 6 committee hearing, pulling back the curtain to reveal an orchestrated scheme

to steal the presidency that involved some of the most powerful figures in government, her testimony reportedly came as a surprise to DOJ. Hutchinson's testimony made clear that the DOJ's "bottom-up" approach would allow some of the most important figures in the alleged coup to evade responsibility for their actions. The loud and public grumblings from January 6 committee's members were therefore understandable: many of them were former prosecutors and they knew how unusual it was for Congress to be ahead of the DOJ.

So, what changed? How did DOJ get to the point where it charged Trump on August 1, 2023, for the attempted coup? Two developments were pivotal to getting the DOJ to change course. First was the success of the January 6 congressional hearings, which produced new evidence, while simultaneously shaming the DOJ into action and giving it cover for that action. After all, during the hearings, a sizable part of the public saw for themselves the mounting evidence pointing to corruption and fraud, and started wondering, along with the House members conducting the hearings, "Where is DOJ?"

The second development was, ironically, Trump himself. Because Trump wanted to be able to claim that any federal indictment was a political attack against him for challenging Biden for the presidency, he declared on November 16, 2022, that he would run for president in 2024—almost two years before the election and earlier in the cycle than any candidate in recent memory. It was all for show: Trump hoped to be able to say that he was charged only *after* he declared he was running. He was silent on one of his main motivations: he was hearing very loud DOJ footsteps. The political effects are difficult to read, but in one respect Trump's move backfired. Once Trump was a declared candidate, and Biden, too, indicated that he would be a candidate, Attorney General Merrick Garland, in an effort to insulate the Biden administration and the DOJ from claims of political brinksmanship, made a fateful move for Trump: he appointed a special counsel. Functioning much as an independent prosecutor would, the special counsel was authorized to investigate the events of January 6 and prosecute any crimes arising from that investigation. And, as explored in this book's introduction, Garland tapped a DOJ veteran with particular expertise in political accountability here in the United States and across the globe: Jack Smith.

Smith was tailor-made for this case. His actions to date show that despite being dealt a tough hand in terms of timing, he has risen to the challenge. Both the DC and Florida cases were clearly going to be extremely strong, but only an experienced prosecutor like Smith could get them quickly to the finish line. Smith does not "play with his food"—to use a phrase Robert Mueller frequently used. In this way, the DC January 6 indictment is the work of a seasoned prosecutor who was focused, realistic, and fearless. Smith did not shy away from anything needed to advance the case and bring it to fruition. He insisted on subpoenaing the grand jury testimony of former vice president Mike Pence, and former White House counsels, among many others. He treated these high-level figures like anyone else—the grand jury was entitled under the law to every person's evidence and Smith was going to ensure that is what it got.

The final indictment charges only a single defendant: Donald Trump, the forty-fifth president of the United States. In this regard, the indictment was built for speed—to get a trial date so that the American public could see the evidence and hear the jury's conclusion. This "lean and mean" approach worked: as of this writing, the trial is set for March 4, 2024. That date is of historic significance: it is the date in 1789 when our Constitution went into effect and the first Congress was convened. And, until 1937, when the Twentieth Amendment went into effect, March 4 was Inauguration Day.

So, once again, in 2024, it is possible that March 4 will be a date of historic importance.

CAST OF CHARACTERS

M ANY OF THE INDICTMENTS REFERENCE UNNAMED individuals by descriptions such as "Employee 1," "Woman 2," and "Co-Conspirator 3." To be clear, these unnamed individuals have not been charged with any crime. They are referenced because they play some role in the events alleged. Relying on media reports identifying these individuals, we have named them here in order to facilitate the reader's comprehension of these documents and the alleged conduct they describe. That said, it must be remembered that none of these individuals has been charged with any wrongdoing.

▲ = involved in multiple cases

Rusty Bowers ("Arizona House Speaker")—The former Speaker of the Arizona House of Representatives. According to Bowers's sworn testimony before the January 6 committee, Trump and his team repeatedly pressured Bowers, a Republican loyalist, not to recognize Arizona's legitimate electors. Bowers declined to comply with these entreaties and issued a public statement that his constitutional duty required him to honor the popular vote.

Lee Chatfield ("Michigan House Speaker")—The former Speaker of the Michigan House of Representatives whom, according to the January 6 congressional report, Trump and Giuliani unsuccessfully pressured to reject Michigan's legitimate electors.

Kenneth Chesebro▲ ("Co-Conspirator 5")—Trump's former legal advisor. Chesebro, who was a defendant in the Fulton County indictment and referred to as "co-conspirator 5" in the DOJ's January 6 indictment, was charged with his role in devising a plan to appoint slates of fraudulent electors in seven states that Trump lost. According to the Georgia and the January 6 indictments, the plan called for slates of Trump electors—individuals who would have served as electors if Trump had won the popular vote in those states—to convene to mimic the actions of real electors by casting fraudulent "votes" and signing false certifications that they were the legitimate electors. The fraudulent certificates were then provided to the President of the Senate and others. The plan was supposed to culminate on January 6, 2021, with Vice President Pence opening the fraudulent certificates on the Senate floor and counting them as real votes, but Pence never complied. Chesebro faced seven criminal charges in Fulton County. On October 20, 2023, just days before his trial was scheduled to begin, Chesebro pleaded guilty to one felony count of conspiracy to commit filing false documents. As part of his Fulton County plea deal, Chesebro is sentenced to five years' probation and will pay $5,000 in restitution. He has also agreed to testify truthfully in all future proceedings.

Judge Tanya Chutkan—The Washington, DC, federal judge presiding over the DOJ's January 6 case. Chutkan, a former public defender and law firm partner, was nominated by Barack Obama and began serving in 2014.

Pat Cipollone—Trump's White House Counsel from 2018 to January 20, 2021. Cipollone allegedly pushed back on Trump's false claims about election fraud and threatened to resign if Trump fired Acting Attorney General Jeffrey Rosen. A few hours after Trump's supporters attacked the Capitol on January 6, Cipollone called Trump to ask him to withdraw his objection to the certification of the election—a request Trump declined. Cipollone defended Trump during his first impeachment trial.

Jeffrey Clark▲ ("Co-Conspirator 4")—Trump's former acting head of the DOJ's civil division. On January 3, 2021, Trump briefly appointed Clark Acting Attorney General so that he could lend the DOJ's backing to Trump's efforts to overturn the election. Trump rescinded the appointment later that day when threatened with the prospect of mass resignations. According to the DOJ January 6 indictment, Clark drafted a letter (never ultimately sent) to Georgia lawmakers stating the DOJ had significant concerns about election fraud and viewed Trump's fraudulent Georgia electors—the individuals who would have served as electors if Trump had won the popular vote—as legitimate electors. Clark's bosses at the DOJ, Acting Attorney General Jeffrey Rosen and Acting Deputy Attorney General Richard Donoghue, refused to sign the Georgia letter.

Richard Donoghue—Former Acting Deputy Attorney General to Trump. Donoghue, along with Acting Attorney General Jeffrey Rosen, refused to lend the DOJ's support to Trump's efforts to overturn the election.

John Eastman▲ ("Co-Conspirator 2")—Trump's former legal advisor. Eastman is a defendant in the Fulton County District Attorney's indictment and referred to as "co-conspirator 2" in the DOJ's January 6 indictment. Prosecutors allege that Eastman was an architect of the plan to have Mike Pence leverage his ceremonial role as President of the Senate to obstruct the certification of the 2020 election by rejecting the electoral votes of seven states that Biden won. Eastman later devised a second plan whereby Pence, instead of outright rejecting the seven "disputed" states' electoral votes, would send dueling slates of electors to those seven states' legislatures and ask the legislatures to determine which electors to count. Eastman and Trump met with Pence in the White House on January 4, 2021, and attempted to convince Pence to adopt either of the two plans, even though Eastman acknowledged in communications cited by prosecutors that the plans violated the Electoral Count Act and would be rejected by courts. Eastman spoke to the crowd of Trump supporters gathered in Washington, DC, on the morning of January 6, 2021, and, hours after the attack on the Capitol, emailed Pence's counsel to "implore" him to delay the count for another ten days. Eastman faces nine criminal charges in Fulton County.

Boris Epshteyn▲ (reported as possibly "Co-Conspirator 6")—A political consultant who has publicly said he helped Trump implement the plan to submit slates of electors claiming that they were "alternate" electors, rather than fraudulent electors. The Fulton County indictment states that "Individual 3"—reportedly Epshteyn—made false statements about election fraud at a November 19, 2020, press conference at Republican National Committee ("RNC") headquarters.

Rudy Giuliani▲ ("Co-Conspirator 1")—Trump's former personal attorney. He is named as a defendant in the Fulton County District Attorney's indictment and referred to as "co-conspirator 1" in the DOJ's January 6 indictment. Prosecutors claim that Giuliani spearheaded the Trump legal team's efforts to overturn the results of the 2020 presidential election. Giuliani repeatedly spread bogus claims about fraud in the 2020 presidential election and personally met with lawmakers in several states that Biden won in an attempt to convince them to adopt his baseless theories. Giuliani arranged a presentation to Georgia lawmakers at which he and other Trump lawyers promoted debunked theories of voter fraud and asked the Georgia state legislature not to recognize Georgia's legitimate, Biden-chosen electors. After Giuliani failed to persuade state legislatures not to recognize the legitimate electors, he helped carry out a new scheme to have slates of fake electors meet to declare themselves the true electors and send fraudulent certifications to the President of the Senate. In addressing the crowd of Trump supporters gathered in Washington, DC, on January 6, 2021, Giuliani called for "trial by combat" and declared that Mike Pence had the power to unilaterally stop the certification of the election. That night, after rioters had violently stormed the Capitol, Giuliani reportedly called seven members of Congress to ask them to further delay the certification of the election. Giuliani faces thirteen criminal charges in Fulton County.

Eric Herschmann ("Senior Advisor")—A senior White House attorney who challenged Trump's attorneys' legal theories for keeping Trump in power.

Greg Jacob ("Vice President's Counsel")—Former Counsel to Vice President Pence. According to the January 6 committee report, Jacob met with John Eastman on multiple occasions and was present at the meeting in which Trump and Eastman tried to convince Pence to reject the electoral votes of seven states. Jacob testified that Pence rejected their idea that as vice president he could reject the electoral votes.

Ronna McDaniel▲ ("RNC Chair")—The chairwoman of the Republican National Committee. As revealed during the January 6 committee hearings and the Georgia indictment, Trump and John Eastman called McDaniel to seek her help in arranging the gatherings of Trump electors. McDaniel testified in the congressional investigation that Eastman assured McDaniel that the "contingent" electors' votes would be used only if Trump's litigation succeeded. McDaniel agreed to help and later updated Trump with the news that his electors had successfully met and cast their "votes."

Mark Meadows▲ ("Chief of Staff")— Meadows served as Trump's last Chief of Staff, from March 2020 until January 20, 2021. Prior to that, he served for seven years as a congressman from North Carolina and was a leading member of the Freedom Caucus. In connection with his effort to "remove" the State of Georgia criminal charges against him to federal court for trial, Meadows testified at a federal hearing that all the alleged acts in the state indictment were undertaken by him as part of his official position as Chief of Staff. News reports have also suggested that Meadows may have testified under a grant of immunity before a federal grand jury investigating the January 6 insurrection.

Jason Miller ("Senior Campaign Advisor")—A senior campaign advisor to Trump who allegedly spoke with Trump frequently and repeatedly told him that the election fraud claims being promoted by Rudy Giuliani's legal team were untrue.

Sidney Powell▲ ("Co-Conspirator 3")—Trump's former attorney. Powell, who was a defendant in the Fulton County indictment and referred to as "co-conspirator 3" in the DOJ's January 6 indictment, is alleged to have concocted and promulgated several outlandish election fraud claims advanced by Trump and his team. Though Trump privately acknowledged that Powell sounded "crazy," he promoted her theories and considered appointing her special counsel with broad authority to investigate voter fraud. Powell claimed that a network of rigged voting machines—set up by former Venezuelan president Hugo Chávez, who died in 2013, and controlled by the likes of Democratic billionaire George Soros and Antifa—had switched Trump votes to Biden votes. Powell claimed without basis that the manufacturer of the voting machines, Dominion Voting Systems, had bribed the governor and secretary of state of Georgia, and she launched a failed lawsuit against the governor of Georgia that alleged "massive election fraud" accomplished through voting machine software and hardware. The Georgia indictment charges Powell with engaging a private forensic data company to access voting machines in Georgia and Michigan. Powell pleaded guilty in Georgia to misdemeanor criminal charges related to her participation in this scheme. She will serve six years' probation, pay a $6,000 fine, as well as $2,700 to the Georgia Secretary of State's Office, and is required to testify truthfully at future hearings and trials related to the Georgia criminal case.

Jeffrey Rosen ("Acting Attorney General")—The former Acting Attorney General who repeatedly told Trump that his various claims about election fraud were untrue. Trump asked Rosen to announce that the DOJ was investigating fraud in the election and, when Rosen refused, threatened to replace him with Jeffrey Clark (which he did for part of January 3, 2021). Trump ultimately backed down when attorneys from the DOJ and White House Counsel's Office threatened to resign if Rosen was fired.

Mike Shirkey ("Michigan Senate Majority Leader")—The former Michigan Senate Majority Leader whom Trump unsuccessfully pressured to reject Michigan's legitimate electors and instead appoint Trump's fraudulent slate of electors.

Marc Short ("Vice President's Chief of Staff")—Former Chief of Staff to Vice President Pence. Short testified in the January 6 committee investigation that he was present at the meeting in which Trump and John Eastman tried to convince Pence to reject the electoral votes of seven states and declare Trump president. According to the January 6 indictment, on January 5, 2021, Short became so concerned about Pence's safety the following day that he alerted the head of Pence's Secret Service detail to his concerns.

Bill Stepien ("Campaign Manager")—Trump's 2020 campaign manager. Stepien has testified that he told the Trump team that claims about thousands of noncitizens voting in Arizona were false and that when Trump was dissatisfied with what he was hearing from his legal team headed by Justin Clark, he replaced Clark with Giuliani.

PROSECUTORS

J. P. Cooney—A veteran prosecutor who worked under Jack Smith and Raymond Hulser in the DOJ's Public Integrity Section. Cooney, now an Assistant United States Attorney for the District of Columbia, worked on the unsuccessful prosecutions of Senator Bob Menendez and former Obama White House Counsel Gregory Craig, and he worked on the successful prosecutions of Steve Bannon and Roger Stone. Cooney also played a role in the DOJ's investigation of former FBI Acting Director Andrew McCabe, whom the grand jury reportedly declined to charge.

Mary Dohrmann—An Assistant United States Attorney for the District of Columbia who prosecuted several Capitol rioters.

Molly Gaston—An experienced federal prosecutor in the District of Columbia who worked alongside J. P. Cooney on the high-profile investigations of Gregory Craig, Andrew McCabe, Roger Stone, and Steve Bannon.

Raymond Hulser—An experienced prosecutor from the Justice Department's Public Integrity Section. Hulser served as Jack Smith's deputy at the Public Integrity Section and later succeeded Smith as the section's chief. Hulser's notable cases include prosecutions of Senator Bob Menendez and Trump White House trade advisor Peter Navarro. Menendez's case ended with a hung jury and was not retried; Navarro was convicted of contempt of Congress.

Jack Smith▲—The Special Counsel overseeing the DOJ's investigation of Donald Trump. Smith, who was appointed by Attorney General Merrick Garland in November 2022, is heading both federal prosecutions of Trump—the classified documents case and the January 6 case. Smith is a longtime federal and state prosecutor whose former roles include serving as the Chief of the DOJ's Public Integrity Section, the Acting US Attorney for the Middle District of Tennessee, an Assistant US Attorney in the Eastern District of New York, and an Assistant District Attorney in the Manhattan District Attorney's Office. Smith left his post as the chief prosecutor in the Kosovo Specialist Prosecutor's Office to become DOJ Special Counsel.

Alex Whiting—A former Harvard Law School professor of practice and Jack Smith's successor as the acting specialist prosecutor at the Kosovo Specialist Prosecutor's Office. Whiting, who has also served as a federal prosecutor and as the Prosecutions Coordinator for the International Criminal Court, joined Smith's team in 2023.

Thomas Windom—A Maryland-based federal prosecutor who, since 2021, has been investigating Trump and his allies for election obstruction. Windom, whose investigation predated Smith's appointment as Special Counsel, was one of the first lawyers to join Smith's team.

DEFENSE ATTORNEYS

Todd Blanche▲—A white-collar criminal defense lawyer and former federal prosecutor. Blanche, previously a partner at a well-known New York law firm, launched his own firm in 2023 to represent Trump in three criminal investigations: the New York case and both federal cases. Blanche successfully represented Trump's former presidential campaign manager Paul Manafort in the Manhattan District Attorney's prosecution that was ultimately dismissed on state double-jeopardy grounds.

Evan Corcoran▲—Trump's lawyer who participated in the response to the DOJ's 2022 grand jury subpoena for documents bearing classified markings. According to prosecutors, Corcoran informed Trump that he would search the Mar-a-Lago storage room for responsive documents. Before Corcoran could do so, Trump allegedly had aides remove boxes from the storage room and bring them to Trump's personal residence. Corcoran searched the storage room and found only thirty-eight classified documents, all of which he turned over to the FBI. Corcoran—apparently unaware of the removal of the boxes—asked Christina Bobb to sign a certification stating that all responsive documents had been returned. Corcoran's personal meeting notes feature prominently in the DOJ's Florida indictment and record that Trump repeatedly intimated that Corcoran should destroy or hide the documents that the DOJ requested. Corcoran recused himself as Trump's lawyer in the Florida documents case but apparently continues to represent Trump in other cases, including the DOJ's January 6 case.[*]

John Lauro—A former federal prosecutor in the Eastern District of New York and longtime white-collar criminal defense attorney. Lauro appeared on several Sunday talk shows as the public face of Trump's defense. In those appearances, Lauro has argued that Trump believed he won the election and was exercising his First Amendment rights to protest the results. Lauro is known for his defense of Tim Donaghy, a former NBA referee who admitted to betting on games he officiated.

PROUD BOYS AND OATH KEEPERS

Joe Biggs—The former head of the Florida chapter of the Proud Boys. Biggs, an army veteran, commanded a large group of Trump supporters in attacking the Capitol on January 6. Biggs was convicted of seditious conspiracy and sentenced to seventeen years in prison.

Joseph Hackett—A former member of the Oath Keepers who stormed the Capitol on January 6. Hackett was convicted of seditious conspiracy and destruction of evidence and received a three-and-a-half-year prison sentence.

---

[*] Jacqueline Alemany, Josh Dawsey, and Spencer S. Hsu, "A Top Trump Lawyer Has Recused Himself from Mar-a-Lago Documents Case," *Washington Post*, April 15, 2023.

Kenneth Harrelson—A ground leader of the Oath Keepers' January 6 attack on the Capitol. Harrelson was convicted of several felonies and sentenced to four years in prison.

Kelly Meggs—The former leader of the Florida chapter of the Oath Keepers. Meggs was convicted of seditious conspiracy for his role in the January 6 attack on the Capitol and received a twelve-year prison sentence.

Roberto Minuta—A member of the Oath Keepers who attacked the Capitol on January 6. Minuta was convicted of seditious conspiracy and other felonies and sentenced to four-and-a-half years in prison.

David Moerschel—A former member of the Oath Keepers who acted as a "battering ram" in the Oath Keepers' military-style stack formation that attacked the Capitol on January 6. Moerschel was convicted of seditious conspiracy and sentenced to three years in prison.

Ethan Nordean—A former Proud Boys leader and commander in the January 6 attack on the Capitol. Nordean was convicted of multiple felonies, including seditious conspiracy, and sentenced to eighteen years in prison.

Dominic Pezzola—A New York Proud Boy who attacked the Capitol on January 6. Pezzola, who helped ignite the breach of the Capitol by smashing a window with a stolen police riot shield, was convicted of multiple felonies and sentenced to ten years in prison.

Zachary Rehl—The former leader of the Philadelphia chapter of the Proud Boys and a commander in the January 6 attack on the Capitol. Rehl, an ex-Marine, was convicted of seditious conspiracy and received a fifteen-year prison sentence.

Elmer Stewart Rhodes—The founder of the far-right extremist group known as the Oath Keepers and a leader of the January 6 attack on the Capitol. Rhodes was convicted of seditious conspiracy and sentenced to eighteen years in prison.

Enrique Tarrio—The former national leader of the Proud Boys and a plotter of the January 6 attack on the Capitol. Tarrio was convicted of seditious conspiracy and received a twenty-two-year prison sentence.

Edward Vallejo—A former member of the Oath Keepers who helped plot the January 6 attack on the Capitol. Vallejo did not enter the Capitol on January 6 and instead remained on standby from a heavily armed Virginia hotel room. Vallejo was convicted of seditious conspiracy and sentenced to three years in prison.

Jessica Watkins—A former Oath Keepers leader and Army veteran who commanded an Ohio militia in the January 6 attack on the Capitol. Watkins was convicted of several felony charges and received an eight-and-a-half-year sentence.

IN THE UNITED STATES DISTRICT COURT
FOR THE DISTRICT OF COLUMBIA*

UNITED STATES	*	CRIMINAL NO.
OF AMERICA	*	
	*	GRAND JURY ORIGINAL
v.	*	
	*	VIOLATIONS:
	*	
DONALD J. TRUMP,†	*	Count 1: 18 U.S.C. § 371
	*	(Conspiracy to Defraud the
Defendant.	*	United States)
	*	
	*	Count 2: 18 U.S.C. § 1512(k)
	*	(Conspiracy to Obstruct an
	*	Official Proceeding)

---

* This case was brought in the federal district court in the District of Columbia (DC), the federal district that encompasses Washington, DC. This district was an appropriate location because the crimes Donald Trump is charged with are alleged to have been orchestrated from the White House.

INSIDER NOTE: The US Constitution requires that a case be brought where the crime occurred. When a crime may have occurred in multiple places, the government has substantial discretion to choose where to bring the case. Here, Jack Smith appears to have played it straight: bringing the documents case in the Southern District of Florida because the gravamen of the case occurred at Mar-a-Lago, which is in that district, and filing this case in DC.

† The indictment identifies six people who are alleged to have participated with Trump in the alleged crimes. Yet, the indictment charges only Donald Trump with these crimes. Why? Jack Smith likely determined that limiting the scope of the trial to a single defendant would surely make it easier for the case to be tried and concluded expeditiously. Further, Smith no doubt understands that getting this case to trial before the November 2024 election is crucial to our democracy: the electorate is entitled to know, one way or the other, the jury's conclusions as to the most serious charges involving the effort to thwart the 2020 presidential election.

INSIDER NOTE: Smith's strategy of keeping the indictment "lean and mean" appears to have worked. When selecting a March 4, 2024, trial date, the assigned judge, US District Judge Tanya Chutkan, cited the fact that the case involved a single defendant and only four charges.

*

*   Count 3: 18 U.S.C. §§ 1512(c)(2), 2

*   (Obstruction of and Attempt to

*   Obstruct an Official Proceeding)

*

*   Count 4: 18 U.S.C. § 241

*   (Conspiracy Against Rights)

*

INDICTMENT

The Grand Jury charges that, at all times material to this Indictment, on or about the dates and at the approximate times stated below:

INTRODUCTION

1.   The Defendant, **DONALD J. TRUMP,** was the forty-fifth President of the United States and a candidate for re-election in 2020. The Defendant lost the 2020 presidential election.*

2.   Despite having lost, the Defendant was determined to remain in power. So for more than two months following election day on November 3, 2020, the Defendant spread lies that there had been outcome-determinative fraud in the election and that he had actually won. These claims were false, and the Defendant knew that

---

* The indictment does not mince words here. And, despite conspiracy theories to the contrary, election experts (including Chris Krebs, the Trump official who was in charge of election integrity at the Department of Homeland Security) maintain that the 2020 election was secure and properly conducted. Throughout, the indictment emphasizes the proof that Trump lost.

Insider Note: It is not clear yet whether the government will have to prove that Trump knew he lost the election—there is likely to be considerable disagreement between the government and the defense on that issue. The government will likely contend that it is sufficient that Trump knew that he legally lost; i.e., that the courts rejected his many efforts to challenge the state votes. In other words, if Trump believed he lost, he had the option of challenging the election results in court; he did so, and lost. Thereafter, the government may well contend that the law does not permit a person to take the law into their own hands. It remains to be seen, however, exactly how Judge Chutkan will instruct the jury as to what it must find to convict.

they were false.* But the Defendant repeated and widely disseminated them anyway—to make his knowingly false claims appear legitimate, create an intense national atmosphere of mistrust and anger, and erode public faith in the administration of the election.

3.   The Defendant had a right, like every American, to speak publicly about the election and even to claim, falsely, that there had been outcome-determinative fraud during the election and that he had won. He was also entitled to formally challenge the results of the election through lawful and appropriate means, such as by seeking recounts or audits of the popular vote in states or filing lawsuits challenging ballots and procedures. Indeed, in many cases, the Defendant did pursue these methods of contesting the election results. His efforts to change the outcome in any state through recounts, audits, or legal challenges were uniformly unsuccessful.†

4.   Shortly after election day, the Defendant also pursued unlawful means of discounting legitimate votes and subverting the

---

* The indictment makes clear not only that Trump lost, but that he *knew* he lost. Trump, to this day, claims that he believed he won, and in fact, did win, the election. Tellingly, he has yet to offer proof to substantiate this claim, either in court or elsewhere. Notably, he was scheduled to give a press conference in August 2023 where he would present "irrefutable" proof of electoral fraud, but he called off the conference, saying that he would present the proof later to a court. As of this writing, that has not yet happened.

INSIDER NOTE: Trump's litany of "proof" at the Ellipse on January 6 that he won the election was nonexistent, and rehashed unsupported claims of electoral fraud that members of his own administration told him were proven erroneous.

† This paragraph has been widely praised, deservedly. It is unusual for an indictment to allege what a defendant can legally do. Here, Smith "prebuts" what is likely to be one of Trump's major lines of defense, in and out of court: that the government is attacking Trump's right to challenge the election. The indictment makes clear that the government is not prosecuting Trump for voicing his views or challenging the election results; indeed, the indictment makes clear Trump had every right to challenge the election in court, and even to lie about it publicly. These acknowledgments set up the next paragraphs, which detail Trump's alleged illegal activity. In addition to acknowledging Trump's right to challenge the election, this paragraph also alleges a key fact that the prosecution will surely stress at trial: all but one of Trump's lawsuits challenging election procedures and results failed. In the lone successful Trump lawsuit, a Pennsylvania lower court judge ruled that voters had three days after the election to provide proper identification and "cure" their ballots.

election results. In so doing, the Defendant perpetrated three criminal conspiracies:*

a. A conspiracy to defraud the United States by using dishonesty, fraud, and deceit to impair, obstruct, and defeat the lawful federal government function by which the results of the presidential election are collected, counted, and certified by the federal government, in violation of 18 U.S.C. § 371;

b. A conspiracy to corruptly obstruct and impede the January 6 congressional proceeding at which the collected results of the presidential election are counted and certified ("the certification proceeding"), in violation of 18 U.S.C. § 1512(k); and

c. A conspiracy against the right to vote and to have one's vote counted, in violation of 18 U.S.C. § 241.†

Each of these conspiracies—which built on the widespread mistrust the Defendant was creating through pervasive and destabilizing lies about election fraud—targeted a bedrock function of the United States federal government: the nation's process of collecting, count-

---

* The indictment's introduction clearly sets out how the alleged conduct triggers three separate federal conspiracy charges. The remainder of the indictment spells out the facts and crimes, but this section is intended to make sure that the public understands *why* Trump is being charged and the crimes with which he is being charged.

† There are four criminal charges. But what is missing? Two potential charges were conspicuously absent in the indictment. The first is a charge of insurrection, which was one of the charges that the House Select Committee to Investigate the January 6th Attack on the United States Capitol (January 6 committee) referred to the DOJ. Another is a charge of seditious conspiracy, which was charged against members of the Oath Keepers and Proud Boys for their roles in the events of January 6. Jack Smith had good reasons to steer clear of these charges.

First, insurrection had not been charged since the nineteenth century and would have raised questions of selective prosecution if it was charged here (although one could argue that the circumstances here were truly extraordinary and warranted such a charge). Second, a charge of seditious conspiracy requires proof of *intentional* use of force in the seditious act—an element that would require proof beyond a reasonable doubt that Trump *intended* for those storming the Capitol on January 6 to overthrow the government through force. Forgoing both charges, Smith instead has opted for more straightforward charges, and in doing so, has avoided needless trial and appellate litigation that would surely slow things down.

ing, and certifying the results of the presidential election ("the federal government function").

COUNT ONE

(Conspiracy to Defraud the United States—18 U.S.C. § 371)

5.   The allegations contained in paragraphs 1 through 4 of this Indictment are re-alleged and fully incorporated here by reference.[*]

The Conspiracy

6.   From on or about November 14, 2020,[†] through on or about January 20, 2021, in the District of Columbia and elsewhere, the Defendant,

DONALD J. TRUMP,

did knowingly combine, conspire, confederate, and agree with coconspirators, known and unknown to the Grand Jury, to defraud the United States by using dishonesty, fraud, and deceit to impair, obstruct, and defeat the lawful federal government function by which the results of the presidential election are collected, counted, and certified by the federal government.

Purpose of the Conspiracy

7.   The purpose of the conspiracy was to overturn the legitimate results of the 2020 presidential election by using knowingly false claims of election fraud to obstruct the federal government function by which those results are collected, counted, and certified.

---

[*] INSIDER NOTE: "Incorporating by reference" is a standard prosecutorial practice. Rather than repeating verbatim text that is used elsewhere, the indictment simply refers back to the earlier text—"incorporating" it by reference. This approach makes the indictment easier to read and understand.

[†] It is interesting that this is the start date of the alleged conspiracy. It is tied to the date that the election was declared for Biden, but there is evidence that Trump was planning to claim election fraud even before the election was decided and would claim victory regardless of the actual vote. That earlier evidence may be admitted at trial as proof of Trump's intent, plan, and motive, even though this later date was selected.

The Defendant's Co-Conspirators[*]

8.　The Defendant enlisted co-conspirators to assist him in his criminal efforts to overturn the legitimate results of the 2020 presidential election and retain power. Among these were:

a.　Co-Conspirator 1,[†] an attorney who was willing to spread knowingly false claims and pursue strategies that the Defendant's 2020 re-election campaign attorneys would not.

b.　Co-Conspirator 2, an attorney who devised and attempted to implement a strategy to leverage the Vice President's ceremonial role overseeing the certification proceeding to obstruct the certification of the presidential election.

c.　Co-Conspirator 3, an attorney whose unfounded claims of election fraud the Defendant privately acknowledged to others sounded "crazy." Nonetheless, the Defendant embraced and publicly amplified Co-Conspirator 3's disinformation.

d.　Co-Conspirator 4, a Justice Department official who worked on civil matters and who, with the Defendant, attempted to use the Justice Department to open sham election crime investigations and influence state legislatures with knowingly false claims of election fraud.

---

[*] A criminal conspiracy requires at least two people. In order to prove a conspiracy, the government must show that there was an agreement with at least one other person. But the government need not charge all—or indeed, any—of the conspirators. Here, the government charged only Trump, even as the indictment lists six unindicted co-conspirators. The indictment makes clear that it has not identified *all* of the co-conspirators. The prosecution can always file another indictment charging co-conspirators. It is doubtful it would seek to add new defendants, however, to this Trump indictment (as it did in the Florida documents case), because it wouldn't want to jeopardize the March 4 trial date.

[†] Why is this terminology used, as opposed to naming the actual person, since the government clearly knows the person's identity? Because the DOJ has a policy that is euphemistically known as "put up, or shut up," meaning you either charge someone, or you stay silent as to that person's alleged guilt, out of respect for the person's right not to be subject to public opprobrium unless and until they are charged with a crime, or the law otherwise requires that the person be named. The latter could happen during the trial where the government will have to adduce proof of at least one co-conspirator and the jury will need to know that co-conspirator's identity to find that there was a conspiracy.

e.   Co-Conspirator 5, an attorney who assisted in devising and attempting to implement a plan to submit fraudulent slates of presidential electors to obstruct the certification proceeding.

f.   Co-Conspirator 6, a political consultant who helped implement a plan to submit fraudulent slates of presidential electors to obstruct the certification proceeding.*

The Federal Government Function

9.   The federal government function by which the results of the election for President of the United States are collected, counted, and certified was established through the Constitution and the Electoral Count Act (ECA), a federal law enacted in 1887. The Constitution provided that individuals called electors select the president, and that each state determine for itself how to appoint the electors apportioned to it. Through state laws, each of the fifty states and the District of Columbia chose to select their electors based on the popular vote in the state. After election day, the ECA required each state to formally determine—or "ascertain"—the electors who would represent the state's voters by casting electoral votes on behalf of the candidate who had won the popular vote, and required the executive of each state to certify to the federal government the identities of those electors. Then, on a date set by the ECA, each state's ascertained electors were required to meet and collect the results of the presidential election—that is, to cast electoral votes based on their state's popular vote, and to send their electoral votes, along with the state executive's certification that they were the state's legitimate electors, to the United States Congress to be counted and certified in

---

* For ease of reading, we have noted the names of the people who have been publicly reported to be the six unindicted co-conspirators, based on evidence and reporting from which their identities can reasonably be ascertained. Thus, in these notes, we refer to "Co-Conspirator 1" as "Rudy Giuliani." The other unindicted co-conspirators are similarly identified as: (2) John Eastman, (3) Sidney Powell, (4) Jeffrey Clark, and (5) Kenneth Chesebro. There has been more speculation as to the identity of the sixth unindicted co-conspirator, but details in the indictment and media reporting suggest it may be political operative Boris Epshteyn.

an official proceeding. Finally, the Constitution and ECA required that on the sixth of January* following election day, the Congress meet in a Joint Session for a certification proceeding, presided over by the Vice President as President of the Senate, to count the electoral votes, resolve any objections, and announce the result—thus certifying the winner of the presidential election as president-elect. This federal government function—from the point of ascertainment to the certification—is foundational to the United States' democratic process, and until 2021, had operated in a peaceful and orderly manner for more than 130 years.†

Manner and Means‡

10.   The Defendant's conspiracy to impair, obstruct, and defeat the federal government function through dishonesty, fraud, and deceit included the following manner and means:

a.   The Defendant and co-conspirators used knowingly false claims of election fraud to get state legislators and election officials to subvert the legitimate election results and change electoral votes for the Defendant's opponent, Joseph R. Biden, Jr., to electoral votes for the Defendant. That is, on the pretext of baseless fraud claims, the Defendant pushed officials in certain states to ignore the popular vote; disenfranchise millions of voters; dismiss legitimate electors; and ultimately,

---

* Why did the plot to overturn the election culminate on January 6, 2021? As the indictment explains, by congressional statute, January 6 is the day the electoral votes are counted in Congress, and thus the date on which Trump and his co-conspirators could try to stop or delay the congressional recording of the votes for Biden, and thwart for the first time in US history the peaceful transfer of power—a record that has distinguished the United States from countries around the world for centuries.
† This date is linked to the 1887 passage of the Electoral Count Act, but the peaceful transfer of power has been a hallmark of our country since 1796 when President George Washington refused entreaties for a third presidential term, insisting instead on an election and the transfer of the presidency to the winner of that election.
‡ This is traditional indictment language: lawyers speak about the "methods and means" or "manner and means" used to carry out a conspiracy. This section permits the government to provide an overview of the scheme in plain English, before the more detailed factual allegations and the technical charging language of the criminal statute, which follow this section.

cause the ascertainment of and voting by illegitimate electors in favor of the Defendant.

b.   The Defendant and co-conspirators organized fraudulent slates of electors in seven targeted states (Arizona, Georgia, Michigan, Nevada, New Mexico, Pennsylvania, and Wisconsin), attempting to mimic the procedures that the legitimate electors were supposed to follow under the Constitution and other federal and state laws. This included causing the fraudulent electors to meet on the day appointed by federal law on which legitimate electors were to gather and cast their votes; cast fraudulent votes for the Defendant; and sign certificates falsely representing that they were legitimate electors. Some fraudulent electors were tricked into participating based on the understanding that their votes would be used only if the Defendant succeeded in outcome-determinative lawsuits within their state, which the Defendant never did. The Defendant and co-conspirators then caused these fraudulent electors to transmit their false certificates to the Vice President and other government officials to be counted at the certification proceeding on January 6.[*]

c.   The Defendant and co-conspirators attempted to use the power and authority of the Justice Department to conduct sham election crime investigations and to send a letter to the targeted states that falsely claimed that the Justice Department had identified significant concerns that may have impacted the election outcome; that sought to advance the Defendant's fraudulent elector plan by using the Justice Department's

---

[*] The indictment does not treat all of the "fake electors" as knowing participants in election fraud, noting that some were tricked by the conspirators into believing that they were contingent electors who would participate in the Electoral College process only if a court found that the state vote was for Trump, and not Biden. Many electors have been charged in Georgia and Michigan and will be mounting as a defense to those charges that they were mere innocent dupes, rather than knowing participants. (One Michigan elector has pleaded guilty already and is reported to be cooperating with that state's case.) Regardless of which side these electors fall on, the Trump campaign is alleged to have tried to use the slate of "fake" electors as real electors, even though no court had reversed any state election. That there were some unwitting dupes would just mean that the conspirators would stoop to fraud to induce those electors to sign up.

authority to falsely present the fraudulent electors as a valid alternative to the legitimate electors; and that urged, on behalf of the Justice Department, the targeted states' legislatures to convene to create the opportunity to choose the fraudulent electors over the legitimate electors.*

d. The Defendant and co-conspirators attempted to enlist the Vice President to use his ceremonial role at the January 6 certification proceeding to fraudulently alter the election results. First, using knowingly false claims of election fraud, the Defendant and co-conspirators attempted to convince the Vice President to use the Defendant's fraudulent electors, reject legitimate electoral votes, or send legitimate electoral votes to state legislatures for review rather than counting them. When that failed, on the morning of January 6, the Defendant and co-conspirators repeated knowingly false claims of election fraud to gathered supporters, falsely told them that the Vice President had the authority to and might alter the election results, and directed them to the Capitol to obstruct the certification proceeding and exert pressure on the Vice President to take the fraudulent actions he had previously refused.†

---

* A second major "manner and means" involved efforts to solicit the DOJ's assistance to falsely say that it was investigating credible allegations of material fraud; the problem is that former attorney general Bill Barr, and the then-acting attorney general and deputy attorney general, all said there were no credible allegations of fraud—and averred that they relayed this to Trump. This part of the conspiracy has particularly compelling proof that, by insisting that he won the election, Trump was knowingly perpetrating a fraud.

INSIDER NOTE: Some readers may have already observed that these allegations are strikingly reminiscent of facts that surfaced in the *first* Trump impeachment. There, evidence was presented that Trump instructed Ukrainian president Volodymyr Zelenskyy to open an investigation into Joe Biden and his son Hunter, allowing Trump an opportunity to attack Biden, if he were the 2020 Democratic nominee. Here, Trump is alleged to have instructed the DOJ to say it was investigating nonexistent electoral fraud, allowing him to use the fact of an investigation to continue to peddle the myth that the election was stolen from him. As Trump is alleged to have said to top DOJ officials: "Just call it corrupt and leave the rest to me."

† Trump's vice president, Mike Pence, is a clear target of the fraud—but resisted efforts to enlist his participation.

INSIDER NOTE: Although Mike Pence resisted testifying before the January 6 committee, Jack Smith compelled his testimony before a federal grand jury, and the allegations in the indictment reflect that development. This trial will thus likely feature

e.   After it became public on the afternoon of January 6 that the Vice President would not fraudulently alter the election results, a large and angry crowd—including many individuals whom the Defendant had deceived into believing the Vice President could and might change the election results—violently attacked the Capitol and halted the proceeding. As violence ensued, the Defendant and co-conspirators exploited the disruption by redoubling efforts to levy false claims of election fraud and convince Members of Congress to further delay the certification based on those claims.*

The Defendant's Knowledge of the Falsity of His Election Fraud Claims

11.   The Defendant, his co-conspirators, and their agents made knowingly false claims that there had been outcome-determinative† fraud in the 2020 presidential election. These prolific lies about election fraud included dozens of specific claims that there had been substantial fraud in certain states, such as that large numbers of dead,

---

a former vice president of the United States testifying for the prosecution against the former president under whom he served.

* The indictment's discussion of the January 6 violence is important to note. Trump is not charged with inciting the violence, although there is evidence to support that conclusion. Here, Smith decided not to raise the legal issue of whether Trump's speech at the Ellipse and in social media posts met the high legal standard for proving incitement—a standard that is purposely high in order to protect our free speech rights. Instead, Smith skillfully weaves the violence into the indictment by showing how Trump and his conspirators opportunistically used it to further their criminal scheme, regardless of whether the conspirators intentionally incited the violence.

INSIDER NOTE: The defense will surely try to strike or limit evidence of this violence at trial, on the ground that it is unduly prejudicial since Trump is not charged with incitement. Judge Chutkan might agree, preventing the prosecution from presenting such evidence at trial. Alternatively, she might choose to deny the motion, but limit the scope of such evidence and instruct the jury that it may not use evidence of the violence against Trump, except to the extent the jury finds it relevant to how Trump relied on the violent acts to further his alleged scheme to maintain the presidency.

† It is worth noting this phrasing; the government is not contending that there was no fraud at all in the election (there inevitably is some low-level fraud in any significant election). Instead, the government maintains that there is no evidence to date that there was outcome-determinative fraud in the 2020 election.

non-resident, non-citizen, or otherwise ineligible voters had cast ballots, or that voting machines had changed votes for the Defendant to votes for Biden. These claims were false, and the Defendant knew that they were false. In fact, the Defendant was notified repeatedly that his claims were untrue—often by the people on whom he relied for candid advice on important matters, and who were best positioned to know the facts—and he deliberately disregarded the truth. For instance:

a.   The Defendant's Vice President—who personally stood to gain by remaining in office as part of the Defendant's ticket and whom the Defendant asked to study fraud allegations—told the Defendant that he had seen no evidence of outcome-determinative fraud.*

b.   The senior leaders of the Justice Department—appointed by the Defendant and responsible for investigating credible allegations of election crimes—told the Defendant on multiple occasions that various allegations of fraud were unsupported.

c.   The Director of National Intelligence—the Defendant's principal advisor on intelligence matters related to national security—disabused the Defendant of the notion that the Intelligence Community's findings regarding foreign interference would change the outcome of the election.

d.   The Department of Homeland Security's Cybersecurity and Infrastructure Security Agency ("CISA")—whose existence the Defendant signed into law to protect the nation's cybersecurity infrastructure from attack—joined an official multi-agency statement that there was no evidence any voting system had been compromised and that declared the 2020 election "the most secure in American history." Days later, after the CISA Director—whom the Defendant had appointed—announced publicly that election security experts were in

---

* Here, the government maintains that Pence, like Trump, had strong incentives to win the election, and Pence's willingness to admit defeat is a notable contrast to Trump. At trial, the government will hold Pence up to the jury as an example of how to behave in the wake of an election loss—in contrast to what Trump is alleged to have done.

agreement that claims of computer-based election fraud were unsubstantiated, the Defendant fired him.

e. Senior White House attorneys—selected by the Defendant to provide him candid advice—informed the Defendant that there was no evidence of outcome-determinative election fraud, and told him that his presidency would end on Inauguration Day in 2021.*

f. Senior staffers on the Defendant's 2020 re-election campaign ("Defendant's Campaign" or "Campaign")—whose sole mission was the Defendant's reelection—told the Defendant on November 7, 2020, that he had only a five to ten percent chance of prevailing in the election, and that success was contingent on the Defendant winning ongoing vote counts or litigation in Arizona, Georgia, and Wisconsin. Within a week of that assessment, the Defendant lost in Arizona—meaning he had lost the election.

g. State legislators and officials—many of whom were the Defendant's political allies, had voted for him, and wanted him to be re-elected—repeatedly informed the Defendant that his claims of fraud in their states were unsubstantiated or false and resisted his pressure to act based upon them.

h. State and federal courts—the neutral arbiters responsible for ensuring the fair and even-handed administration of election laws—rejected every outcome-determinative post-election lawsuit filed by the Defendant, his co-conspirators, and allies, providing the Defendant real-time notice that his allegations were meritless.†

---

* The indictment notes that a number of senior White House counsel told Trump that he lost the election fair and square. If these lawyers testify to this fact—and if a jury credits their testimony—it will be strong proof of Trump's criminal intent and knowledge that he was acting illegally.

† A jury may find this litany of evidence particularly compelling to establish that Trump knew that there was no material fraud in the 2020 election. Notably, the proof comes from Republican Trump loyalists, as well as from judges appointed by both Democrats and Republicans, including Trump. At trial, Trump is likely to say that he still believed he won, but that claim may be hard for a jury to accept in the absence of evidence that refutes the evidence that there was no material fraud in the 2020 election. Further, the prosecution will point to Trump's many unsuccessful post-election

12.   The Defendant widely disseminated his false claims of election fraud for months, despite the fact that he knew, and in many cases had been informed directly, that they were not true. The Defendant's knowingly false statements were integral to his criminal plans to defeat the federal government function, obstruct the certification, and interfere with others' right to vote and have their votes counted. He made these knowingly false claims throughout the post-election time period, including those below that he made immediately before the attack on the Capitol on January 6:

a.   The Defendant insinuated that more than ten thousand dead voters had voted in Georgia. Just four days earlier, Georgia's Secretary of State had explained to the Defendant that this was false.

b.   The Defendant asserted that there had been 205,000 more votes than voters in Pennsylvania. The Defendant's Acting Attorney General and Acting Deputy Attorney General had explained to him that this was false.

c.   The Defendant said that there had been a suspicious vote dump in Detroit, Michigan. The Defendant's Attorney General had explained to the Defendant that this was false, and the Defendant's allies in the Michigan state legislature—the Speaker of the House of Representatives and Majority Leader of the Senate—had publicly announced that there was no evidence of substantial fraud in the state.

d.   The Defendant claimed that there had been tens of thousands of double votes and other fraud in Nevada. The Nevada Secretary of State had previously rebutted the Defendant's fraud claims by publicly posting a "Facts vs. Myths" document explaining that Nevada judges had reviewed and rejected them, and the Nevada Supreme Court had rendered a decision denying such claims.

e.   The Defendant said that more than 30,000 non-citizens had voted in Arizona. The Defendant's own Campaign Manager

---

lawsuits to show that it was simply impermissible for Trump to take the law into his own hands, even if he thought he had won.

had explained to him that such claims were false, and the Speaker of the Arizona House of Representatives, who had supported the Defendant in the election, had issued a public statement that there was no evidence of substantial fraud in Arizona.

f.   The Defendant asserted that voting machines in various contested states had switched votes from the Defendant to Biden. The Defendant's Attorney General, Acting Attorney General, and Acting Deputy Attorney General all had explained to him that this was false, and numerous recounts and audits had confirmed the accuracy of voting machines.[*]

The Criminal Agreement and Acts to Effect the Object of the Conspiracy

The Defendant's Use of Deceit to Get State Officials to Subvert the Legitimate Election Results and Change Electoral Votes

13.   Shortly after[†] election day—which fell on November 3, 2020—the Defendant launched his criminal scheme. On November 13, the Defendant's Campaign attorneys conceded in court that he had lost the vote count in the state of Arizona—meaning, based on the assessment the Defendant's Campaign advisors had given him just a week earlier, the Defendant had lost the election. So the next day, the Defendant turned to Co-Conspirator 1,[‡] whom he

---

[*] Again, the indictment marshals key evidence of alleged false statements by Trump, as well as evidence that Trump knew at the time that his statements were untruthful. The indictment, having alleged that making such false statements alone and in isolation is not a crime, ties the false statements to aspects of the charged scheme— namely to pressure state officials, Congress, the DOJ, and the vice president to thwart the certification of the election results.

[†] The proof that Trump was preparing for this scheme *even prior to the election* is not inconsistent with this start date: Trump would not need to implement the scheme unless he had lost the election.

[‡] As noted, Giuliani is an unindicted co-conspirator here, but he is an actual indicted co-conspirator in the Georgia criminal case. Unless facts change dramatically, he is thus unlikely to be a witness for either side in this case, as his testimony could be used

announced would spearhead his efforts going forward to challenge the election results. From that point on, the Defendant and his co-conspirators executed a strategy to use knowing deceit in the targeted states to impair, obstruct, and defeat the federal government function, including as described below.

*Arizona**

14.   On November 13, 2020, the Defendant had a conversation with his Campaign Manager, who informed him that a claim that had been circulating, that a substantial number of non-citizens had voted in Arizona, was false.

15.   On November 22, eight days before Arizona's Governor certified the ascertainment of the state's legitimate electors based on the popular vote, the Defendant and Co-Conspirator 1 called the Speaker of the Arizona House of Representatives and made knowingly false claims of election fraud aimed at interfering with the ascertainment of and voting by Arizona's electors, as follows:

   a.   The Defendant and Co-Conspirator 1 falsely asserted, among other things, that a substantial number of non-citizens, non-residents, and dead people had voted fraudulently in Arizona. The Arizona House Speaker asked Co-Conspirator 1 for evidence of the claims, which Co-Conspirator 1 did not have, but claimed he would provide. Co-Conspirator 1 never did so.

   b.   The Defendant and Co-Conspirator 1 asked the Arizona House Speaker to call the legislature into session to hold a hearing based on their claims of election fraud. The Arizona House Speaker refused, stating that doing so would require a two-thirds vote of its members, and he would not allow it without actual evidence of fraud.

---

against him in the Georgia criminal case. This is true as to Eastman and Clark, who are unindicted co-conspirators in this indictment, and are also co-defendants in the Georgia case.

* The indictment outlines key evidence from so-called battleground states where Trump and his co-conspirators targeted election officials to pressure them to change the vote tallies.

c.   The Defendant and Co-Conspirator 1 asked the Arizona House Speaker to use the legislature to circumvent the process by which legitimate electors would be ascertained for Biden based on the popular vote, and replace those electors with a new slate for the Defendant. The Arizona House Speaker refused, responding that the suggestion was beyond anything he had ever heard or thought of as something within his authority.

16.   On December 1, Co-Conspirator 1 met with the Arizona House Speaker. When the Arizona House Speaker again asked Co-Conspirator 1 for evidence of the outcome-determinative election fraud he and the Defendant had been claiming, Co-Conspirator 1 responded with words to the effect of, "We don't have the evidence, but we have lots of theories."*

17.   On December 4, the Arizona House Speaker issued a public statement that said, in part:

No election is perfect, and if there were evidence of illegal votes or an improper count, then Arizona law provides a process to contest the election: a lawsuit under state law. But the law does not authorize the Legislature to reverse the results of an election.

As a conservative Republican, I don't like the results of the presidential election. I voted for President Trump and worked

---

* The allegations here rely on the testimony of Rusty Bowers, the Republican Speaker of the Arizona House of Representatives in 2020. He was a key witness in the January 6 committee hearings. The similarity between what Bowers alleges and what is alleged to have occurred in other key states, and is captured on tape in Georgia, will indirectly corroborate Bowers's testimony, while also bolstering the government's argument that proof of the illegal pressure campaign is clear from multiple independent sources who had no incentive to lie or hurt Trump politically.

INSIDER NOTE: The last line—Giuliani's direct admission to Bowers that they had no proof of fraud—will be key evidence in the Georgia case against Giuliani. Jack Smith will contend that it is also admissible against Trump in this case as a "co-conspirator statement." Rule 801(d)(2)(e) of the Federal Rules of Evidence permits statements made by co-conspirators to be admitted into evidence if the statement is in furtherance of the underlying conspiracy and offered against a conspirator, even if the statement is not made *to* a conspirator. Trump likely will contest the admissibility of these statements.

hard to reelect him. But I cannot and will not entertain a suggestion that we violate current law to change the outcome of a certified election.

I and my fellow legislators swore an oath to support the U.S. Constitution and the constitution and laws of the state of Arizona. It would violate that oath, the basic principles of republican government, and the rule of law if we attempted to nullify the people's vote based on unsupported theories of fraud. Under the laws that we wrote and voted upon, Arizona voters choose who wins, and our system requires that their choice be respected.*

18. On the morning of January 4, 2021, Co-Conspirator 2† called the Arizona House Speaker to urge him to use a majority of the legislature to decertify the state's legitimate electors. Arizona's validly ascertained electors had voted three weeks earlier and sent their votes to Congress, which was scheduled to count those votes in Biden's favor in just two days' time at the January 6 certification proceeding. When the Arizona House Speaker explained that state investigations had uncovered no evidence of substantial fraud in the state, Co-Conspirator 2 conceded that he "[didn't] know enough about facts on the ground" in Arizona, but nonetheless told the Arizona House Speaker to decertify and "let the courts sort it out." The Arizona House Speaker refused, stating that he would not "play with

---

* This an example of how the indictment is a "speaking indictment"—and an unusual one at that. An indictment only needs legally to set out the statutes allegedly violated and need not recite facts. A "speaking indictment," however, lays out facts and allows the public, as well as the defendant, to know more about the government's evidence and theory of the case. Further, this paragraph alleges facts that may not be admissible in this form at trial, depending on various factors. It is unusual to include material in a charge unless the government is confident it will be admissible; here, the fact of the statement is indisputable and serves to make plain to the public why Bowers did not go along with the scheme.

† This is a reference to John Eastman, who, through his attorney, confirmed his identity as "co-conspirator 2" to multiple news outlets. Eastman is criminally charged in the Georgia indictment. Bowers recounts here something Eastman is alleged to have said. If a jury credits Bowers, this is a highly incriminating statement.

the oath" he had taken to uphold the United States Constitution and Arizona law.

19.   On January 6, the Defendant publicly repeated the knowingly false claim that 36,000 non-citizens had voted in Arizona.

Georgia

20.   On November 16, 2020, on the Defendant's behalf, his executive assistant sent Co-Conspirator 3[*] and others a document containing bullet points critical of a certain voting machine company, writing, "See attached – Please include as is, or almost as is, in lawsuit." Co-Conspirator 3 responded nine minutes later, writing, "IT MUST GO IN ALL SUITS IN GA AND PA IMMEDIATELY WITH A FRAUD CLAIM THAT REQUIRES THE ENTIRE ELECTION TO BE SET ASIDE in those states and machines impounded for non-partisan professional inspection." On November 25, Co-Conspirator 3 filed a lawsuit against the Governor of Georgia falsely alleging "massive election fraud" accomplished through the voting machine company's election software and hardware. Before the lawsuit was even filed, the Defendant retweeted a post promoting it. The Defendant did this despite the fact that when he had discussed Co-Conspirator 3's far-fetched public claims regarding the voting machine company in private with advisors, the Defendant had conceded that they were unsupported and that Co-

---

[*] Media reporting and extant evidence suggest that this is a reference to Sidney Powell, who was criminally charged with this scheme in Georgia. On October 19, 2023, Powell pleaded guilty to six Georgia misdemeanors relating to a conspiracy to intentionally interfere with the performance of election duties. As a result of her plea bargain, Powell will serve six years of probation, was fined $6,000, and wrote an apology letter to Georgia and its residents. She also recorded a statement for prosecutors (the contents of which are publicly unknown) and agreed to testify truthfully against her Georgia co-defendants at future trials as a condition of her probation. If she is found to have testified falsely, her probation term could be revoked.

INSIDER NOTE: Powell has no known federal agreement with Jack Smith. It is highly unusual for a defendant not to negotiate a global disposition for her criminal exposure. Because Powell does not appear to have done so, federal prosecutors could use her statements in the Georgia case against her to charge her with federal crimes.

Conspirator 3 sounded "crazy." Co-Conspirator 3's Georgia lawsuit was dismissed on December 7.*

21.   On December 3, Co-Conspirator 1 orchestrated a presentation to a Judiciary Subcommittee of the Georgia State Senate, with the intention of misleading state senators into blocking the ascertainment of legitimate electors. During the presentation:

a.   An agent of the Defendant and Co-Conspirator 1 falsely claimed that more than 10,000 dead people voted in Georgia. That afternoon, a Senior Advisor to the Defendant told the Defendant's Chief of Staff through text messages, "Just an FYI. [A Campaign lawyer] and his team verified that the 10k+ supposed dead people voting in GA is not accurate. . . . It was alleged in [Co-Conspirator 1's] hearing today." The Senior Advisor clarified that he believed that the actual number was 12.

b.   Another agent of the Defendant and Co-Conspirator 1 played a misleading excerpt of a video recording of ballot-counting at State Farm Arena in Atlanta and insinuated that it showed election workers counting "suitcases" of illegal ballots.

c.   Co-Conspirator 2 encouraged the legislators to decertify the state's legitimate electors based on false allegations of election fraud.

22.   Also on December 3, the Defendant issued a Tweet amplifying the knowingly false claims made in Co-Conspirator 1's presentation in Georgia: "Wow! Blockbuster testimony taking place right now in Georgia. Ballot stuffing by Dems when Republicans were forced to leave the large counting room. Plenty more coming, but this alone leads to an easy win of the State!"

---

* The voting machine company referenced is Dominion Voting Systems, which has sued Giuliani and Powell, among others. Dominion also sued Fox News Network in a suit that settled for hundreds of millions of dollars. In that civil case, the court ruled that there was no evidence that Dominion had perpetrated election fraud. In *Trump v. Kemp*, Trump's effort to contest the Georgia election results, a judge also concluded that there had been no outcome-determinative fraud. Notably, despite privately dismissing Powell's allegations as "unsupported" and "crazy," Trump repeated these allegations, including during his speech at the Ellipse on the morning of January 6.

23. On December 4, the Georgia Secretary of State's Chief Operating Officer* debunked the claims made at Co-Conspirator 1's presentation the previous day, issuing a Tweet stating, "The 90 second video of election workers at State Farm arena, purporting to show fraud was watched in its entirety (hours) by @GaSecof-State investigators. Shows normal ballot processing. Here is the fact check on it." On December 7, he reiterated during a press conference that the claim that there had been misconduct at State Farm Arena was false.

24. On December 8, the Defendant called the Georgia Attorney General to pressure him to support an election lawsuit filed in the Supreme Court by another state's attorney general. The Georgia Attorney General told the Defendant that officials had investigated various claims of election fraud in the state and were not seeing evidence to support them.

25. Also on December 8, a Senior Campaign Advisor—who spoke with the Defendant on a daily basis and had informed him on multiple occasions that various fraud claims were untrue—expressed frustration that many of Co-Conspirator 1 and his legal team's claims could not be substantiated. As early as mid-November, for instance, the Senior Campaign Advisor had informed the Defendant that his claims of a large number of dead voters in Georgia were untrue. With respect to the persistent false claim regarding State Farm Arena, on December 8, the Senior Campaign Advisor wrote in an email, "When our research and campaign legal team can't back up any of the claims made by our Elite Strike Force Legal Team, you can see why we're 0-32 on our cases. I'll obviously hustle to help on all fronts, but it's tough to own any of this when it's all just conspiracy shit beamed down from the mothership."

26. On December 10, four days before Biden's validly ascertained electors were scheduled to cast votes and send them to Congress, Co-Conspirator 1 appeared at a hearing before the Georgia

---

* The context and extant media reporting indicate that this is a reference to Robert Gabriel Sterling, a Georgia Republican state official.

House of Representatives' Government Affairs Committee. Co-Conspirator 1 played the State Farm Arena video again, and falsely claimed that it showed "voter fraud right in front of people's eyes" and was "the tip of the iceberg." Then, he cited two election workers by name, baselessly accused them of "quite obviously surreptitiously passing around USB ports as if they are vials of heroin or cocaine," and suggested that they were criminals whose "places of work, their homes, should have been searched for evidence of ballots, for evidence of USB ports, for evidence of voter fraud." Thereafter, the two election workers received numerous death threats.*

27. On December 15, the Defendant summoned the incoming Acting Attorney General, the incoming Acting Deputy Attorney General, and others to the Oval Office to discuss allegations of election fraud.† During the meeting, the Justice Department officials specifically refuted the Defendant's claims about State Farm Arena, explaining to him that the activity shown on the tape Co-Conspirator 1 had used was "benign."

28. On December 23, a day after the Defendant's Chief of Staff personally observed the signature verification process at the Cobb County Civic Center and notified the Defendant that state election officials were "conducting themselves in an exemplary fashion" and would find fraud if it existed, the Defendant tweeted that

---

* This is a reference to Ruby Freeman and her daughter Shaye Moss. Freeman and Moss filed a civil suit against Rudy Giuliani in a federal court in Washington, DC, for defamation arising from his claims that they engaged in electoral fraud. There, US District Judge Beryl Howell granted Freeman and Moss's motion for summary judgment as to liability, resolving the case in their favor. Giuliani has admitted that he intentionally lied about Freeman and Moss. That admission may come back to haunt him, as he is charged criminally in connection with this scheme in Georgia. Additionally, the racial subtext of his slander—Freeman and Moss are Black women and Giuliani claimed that they were "passing around USB ports [at a Georgia polling site] like they were vials of heroin or cocaine"—may create additional difficulties for him at trial.

† This is a reference to Jeffrey Rosen and Richard Donahue, respectively, as well as members of the White House counsel staff. Many White House and DOJ lawyers will be government witnesses in the trial; they have testified to many of these details before the January 6 committee. Like Pence, they are all Republicans and would lose their jobs if Trump lost the election.

the Georgia officials administering the signature verification process were trying to hide evidence of election fraud and were "[t]erri-
ble people!"*

29.   In a phone call on December 27, the Defendant spoke with
the Acting Attorney General and Acting Deputy Attorney General.
During the call, the Defendant again pressed the unfounded claims
regarding State Farm Arena, and the two top Justice Department
officials again rebutted the allegations, telling him that the Justice
Department had reviewed videotape and interviewed witnesses, and
had not identified any suspicious conduct.

30.   On December 31, the Defendant signed a verification
affirming false election fraud allegations made on his behalf in a
lawsuit filed in his name against the Georgia Governor. In advance
of the filing, Co-Conspirator 2—who was advising the Defendant
on the lawsuit—acknowledged in an email that he and the Defendant had, since signing a previous verification, "been made aware
that some of the allegations (and evidence proffered by the experts)
has been inaccurate" and that signing a new affirmation "with that
knowledge (and incorporation by reference) would not be accurate."
The Defendant and Co-Conspirator 2 caused the Defendant's signed
verification to be filed nonetheless.†

31.   On January 2, four days before Congress's certification
proceeding, the Defendant and others called Georgia's Secretary of

---

* This is a reference to Mark Meadows, Trump's White House chief of staff. It is
interesting that this statement is included here. It would be unusual to be actively
cooperating with federal prosecutors while simultaneously being subject to charges
in a state-level prosecution. Meadows has been charged in Georgia and also appears
to have testified in Georgia falsely in connection with his effort to remove the case
against him to federal court. Of course, it is entirely possible that Meadows is not the
source of this statement. In that case, the federal government may be able to prove
this statement using the testimony of someone who heard Meadows when Meadows
reported his findings to Trump.

INSIDER NOTE: The indictment includes this illustration of Trump's common tac-
tic of using adjectives and epithets, in lieu of facts or reasoning, to undermine his
adversaries.

† Of note, it is a crime to make a knowingly false filing to a court, although this is not
separately charged. Here, it is offered as important proof of Trump's intent.

State. During the call, the Defendant lied* to the Georgia Secretary of State to induce him to alter Georgia's popular vote count and call into question the validity of the Biden electors' votes, which had been transmitted to Congress weeks before, including as follows:

a. The Defendant raised allegations regarding the State Farm Arena video and repeatedly disparaged one of the same election workers that Co-Conspirator 1 had maligned on December 10, using her name almost twenty times and falsely referring to her as "a professional vote scammer and hustler." In response, the Georgia Secretary of State refuted this: "You're talking about the State Farm video. And I think it's extremely unfortunate that [Co-Conspirator 1] or his people, they sliced and diced that video and took it out of context." When the Georgia Secretary of State then offered a link to a video that would disprove Co-Conspirator 1's claims, the Defendant responded, "I don't care about a link, I don't need it. I have a much, [Georgia Secretary of State], I have a much better link."

b. The Defendant asked about rumors that paper ballots cast in the election were being destroyed, and the Georgia Secretary of State's Counsel explained to him that the claim had been investigated and was not true.

c. The Defendant claimed that 5,000 dead people voted in Georgia, causing the Georgia Secretary of State to respond, "Well, Mr. President, the challenge that you have is the data you have is wrong. . . . The actual number were two. Two. Two people that were dead that voted. And so [your information]'s wrong, that was two."

d. The Defendant claimed that thousands of out-of-state voters had cast ballots in Georgia's election, which the Georgia Secretary of State's Counsel refuted, explaining, "We've been

---

* Again, the indictment pulls no punches, directly alleging that Trump lied to Georgia secretary of state Brad Raffensperger on the infamous telephone call. Notably, this call occurred *after* a Georgia recount had occurred and the vote had been certified.

INSIDER NOTE: The fact that Raffensperger taped the call is, by itself, revealing. Presumably, Raffensperger believed that he needed to do so because Trump might lie about what had occurred during the call.

going through each of those as well, and those numbers that we got, that [Defendant's counsel] was just saying, they're not accurate. Every one we've been through are people that lived in Georgia, moved to a different state, but then moved back to Georgia legitimately . . . they moved back in years ago. This was not like something just before the election."

e.　In response to multiple other of the Defendant's allegations, the Georgia Secretary of State's Counsel told the Defendant that the Georgia Bureau of Investigation was examining all such claims and finding no merit to them.

f.　The Defendant said that he needed to "find" 11,780 votes, and insinuated that the Georgia Secretary of State and his Counsel could be subject to criminal prosecution if they failed to find election fraud as he demanded, stating, "And you are going to find that they are—which is totally illegal—it's, it's, it's, more illegal for you than it is for them because you know what they did and you're not reporting it. That's a criminal, you know, that's a criminal offense. And you know, you can't let that happen. That's a big risk to you and to [the Georgia Secretary of State's Counsel], your lawyer."*

32.　The next day, on January 3, the Defendant falsely claimed that the Georgia Secretary of State had not addressed the Defendant's allegations, publicly stating that the Georgia Secretary of State "was unwilling, or unable, to answer questions such as the 'ballots under table' scam, ballot destruction, out of state 'voters', dead voters, and more. He has no clue!"†

33.　On January 6, the Defendant publicly repeated the knowingly false insinuation that more than 10,300 dead people had voted in Georgia.

---

* This threat of criminal prosecution is one of the more damning pieces of proof. For Raffensperger to face any legitimate criminal prosecution, he would have to be knowingly engaged in a crime; there is nothing about what he was reporting that has been shown to be factually incorrect, let alone intentionally wrong. For the president to nonetheless threaten the prospect of criminal prosecution was thus a ham-handed way to induce Raffensperger to "find" the votes needed to overturn the Georgia election result.

† Unbeknownst to Trump at this point, the call had been taped.

Michigan

34.   On November 5, 2020, the Defendant claimed that there had been a suspicious dump of votes—purportedly illegitimate ballots—stating, "In Detroit, there were hours of unexplained delay in delivering many of the votes for counting. The final batch did not arrive until four in the morning and—even though the polls closed at eight o'clock. So they brought it in, and the batches came in, and nobody knew where they came from."

35.   On November 20, three days before Michigan's Governor signed a certificate of ascertainment notifying the federal government that, based on the popular vote, Biden's electors were to represent Michigan's voters, the Defendant held a meeting in the Oval Office with the Speaker of the Michigan House of Representatives and the Majority Leader of the Michigan Senate. In the meeting, the Defendant raised his false claim, among others, of an illegitimate vote dump in Detroit. In response, the Michigan Senate Majority Leader told the Defendant that he had lost Michigan not because of fraud, but because the Defendant had underperformed with certain voter populations in the state. Upon leaving their meeting, the Michigan House Speaker and Michigan Senate Majority Leader issued a statement reiterating this:

> The Senate and House Oversight Committees are actively engaged in a thorough review of Michigan's elections process and we have faith in the committee process to provide greater transparency and accountability to our citizens. We have not yet been made aware of any information that would change the outcome of the election in Michigan and as legislative leaders, we will follow the law and follow the normal process regarding Michigan's electors, just as we have said throughout this election.

36.   On December 1, the Defendant raised his Michigan vote dump claim with the Attorney General, who responded that what had occurred in Michigan had been the normal vote-counting process and that there was no indication of fraud in Detroit.

37.   Despite this, the next day, the Defendant made a know-ingly false statement that in Michigan, "[a]t 6:31 in the morning, a vote dump of 149,772 votes came in unexpectedly. We were winning by a lot. That batch was received in horror. Nobody knows anything about it. . . . It's corrupt. Detroit is corrupt. I have a lot of friends in Detroit. They know it. But Detroit is totally corrupt."*

38.   On December 4, Co-Conspirator 1 sent a text message to the Michigan House Speaker reiterating his unsupported claim of election fraud and attempting to get the Michigan House Speaker to assist in reversing the ascertainment of the legitimate Biden electors, stating, "Looks like Georgia may well hold some factual hearings and change the certification under ArtII sec 1 cl 2 of the Constitu-tion. As [Co-Conspirator 2] explained they don't just have the right to do it but the obligation. . . . Help me get this done in Michigan."

39.   Similarly, on December 7, despite still having established no fraud in Michigan, Co-Conspirator 1 sent a text intended for the Michigan Senate Majority Leader: "So I need you to pass a joint res-olution from the Michigan legislature that states that, * the election is in dispute, * there's an ongoing investigation by the Legislature, and * the Electors sent by Governor Whitmer are not the official Electors of the State of Michigan and do not fall within the Safe Harbor deadline of Dec 8 under Michigan law."†

40.   On December 14—the day that electors in states across the country were required to vote and submit their votes to Congress— the Michigan House Speaker and Michigan Senate Majority Leader announced that, contrary to the Defendant's requests, they would not decertify the legitimate election results or electors in Michigan. The Michigan Senate Majority Leader's public statement included,

---

* The indictment reprises a consistent theme: Trump's excessive use of adjectives, rather than facts, to rebut the information that experts provided to him showing that there had been no electoral fraud.

† This illustrates another theme: Trump's efforts to convince officials to make state-ments confirming that the election was in dispute, even though there was scant evi-dence to support Trump's claim of genuinely disputed election results.

"[W]e have not received evidence of fraud on a scale that would change the outcome of the election in Michigan." The Michigan House Speaker's public statement read, in part:

> We've diligently examined these reports of fraud to the best of our ability. . . .
>
> . . . I fought hard for President Trump. Nobody wanted him to win more than me. I think he's done an incredible job. But I love our republic, too. I can't fathom risking our norms, traditions and institutions to pass a resolution retroactively changing the electors for Trump, simply because some think there may have been enough widespread fraud to give him the win. That's unprecedented for good reason. And that's why there is not enough support in the House to cast a new slate of electors. I fear we'd lose our country forever. This truly would bring mutually assured destruction for every future election in regards to the Electoral College. And I can't stand for that. I won't.

41.   On January 6, 2021, the Defendant publicly repeated his knowingly false claim regarding an illicit dump of more than a hundred thousand ballots in Detroit.

Pennsylvania

42.   On November 11, 2020, the Defendant publicly maligned a Philadelphia City Commissioner for stating on the news that there was no evidence of widespread fraud in Philadelphia. As a result, the Philadelphia City Commissioner and his family received death threats.*

---

* Another important theme throughout the indictment is Trump's imperviousness to concerns that his false statements about the election would lead to violence—a callousness that continues to this day in spite of threats and actual violence against judges, grand jurors, election officials, prosecutors, law enforcement officials, state and federal elected officials, and their family members.

INSIDER NOTE: Violence and threats of violence may have helped Trump cling to power for as long as he did. Utah senator Mitt Romney reports that certain senators declined to vote to convict Trump during his second impeachment trial out of concern for their safety and the safety of their families, despite their oaths of office.

43.   On November 25, the day after Pennsylvania's Governor signed a certificate of ascertainment and thus certified to the federal government that Biden's electors were the legitimate electors for the state, Co-Conspirator 1 orchestrated an event at a hotel in Gettysburg attended by state legislators. Co-Conspirator 1 falsely claimed that Pennsylvania had issued 1.8 million absentee ballots and received 2.5 million in return. In the days thereafter, a Campaign staffer wrote internally that Co-Conspirator 1's allegation was "just wrong" and "[t]here's no way to defend it." The Deputy Campaign Manager responded, "We have been saying this for a while. It's very frustrating."*

44.   On December 4, after four Republican leaders of the Pennsylvania legislature issued a public statement that the General Assembly lacked the authority to overturn the popular vote and appoint its own slate of electors, and that doing so would violate the state Election Code and Constitution, the Defendant re-tweeted a post labeling the legislators cowards.

45.   On December 31 and January 3, the Defendant repeatedly raised with the Acting Attorney General and Acting Deputy Attorney General the allegation that in Pennsylvania, there had been 205,000 more votes than voters. Each time, the Justice Department officials informed the Defendant that his claim was false.

46.   On January 6, 2021, the Defendant publicly repeated his knowingly false claim that there had been 205,000 more votes than voters in Pennsylvania.†

Wisconsin

47.   On November 29, 2020, a recount in Wisconsin that the Defendant's Campaign had petitioned and paid for did not change

---

* The indictment is notable for the unusually wide array of people—within the Republican party and Trump's own administration, and from across the nation—who will likely bear witness at trial to Trump's false claims of election fraud.

† INSIDER NOTE: The Pennsylvania lawsuit that Rudy Giuliani filed to overturn that state's election results is the subject of DC bar proceeding against him. There, it is recommended that Giuliani be disbarred because he acted in bad faith, filing a baseless lawsuit.

the election result, and in fact increased the Defendant's margin of defeat.

48.   On December 14, the Wisconsin Supreme Court rejected an election challenge by the Campaign. One Justice wrote, "[N]othing in this case casts any legitimate doubt that the people of Wisconsin lawfully chose Vice President Biden and Senator Harris to be the next leaders of our great country."

49.   On December 21, as a result of the state Supreme Court's decision, the Wisconsin Governor—who had signed a certificate of ascertainment on November 30 identifying Biden's electors as the state's legitimate electors—signed a certificate of final determination in which he recognized that the state Supreme Court had resolved a controversy regarding the appointment of Biden's electors, and confirmed that Biden had received the highest number of votes in the state and that his electors were the state's legitimate electors.

50.   That same day, in response to the court decision that had prompted the Wisconsin Governor to sign a certificate of final determination, the Defendant issued a Tweet repeating his knowingly false claim of election fraud and demanding that the Wisconsin legislature overturn the election results that had led to the ascertainment of Biden's electors as the legitimate electors.

51.   On December 27, the Defendant raised with the Acting Attorney General and Acting Deputy Attorney General a specific fraud claim—that there had been more votes than voters in Wisconsin. The Acting Deputy Attorney General informed the Defendant that the claim was false.

52.   On January 6, 2021, the Defendant publicly repeated knowingly false claims that there had been tens of thousands of unlawful votes in Wisconsin.*

---

* The Wisconsin allegations clearly indicate that Trump was engaged in lying to the public, but it remains to be seen how the prosecution will link these public lies to the campaign to pressure Wisconsin state officials (as the indictment alleges regarding other states like Georgia and Arizona). The Wisconsin allegations, however, may well be relevant to the fake elector aspect of the scheme, to which the indictment turns next.

The Defendant's Use of Dishonesty, Fraud, and Deceit to Organize Fraudulent Slates of Electors and Cause Them to Transmit False Certificates to Congress

53.   As the Defendant's attempts to obstruct the electoral vote through deceit of state officials met with repeated failure, beginning in early December 2020, he and co-conspirators developed a new plan: to marshal individuals who would have served as the Defendant's electors, had he won the popular vote, in seven targeted states—Arizona, Georgia, Michigan, Nevada, New Mexico, Pennsylvania, and Wisconsin—and cause those individuals to make and send to the Vice President and Congress false certifications that they were legitimate electors. Under the plan, the submission of these fraudulent slates would create a fake controversy at the certification proceeding and position the Vice President—presiding on January 6 as President of the Senate—to supplant legitimate electors with the Defendant's fake electors and certify the Defendant as president.*

54.   The plan capitalized on ideas presented in memoranda drafted by Co-Conspirator 5,† an attorney who was assisting the Defendant's Campaign with legal efforts related to a recount in Wis-

---

* The key phrase here is "fake controversy," which is a leitmotif description of Trump's frequent strategy, whether it be coercing Ukraine to open a fake investigation into the Bidens, pressuring DOJ to open a fake fraud case, filing false court cases, or putting together slates of fake electors.

† Media reporting and extant evidence suggest that this is a reference to Kenneth Chesebro, who was criminally charged in Georgia. On October 20, 2023, Chesebro pled guilty to a felony count of conspiracy to commit filing false documents (count 15 of the Georgia indictment). As a result of his Georgia plea bargain, Chesebro will serve five years of probation and 100 hours of community service, and must pay $5,000 in restitution. He has written an apology letter to Georgia and its residents. He also recorded a statement for prosecutors (the contents of which are unknown publicly) and agreed to testify truthfully against his Georgia co-defendants at future trials as a condition of his probation. If he is found to have testified falsely, his probation term could be revoked. Like Powell, he has no known federal plea agreement. Notably, Trump, Giuliani, and Eastman are Chesebro's co-defendants in the very conspiracy to which Chesebro pled guilty (count 15). Accordingly, Chesebro may be in a position to provide inculpatory evidence as to some or all of his alleged co-conspirators.

INSIDER NOTE: Although his college nickname was "the Cheese," Chesebro's last name is pronounced "chez-bro" (rhymes with fez-bro, not "cheese-bro").

consin. The memoranda evolved over time from a legal strategy to preserve the Defendant's rights to a corrupt plan to subvert the federal government function by stopping Biden electors' votes from being counted and certified, as follows:

a. The November 18 Memorandum ("Wisconsin Memo") advocated that, because of the ongoing recount in Wisconsin, the Defendant's electors there should meet and cast votes on December 14—the date the ECA required appointed electors to vote—to preserve the alternative of the Defendant's Wisconsin elector slate in the event the Defendant ultimately prevailed in the state.

b. The December 6 Memorandum ("Fraudulent Elector Memo") marked a sharp departure from Co-Conspirator 5's Wisconsin Memo, advocating that the alternate electors originally conceived of to preserve rights in Wisconsin instead be used in a number of states as fraudulent electors to prevent Biden from receiving the 270 electoral votes necessary to secure the presidency on January 6. The Fraudulent Elector Memo suggested that the Defendant's electors in six purportedly "contested" states (Arizona, Georgia, Michigan, Nevada, Pennsylvania, and Wisconsin) should meet and mimic as best as possible the actions of the legitimate Biden electors, and that on January 6, the Vice President should open and count the fraudulent votes, setting up a fake controversy that would derail the proper certification of Biden as president-elect.

c. The December 9 Memorandum ("Fraudulent Elector Instructions") consisted of Co-Conspirator 5's instructions on how fraudulent electors could mimic legitimate electors in Arizona, Georgia, Michigan, Nevada, Pennsylvania, and Wisconsin. Co-Conspirator 5 noted that in some states, it would be virtually impossible for the fraudulent electors to successfully take the same steps as the legitimate electors because state law required formal participation in the process by state officials, or access to official resources.

55. The plan began in early December, and ultimately, the conspirators and the Defendant's Campaign took the Wisconsin Memo and expanded it to any state that the Defendant claimed was

"contested"—even New Mexico, which the Defendant had lost by more than ten percent of the popular vote. This expansion was forecast by emails the Defendant's Chief of Staff sent on December 6, forwarding the Wisconsin Memo to Campaign staff and writing, "We just need to have someone coordinating the electors for states."*

56.   On December 6, the Defendant and Co-Conspirator 2 called the Chairwoman of the Republican National Committee to ensure that the plan was in motion. During the call, Co-Conspirator 2 told the Chairwoman that it was important for the RNC to help the Defendant's Campaign gather electors in targeted states, and falsely represented to her that such electors' votes would be used only if ongoing litigation in one of the states changed the results in the Defendant's favor.† After the RNC Chairwoman consulted the Campaign and heard that work on gathering electors was underway, she called and reported this information to the Defendant, who responded approvingly.

57.   On December 7, Co-Conspirator 1 received the Wisconsin Memo and the Fraudulent Elector Memo. Co-Conspirator 1 spoke with Co-Conspirator 6 regarding attorneys who could assist in the fraudulent elector effort in the targeted states, and he received from Co-Conspirator 6 an email identifying attorneys in Arizona, Georgia, Michigan, Nevada, New Mexico, Pennsylvania, and Wisconsin.

58.   The next day, on December 8, Co-Conspirator 5 called the Arizona attorney on Co-Conspirator 6's list. In an email after

---

* The allegations are that the scheme was orchestrated from the top down and did not arise organically in states that were, in fact, close calls.

† This allegation is important; if the electors were clearly denominated as contingent—and were publicly relied upon on if and only if the state later called the election for Trump—then such a scheme likely would have been legal. But the indictment makes clear that Trump wanted the electors in place to create the illusion of a controversy as to who won the election in each affected state. Nowhere was the illegal goal of the scheme better illustrated than in Pennsylvania, where the Trump campaign had to accede to Pennsylvania electors' request that the elector certifications explicitly state that they were there only if the Pennsylvania vote was called for Trump. The Trump campaign is alleged to have been worried that other states would insist on similar language, which would defeat the intended use of the slates of fake electors. (See paragraph 61, below.)

the call, the Arizona attorney recounted his conversation with Co-Conspirator 5 as follows:

> I just talked to the gentleman who did that memo, [Co-Conspirator 5]. His idea is basically that all of us (GA, WI, AZ, PA, etc.) have our electors send in their votes (even though the votes aren't legal under federal law -- because they're not signed by the Governor); so that members of Congress can fight about whether they should be counted on January 6th. (They could potentially argue that they're not bound by federal law because they're Congress and make the law, etc.) Kind of wild/creative -- I'm happy to discuss. My comment to him was that I guess there's no harm in it, (legally at least) -- i.e. we would just be sending in "fake" electoral votes to Pence so that "someone" in Congress can make an objection when they start counting votes, and start arguing that the "fake" votes should be counted.*

59.   At Co-Conspirator 1's direction, on December 10, Co-Conspirator 5 sent to points of contact in all targeted states except Wisconsin (which had already received his memos) and New Mexico a streamlined version of the Wisconsin Memo—which did not reveal the intended fraudulent use of the Defendant's electors—and the Fraudulent Elector Instructions, along with fraudulent elector certificates that he had drafted.

60.   The next day, on December 11, through Co-Conspirator 5, Co-Conspirator 1 suggested that the Arizona lawyer file a petition for certiorari in the Supreme Court as a pretext to claim that litigation was pending in the state, to provide cover for the convening and voting of the Defendant's fraudulent electors there. Co-Conspirator 5 explained that Co-Conspirator 1 had heard from a state official

---

* Trump and his allies have claimed that on December 14, 2020—the same day the real electors met and cast their votes—the fake electors convened in seven states that Biden had won in order to preserve Trump's rights in the event that any of the Trump lawsuits succeeded in reversing the election outcome in any of those states. The indictment, in this section, repeatedly sets out allegations that, if proved, demonstrate that this contention that the electors were a mere contingency slate is false. (See, for example, paragraph 62.)

and state provisional elector that "it could appear **treasonous** for the AZ electors to vote on Monday if there is no pending court proceeding. . . ."

61.   To manage the plan in Pennsylvania, on December 12, Co-Conspirator 1, Co-Conspirator 5, and Co-Conspirator 6 participated in a conference call organized by the Defendant's Campaign with the Defendant's electors in that state. When the Defendant's electors expressed concern about signing certificates representing themselves as legitimate electors, Co-Conspirator 1 falsely assured them that their certificates would be used only if the Defendant succeeded in litigation. Subsequently, Co-Conspirator 6 circulated proposed conditional language to that effect for potential inclusion in the fraudulent elector certificates. A Campaign official cautioned not to offer the conditional language to other states because "[t]he other States are signing what he prepared – if it gets out we changed the language for PA it could snowball." In some cases, the Defendant's electors refused to participate in the plan.

62.   On December 13, Co-Conspirator 5 sent Co-Conspirator 1 an email memorandum that further confirmed that the conspirators' plan was not to use the fraudulent electors only in the circumstance that the Defendant's litigation was successful in one of the targeted states—instead, the plan was to falsely present the fraudulent slates as an alternative to the legitimate slates at Congress's certification proceeding.

63.   On December 13, the Defendant asked the Senior Campaign Advisor for an update on "what was going on" with the elector plan and directed him to "put out [a] statement on electors." As a result, Co-Conspirator 1 directed the Senior Campaign Advisor to join a conference call with him, Co-Conspirator 6, and others. When the Senior Campaign Advisor related these developments in text messages to the Deputy Campaign Manager, a Senior Advisor to the Defendant, and a Campaign staffer, the Deputy Campaign Manager responded, "Here's the thing the way this has morphed it's a crazy play so I don't know who wants to put their name on it." The Senior Advisor wrote, "Certifying illegal votes." In turn, the

participants in the group text message refused to have a statement regarding electors attributed to their names because none of them could "stand by it."

64.   Also on December 13, at a Campaign staffer's request, Co-Conspirator 5 drafted and sent fraudulent elector certificates for the Defendant's electors in New Mexico, which had not previously been among the targeted states, and where there was no pending litigation on the Defendant's behalf. The next day, the Defendant's Campaign filed an election challenge suit in New Mexico at 11:54 a.m., six minutes before the noon deadline for the electors' votes, as a pretext so that there was pending litigation there at the time the fraudulent electors voted.

65.   On December 14, the legitimate electors of all 50 states and the District of Columbia met in their respective jurisdictions to formally cast their votes for president, resulting in a total of 232 electoral votes for the Defendant and 306 for Biden. The legitimate electoral votes that Biden won in the states that the Defendant targeted, and the Defendant's margin of defeat, were as follows: Arizona (11 electoral votes; 10,457 votes), Georgia (16 electoral votes; 11,779 votes), Michigan (16 electoral votes; 154,188 votes), Nevada (6 electoral votes; 33,596 votes), New Mexico (5 electoral votes; 99,720 votes), Pennsylvania (20 electoral votes; 80,555 votes), and Wisconsin (10 electoral votes; 20,682 votes).

66.   On the same day, at the direction of the Defendant and Co-Conspirator 1, fraudulent electors convened sham proceedings in the seven targeted states to cast fraudulent electoral ballots in favor of the Defendant. In some states, in order to satisfy legal requirements set forth for legitimate electors under state law, state officials were enlisted to provide the fraudulent electors access to state capitol buildings so that they could gather and vote there. In many cases, however, as Co-Conspirator 5 had predicted in the Fraudulent Elector Instructions, the fraudulent electors were unable to satisfy the legal requirements.

67.   Nonetheless, as directed in the Fraudulent Elector Instructions, shortly after the fraudulent electors met on December

14, the targeted states' fraudulent elector certificates were mailed to the President of the Senate, the Archivist of the United States, and others. The Defendant and co-conspirators ultimately used the certificates of these fraudulent electors to deceitfully target the government function, and did so contrary to how fraudulent electors were told they would be used.

68.   Unlike those of the fraudulent electors, consistent with the ECA, the legitimate electors' signed certificates were annexed to the state executives' certificates of ascertainment before being sent to the President of the Senate and others.

69.   That evening, at 6:26 p.m., the RNC Chairwoman forwarded to the Defendant, through his executive assistant, an email titled, "Electors Recap – Final," which represented that in "Six Contested States"—Arizona, Georgia, Michigan, Nevada, Pennsylvania, and Wisconsin—the Defendant's electors had voted in parallel to Biden's electors. The Defendant's executive assistant responded, "It's in front of him!"

The Defendant's Attempt to Leverage the Justice Department to Use Deceit to Get State Officials to Replace Legitimate Electors and Electoral Votes with the Defendant's[*]

70.   In late December 2020, the Defendant attempted to use the Justice Department to make knowingly false claims of election fraud to officials in the targeted states through a formal letter under the Acting Attorney General's signature, thus giving the Defendant's lies the backing of the federal government and attempting to improperly influence the targeted states to replace legitimate Biden electors with the Defendant's.

---

[*] This section alleges an overview of how Trump sought to use the DOJ's clout to help him overturn the 2020 election by replacing legitimate electors with fake electors. Trump found Jeffrey Clark, a senior ally in the department, who was willing to oblige. Trump decided against pursuing this plan when the most senior DOJ personnel as well as lawyers in the White House Counsel's Office threatened to resign, which Trump was advised would result in his scheme becoming public and thereby backfiring.

71.   On December 22, the Defendant met with Co-Conspirator 4* at the White House. Co-Conspirator 4 had not informed his leadership at the Justice Department of the meeting, which was a violation of the Justice Department's written policy restricting contacts with the White House to guard against improper political influence.

72.   On December 26, Co-Conspirator 4 spoke on the phone with the Acting Attorney General and lied about the circumstances of his meeting with the Defendant at the White House, falsely claiming that the meeting had been unplanned.† The Acting Attorney General directed Co-Conspirator 4 not to have unauthorized contacts with the White House again, and Co-Conspirator 4 said he would not.

73.   The next morning, on December 27, contrary to the Acting Attorney General's direction, Co-Conspirator 4 spoke with the Defendant on the Defendant's cell phone for nearly three minutes.

74.   That afternoon, the Defendant called the Acting Attorney General and Acting Deputy Attorney General and said, among other things, "People tell me [Co-Conspirator 4] is great. I should put him in." The Defendant also raised multiple false claims of election fraud, which the Acting Attorney General and Acting Deputy Attorney General refuted. When the Acting Attorney General told the Defendant that the Justice Department could not and would not change the outcome of the election, the Defendant responded, "Just say that the election was corrupt and leave the rest to me and the Republican congressmen."

---

* Media reporting and extant evidence suggest that this is a reference to Jeffrey Clark, then the acting head of the DOJ's Civil Division, who is indicted in the Georgia criminal case.

† This paragraph alleges that Jeffrey Clark knowingly made a materially false statement to a federal official—the acting attorney general. Under 18 U.S.C. § 1001, it is a crime to knowingly make a materially false statement to a federal official. Accordingly, these allegations indicate separate potential crimes for which Clark could be charged federally. In order to maintain his focus on Trump and avoid potential delays in Trump's DC trial, which is scheduled to begin on March 4, 2024, Smith may be deferring for the time being a criminal case against Clark.

75.   On December 28, Co-Conspirator 4 sent a draft letter to the Acting Attorney General and Acting Deputy Attorney General, which he proposed they all sign. The draft was addressed to state officials in Georgia, and Co-Conspirator 4 proposed sending versions of the letter to elected officials in other targeted states. The proposed letter contained numerous knowingly false claims* about the election and the Justice Department, including that:

   a.   The Justice Department had "identified significant concerns that may have impacted the outcome of the election in multiple States[.]"

   b.   The Justice Department believed that in Georgia and other states, two valid slates of electors had gathered at the proper location on December 14, and that both sets of ballots had been transmitted to Congress. That is, Co-Conspirator 4's letter sought to advance the Defendant's fraudulent elector plan by using the authority of the Justice Department to falsely present the fraudulent electors as a valid alternative to the legitimate electors.

   c.   The Justice Department urged that the state legislature convene a special legislative session to create the opportunity to, among other things, choose the fraudulent electors over the legitimate electors.

76.   The Acting Deputy Attorney General promptly responded to Co-Conspirator 4 by email and told him that his proposed letter was false, writing, "Despite dramatic claims to the contrary, we have not seen the type of fraud that calls into question the reported (and certified) results of the election." In a meeting shortly thereafter,

---

* Given these specific and detailed allegations, it is hard to avoid the conclusion that Clark, at some point, will be charged federally in connection with this scheme. We surmise that the reason he (and others) were not charged along with Trump was to ensure that the Trump trial could be scheduled expeditiously. Multi-defendant trials can be time-consuming and unwieldy. The strategy seems to have worked: Judge Chutkan cited the fact that the indictment involved a single defendant as one of the factors she relied on in setting a March 2024 trial date, and in rejecting Trump's proposed 2026 start date.

the Acting Attorney General and Acting Deputy Attorney General again directed Co-Conspirator 4 not to have unauthorized contact with the White House.

77.   On December 31, the Defendant summoned to the Oval Office the Acting Attorney General, Acting Deputy Attorney General, and other advisors. In the meeting, the Defendant again raised claims about election fraud that Justice Department officials already had told him were not true—and that the senior Justice Department officials reiterated were false—and suggested he might change the leadership in the Justice Department.

78.   On January 2, 2021, just four days before Congress's certification proceeding, Co-Conspirator 4 tried to coerce the Acting Attorney General and Acting Deputy Attorney General to sign and send Co-Conspirator 4's draft letter, which contained false statements, to state officials. He told them that the Defendant was considering making Co-Conspirator 4 the new Acting Attorney General, but that Co-Conspirator 4 would decline the Defendant's offer if the Acting Attorney General and Acting Deputy Attorney General would agree to send the proposed letter to the targeted states. The Justice Department officials refused.

79.   The next morning, on January 3, despite having uncovered no additional evidence of election fraud, Co-Conspirator 4 sent to a Justice Department colleague an edited version of his draft letter to the states, which included a change from its previous claim that the Justice Department had "concerns" to a stronger false claim that "[a]s of today, there is evidence of significant irregularities that may have impacted the outcome of the election in multiple States. . . ."*

80.   Also on the morning of January 3, Co-Conspirator 4 met with the Defendant at the White House—again without hav-

---

* This allegation is striking, as it is both damning and relates solely to Clark; there is no allegation that Trump was aware of this letter or its stated change in the DOJ's position on election fraud. It is further reason to think that Clark will at some point be charged federally.

ing informed senior Justice Department officials—and accepted the Defendant's offer that he become Acting Attorney General.*

81.   On the afternoon of January 3, Co-Conspirator 4 spoke with a Deputy White House Counsel. The previous month, the Deputy White House Counsel had informed the Defendant that "there is no world, there is no option in which you do not leave the White House [o]n January 20th."† Now, the same Deputy White House Counsel tried to dissuade Co-Conspirator 4 from assuming the role of Acting Attorney General. The Deputy White House Counsel reiterated to Co-Conspirator 4 that there had not been outcome-determinative fraud in the election and that if the Defendant remained in office nonetheless, there would be "riots in every major city in the United States." Co-Conspirator 4 responded, "Well, [Deputy White House Counsel], that's why there's an Insurrection Act."‡

82.   Also that afternoon, Co-Conspirator 4 met with the Acting Attorney General and told him that the Defendant had decided to put Co-Conspirator 4 in charge of the Justice Department. The Acting Attorney General responded that he would not accept being fired by a subordinate and immediately scheduled a meeting with the Defendant for that evening.

83.   On the evening of January 3, the Defendant met for a briefing on an overseas national security issue with the Chairman

---

* This allegation is the first time that the public learned the actual date on which Trump attempted to appoint Clark the acting attorney general of the United States: January 3, 2021.

† The reference to the Deputy White House Counsel is to Pat Philbin, a loyal Republican public official who defended Trump during his first impeachment trial. Philbin and others did not disclose direct communications with former President Trump when testifying before the January 6 committee. This allegation is new—and an example of Smith's ability to compel full disclosure of such communications. The allegation is particularly compelling as it is from a White House lawyer who directly advised Trump that he legally could not remain in office.

‡ This alleged statement is ominous as it suggests Clark's support for deploying the military to advance the coup and to thwart protests, something that has been associated primarily with military juntas, such as that in Argentina in the 1980s.

of the Joint Chiefs of Staff and other senior national security advisors. The Chairman briefed the Defendant on the issue—which had previously arisen in December—as well as possible ways the Defendant could handle it. When the Chairman and another advisor recommended that the Defendant take no action because Inauguration Day was only seventeen days away and any course of action could trigger something unhelpful, the Defendant calmly agreed, stating, "Yeah, you're right, it's too late for us. We're going to give that to the next guy."*

84. The Defendant moved immediately from this national security briefing to the meeting that the Acting Attorney General had requested earlier that day, which included Co-Conspirator 4, the Acting Attorney General, the Acting Deputy Attorney General, the Justice Department's Assistant Attorney General for the Office of Legal Counsel, the White House Counsel, a Deputy White House Counsel, and a Senior Advisor. At the meeting, the Defendant expressed frustration with the Acting Attorney General for failing to do anything to overturn the election results, and the group discussed Co-Conspirator 4's plans to investigate purported election fraud and to send his proposed letter to state officials—a copy of which was provided to the Defendant during the meeting. The Defendant relented in his plan to replace the Acting Attorney General with Co-Conspirator 4 only when he was told that it would result in mass resignations at the Justice Department and of his own White House Counsel.†

85. At the meeting in the Oval Office on the night of January 3, Co-Conspirator 4 suggested that the Justice Department should opine that the Vice President could exceed his lawful author-

---

* This allegation is included to show Trump's recognition, at least at this time, that he had lost the election.

† The head of the Office of Legal Counsel took a wise tack in talking Trump out of this plan: he testified to the January 6 committee that he warned Trump that such resignations would result in a public spectacle that would backfire (akin to when President Nixon fired the leadership of the DOJ in the Saturday Night Massacre).

ity during the certification proceeding and change the election outcome. When the Assistant Attorney General for the Office of Legal Counsel began to explain why the Justice Department should not do so, the Defendant said, "No one here should be talking to the Vice President. I'm talking to the Vice President," and ended the discussion.*

The Defendant's Attempts to Enlist the Vice President to Fraudulently Alter the Election Results at the January 6 Certification Proceeding

86.   As the January 6 congressional certification proceeding approached and other efforts to impair, obstruct, and defeat the federal government function failed, the Defendant sought to enlist the Vice President to use his ceremonial role at the certification to fraudulently alter the election results. The Defendant did this first by using knowingly false claims of election fraud to convince the Vice President to accept the Defendant's fraudulent electors, reject legitimate electoral votes, or send legitimate electoral votes to state legislatures for review rather than count them. When that failed, the Defendant attempted to use a crowd of supporters that he had gathered in Washington, D.C., to pressure the Vice President to fraudulently alter the election results.†

87.   On December 19, 2020, after cultivating widespread anger and resentment for weeks with his knowingly false claims of election fraud, the Defendant urged his supporters to travel to Washington on the day of the certification proceeding, tweeting, "Big protest in D.C. on January 6th. Be there, will be wild!" Throughout late

---

* This is a tantalizing detail—it suggests that Trump wanted to be the one to pressure the vice president, before the White House counsel could advise Pence that Trump's proposed course of action was illegal. Pence nevertheless received such advice from his own legal advisors, and did not succumb to Trump's pressure.

† Here, the indictment gestures toward the prospect of Trump's inciting the Capitol riot—though it stops short of making any legal claim or charge to this effect. Instead, it alleges that Trump used the crowd to pressure Pence.

December, he repeatedly urged his supporters to come to Washington for January 6.*

88.   On December 23, the Defendant re-tweeted a memo titled "Operation 'PENCE' CARD," which falsely asserted that the Vice President could, among other things, unilaterally disqualify legitimate electors from six targeted states.

89.   On the same day, Co-Conspirator 2 circulated a two-page memorandum outlining a plan for the Vice President to unlawfully declare the Defendant the certified winner of the presidential election. In the memorandum, Co-Conspirator 2 claimed that seven states had transmitted two slates of electors and proposed that the Vice President announce that "because of the ongoing disputes in the 7 States, there are no electors that can be deemed validly appointed in those States." Next, Co-Conspirator 2 proposed steps that he acknowledged violated the ECA, advocating that, in the end, "Pence then gavels President Trump as re-elected." Just two months earlier, on October 11, Co-Conspirator 2 had taken the opposite position, writing that neither the Constitution nor the ECA provided the Vice President discretion in the counting of electoral votes, or permitted him to "make the determination on his own."

90.   On several private phone calls in late December and early January, the Defendant repeated knowingly false claims of election fraud and directly pressured the Vice President to use his ceremonial role at the certification proceeding on January 6 to fraudulently overturn the results of the election, and the Vice President resisted,† including:

---

* The allegation here recalls former congresswoman Liz Cheney's approach during the January 6 committee hearings. Instead of blaming Trump's most radical supporters, Cheney noted that Trump misled these supporters. The indictment here makes the same point.

† These allegations surely come from Pence, who testified before the DC federal grand jury that charged Trump. Pence declined to testify before the January 6 committee. These are allegations of direct falsehoods about election fraud that Trump made to Pence. They also allege that Trump falsely claimed that Pence agreed with Trump that Pence had the authority to reject certified electoral votes. That it was false comes from Pence himself, and others.

a.   On December 25, when the Vice President called the Defendant to wish him a Merry Christmas, the Defendant quickly turned the conversation to January 6 and his request that the Vice President reject electoral votes that day. The Vice President pushed back, telling the Defendant, as the Vice President already had in previous conversations, "You know I don't think I have the authority to change the outcome."

b.   On December 29, as reflected in the Vice President's contemporaneous notes, the Defendant falsely told the Vice President that the "Justice Dept [was] finding major infractions."

c.   On January 1, the Defendant called the Vice President and berated him because he had learned that the Vice President had opposed a lawsuit seeking a judicial decision that, at the certification, the Vice President had the authority to reject or return votes to the states under the Constitution. The Vice President responded that he thought there was no constitutional basis for such authority and that it was improper. In response, the Defendant told the Vice President, "You're too honest." Within hours of the conversation, the Defendant reminded his supporters to meet in Washington before the certification proceeding, tweeting, "The BIG Protest Rally in Washington, D.C., will take place at 11.00 A.M. on January 6th. Locational details to follow. StopTheSteal!"

d.   On January 3, the Defendant again told the Vice President that at the certification proceeding, the Vice President had the absolute right to reject electoral votes and the ability to overturn the election. The Vice President responded that he had no such authority, and that a federal appeals court had rejected the lawsuit making that claim the previous day.

91.   On January 3, Co-Conspirator 2 circulated a second memorandum that included a new plan under which, contrary to the ECA, the Vice President would send the elector slates to the state legislatures to determine which slate to count.

92.   On January 4, the Defendant held a meeting with Co-Conspirator 2, the Vice President, the Vice President's Chief of Staff, and the Vice President's Counsel for the purpose of convinc-

ing the Vice President, based on the Defendant's knowingly false claims of election fraud, that the Vice President should reject or send to the states Biden's legitimate electoral votes, rather than count them. The Defendant deliberately excluded his White House Counsel from the meeting because the White House Counsel previously had pushed back on the Defendant's false claims of election fraud.[*]

93. During the meeting, as reflected in the Vice President's contemporaneous notes,[†] the Defendant made knowingly false claims of election fraud, including, "Bottom line—won every state by 100,000s of votes" and "We won every state," and asked—regarding a claim his senior Justice Department officials previously had told him was false, including as recently as the night before—"What about 205,000 votes more in PA than voters?" The Defendant and Co-Conspirator 2 then asked the Vice President to either unilaterally reject the legitimate electors from the seven targeted states, or send the question of which slate was legitimate to the targeted states' legislatures. When the Vice President challenged Co-Conspirator 2 on whether the proposal to return the question to the states was defensible, Co-Conspirator 2 responded, "Well, nobody's tested it before." The Vice President then told the Defendant, "Did you hear that? Even your own counsel is not saying I have that authority." The Defendant responded, "That's okay, I prefer the other suggestion" of the Vice President rejecting the electors unilaterally.

---

[*] Trump's exclusion of the White House counsel—the White House's top lawyer—is potentially fatal to any claim that Trump was simply relying in good faith on legal advice. If a president were open to candid legal advice on an issue, he would likely welcome debate among key lawyers. The fact that he allegedly excluded from a meeting a lawyer whose views contradicted his own may not convince a jury that Trump was acting in bad faith. Rather, the government will argue that it is evidence that he was simply shopping for advice that aligned with his preferred path.

[†] It is unusual to include this evidentiary detail in an indictment; it is new information that Pence's recollection was contemporaneously recorded, something that Pence presumably did for the same reasons that Raffensperger recorded the Georgia call with Trump. Each likely knew they would need to have a record in the event that Trump lied about what had transpired.

94. Also on January 4, when Co-Conspirator 2 acknowledged to the Defendant's Senior Advisor that no court would support his proposal, the Senior Advisor told Co-Conspirator 2, "[Y]ou're going to cause riots in the streets." Co-Conspirator 2 responded that there had previously been points in the nation's history where violence was necessary to protect the republic. After that conversation, the Senior Advisor notified the Defendant that Co-Conspirator 2 had conceded that his plan was "not going to work."*

95. On the morning of January 5, at the Defendant's direction, the Vice President's Chief of Staff and the Vice President's Counsel met again with Co-Conspirator 2. Co-Conspirator 2 now advocated that the Vice President do what the Defendant had said he preferred the day before: unilaterally reject electors from the targeted states. During this meeting, Co-Conspirator 2 privately acknowledged to the Vice President's Counsel that he hoped to prevent judicial review of his proposal because he understood that it would be unanimously rejected by the Supreme Court. The Vice President's Counsel expressed to Co-Conspirator 2 that following through with the proposal would result in a "disastrous situation" where the election might "have to be decided in the streets."

96. That same day, the Defendant encouraged supporters to travel to Washington on January 6, and he set the false expectation that the Vice President had the authority to and might use his ceremonial role at the certification proceeding to reverse the election outcome in the Defendant's favor, including issuing the following Tweets:

---

* This is a key allegation that undermines Trump's claim that he was acting pursuant to advice from counsel. Here, the indictment alleges that Trump's lawyer directly advised him that Eastman's proposed plan would not work.

INSIDER NOTE: If Trump asserts advice of counsel as a defense—that is, that he was acting pursuant to legal advice from his attorney—he would have to waive attorney-client privilege. Further, to rebut advice of counsel as a defense, the government can offer evidence of other instances where Trump did not follow his counsel's legal advice, including ignoring advice from Evan Corcoran (as alleged in the Florida documents case) and Don McGahn (as alleged in the Mueller Report).

a.   At 11:06 a.m., "The Vice President has the power to reject fraudulently chosen electors." This was within 40 minutes of the Defendant's earlier reminder, "See you in D.C."

b.   At 5:05 p.m., "Washington is being inundated with people who don't want to see an election victory stolen. . . . Our Country has had enough, they won't take it anymore! We hear you (and love you) from the Oval Office."

c.   At 5:43 p.m., "I will be speaking at the SAVE AMERICA RALLY tomorrow on the Ellipse at 11AM Eastern. Arrive early — doors open at 7AM Eastern. BIG CROWDS!"

97.   Also on January 5, the Defendant met alone with the Vice President. When the Vice President refused to agree to the Defendant's request that he obstruct the certification, the Defendant grew frustrated and told the Vice President that the Defendant would have to publicly criticize him.* Upon learning of this, the Vice President's Chief of Staff was concerned for the Vice President's safety and alerted the head of the Vice President's Secret Service detail.†

98.   As crowds began to gather in Washington and were audible from the Oval Office, the Defendant remarked to advisors that the crowd the following day on January 6 was going to be "angry."

99.   That night, the Defendant approved and caused the Defendant's Campaign to issue a public statement that the Defendant knew, from his meeting with the Vice President only hours earlier, was false: "The Vice President and I are in total agreement that the Vice President has the power to act."‡

---

* This allegation is striking as it avers Trump's very conscious and deliberate decision and strategy to attack publicly his own vice president.

† Pence's chief of staff was Marc Short—and Short's concern was prescient. The next day, the crowd, riled up by Trump's false claims, chanted "Hang Mike Pence."

‡ Trump may contend at trial that he was simply reiterating certain lawyers' views about the vice president's power, and that, even if he was wrong, he was acting in good faith. That defense would not explain why he did not simply recite that advice publicly and instead falsely stated on January 5 that Pence himself agreed with Trump's position, something that Pence and others have flatly denied. Nor did Trump reveal the advice he received from White House lawyers that Pence did not have this power

100. On January 6, starting in the early morning hours, the Defendant again turned to knowingly false statements aimed at pressuring the Vice President to fraudulently alter the election outcome, and raised publicly the false expectation that the Vice President might do so:

> a. At 1:00 a.m., the Defendant issued a Tweet that falsely claimed, "If Vice President @Mike_Pence comes through for us, we will win the Presidency. Many States want to decertify the mistake they made in certifying incorrect & even fraudulent numbers in a process NOT approved by their State Legislatures (which it must be). Mike can send it back!"

> b. At 8:17 a.m., the Defendant issued a Tweet that falsely stated, "States want to correct their votes, which they now know were based on irregularities and fraud, plus corrupt process never received legislative approval. All Mike Pence has to do is send them back to the States, AND WE WIN. Do it Mike, this is a time for extreme courage!"

101. On the morning of January 6, an agent of the Defendant contacted a United States Senator[*] to ask him to hand-deliver documents to the Vice President. The agent then facilitated the receipt by the Senator's staff of the fraudulent certificates signed by the Defendant's fraudulent electors in Michigan and Wisconsin, which were believed not to have been delivered to the Vice President or Archivist by mail. When one of the Senator's staffers contacted a staffer for the Vice President by text message to arrange for delivery of what the Senator's staffer had been told were "[a]lternate slate[s] of electors for MI and WI because archivist didn't receive them," the Vice President's staffer rejected them.

---

and, in any event, the facts did not support Pence's actions, even if he had the legal authority to reject the electoral votes.

[*] Media reporting and known evidence suggest that this is a reference to Wisconsin senator Ron Johnson, as was revealed from text messages obtained by the January 6 committee investigators.

102. At 11:15 a.m., the Defendant called the Vice President and again pressured him to fraudulently reject or return Biden's legitimate electoral votes. The Vice President again refused. Immediately after the call, the Defendant decided to single out the Vice President in public remarks he would make within the hour, reinserting language that he had personally drafted earlier that morning—falsely claiming that the Vice President had authority to send electoral votes to the states—but that advisors had previously successfully advocated be removed.

103. Earlier that morning, the Defendant had selected Co-Conspirator 2 to join Co-Conspirator 1 in giving public remarks before his own. When they did so, based on knowingly false election fraud claims, Co-Conspirator 1 and Co-Conspirator 2 intensified pressure on the Vice President to fraudulently obstruct the certification proceeding:

  a.   Co-Conspirator 1 told the crowd that the Vice President could "cast [the ECA] aside" and unilaterally "decide on the validity of these crooked ballots[.]" He also lied when he claimed to "have letters from five legislatures begging us" to send elector slates to the legislatures for review, and called for "trial by combat."

  b.   Co-Conspirator 2 told the crowd, "[A]ll we are demanding of Vice President Pence is this afternoon at one o'clock he let the legislatures of the state look into this so we get to the bottom of it and the American people know whether we have control of the direction of our government or not. We no longer live in a self-governing republic if we can't get the answer to this question."

104. Next, beginning at 11:56 a.m., the Defendant made multiple knowingly false statements integral to his criminal plans to defeat the federal government function, obstruct the certification, and interfere with others' right to vote and have their votes counted. The Defendant repeated false claims of election fraud, gave false hope that the Vice President might change the election outcome, and directed the crowd in front of him to go to the Capitol as a

means to obstruct the certification and pressure the Vice President to fraudulently obstruct the certification. The Defendant's knowingly false statements for these purposes included:

a.   The Defendant falsely claimed that, based on fraud, the Vice President could alter the outcome of the election results, stating:

> I hope Mike is going to do the right thing. I hope so. I hope so.
>
> Because if Mike Pence does the right thing, we win the election. All he has to do—all, this is, this is from the number one, or certainly one of the top, Constitutional lawyers in our country—he has the absolute right to do it. We're supposed to protect our country, support our country, support our Constitution, and protect our Constitution.
>
> States want to revote. The states got defrauded. They were given false information. They voted on it. Now they want to recertify. They want it back. All Vice President Pence has to do is send it back to the states to recertify and we become president and you are the happiest people.

b.   After the Defendant falsely stated that the Pennsylvania legislature wanted "to recertify their votes. They want to recertify. But the only way that can happen is if Mike Pence agrees to send it back," the crowd began to chant, "Send it back."

c.   The Defendant also said that regular rules no longer applied, stating, "And fraud breaks up everything, doesn't it? When you catch somebody in a fraud, you're allowed to go by very different rules."

d.   Finally, after exhorting that "we fight. We fight like hell. And if you don't fight like hell, you're not going to have a country anymore," the Defendant directed the people in front of him to head to the Capitol, suggested he was going with them, and told them to give Members of Congress "the kind of pride and boldness that they need to take back our country."

105. During and after the Defendant's remarks, thousands of people marched toward the Capitol.

The Defendant's Exploitation of the Violence and Chaos at the Capitol

106. Shortly before 1:00 p.m., the Vice President issued a public statement explaining that his role as President of the Senate at the certification proceeding that was about to begin did not include "unilateral authority to determine which electoral votes should be counted and which should not."

107. Before the Defendant had finished speaking, a crowd began to gather at the Capitol. Thereafter, a mass of people—including individuals who had traveled to Washington and to the Capitol at the Defendant's direction—broke through barriers cordoning off the Capitol grounds and advanced on the building, including by violently attacking law enforcement officers trying to secure it.

108. The Defendant, who had returned to the White House after concluding his remarks, watched events at the Capitol unfold on the television in the dining room next to the Oval Office.*

109. At 2:13 p.m., after more than an hour of steady, violent advancement, the crowd at the Capitol broke into the building.

110. Upon receiving news that individuals had breached the Capitol, the Defendant's advisors told him that there was a riot there and that rioters had breached the building. When advisors urged the Defendant to issue a calming message aimed at the rioters, the

---

* INSIDER NOTE: It is a bit surprising that the indictment omits completely an event that was the focus of significant attention during the January 6 committee hearings: Mark Meadows's staffer Cassidy Hutchinson's testimony revealing what she was told about Trump's desire to be at the Capitol with his supporters after the rally at the Ellipse. Although not alleged in the indictment, this still may be an area where evidence is submitted at trial. An indictment is not required to—and often does not—set out all proof. But the absence of such allegations may suggest Smith's wariness to pursue this line of evidence as an unnecessary sideshow for which there may be conflicting accounts.

Defendant refused, instead repeatedly remarking that the people at the Capitol were angry because the election had been stolen.

111. At 2:24 p.m., after advisors had left the Defendant alone in his dining room, the Defendant issued a Tweet intended to further delay and obstruct the certification: "Mike Pence didn't have the courage to do what should have been done to protect our Country and our Constitution, giving States a chance to certify a corrected set of facts, not the fraudulent or inaccurate ones which they were asked to previously certify. USA demands the truth!"

112. One minute later, at 2:25 p.m., the United States Secret Service was forced to evacuate the Vice President to a secure location.

113. At the Capitol, throughout the afternoon, members of the crowd chanted, "Hang Mike Pence!"; "Where is Pence? Bring him out!"; and "Traitor Pence!"

114. The Defendant repeatedly refused to approve a message directing rioters to leave the Capitol, as urged by his most senior advisors—including the White House Counsel, a Deputy White House Counsel, the Chief of Staff, a Deputy Chief of Staff, and a Senior Advisor. Instead, the Defendant issued two Tweets that did not ask rioters to leave the Capitol but instead falsely suggested that the crowd at the Capitol was being peaceful, including:

   a.   At 2:38 p.m., "Please support our Capitol Police and Law Enforcement. They are truly on the side of our Country. Stay peaceful!"

   b.   At 3:13 p.m., "I am asking for everyone at the U.S. Capitol to remain peaceful. No violence! Remember, WE are the Party of Law & Order – respect the Law and our great men and women in Blue. Thank you!"

115. At 3:00 p.m., the Defendant had a phone call with the Minority Leader of the United States House of Representatives. The Defendant told the Minority Leader that the crowd at the Capitol was more upset about the election than the Minority Leader was.*

---

* Evidence about this call could come from people who heard it from the White House side of the conversation, or from Kevin McCarthy (the then–minority leader

116. At 4:17 p.m., the Defendant released a video message on Twitter that he had just taped in the White House Rose Garden. In it, the Defendant repeated the knowingly false claim that "[w]e had an election that was stolen from us," and finally asked individuals to leave the Capitol, while telling them that they were "very special" and that "we love you."*

117. After the 4:17 p.m. Tweet, as the Defendant joined others in the outer Oval Office to watch the attack on the Capitol on television, the Defendant said, "See, this is what happens when they try to steal an election. These people are angry. These people are really angry about it. This is what happens."

118. At 6:01 p.m., the Defendant tweeted, "These are the things and events that happen when a sacred landslide election victory is so unceremoniously & viciously stripped away from great patriots who have been badly & unfairly treated for so long. Go home with love & in peace. Remember this day forever!"

119. On the evening of January 6, the Defendant and Co-Conspirator 1 attempted to exploit the violence and chaos at the Capitol by calling lawmakers to convince them, based on knowingly false claims of election fraud, to delay the certification, including:

    a.   The Defendant, through White House aides, attempted to reach two United States Senators at 6:00 p.m.

    b.   From 6:59 p.m. until 7:18 p.m., Co-Conspirator 1 placed calls to five United States Senators and one United States Representative.

---

of the House of Representatives), or both. New reports contend that, on the call, Trump also falsely claimed that the riots were caused by antifa—a claim that made McCarthy scoff.

* This evidence of Trump's actions while the attack on the Capitol was unfolding speaks to his intent. Americans of all political stripes were appalled by what they saw play out on their television screens. Yet, the person in the best position to quell the violence was instead praising the perpetrators and only belatedly calling on them to stand down.

c.   Co-Conspirator 6 attempted to confirm phone numbers for six United States Senators whom the Defendant had directed Co-Conspirator 1 to call and attempt to enlist in further delaying the certification.

d.   In one of the calls, Co-Conspirator 1 left a voicemail intended for a United States Senator that said, "We need you, our Republican friends, to try to just slow it down so we can get these legislatures to get more information to you. And I know they're reconvening at eight tonight but the only strategy we can follow is to object to numerous states and raise issues so that we get ourselves into tomorrow—ideally until the end of tomorrow."*

e.   In another message intended for another United States Senator, Co-Conspirator 1 repeated knowingly false allegations of election fraud, including that the vote counts certified by the states to Congress were incorrect and that the governors who had certified knew they were incorrect; that "illegal immigrants" had voted in substantial numbers in Arizona; and that "Georgia gave you a number in which 65,000 people who were underage voted." Co-Conspirator 1 also claimed that the Vice President's actions had been surprising and asked the Senator to "object to every state and kind of spread this out a little bit like a filibuster[.]"

120. At 7:01 p.m., while Co-Conspirator 1 was calling United States Senators on behalf of the Defendant, the White House Counsel called the Defendant to ask him to withdraw any objections and allow the certification. The Defendant refused.

121. The attack on the Capitol obstructed and delayed the certification for approximately six hours, until the Senate and House of Representatives came back into session separately at 8:06 p.m. and 9:02 p.m., respectively, and came together in a Joint Session at 11:35 p.m.

---

* These are references to the efforts to delay the certification of the Electoral College.

122. At 11:44 p.m., Co-Conspirator 2 emailed the Vice President's Counsel advocating that the Vice President violate the law and seek further delay of the certification. Co-Conspirator 2 wrote, "I implore you to consider one more relatively minor violation [of the ECA] and adjourn for 10 days to allow the legislatures to finish their investigations, as well as to allow a full forensic audit of the massive amount of illegal activity that has occurred here."

123. At 3:41 a.m. on January 7, as President of the Senate, the Vice President announced the certified results of the 2020 presidential election in favor of Biden.

124. The Defendant and his co-conspirators committed one or more of the acts to effect the object of the conspiracy alleged above in Paragraphs 13, 15-16, 18-22, 24, 26, 28, 30-33, 35, 37-39, 41, 43-44, 46, 50, 52, 54, 56, 57-64, 67, 71-75, 78-82, 84, 85, 87-97, 99-100, 102-104, 111, 114, 116, 118-119, and 122.*

(In violation of Title 18, United States Code, Section 371)

COUNT TWO

(Conspiracy to Obstruct an Official Proceeding—
18 U.S.C. § 1512(k))

125. The allegations contained in paragraphs 1 through 4 and 8 through 123 of this Indictment are re-alleged and fully incorporated here by reference.

126. From on or about November 14, 2020, through on or about January 7, 2021, in the District of Columbia and elsewhere, the Defendant,

DONALD J. TRUMP,

did knowingly combine, conspire, confederate, and agree with co-conspirators, known and unknown to the Grand Jury, to corruptly

---

* Because a conspiracy under 18 U.S.C. § 371 requires the jury to find that at least one conspirator committed an overt act in furtherance of the conspiracy, the indictment here sets out numerous possible overt acts. A jury will not be limited to this list, but the prosecution should have to give notice of any other acts on which it intends to rely.

obstruct and impede an official proceeding, that is, the certification of the electoral vote, in violation of Title 18, United States Code, Section 1512(c)(2).

(In violation of Title 18, United States Code, Section 1512(k))

COUNT THREE

(Obstruction of, and Attempt to Obstruct, an Official Proceeding—18 U.S.C. §§ 1512(c)(2), 2)

127. The allegations contained in paragraphs 1 through 4 and 8 through 123 of this Indictment are re-alleged and fully incorporated here by reference.

128. From on or about November 14, 2020, through on or about January 7, 2021, in the District of Columbia and elsewhere, the Defendant,

DONALD J. TRUMP,

attempted to, and did, corruptly obstruct and impede an official proceeding, that is, the certification of the electoral vote.

(In violation of Title 18, United States Code, Sections 1512(c)(2), 2)

COUNT FOUR

(Conspiracy Against Rights—18 U.S.C. § 241)

129. The allegations contained in paragraphs 1 through 4 and 8 through 123 of this Indictment are re-alleged and fully incorporated here by reference.

130. From on or about November 14, 2020, through on or about January 20, 2021, in the District of Columbia and elsewhere, the Defendant,

DONALD J. TRUMP,

did knowingly combine, conspire, confederate, and agree with co-conspirators, known and unknown to the Grand Jury, to injure, oppress, threaten, and intimidate one or more persons in the free exercise and enjoyment of a right and privilege secured to them by the Constitution and laws of the United States—that is, the right to vote, and to have one's vote counted.

(In violation of Title 18, United States Code, Section 241)

A TRUE BILL

_____

FOREPERSON*

_____

JACK SMITH
SPECIAL COUNSEL
UNITED STATES DEPARTMENT OF JUSTICE†

---

* To protect the person's privacy, the publicly filed indictment does not contain the name of the grand jury foreperson who signed the indictment (by contrast, Georgia law requires the names of grand jurors to be public). For these charges to be brought by the grand jury, at least twelve out of twenty-three grand jurors had to agree that there was probable cause that Trump committed each of the crimes charged.
† Jack Smith, although a "special counsel," is a part of the DOJ. There are internal DOJ rules governing a special counsel's duties and responsibilities, but the special counsel remains a "subordinate officer" to the attorney general. Attorney General Merrick Garland need not, and has said he did not, make the decision to bring these charges, although he had the power to approve or reject them if he so chose.

THE STATE OF GEORGIA V. DONALD JOHN TRUMP, ET AL.

(FULTON COUNTY, GEORGIA, INDICTMENT)

INTRODUCTION

P UNDITS EXPECTED THE GEORGIA INDICTMENT TO BE A subset of the charges filed in the DC January 6 indictment. As the substance of the Georgia indictment makes clear, that is not the case. To be sure, the gravamen of the cases is similar—both concern the former president's efforts to resist illegally the peaceful transfer of power. But while the DC January 6 indictment emphasized a DC-centered scheme, the Georgia indictment focuses granularly on the efforts to overturn Georgia's results in the 2020 election.

In doing so, the Georgia indictment broke new ground. For starters, unlike the DC January 6 indictment, it did not level charges exclusively at Donald Trump. Instead, the Fulton County grand jury issued a sprawling indictment charging *all* of the president's men and women—eighteen other co-defendants, to be precise. This was in stark contrast to the DC January 6 indictment, which only charged Trump, even as it identified six *unindicted* co-conspirators. The Georgia indictment charged nineteen individuals in total and indicated that there were thirty *unindicted* individuals involved in a wide-ranging scheme to overturn the election results.

The Georgia indictment also digs deep into how Trump's national election interference scheme was carried out in Georgia. It details the effort to infiltrate voting machines in Coffee County, as well as the effort to advance a slate of alternate electors. And the indictment has moments of real pathos: it explains how two honorable election workers—Ruby Freeman and her daughter Shaye Moss—were smeared with false and racist assertions that they engaged in election fraud, and how and why Trump supporters targeted them for harassment. The indictment outlines an effort to persuade the two women to claim falsely the election had been corrupted in favor of Joe Biden, which they refused to do.

Such a broad array of defendants and charges presents challenges.

Some of these challenges are procedural—exactly how and when the case will proceed to trial, and whether the co-defendants will receive separate trials, are open questions as of this writing. It is also unclear whether the case will remain in state court or will be removed, whether in whole or in part, to federal court. In addition, there are also substantive challenges—how to present a complicated, multivarious election interference scheme in a way that is both comprehensive and coherent to a jury.

Despite these challenges, the case could hold Donald Trump accountable for the events preceding and occurring on January 6, 2021. In multi-defendant cases, it is not unusual for defendants to enter a change of plea—that is, enter a guilty plea—and begin cooperating with the prosecution in exchange for reducing the charges and the ultimate sentence imposed. Indeed, in this case, some of the lower-level operatives who had more limited involvement in the alleged criminal scheme may be especially interested in providing evidence to the state in exchange for more limited legal liability. As of this writing, four codefendants—Scott Hall, Sidney Powell, and Kenneth Chesebro, and Jenna Ellis—have pleaded guilty and agreed to provide evidence to the prosecution. To be sure, given the sources and the incentives to cooperate, such evidence may face a high threshold for credibility at trial. Nevertheless, eyewitness testimony from co-conspirators could be quite helpful to the state as it seeks to prove its case to a jury.

But even leaving aside the prospect of co-defendants flipping, the Georgia case has other notable features. Unlike the DC January 6 indictment, it seeks to hold the many members of the alleged criminal conspiracy accountable, not just Donald Trump. This underscores for the public the wrongfulness of *all* the conduct that scaffolded Trump's effort to obstruct the election and democracy—the case should be a strong deterrent to future election obstructors and deniers. And critically, because the Georgia case involves violations of *state* law, any resulting convictions are ineligible for a federal presidential pardon. Under our Constitution, the president's Article II clemency powers extend only to *federal* crimes. Accordingly, even if he is reelected in 2024, Trump would be unable to pardon himself or any convicted co-defendants for these alleged crimes.

CAST OF CHARACTERS

Many of the indictments reference unnamed individuals by descriptions such as "Employee 1," "Woman 2," and "Co-Conspirator 3." To be clear, these unnamed individuals have not been charged with any crime. They are referenced because they play some role in the events alleged. Relying on media reports identifying these individuals, we have named them here in order to facilitate the reader's comprehension of these documents and the alleged conduct they describe. That said, it must be remembered that none of these individuals has been charged with any wrongdoing.

○ = defendant (To charge a defendant, a grand jury has to determine that there is probable cause that the person committed the crime. At trial, the government needs to establish guilt beyond a reasonable doubt and the defendant is presumed innocent unless and until such time.)

▲ = involved in multiple cases

Joseph Brannan (Unindicted Co-Conspirator)[*]—The former treasurer of the Georgia GOP and, according to prosecutors, one of Trump's sixteen fraudulent Georgia electors.

Robert Cheeley○—A Georgia-based lawyer who prosecutors say worked with Trump's attorneys to overturn Georgia's election results. Cheeley presented at a Georgia Senate subcommittee meeting and told lawmakers that election workers had double- and triple-counted votes. The Fulton County indictment alleges that Cheeley later committed perjury by lying to the Fulton County grand jury about his involvement in Trump's efforts to overturn Georgia's election results. Cheeley faces ten criminal charges in Fulton County.

---

[*] The identities of unnamed Fulton County co-conspirators are reported in the following article: Ryan Goodman, Norman L. Eisen, Siven Watt, Allison Rice, Francois Barrilleaux, Beth Markman, and Michael Nevett, "Chart: Names of the 'Unindicted Co-Conspirators' in Fulton County, Georgia Indictment," Just Security, August 25, 2023.

Kenneth Chesebro○▲—Trump's co-defendant and former legal advisor. Chesebro, who was a defendant in the Fulton County indictment and referred to as "co-conspirator 5" in the DOJ's January 6 indictment, was charged with his role in devising a plan to appoint slates of fraudulent electors in seven states that Trump lost. According to the Georgia and the January 6 indictments, the plan called for slates of Trump electors—individuals who would have served as electors if Trump had won the popular vote in those states—to convene to mimic the actions of real electors by casting fraudulent "votes" and signing false certifications that they were the legitimate electors. The fraudulent certificates were then provided to the President of the Senate and others. The plan was supposed to culminate on January 6, 2021, with Vice President Pence opening the fraudulent certificates on the Senate floor and counting them as real votes, but Pence never complied. Chesebro faced seven criminal charges in Fulton County. On October 20, 2023, just days before his trial was scheduled to begin, Chesebro pleaded guilty to one felony count of conspiracy to commit filing false documents. As part of his Fulton County plea deal, Chesebro is sentenced to five years' probation and will pay $5,000 in restitution. He has also agreed to testify truthfully in all future proceedings.

Clark, Jeffrey○▲—Trump's co-defendant and the former acting head of the DOJ's civil division. On January 3, 2021, Trump briefly appointed Clark Acting Attorney General so that he could lend the DOJ's backing to Trump's efforts to overturn the election. Trump rescinded the appointment later that day when threatened with the prospect of mass resignations. According to the DOJ January 6 indictment, Clark drafted a letter (never ultimately sent) to Georgia lawmakers stating the DOJ had significant concerns about election fraud and viewed Trump's fraudulent Georgia electors—the individuals who would have served as electors if Trump had won the popular vote—as legitimate electors. Clark's bosses at the DOJ, Acting Attorney General Jeffrey Rosen and Acting Deputy Attorney General Richard Donoghue, refused to sign the Georgia letter.

Vikki Townsend Consiglio (Unindicted Co-Conspirator 10 or 11)—One of Georgia's sixteen illegitimate Trump electors.

Alex Cruce (Unindicted Co-Conspirator)—A Trump supporter who, according to the indictment, flew to Coffee County, Georgia, to assist with the illegal breach of voting machines.

Eastman, John○▲—Trump's co-defendant and former legal advisor. Eastman is a defendant in the Fulton County District Attorney's indictment and referred to as "co-conspirator 2" in the DOJ's January 6 indictment. Prosecutors allege that Eastman was an architect of the plan to have Mike Pence leverage his ceremonial role as President of the Senate to obstruct the certification of the 2020 election by rejecting the electoral votes of seven states that

Biden won. Eastman later devised a second plan whereby Pence, instead of outright rejecting the seven "disputed" states' electoral votes, would send dueling slates of electors to those seven states' legislatures and ask the legislatures to determine which electors to count. Eastman and Trump met with Pence in the White House on January 4, 2021, and attempted to convince Pence to adopt either of the two plans, even though Eastman acknowledged in communications cited by prosecutors that the plans violated the Electoral Count Act and would be rejected by courts. Eastman spoke to the crowd of Trump supporters gathered in Washington, DC, on the morning of January 6, 2021, and, hours after the attack on the Capitol, emailed Pence's counsel to "implore" him to delay the count for another ten days. Eastman faces nine criminal charges in Fulton County.

Jenna Ellis○—A former Trump campaign attorney. Prosecutors claim that Ellis was among the lawyers who presented false claims about election fraud to Georgia lawmakers at a Georgia Senate subcommittee meeting. Ellis also met with legislators in Arizona, Pennsylvania, and Michigan to promote similarly baseless claims of election fraud. Facing two criminal charges in Fulton County, on October 24, 2023, Ellis pleaded guilty to one felony charge of aiding and abetting false statements and writings. Under the terms of her plea deal with the Georgia prosecutors, Ellis will serve five years' probation, will pay $5,000 in restitution, and will perform one hundred hours of community service. She has written a letter of apology to the citizens of Georgia, and she has agreed to cooperate fully with the prosecution as it progresses.

Epshteyn, Boris▲—A political consultant who has publicly said he helped Trump implement the plan to submit slates of electors claiming that they were "alternate" electors, rather than fraudulent electors. The Fulton County indictment states that "Individual 3"—reportedly Epshteyn—made false statements about election fraud at a November 19, 2020, press conference at Republican National Committee ("RNC") headquarters.

Carolyn Fisher (Unindicted Co-Conspirator 10 or 11)—Alleged to be one of Georgia's sixteen illegitimate Trump electors.

Tom Fitton (Unindicted Co-Conspirator 1)—A conservative activist reported to be unindicted co-conspirator 1 in the Fulton County indictment. The indictment alleges that Trump spoke with Fitton four days before the 2020 presidential election and discussed a draft of a speech that falsely claimed voter fraud and declared a Trump electoral victory.

Harrison Floyd○—A Trump supporter who, according to Fulton County prosecutors, attempted to intimidate a Georgia election worker. The indictment asserts that Floyd, the former leader of a group called "Black Voices for Trump," arranged a meeting between election worker Ruby Freeman and former Kanye West publicist Trevian Kutti. At the meeting, which Floyd joined by telephone, Kutti and Floyd allegedly pressured Freeman to admit to election fraud. Floyd faces two criminal charges in Fulton County.

Ruby Freeman—A Georgia election worker whom Trump and Giuliani falsely accused of committing election fraud. Trump repeatedly targeted Freeman by name, and she was harassed and threatened by Trump supporters who attempted to pressure her to admit to fraud.

Giuliani, Rudy○▲—Trump's co-defendant and former personal attorney. He is named as a defendant in the Fulton County District Attorney's indictment and referred to as "co-conspirator 1" in the DOJ's January 6 indictment. Prosecutors claim that Giuliani spearheaded the Trump legal team's efforts to overturn the results of the 2020 presidential election. Giuliani repeatedly spread bogus claims about fraud in the 2020 presidential election and personally met with lawmakers in several states that Biden won in an attempt to convince them to adopt his baseless theories. Giuliani arranged a presentation to Georgia lawmakers at which he and other Trump lawyers promoted debunked theories of voter fraud and asked the Georgia state legislature not to recognize Georgia's legitimate, Biden-chosen electors. After Giuliani failed to persuade state legislatures not to recognize the legitimate electors, he helped carry out a new scheme to have slates of fake electors meet to declare themselves the true electors and send fraudulent certifications to the President of the Senate. In addressing the crowd of Trump supporters gathered in Washington, DC, on January 6, 2021, Giuliani called for "trial by combat" and declared that Mike Pence had the power to unilaterally stop the certification of the election. That night, after rioters had violently stormed the Capitol, Giuliani reportedly called seven members of Congress to ask them to further delay the certification of the election. Giuliani faces thirteen criminal charges in Fulton County.

Scott Graham Hall○—A pro-Trump poll watcher who prosecutors claim participated in Trump attorney Sidney Powell's plan to illegally access and tamper with Georgia voting machines. Hall faced seven criminal charges in Fulton County. On September 29, 2023, Hall became the first defendant to enter into a plea agreement with the prosecution, pleading guilty to five misdemeanor counts of conspiracy to commit intentional interference with the performance of election duties. As part of his plea deal, Hall will receive five years of probation and agreed to testify in further proceedings. He was also required to write a letter of apology to the citizens of Georgia and is barred from participating in polling activities.

Misty Hampton○—A former Georgia election supervisor who, the indictment alleges, breached Georgia voting machines and provided illegal access to those machines to forensic data analysts working for Sidney Powell.

Conan Hayes (Unindicted Co-Conspirator)—A former professional surfer, according to media reports, who was involved in Sidney Powell's alleged efforts to infiltrate voting machines in Coffee County, Georgia; Hayes was designated to receive data obtained from Georgia voting machines.

Burt Jones (Unindicted Co-Conspirator 8)—The Lieutenant Governor of Georgia and one of Georgia's sixteen illegitimate electors for Trump. On December 7, 2020, Jones sent a tweet telling Georgians to call their representatives and demand a special session of the General Assembly—a session he allegedly sought for the purpose of appointing fake electors.

Brian Kemp—The Governor of Georgia. Trump repeatedly tried to enlist Kemp, a Republican, to help him overturn the results of the 2020 presidential election in Georgia. Kemp pushed back on Trump's claims of voter fraud and declined to interfere with the legitimate election results.

Bernard Kerik (Unindicted Co-Conspirator 5)—The former Commissioner of the New York City Police Department under then-Mayor Rudy Giuliani. Kerik, a Trump supporter and convicted felon, allegedly accompanied Giuliani to meetings with Arizona and Pennsylvania lawmakers in which Giuliani promoted false claims about election fraud.

Trevian C. Kutti○—A Chicago-based publicist and Trump supporter who prosecutors allege traveled to Georgia to pressure an election worker. Kutti, formerly the publicist to R. Kelly and Kanye West, traveled to election worker Ruby Freeman's Fulton County home and unsuccessfully attempted to speak with her. Kutti then called Freeman on the phone and warned her that she was in danger and offered to meet with her at a police department precinct. According to the Georgia indictment, Kutti met with Freeman at the precinct and pressured her to admit to election fraud. Kutti faces three criminal charges in Fulton County.

Stefanie Lambert (Unindicted Co-Conspirator)—A Michigan lawyer who prosecutors allege worked with Sidney Powell to overturn the 2020 election. According to media reporting, Lambert was one of the individuals designated to receive data obtained from Georgia voting machines. A Michigan special prosecutor charged Lambert with four felonies, including one related to willfully damaging a Michigan voting machine.

Cathleen Alston Latham○—The former head of the Republican Party in Coffee County, Georgia. According to the Fulton County indictment, Latham was both a fake elector for Trump and a participant in Trump attorney Sidney Powell's alleged efforts to illegally access Georgia voting machines. The Fulton County indictment alleges that Latham also committed perjury by lying to the grand jury about her role in the scheme. Latham faces eleven criminal charges in Fulton County.

Stephen Lee○—A Lutheran pastor from Illinois who, according to prosecutors, traveled to Georgia for the purpose of addressing so-called election fraud. According to the Georgia indictment, Lee knocked on the front door of Ruby Freeman's home in an attempt to get the election worker, whom Trump allies had targeted, to admit to election fraud. Lee faces five criminal charges in Fulton County.

Jeffrey Lenberg (Unindicted Co-Conspirator)—A former employee at a National Nuclear Security Administration laboratory in New Mexico who, according to media reports, entered nonpublic areas of the Coffee County, Georgia, elections office as part of an effort to gain access to voting machines.

Doug Logan (Unindicted Co-Conspirator)—The former head of cybersecurity firm Cyber Ninjas. Media reports allege that Logan entered nonpublic areas of a Georgia election office and downloaded election data. Logan's firm was later hired by Republican state lawmakers in Arizona to conduct an audit of the Arizona election.

Judge Scott McAfee—The Georgia trial judge presiding over the Fulton County case. Previously the Georgia inspector general and a state and federal prosecutor, McAfee became a state court judge in 2023. McAfee once worked under Fani Willis at the Fulton County District Attorney's Office.

Mark Meadows○▲—Trump's co-defendant and last Chief of Staff, from March 2020 until January 20, 2021. Prior to that, he served for seven years as a congressman from North Carolina and was a leading member of the Freedom Caucus. In connection with his effort to "remove" the State of Georgia criminal charges against him to federal court for trial, Meadows testified at a federal hearing that all the alleged acts in the state indictment were undertaken by him as part of his official position as Chief of Staff. News reports have also suggested that Meadows may have testified under a grant of immunity before a federal grand jury investigating the January 6 insurrection.

Butch Miller—The former President Pro Tempore of the Georgia Senate. Trump and Giuliani made phone calls to Miller, a Republican, to attempt to convince him to call a special session of the Georgia General Assembly to appoint Trump's fraudulent slate of Georgia electors. Miller rejected Trump and Giuliani's requests.

Shaye Moss—A former Georgia poll worker falsely accused of running an illegal ballot scheme by Trump and his team. Trump supporters repeatedly threatened and harassed Moss and her mother, fellow poll worker Ruby Freeman, after Trump publicly alleged that they were responsible for election fraud.

Jim Penrose (Unindicted Co-Conspirator)—A former NSA officer and the current president of a cybersecurity company. Media reporting maintains that

Penrose downloaded data from Georgia voting machines and instructed the Chief Operating Officer of SullivanStrickler, the company that collected the data, to send the data to Trump attorney Sidney Powell.

Powell, Sidney○▲—Trump's co-defendant and former attorney. Powell was a defendant in the Fulton County indictment and is referred to as "co-conspirator 3" in the DOJ's January 6 indictment. Powell is alleged to have concocted and promulgated several outlandish election fraud claims advanced by Trump and his team. Though Trump privately acknowledged that Powell sounded "crazy," he promoted her theories and considered appointing her special counsel with broad authority to investigate voter fraud. Powell claimed that a network of rigged voting machines—set up by former Venezuelan president Hugo Chávez, who died in 2013, and controlled by the likes of Democratic billionaire George Soros and Antifa—had switched Trump votes to Biden votes. Powell claimed without basis that the manufacturer of the voting machines, Dominion Voting Systems, had bribed the governor and secretary of state of Georgia, and she launched a failed lawsuit against the governor of Georgia that alleged "massive election fraud" accomplished through voting machine software and hardware. The Georgia indictment charged Powell with engaging a private forensic data company to access voting machines in Georgia and Michigan. Powell pleaded guilty in Georgia to misdemeanor criminal charges related to her participation in this scheme. She will serve six years' probation, pay a $6,000 fine, as well as $2,700 to the Georgia Secretary of State's Office, and is required to testify truthfully at future hearings and trials related to the Georgia criminal case.

Brad Raffensperger—The Secretary of State of Georgia. Raffensperger repeatedly refused Trump's requests that he overturn Georgia's election results and declare Trump the rightful winner. Trump, in a phone call with Raffensperger and other Georgia officials, asked Raffensperger to "find" him 11,780 votes—enough to overturn Trump's loss in Georgia.

David Ralston—The former Speaker of the Georgia House of Representatives. Ralston, who died in November 2022, received phone calls from Trump urging him to call a special session of the Georgia General Assembly to recognize Trump's fraudulent slate of Georgia electors.

Michael Roman○—Trump's co-defendant and former campaign staffer. Prosecutors allege that Roman helped coordinate Trump's attorneys' efforts to convene slates of illegitimate electors in seven states so that those electors could submit fraudulent electoral votes for Trump. Roman faces seven criminal charges in Fulton County.

Todd Sanders (Unindicted Co-Conspirator)—A cybersecurity analyst. Media reports claim that Sidney Powell designated Sanders to receive data obtained from Georgia voting machines.

David Shafer○—The former chairman of the Republican Party in Georgia and a former Georgia State Senator. According to the Georgia indictment, Shafer falsely portrayed himself as the "chairman" of the electoral college in Georgia and convened a meeting of Georgia's sixteen fake electors at the Georgia State Capitol in which the fraudulent electors signed a certificate falsely representing that they were Georgia's legitimate electors. Prosecutors maintain that Shafer, who was himself one of the sixteen fake electors, subsequently helped transmit the fraudulent electoral votes to the Archivist of the United States and President of the United States Senate. Shafer faces eight criminal charges in Fulton County.

Robert Sinners (Unindicted Co-Conspirator 4)—A former Trump campaign staffer. Media reports indicate that Sinners, who is apparently identified as Individual 4 in the Georgia indictment, played a role in carrying out the fake elector scheme. Documents uncovered by the January 6 congressional committee show that Sinners instructed Georgia's fake electors to maintain "complete secrecy" about their work. Sinners is now a spokesman for Georgia Secretary of State Brad Raffensperger and has renounced his views about election fraud.

Ray Smith III○—A former Trump campaign attorney. Smith, along with several other Trump campaign lawyers, presented false claims about election fraud to a group of Georgia lawmakers who were present at a Georgia Senate subcommittee meeting. Smith's false statements included allegations that over 10,000 dead people and over 60,000 underaged people voted in Georgia during the 2020 presidential election. Smith faces twelve criminal charges in Fulton County.

Shawn Micah Tresher Still○—One of Georgia's sixteen fake electors and, since 2023, a Georgia State Senator. Prosecutors allege that Still signed a fraudulent certificate in which he represented himself to be a legitimate elector of Georgia. Still faces seven criminal charges in Fulton County.

Phil Waldron (Unindicted Co-Conspirator 6)—A former Army colonel trained in information warfare who, according to media reports, worked with Trump attorneys to spread false theories about election fraud. Waldron was present at a White House meeting between Rudy Giuliani and Pennsylvania legislators.

PROSECUTORS

Alex Bernick—An Assistant District Attorney in the Fulton County DA's Office. Bernick became a Fulton County prosecutor in 2023 and previously worked in the Georgia Attorney General's Office.

Anna Green Cross—A private attorney and former prosecutor who Fani Willis brought on to the Trump investigation. Cross, who currently works at a firm she co-founded, spent twenty years as a Georgia prosecutor and has considerable appellate experience.

John Floyd—An Atlanta-based lawyer tapped by Fani Willis to work on the Trump investigation. Floyd is viewed as an expert in Georgia's racketeering law.

Adam Ney—An Assistant District Attorney in the Fulton County DA's Office.

Grant Root—A senior attorney in the Civil Forfeiture Unit of the Fulton County DA's Office.

Nathan Wade—A private attorney and former prosecutor tapped by Fani Willis to lead the Trump investigation. Wade, who also serves as a municipal court judge in Cobb County, has been on Willis's team since early 2022.

Donald Wakeford—A senior attorney in the Anti-Corruption Unit of the Fulton County DA's Office. Wakeford has been a prosecutor since 2016.

Fani Willis—The Fulton County District Attorney. Willis, a longtime Fulton County prosecutor, was elected in 2020.

Will Wooten—A Deputy District Attorney in the White-Collar Crime Unit of the Fulton County DA's Office. Wooten, a former public defender, has worked in the Fulton County DA's Office since 2021.

Daysha Young—An Executive District Attorney in the Special Victims Division of the Fulton County DA's Office. Young is a veteran prosecutor who has also worked in the DeKalb County DA's Office.

DEFENSE ATTORNEYS

Jennifer Little▲—A former Georgia prosecutor and current Trump defense lawyer. Little has been identified as "Trump Attorney 2" in the DOJ's classified documents indictment, which maintains that she, along with Evan Corcoran, met with Trump at Mar-a-Lago to plan Trump's response to the DOJ's subpoena for classified documents. Little runs her own law firm in Atlanta and has been a member of Trump's Fulton County defense team since the case's inception.

Steven Sadow—A veteran criminal defense lawyer based in Atlanta. In August 2023, Trump overhauled his Fulton County defense team, hiring Sadow to replace his former lead counsel. Sadow rose to prominence defending several high-profile recording artists, including Usher, Rick Ross, and T.I. More recently, Sadow represented Atlanta rapper Gunna in a racketeering case brought by Willis's office. In that case, the rapper entered a negotiated deal, pleading guilty without admitting to criminal conduct, and was released from jail.

Notes to Facing Page

---

* Unlike the Florida documents indictment and the DC January 6 indictment, which will proceed in federal court, this is a state court indictment charging violations of state law—specifically, Georgia law. Although presidents have the authority to pardon individuals for *federal* crimes, they do not have the authority to pardon *state* crimes. Accordingly, in the event that Donald Trump is reelected in the 2024 presidential election, he would not be able to issue pardons to any of the defendants charged here—including himself.

INSIDER NOTE: even if this state case is removed to federal court with regard to the defendants who are former federal officials, the crimes alleged are still state crimes and cannot be pardoned by the next president.

† In certain respects, this indictment overlaps with the DC January 6 indictment. However, despite the similar subject matter, there should be no concerns about double jeopardy, which prohibits a defendant from being prosecuted more than once for the same crime by the same "sovereign." The US Supreme Court has held that prosecutions by separate sovereigns—here, the State of Georgia and the federal government—do not raise double jeopardy concerns.

‡ In the DC January 6 indictment, Trump was charged with just four offenses—three conspiracy charges (one to defraud the United States; a second to obstruct an official government proceeding; and a third to deprive people of civil rights provided by federal law or the Constitution) and attempting to obstruct an official proceeding. By contrast, this indictment charges Trump with multiple violations of Georgia law.

§ Giuliani was not indicted in the DC January 6 indictment, although he is widely reported to be "unindicted co-conspirator 1" in that indictment. By contrast, in this indictment, he is among Trump's most high-profile co-defendants. And notably, he is charged with violating Georgia's RICO (Racketeer Influenced and Corrupt Organizations) statute. Giuliani, as the US Attorney for the Southern District of New York, made a name for himself prosecuting organized crime families and white-collar criminals under the federal RICO statute.

¶ Initially used to target organized crime syndicates like the Mafia, RICO statutes exist at both the state and federal levels and have been used by prosecutors in a wide variety of contexts. Georgia's RICO statute was modeled after the federal RICO statute, but meaningfully, the Georgia statute is broader than the federal statute in its definition of racketeering and the predicate acts that go to show the existence of a criminal conspiracy. Under the Georgia RICO conspiracy statute, the state must prove beyond a reasonable doubt: (1) that a defendant committed or conspired to commit two or more predicate crimes; (2) that the predicate acts were part of an enterprise engaging in a pattern of racketeering activity; and (3) that either: one or more of the acts that form the pattern resulted or would result in a defendant acquiring or maintaining control of any enterprise, real property, or personal property (including money), or the defendant was employed by or associated with an enterprise through a pattern of racketeering.

GC

Fulton County Superior Court
INDICTMENT
FILED CA

E. J15. McAfee

Date: August 14, 2023
Che Alexander, Clerk of Court

INDICTMENT

Clerk No. *23SC188947*

FULTON SUPERIOR COURT*

THE STATE OF GEORGIA†	1	**VIOLATION OF THE GEORGIA RICO (RACKETEER INFLUENCED AND CORRUPT ORGANIZATIONS) ACT¶** O.C.G.A. § 16-14-4(c)
V.		
DONALD JOHN TRUMP Counts 1, 5, 9, 11, 13, 15, 17, 19, 27-29, 38-39‡	2	**SOLICITATION OF VIOLATION OF OATH BY PUBLIC OFFICER** O.C.G.A. §§ 16-4-7 & 16-10-1
RUDOLPH WILLIAM LOUIS GIULIANI§ Counts 1-3, 6-7, 9, 11, 13, 15, 17, 19, 23-24	3	**FALSE STATEMENTS AND WRITINGS** O.C.G.A. § 16-10-20
JOHN CHARLES EASTMAN Counts 1-2, 9, 11, 13, 15, 17, 19, 27	4	**FALSE STATEMENTS AND WRITINGS** O.C.G.A. § 16-10-20
MARK RANDALL MEADOWS Counts 1, 28	5	**SOLICITATION OF VIOLATION OF OATH BY PUBLIC OFFICER** O.C.G.A. §§ 16-4-7 & 16-10-1
KENNETH JOHN CHESEBRO Counts 1, 9, 11, 13, 15, 17, 19	6	**SOLICITATION OF VIOLATION OF OATH BY PUBLIC OFFICER** O.C.G.A. §§ 16-4-7 & 16-10-1

JEFFREY BOSSERT CLARK
Counts 1, 22

7 **FALSE STATEMENTS AND WRITINGS**
O.C.G.A. § 16-10-20

JENNA LYNN ELLIS
Counts 1-2

8 **IMPERSONATING A PUBLIC OFFICER**
O.C.G.A. § 16-10-23

RAY STALLINGS SMITH III
Counts 1-2, 4, 6, 9, 11, 13, 15, 17, 19, 23, 25

9 **CONSPIRACY TO COMMIT IMPERSONATING A PUBLIC OFFICER**
O.C.G.A. §§ 16-4-8 & 16-10-23

ROBERT DAVID CHEELEY
Counts 1, 9, 11, 13, 15, 17, 19, 23, 26, 41

10 **FORGERY IN THE FIRST DEGREE**
O.C.G.A. § 16-9-1(b)

MICHAEL A. ROMAN
Counts 1, 9, 11, 13, 15, 17, 19

11 **CONSPIRACY TO COMMIT FORGERY IN THE FIRST DEGREE**
O.C.G.A. §§ 16-4-8 & 16-9-1(b)

DAVID JAMES SHAFER
Counts 1, 8, 10, 12, 14, 16, 18, 40

12 **FALSE STATEMENTS AND WRITINGS**
O.C.G.A. § 16-10-20

SHAWN MICAH TRESHER STILL
Counts 1, 8, 10, 12, 14, 16, 18

13 **CONSPIRACY TO COMMIT FALSE STATEMENTS AND WRITINGS**
O.C.G.A. §§ 16-4-8 & 16-10-20

STEPHEN CLIFFGARD LEE
Counts 1, 20-21, 30-31

14 **CRIMINAL ATTEMPT TO COMMIT FILING FALSE DOCUMENTS**
O.C.G.A. §§ 16-4-1 & 16-10-20.1(b)(1)

HARRISON WILLIAM PRESCOTT FLOYD Counts 1, 30-31	**15**	**CONSPIRACY TO COMMIT FILING FALSE DOCUMENTS** O.C.G.A. §§ 16-4-8 & 16-10-20.1(b)(1)
TREVIAN C. KUTTI Counts 1, 30-31	**16**	**FORGERY IN THE FIRST DEGREE** O.C.G.A. § 16-9-1(b)
SIDNEY KATHERINE POWELL Counts 1, 32-37	**17**	**CONSPIRACY TO COMMIT FORGERY IN THE FIRST DEGREE** O.C.G.A. §§ 16-4-8 & 16-9-1(b)
CATHLEEN ALSTON LATHAM Counts 1, 8, 10, 12, 14, 32-37	**18**	**FALSE STATEMENTS AND WRITINGS** O.C.G.A. § 16-10-20
SCOTT GRAHAM HALL[*] Counts 1, 32-37	**19**	**CONSPIRACY TO COMMIT FALSE STATEMENTS AND WRITINGS** O.C.G.A. §§ 16-4-8 & 16-10-20

---

[*] Hall was the first of the Georgia codefendants to plead guilty, on September 29, 2023. He pled to five misdemeanors in connection with infiltration of the Coffee County election office. He was sentenced to five years of probation and fined $5,000. He must perform 200 hours of community service and provide a letter of apology to the citizens of Georgia. He was also required to provide a recorded statement to the DA and to testify truthfully at any future proceeding in the case.

INSIDER NOTE: It is common for prosecutors to pursue pleas as to lower-level members of a conspiracy and work their way up the chain, as appears to be occurring here, with Hall, then Powell, and then Chesbro and Ellis. It is also common for plea deals to be worked out on the courthouse steps, just before a trial is scheduled to begin, as occurred with Powell and Chesebro, whose joint trial was scheduled to begin on October 23, 2023.

**MISTY HAMPTON AKA
EMILY MISTY HAYES**
Counts 1, 32-37

**20   CRIMINAL ATTEMPT TO
COMMIT INFLUENCING
WITNESSES**
O.C.G.A. §§ 16-4-1 & 16-10-93 (b)
(1)(A)

**21   CRIMINAL ATTEMPT TO
COMMIT INFLUENCING
WITNESSES**
O.C.G.A. §§ 16-4-1 & 16-10-93(b)
(1)(A)

**22   CRIMINAL ATTEMPT TO
COMMIT FALSE
STATEMENTS AND
WRITINGS**
O.C.G.A. §§ 16-4-1 & 16-10-20

**23   SOLICITATION OF
VIOLATION OF OATH BY
PUBLIC OFFICER**
O.C.G.A. §§ 16-4-7 & 16-10-1

**24   FALSE STATEMENTS
AND WRITINGS**
O.C.G.A. § 16-10-20

**25   FALSE STATEMENTS AND
WRITINGS**
O.C.G.A. § 16-10-20

**26   FALSE STATEMENTS AND
WRITINGS**
O.C.G.A. § 16-10-20

**27   FILING FALSE
DOCUMENTS**
O.C.G.A. § 16-10-20.1(b)(1)

28 SOLICITATION OF VIOLATION OF OATH BY PUBLIC OFFICER
O.C.G.A. §§ 16-4-7 & 16-10-1

29 FALSE STATEMENTS AND WRITINGS
O.C.G.A. § 16-10-20

30 CONSPIRACY TO COMMIT SOLICITATION OF FALSE STATEMENTS AND WRITINGS
O.C.G.A. §§ 16-4-8, 16-4-7 & 16-10-20

31 INFLUENCING WITNESSES
O.C.G.A. § 16-10-93(b)(1)(A)

32 CONSPIRACY TO COMMIT ELECTION FRAUD
O.C.G.A. §§ 21-2-603 & 21-2-566

33 CONSPIRACY TO COMMIT ELECTION FRAUD
O.C.G.A. §§ 21-2-603 & 21-2-574

34 CONSPIRACY TO COMMIT COMPUTER THEFT
O.C.G.A. §§ 16-4-8 & 16-9-93(a)

35 CONSPIRACY TO COMMIT COMPUTER TRESPASS
O.C.G.A. §§ 16-4-8 & 16-9-93(b)

36 CONSPIRACY TO COMMIT COMPUTER INVASION OF PRIVACY
O.C.G.A. §§ 16-4-8 & 16-9-93(c)

37 CONSPIRACY TO DEFRAUD THE STATE
O.C.G.A. § 16-10-21

38 SOLICITATION OF VIOLATION OF OATH BY PUBLIC OFFICER
O.C.G.A. §§ 16-4-7 & 16-10-1

39 FALSE STATEMENTS AND WRITINGS
O.C.G.A. § 16-10-20

40 FALSE STATEMENTS AND WRITINGS
O.C.G.A. § 16-10-20

41 PERJURY
O.C.G.A. § 16-10-70(a)

True BILL

Aug. 14, 2023

Grand Jury Foreperson

_____   **FANI T. WILLIS, District Attorney**[*]

---

[*] The district attorney of Fulton County is the prosecutor for the metropolitan Atlanta area. It is an elected position—Willis was elected in 2020, after defeating her former boss, the incumbent DA, Paul Howard. She campaigned on the premise of restoring integrity to the Fulton County district attorney's office. She is the first woman to serve as Fulton County DA.

INSIDER NOTE: Although Trump pointedly mispronounces Willis's first name, it is pronounced Faw-knee, not Fan-knee. Willis's father was a Black Panther and was, in her description, "very Afrocentric." "Fani" means "prosperous" in Swahili.

| The Defendant waives copy of indictment, list of witnesses, formal arraignment and pleads _____ Guilty.[*] | The Defendant waives copy of indictment, list of witnesses, formal arraignment and pleads _____ Guilty. | The Defendant waives copy of indictment, list of witnesses, formal arraignment and pleads _____ Guilty. |

_____
Defendant

_____
Attorney for Defendant

_____
Assistant District Attorney[†]

This ____ day of _____, ___

_____
Defendant

_____
Attorney for Defendant

_____
Assistant District Attorney

This ____ day of _____, ___

_____
Defendant

_____
Attorney for Defendant

_____
Assistant District Attorney

This ____ day of _____, ___[‡]

---

[*] As is standard, the defendants must enter a plea of guilty or not guilty to some or all of the charges. Often, the prosecutor and the defendant enter into a plea bargain—an agreement that resolves the criminal case against the defendant, typically to less than all the charges. In some cases, the plea agreement may entail the defendant's cooperation as a witness in exchange for more limited charges, the prospect of a reduced sentence, or both. It is estimated that roughly 95 percent of state and federal criminal cases are resolved via plea agreement. Here, as of this writing, four of the defendants—Scott Hall, Sidney Powell, and Kenneth Chesebro, and Jenna Ellis—have entered guilty pleas pursuant to Georgia plea agreements.

[†] "Assistant District Attorney" refers to the so-called "line prosecutors," who report to the DA and handle most aspects of the prosecution and trial, including court appearances.

[‡] There are thirty-nine of these waivers in the original document, condensed here to three representative blocks.

STATE OF GEORGIA, COUNTY OF FULTON
IN THE SUPERIOR COURT OF SAID COUNTY
THE GRAND JURORS, * selected, chosen, and sworn for the County of Fulton, to wit:

---

* Initially, a "special" grand jury was convened to investigate the effort to overturn the results of the 2020 election in Georgia. Like a "regular" grand jury, a special grand jury is composed of twenty-three Georgia citizens (plus three alternates) serving jury duty, but a special grand jury has different purposes and powers. In Fulton County, a regular grand jury generally serves for a two-month period and has the authority to issue indictments. By contrast, a Fulton County special grand jury is reserved for more involved cases with more witnesses and evidence to be reviewed. Special grand juries are not limited to a two-month period and, critically, they cannot vote indictments, but they can issue reports and recommendations. In this case, the special grand jury heard testimony and collected evidence—including from high-profile individuals in and outside of Fulton County—for nearly nine months. Notably, the special grand jurors unanimously found that there was no material voter fraud in the Georgia election; i.e., no fraud that was outcome determinative—a clear rebuke of Trump and his allies who made allegations of widespread voter fraud in the Georgia election to the public and to various Georgia officials.

In its report, the special grand jury made certain findings and recommendations with respect to potential charges as to various people. The DA and a regular grand jury are not bound to follow these recommendations, and indeed, here they did not (bringing far fewer charges and charging fewer people as defendants than the special grand jury recommended). If the DA decides to seek indictments, she must bring the case before a regular grand jury, which then reviews the evidence and determines whether to issue an indictment. A majority of the regular grand jury must agree on each charge, as to each defendant, for an indictment to issue.

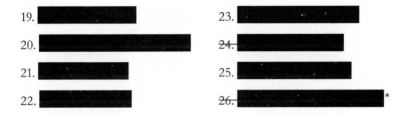

19.

20.

21.

22.

23.

24.

25.

26.

* Georgia law requires that the grand jurors' names be included in the indictment. While this may promote transparency, it exposed the grand jurors to harassment and other unwelcome conduct. In stark contrast, in federal court indictments, like the DOJ January 6 indictment and the Mar-a-Lago documents indictment, the names of the grand jurors are not publicized and the name of the grand jury foreperson who signs an indictment can be redacted from the public charge. To minimize the potential for harassment or intimidation, and consonant with the DC and Florida indictments, which redact identifying information for the grand jury foreperson, we have omitted the names of the Georgia grand jurors.

TABLE OF CONTENTS*

---

* At the heart of the indictment are the violations of Georgia's RICO statute, but DA Willis also charged forty other crimes, including forgery, impersonating a public officer, and false statements.

† The decision to rely on Georgia's RICO statute is significant. Using the Georgia RICO statute, prosecutors seek to connect disparate events to tell a sweeping story about how Trump allies worked together toward the common goal of overturning the results of the election in Georgia. The benefit of a RICO statute is that it allows the prosecution to weave all the strands of a scheme, which is often made up of different crimes, into a coherent narrative for the jury. This is especially important in a multi-defendant trial in which many different crimes are charged.

‡ Page references in this table of contents refer to the pagination in the original document.

COUNT 1 of 41

The Grand Jurors aforesaid, in the name and behalf of the citizens of Georgia, do hereby charge and accuse:

**DONALD JOHN TRUMP,
RUDOLPH WILLIAM LOUIS GIULIANI,
JOHN CHARLES EASTMAN,
MARK RANDALL MEADOWS,***
**KENNETH JOHN CHESEBRO,
JEFFREY BOSSERT CLARK,
JENNA LYNN ELLIS,
RAY STALLINGS SMITH III,
ROBERT DAVID CHEELEY,
MICHAEL A. ROMAN,
DAVID JAMES SHAFER,
SHAWN MICAH TRESHER STILL,
STEPHEN CLIFFGARD LEE,
HARRISON WILLIAM PRESCOTT FLOYD,
TREVIAN C. KUTTI,
SIDNEY KATHERINE POWELL,
CATHLEEN ALSTON LATHAM,
SCOTT GRAHAM HALL, and
MISTY HAMPTON**

with the offense of **VIOLATION OF THE GEORGIA RICO (RACKETEER INFLUENCED AND CORRUPT ORGANIZATIONS) ACT, O.C.G.A. § 16-14-4(c),** for the said accused, individually and as persons concerned in the commission of a crime, and

---

* Notably, Meadows and Giuliani were subpoenaed to testify before the Fulton County special grand jury that was investigating election interference. A subpoenaed witness must testify, absent a valid privilege as to specific questions, such as attorney-client privilege, executive privilege, or the privilege against self-incrimination under the US Constitution's Fifth Amendment.

INSIDER NOTE: A witness who refuses to testify absent such a privilege can be charged with criminal contempt, as happened in DC with respect to Steve Bannon and Peter Navarro, who refused to comply with a congressional subpoena. Both were charged with criminal contempt and were convicted at trial.

together with unindicted co-conspirators, in the State of Georgia and County of Fulton, on and between the **4th day of November 2020 and the 15th day of September 2022,** while associated with an enterprise, unlawfully conspired and endeavored to conduct and participate in, directly and indirectly, such enterprise through a pattern of racketeering activity in violation of **O.C.G.A. § 16-14-4(b),** as described below and incorporated by reference as if fully set forth herein, contrary to the laws of said State, the good order, peace, and dignity thereof;

INTRODUCTION

Defendant Donald John Trump lost the United States presidential election held on November 3, 2020. One of the states he lost was Georgia. Trump and the other Defendants charged in this Indictment refused to accept that Trump lost, and they knowingly and willfully joined a conspiracy to unlawfully change the outcome of the election in favor of Trump. That conspiracy contained a common plan and purpose to commit two or more acts of racketeering activity in Fulton County, Georgia, elsewhere in the State of Georgia, and in other states.

THE ENTERPRISE

At all times relevant to this Count of the Indictment, the Defendants, as well as others not named as defendants, unlawfully conspired and endeavored to conduct and participate in a criminal enterprise in Fulton County, Georgia, and elsewhere. Defendants Donald John Trump, Rudolph William Louis Giuliani, John Charles Eastman, Mark Randall Meadows, Kenneth John Chesebro, Jeffrey Bossert Clark, Jenna Lynn Ellis, Ray Stallings Smith III, Robert David Cheeley, Michael A. Roman, David James Shafer, Shawn Micah Tresher Still, Stephen Cliffgard Lee, Harrison William Prescott Floyd, Trevian C. Kutti, Sidney Katherine Powell, Cathleen Alston Latham, Scott Graham Hall, Misty Hampton, unindicted co-conspirators Individual 1 through Individual 30, and others known and unknown to the Grand Jury, constituted a criminal organization* whose members and associates engaged in various related criminal activities including, but not limited to, false statements and writings, impersonating a public officer, forgery, filing false documents, influencing witnesses, computer theft, computer trespass, computer invasion of privacy, conspiracy to defraud the state, acts involving theft, and perjury.

This criminal organization constituted an enterprise as that term is defined in O.C.G.A. § 16-14-3(3), that is, a group of individuals associated in fact. The Defendants and other members and associates of the enterprise had connections and relationships with one another and with the enterprise. The enterprise constituted an ongoing organization whose members and associates functioned as a continuing unit for a common purpose of achieving the objectives of the enterprise. The enterprise operated in Fulton County, Georgia, elsewhere in the State of Georgia, in other states, including, but not limited to, Arizona, Michigan, Nevada, New Mexico, Pennsylvania, and Wisconsin, and in the District of Columbia.† The enterprise operated for a period of time sufficient to permit its members and associates to pursue its objectives.

---

* Although DA Willis charged nineteen individuals, the indictment alleges an even wider-ranging criminal enterprise that included thirty unnamed, unindicted co-conspirators. Readers may find it helpful to refer to the cast of characters provided in this book to learn more about each alleged participant.

On September 8, 2023, the special grand jury's report was released to the public, revealing that the special grand jury actually recommended filing criminal charges against *thirty-nine* people, including a sitting US senator from South Carolina, Lindsay Graham; former US senators from Georgia, David Perdue and Kelly Loeffler; former Trump national security advisor Michael Flynn; Trump advisor Boris Epshteyn; and attorney Cleta Mitchell. Although some have challenged DA Willis's decision to charge nineteen defendants as sprawling and aggressive, the release of the special grand jury's report makes clear that the DA exercised considerable restraint in her charging decisions.

INSIDER NOTE: A special grand jury finding is only based on proof establishing "probable cause," and found only by a majority of the special grand jurors, whereas DA Willis must consider whether she could ultimately establish any charge unanimously to a trial jury, based on proof "beyond a reasonable doubt," a much higher legal standard.

† The indictment alleges that although the criminal enterprise operated in Fulton County, the acts undertaken in furtherance of the enterprise's goals were not limited to Fulton County. Indeed, they stretched across the country to other so-called battleground states, where the Trump campaign was contesting election results, and to

MANNER AND METHODS
OF THE ENTERPRISE*

The manner and methods used by the Defendants and other members and associates of the enterprise to further the goals of the enterprise and to achieve its purposes included, but were not limited to, the following:

1. **False Statements to and Solicitation of State Legislatures**

Members of the enterprise, including several of the Defendants, appeared at hearings in Fulton County, Georgia, before members of the Georgia General Assembly on December 3, 2020, December 10, 2020, and December 30, 2020. At these hearings, members of the enterprise made false statements concerning fraud in the November 3, 2020, presidential election. The purpose of these false statements was to persuade Georgia legislators to reject lawful electoral votes cast by the duly elected and qualified presidential electors from Georgia. Members of the enterprise corruptly solicited Georgia legislators instead to unlawfully appoint their own presidential electors for the purpose of casting electoral votes for Donald Trump. Members of the enterprise also made false statements to state legislators during hearings and meetings in Arizona, Michigan, and Pennsylvania in November and December 2020 to persuade legislators in those states to unlawfully appoint their own presidential electors.

---

the nation's capital. It makes good sense to include this larger framework as jurors otherwise might wonder why the scheme was limited to Georgia, as even a reversal of Georgia's electoral outcome would not, by itself, change the outcome of the presidential election.

* In many ways, the allegations that give rise to these charges reiterate the allegations underlying the DC January 6 indictment, including the scheme to advance slates of "fake" electors, the effort to enlist state officials in the scheme to overturn election results in battleground states, as well as the effort to pressure DOJ officials and Vice President Mike Pence to participate.

2. False Statements to and Solicitation of High-Ranking State Officials

Members of the enterprise, including several of the Defendants, made false statements in Fulton County and elsewhere in the State of Georgia to Georgia officials, including the Governor, the Secretary of State, and the Speaker of the House of Representatives. Members of the enterprise also corruptly solicited Georgia officials, including the Secretary of State and the Speaker of the House of Representatives, to violate their oaths to the Georgia Constitution and to the United States Constitution by unlawfully changing the outcome of the November 3, 2020, presidential election in Georgia in favor of Donald Trump. Members of the enterprise also made false statements to and solicited state officials in Arizona, Michigan, and Pennsylvania.

3. Creation and Distribution of False Electoral College Documents

Members of the enterprise, including several of the Defendants, created false Electoral College documents and recruited individuals to convene and cast false Electoral College votes at the Georgia State Capitol, in Fulton County, on December 14, 2020. After the false Electoral College votes were cast, members of the enterprise transmitted the votes to the President of the United States Senate, the Archivist of the United States, the Georgia Secretary of State, and the Chief Judge of the United States District Court for the Northern District of Georgia. The false documents were intended to disrupt and delay the joint session of Congress on January 6, 2021, in order to unlawfully change the outcome of the November 3, 2020, presidential election in favor of Donald Trump. Similar schemes were executed by members of the enterprise in Arizona, Michigan, Nevada, New Mexico, Pennsylvania, and Wisconsin.*

---

* The indictment alleges that, in addition to the effort to overturn the election results in Georgia, there were parallel attempts to overturn the election results in other key battleground states that had been called for Biden.

4. **Harassment and Intimidation of
Fulton County Election Worker Ruby Freeman**[*]

Members of the enterprise, including several of the Defendants, falsely accused Fulton County election worker Ruby Freeman of committing election crimes in Fulton County, Georgia. These false accusations were repeated to Georgia legislators and other. Georgia officials in an effort to persuade them to unlawfully change the outcome of the November 3, 2020, presidential election in favor of Donald Trump. In furtherance of this scheme, members of the enterprise traveled from out of state to harass Freeman, intimidate her, and solicit her to falsely confess to election crimes that she did not commit.

5. **Solicitation of High-Ranking United States
Department of Justice Officials**

Members of the enterprise, including several of the Defendants, corruptly solicited high-ranking United States Department of Justice officials to make false statements to government officials in Fulton County, Georgia, including the Governor, the Speaker of the House of Representatives, and the President Pro Tempore of the Senate. In one instance, Donald Trump stated to the Acting United States Attorney General, "Just say that the election was corrupt, and leave the rest to me and the Republican congressmen."

6. **Solicitation of the Vice President of the United States**

Members of the enterprise, including several of the Defendants, corruptly solicited the Vice President of the United States to violate the United States Constitution and federal law by unlawfully rejecting Electoral College votes cast in Fulton County, Georgia, by

---

[*] Although she was only indirectly referenced in the DC January 6 indictment, election worker Ruby Freeman is prominently named here. The indictment alleges that members of the enterprise falsely accused Freeman of committing election crimes— and indeed, repeated these false claims of election fraud to others in order to unlawfully change the outcome of the election in Georgia. Freeman and her daughter, Shaye Moss, testified before the January 6 congressional committee that these accusations completely upended their lives, exposing them to a raft of harassment and hostility.

the duly elected and qualified presidential electors from Georgia. Members of the enterprise also corruptly solicited the Vice President to reject votes cast by the duly elected and qualified presidential electors from several other states.

7. Unlawful Breach of Election Equipment in Georgia and Elsewhere*

Members of the enterprise, including several of the Defendants, corruptly conspired in Fulton County, Georgia, and elsewhere to unlawfully access secure voting equipment and voter data. In Georgia, members of the enterprise stole data, including ballot images, voting equipment software, and personal voter information. The stolen data was then distributed to other members of the enterprise, including members in other states.

8. Obstructive Acts in Furtherance of the Conspiracy and the Cover Up

Members of the enterprise, including several of the Defendants, filed false documents, made false statements to government investigators, and committed perjury in judicial proceedings in Fulton County, Georgia, and elsewhere in furtherance of and to cover up the conspiracy.

ACTS OF RACKETEERING ACTIVITY AND OVERT ACTS IN FURTHERANCE OF THE CONSPIRACY

As part of and on behalf of the criminal enterprise detailed above, the Defendants and other members and associates of the

---

* Although many of the allegations in this indictment reiterate the facts alleged in the DC January 6 indictment, this references new and distinct allegations with respect to specific events in Georgia. If a jury credits all of these allegations, they would point to a nationwide effort to overturn the presidential election results—something one associates with elections in other authoritarian countries and systems.

INSIDER NOTE: The Coffee County allegations spelled out in this indictment are in keeping with the reports of a meeting in the Oval Office in which Trump and his allies seriously contemplated calling on the US military to seize voting machines.

enterprise committed overt acts* to effect the objectives of the enterprise, including but not limited to:

Act 1.

On or about the **4th day of November 2020, DONALD JOHN TRUMP**† made a nationally televised speech falsely declaring victory in the 2020 presidential election. Approximately four days earlier, on or about October 31, 2020, **DONALD JOHN TRUMP** discussed a draft speech with unindicted co-conspirator Individual 1, whose identity is known to the Grand Jury, that falsely declared victory and falsely claimed voter fraud. The speech was an overt act in furtherance of the conspiracy.

Act 2.

On or about the **15th day of November 2020, RUDOLPH WILLIAM LOUIS GIULIANI** placed a telephone call to unindicted co-conspirator Individual 2, whose identity is known to the Grand Jury, and left an approximately 83-second-long voicemail message for unindicted co-conspirator Individual 2 making statements concerning fraud in the November 3, 2020, election in Fulton County, Georgia. This telephone call was an overt act in furtherance of the conspiracy.

---

* The prosecutors detail the "overt acts" undertaken by the criminal enterprise in furtherance of the conspiracy. To be clear, by themselves, many of these acts would not rise to the level of a crime; however, they do not need to be a crime. Instead, the prosecution needs only establish that the alleged conspiracy was not mere talk, but took at least one concrete step forward. Here, the overt acts, when viewed in tandem, form a detailed story of the various steps that went into carrying out a sprawling and complex criminal conspiracy.

† Notably, the prosecutors allege that the first overt act in furtherance of the conspiracy occurred on Election Day 2020, when Trump gave a speech falsely declaring himself the winner of the election.

Act 2.[*]

On or about the **19th day of November 2020, RUDOLPH WILLIAM LOUIS GIULIANI, JENNA LYNN ELLIS, SID-NEY KATHERINE POWELL,**[†] and unindicted coconspirator Individual 3, whose identity is known to the Grand Jury, appeared at a press conference at the Republican National Committee Head-quarters on behalf of **DONALD JOHN TRUMP** and Donald J. Trump for President, Inc. (the "Trump Campaign") and made false statements concerning fraud in the November 3, 2020, presidential election in Georgia and elsewhere. These were overt acts in further-ance of the conspiracy.

Act 4.

On or about the **20th day of November 2020, DAVID JAMES SHAFER** sent an e-mail to unindicted co-conspirator Individual 4, whose identity is known to the Grand Jury, and other individuals. In the e-mail, **DAVID JAMES SHAFER** stated that **SCOTT GRAHAM HALL,**[‡] a Georgia bail bondsman, "has been looking into the election on behalf of the President at the request of David Bossie" and asked unindicted co-conspirator Individual 4 to exchange contact information with **SCOTT GRAHAM HALL** and to "help him as needed." This was an overt act in furtherance of the conspiracy.

---

[*] Misnumbering as per original text.

[†] Jenna Ellis once dubbed this group of Trump lawyers an "elite strike force team."

[‡] On September 29, 2023, Hall became the first of the nineteen Georgia defendants to enter into a plea agreement with the prosecution. Hall pleaded guilty to five mis-demeanor charges and was sentenced to five years of probation. He also agreed to provide evidence to prosecutors and testify in court hearings and trials involving the other eighteen defendants. In the wake of Hall's plea, media reports speculated that Hall's cooperation with prosecutors would be especially relevant to Sidney Pow-ell's (and other conspirators') alleged efforts to infiltrate voting machines in Coffee County, Georgia. On October 18, 2023, Powell became the second defendant to enter a guilty plea.

Act 5.

On or about the **20th day of November 2020, DONALD JOHN TRUMP** and **MARK RANDALL MEADOWS** met with Majority Leader of the Michigan Senate Michael Shirkey, Speaker of the Michigan House of Representatives Lee Chatfield, and other Michigan legislators in the Oval Office at the White House,* and **DONALD JOHN TRUMP** made false statements concerning fraud in the November 3, 2020, presidential election in Michigan. **RUDOLPH WILLIAM LOUIS GIULIANI** joined the meeting by telephone. This meeting was an overt act in furtherance of the conspiracy.

Act 6.

On or about the **21st day of November 2020, MARK RANDALL MEADOWS** sent a text message to United States Representative Scott Perry from Pennsylvania† and stated, "Can you send me the number for the speaker and the leader of PA Legislature.

---

* Notably, this alleged act did not take place in Fulton County—or even Georgia. Under the expansive Georgia RICO statute, the DA need not show that all the acts undertaken in furtherance of the conspiracy occurred in her jurisdiction. She needs only to prove that the act was in furtherance of the alleged conspiracy to overturn the election results in Georgia. A number of the acts alleged did not take place in Fulton County—and the named defendants need never have set foot in Georgia, although many did.

† In August 2022, the FBI seized Representative Perry's phone under a court-authorized search warrant. Perry immediately sought to prevent investigators from accessing the phone's contents, citing his legal privileges as a federal legislator and Congress's authority to be free from interference from the executive branch (a protection under the Speech or Debate Clause of the US Constitution). On January 4, 2023, District Judge Beryl A. Howell, in the District of the District of Columbia, granted the government access to what appeared likely to be most of the files on Perry's phone. On September 5, 2023, a three-judge panel of the Court of Appeals rejected the test applied by Judge Howell that would have given greater leeway to prosecutors to access the contents of Perry's phone related to his communications with third parties, including those in the White House and the Trump campaign. Judge Neomi Rao, a Trump appointee, wrote the majority opinion in which Judge Karen LeCraft Henderson, a George H. W. Bush appointee, joined. Judge Greg Katsas, a Trump appointee, joined the judgment but filed a separate concurrence. As a result of the appellate court's ruling, the government received less access to these files

POTUS wants to chat with them." This was an overt act in further-ance of the conspiracy.*

Act 7.

On or about the **22nd day of November 2020, DON-ALD JOHN TRUMP** and **RUDOLPH WILLIAM LOUIS GIULIANI** placed a telephone call to Speaker of the Arizona House of Representatives Russell "Rusty" Bowers. During the tele-phone call, **RUDOLPH WILLIAM LOUIS GIULIANI** made false statements concerning fraud in the November 3, 2020, presi-dential election in Arizona and solicited, requested, and importuned Bowers to unlawfully appoint presidential electors from Arizona. Bowers declined and later testified to the United States House of Representatives Select Committee to Investigate the January 6th Attack on the United States Capitol that he told **DONALD JOHN TRUMP**, "I would not break my oath." The false statements and solicitations were overt acts in furtherance of the conspiracy.

Act 8.

On or about the **25th day of November 2020, RUDOLPH WILLIAM LOUIS GIULIANI** and **JENNA LYNN ELLIS** appeared, spoke, and presented witnesses at a meeting of Pennsyl-vania legislators in Gettysburg, Pennsylvania. During the meeting, **RUDOLPH WILLIAM LOUIS GIULIANI** made false state-ments concerning fraud in the November 3, 2020, presidential election in Pennsylvania and solicited, requested, and importuned the Pennsylvania legislators present at the meeting to unlawfully appoint presidential electors from Pennsylvania. During the meet-

---

than it sought. It remains to be seen whether Special Counsel Jack Smith will seek further review of this decision.

* This request for the telephone number for the speaker and leader of the Pennsyl-vania legislature is, on its face, a relatively anodyne one—ordinarily, it would not rise to the level of a crime, nor would it normally be outside of the scope of Meadows's duties as chief of staff. However, the prosecution here includes this as a relevant act because it alleges that the request for the telephone number was in furtherance of the charged conspiracy.

ing, **JENNA LYNN ELLIS** solicited, requested, and importuned the Pennsylvania legislators present at the meeting to unlawfully appoint presidential electors from Pennsylvania. **DONALD JOHN TRUMP** joined the meeting by telephone, made false statements concerning fraud in the November 3, 2020, presidential election in Pennsylvania, and solicited, requested, and importuned the Pennsylvania legislators present at the meeting to unlawfully appoint presidential electors from Pennsylvania. These were overt acts in furtherance of the conspiracy.

Act 9.*

On or about the **25th day of November 2020,** immediately after the meeting of Pennsylvania legislators in Gettysburg, Pennsylvania, where **RUDOLPH WILLIAM LOUIS GIULIANI** and **JENNA LYNN ELLIS** appeared, spoke, and presented witnesses, **DONALD JOHN TRUMP** invited a group of the Pennsylvania legislators and others to meet with him at the White House. Later that day, **DONALD JOHN TRUMP, MARK RANDALL MEADOWS, RUDOLPH WILLIAM LOUIS GIULIANI, JENNA LYNN ELLIS** and unindicted co-conspirators Individual 5 and Individual 6, whose identities are known to the Grand Jury, met with the group of Pennsylvania legislators at the White House and discussed holding a special session of the Pennsylvania General Assembly. These were overt acts in furtherance of the conspiracy.

---

* The series of overt acts alleged here make clear that Pennsylvania, as much as Georgia, was a key battleground state on which Trump and his allies were focused as they sought to transform the electoral map to assure a Trump victory.

INSIDER NOTE: Giuliani's role in the Pennsylvania scheme is the focus of Washington, DC, bar proceedings that have recommended Giuliani's disbarment. A hearing in the bar proceedings determined that, in challenging the Pennsylvania election results in court, Giuliani sought to "undermine the integrity" of the election and had "helped destabilize our democracy," doing "lasting damage" to the oath to support the US Constitution that he swore when he was admitted to the bar. A separate disciplinary proceeding in New York resulted in Giuliani's suspension from the bar in that state.

Act 10.

On or about the **26th day of November 2020, RUDOLPH WILLIAM LOUIS GIULIANI** and **JENNA LYNN ELLIS** placed a telephone call to Speaker of the Pennsylvania House of Representatives Bryan Cutler and left Cutler a voicemail message for the purpose of soliciting, requesting, and importuning him to unlawfully appoint presidential electors from Pennsylvania. This was an overt act in furtherance of the conspiracy.

Act 11.

On or about the **26th day of November 2020, RUDOLPH WILLIAM LOUIS GIULIANI** placed a telephone call to President Pro Tempore of the Pennsylvania Senate Jacob "Jake" Corman for the purpose of soliciting, requesting, and importuning Corman to unlawfully appoint presidential electors from Pennsylvania. This was an overt act in furtherance of the conspiracy.

Act 12.

On or about the **27th day of November 2020, RUDOLPH WILLIAM LOUIS GIULIANI** and **JENNA LYNN ELLIS** placed a telephone call to Speaker of the Pennsylvania House of Representatives Bryan Cutler and left Cutler a voicemail message for the purpose of soliciting, requesting, and importuning him to unlawfully appoint presidential electors from Pennsylvania. This was an overt act in furtherance of the conspiracy.

Act 12.*

On or about the **27th day of November 2020, RUDOLPH WILLIAM LOUIS GIULIANI** and **JENNA LYNN ELLIS** placed a telephone call to President Pro Tempore of the Pennsylvania Senate Jake Corman for the purpose of soliciting, requesting, and importuning Corman to unlawfully appoint presidential elec-

---

* Misnumbering as per original text.

tors from Pennsylvania. This was an overt act in furtherance of the conspiracy.

Act 14.

On or about the **27th day of November 2020, DONALD JOHN TRUMP** placed a telephone call to President Pro Tempore of the Pennsylvania Senate Jake Corman for the purpose of soliciting, requesting, and importuning Corman to unlawfully appoint presidential electors from Pennsylvania. This was an overt act in furtherance of the conspiracy.

Act 15.

On or about the **28th day of November 2020, RUDOLPH WILLIAM LOUIS GIULIANI** placed a telephone call to Speaker of the Pennsylvania House of Representatives Bryan Cutler and left Cutler a voicemail message for the purpose of soliciting, requesting, and importuning him to unlawfully appoint presidential electors from Pennsylvania. This was an overt act in furtherance of the conspiracy.

Act 16.

On or about the **29th day of November 2020, RUDOLPH WILLIAM LOUIS GIULIANI** placed a telephone call to Speaker of the Pennsylvania House of Representatives Bryan Cutler and left Cutler a voicemail message for the purpose of soliciting, requesting, and importuning him to unlawfully appoint presidential electors from Pennsylvania. This was an overt act in furtherance of the conspiracy.

Act 17.

On or about the **30th day of November 2020, RUDOLPH WILLIAM LOUIS GIULIANI** and **JENNA LYNN ELLIS** appeared, spoke, and presented witnesses at a meeting of Arizona legislators in Phoenix, Arizona. Unindicted co-conspirators Individual 5 and Individual 6, whose identities are known to the Grand Jury, were also present. During the meeting, **RUDOLPH WILLIAM LOUIS GIULIANI** made false statements concerning fraud in the November 3, 2020, presidential election in Arizona and solicited, requested, and importuned the Arizona legislators present at the meeting to unlawfully appoint presidential electors from Arizona. During the meeting, **JENNA LYNN ELLIS** solicited, requested, and importuned the Arizona legislators present at the meeting to unlawfully appoint presidential electors from Arizona. **DONALD JOHN TRUMP** joined the meeting by telephone and made false statements concerning fraud in the November 3, 2020, presidential election in Arizona. These were overt acts in furtherance of the conspiracy.[*]

Act 18.

On or about the **30th day of November 2020, MICHAEL A. ROMAN**[†] instructed unindicted co-conspirator Individual 7, whose identity is known to the Grand Jury, to coordinate with individuals associated with the Trump Campaign to contact state legislators in Georgia and elsewhere on behalf of **DONALD JOHN TRUMP** and to encourage them to unlawfully appoint presidential electors from their respective states. This was an overt act in furtherance of the conspiracy.

Act 19.

On or between the **1st day of December 2020 and the 31st day of December 2020, DONALD JOHN TRUMP** and **MARK RANDALL MEADOWS** met with John McEntee and requested that McEntee prepare a memorandum outlining a strategy for dis-

---

[*] The prosecution makes clear that Arizona, like Georgia and Pennsylvania, was a key battleground state on which Trump and his allies focused as they sought to secure through fraud, threats, and pressure, a Trump victory.
[†] Roman is a Trump campaign staffer and longtime Republican political operative. Prior to working for the Trump campaign, he ran an in-house intelligence unit for the Koch brothers. He has also been active in promoting claims about widespread voter fraud. During the 2020 election he headed an army of Trump poll watchers.

rupting and delaying the joint session of Congress on January 6, 2021, the day prescribed by law for counting votes cast by the duly elected and qualified presidential electors from Georgia and the other states. The strategy included having Vice President Michael R. "Mike" Pence count only half of the electoral votes from certain states and then return the remaining electoral votes to state legislatures. The request was an overt act in furtherance of the conspiracy.

Act 20.

On or about the **1st day of December 2020, RUDOLPH WILLIAM LOUIS GIULIANI** and **JENNA LYNN ELLIS** met with Speaker of the Arizona House of Representatives Rusty Bowers, President of the Arizona Senate Karen Fann, and other Arizona legislators in Phoenix, Arizona. Unindicted co-conspirator Individual 5, whose identity is known to the Grand Jury, was also present. During the meeting, **RUDOLPH WILLIAM LOUIS GIULIANI** made false statements concerning fraud in the November 3, 2020, presidential election in Arizona and solicited, requested, and importuned the legislators present to call a special session of the Arizona State Legislature. These were overt acts in furtherance of the conspiracy.

Act 21.

On or about the **2nd day of December 2020, RUDOLPH WILLIAM LOUIS GIULIANI** and **JENNA LYNN ELLIS** appeared, spoke, and presented witnesses at a meeting of the Michigan House of Representatives Oversight Committee. During the meeting, **RUDOLPH WILLIAM LOUIS GIULIANI** made false statements concerning fraud in the November 3, 2020, presidential election in Michigan and solicited, requested, and importuned the Michigan legislators present at the meeting to unlawfully appoint presidential electors from Michigan. During the meeting, **JENNA LYNN ELLIS** solicited, requested, and importuned the Michigan legislators present at the meeting to unlawfully appoint presidential electors from Michigan. These were overt acts in furtherance of the conspiracy.

Act 22.

On or about the **3rd day of December 2020, DONALD JOHN TRUMP** caused to be tweeted from the Twitter account @ RealDonaldTrump, "Georgia hearings now on @OANN. Amazing!" This was an overt act in furtherance of the conspiracy.

Act 23.

On or about the **3rd day of December 2020, RUDOLPH WILLIAM LOUIS GIULIANI, JOHN CHARLES EAST-MAN, JENNA LYNN ELLIS,** and **RAY STALLINGS SMITH III** committed the felony offense of **SOLICITATION OF VIO-LATION OF OATH BY PUBLIC OFFICER,** in violation of **O.C.G.A. §§ 16-4-7 & 16-10-1,** in Fulton County, Georgia, by unlawfully soliciting, requesting, and importuning certain public officers then serving as elected members of the Georgia Senate and present at a Senate Judiciary Subcommittee meeting, including unindicted co-conspirator Individual 8, whose identity is known to the Grand Jury, Senators Lee Anderson, Brandon Beach, Matt Brass, Greg Dolezal, Steve Gooch, Tyler Harper, Bill Heath, Jen Jordan, John F. Kennedy, William Ligon, Elena Parent, Michael Rhett, Carden Summers, and Blake Tillery, to engage in conduct constituting the felony offense of Violation of Oath by Public Officer, O.C.G.A. § 16-10-1, by unlawfully appointing presidential electors from Georgia, in willful and intentional violation of the terms of the oath of said persons as prescribed by law, with intent that said persons engage in said conduct. This was an overt act in furtherance of the conspiracy.

Act 24.

On or about the **3rd day of December 2020, RUDOLPH WILLIAM LOUIS GIULIANI** committed the felony offense of **FALSE STATEMENTS AND WRITINGS,*** in violation of **O.C.G.A. § 16-10-20,** in Fulton County, Georgia, by knowingly,

---

* Notably, Giuliani is charged with thirteen crimes, ranging from making false statements and representations to soliciting public officials to violate their oaths of

willfully, and unlawfully making at least one of the following false statements and representations to members of the Georgia Senate present at a Senate Judiciary Subcommittee meeting:*

1.　　That at least 96,600 mail-in ballots were counted in the November 3, 2020, presidential election in Georgia, despite there being no record of those ballots having been returned to a county elections office;

2.　　That Dominion Voting Systems equipment used in the November 3, 2020, presidential election in Antrim County, Michigan, mistakenly recorded 6,000 votes for Joseph R. Biden when the votes were actually cast for Donald John Trump;

said statements being within the jurisdiction of the Office of the Georgia Secretary of State and the Georgia Bureau of Investigation, departments and agencies of state government, and county and city law enforcement agencies. This was an act of racketeering activity under O.C.G.A. § 16-14-3(5)(A)(xxii) and an overt act in furtherance of the conspiracy.

Act 25.

On or about the **3rd day of December 2020, RAY STALL-INGS SMITH III** committed the felony offense of **FALSE STATEMENTS AND WRITINGS,** in violation of **O.C.G.A. § 16-10-20,** in Fulton County, Georgia, by knowingly, willfully, and unlawfully making at least one of the following false statements and representations to members of the Georgia Senate present at a Senate Judiciary Subcommittee meeting:

1.　　That 2,506 felons voted illegally in the November 3, 2020, presidential election in Georgia;

---

office. The only person who has been charged with more crimes in this indictment is Trump himself.

* The prosecution details some of the claims of election fraud that Trump's allies promoted among Georgia legislators in an attempt to persuade these officials to invalidate the results of the Georgia election.

2.   That 66,248 underage people illegally registered to vote before their seventeenth birthday prior to the November 3, 2020, presidential election in Georgia;

3.   That at least 2,423 people voted in the November 3, 2020, presidential election in Georgia who were not listed as registered to vote;

4.   That 1,043 people voted in the November 3, 2020, presidential election in Georgia who had illegally registered to vote using a post office box;

5.   That 10,315 or more dead people voted in the November 3, 2020, presidential election in Georgia;

6.   That Fulton County election workers at State Farm Arena ordered poll watchers and members of the media to leave the tabulation area on the night of November 3, 2020, and continued to operate after ordering everyone to leave;

said statements being within the jurisdiction of the Office of the Georgia Secretary of State and the Georgia Bureau of Investigation, departments and agencies of state government, and county and city law enforcement agencies. This was an act of racketeering activity under O.C.G.A. § 16-14-3(5)(A)(xxii) and an overt act in furtherance of the conspiracy.

Act 26.

On or about the **3rd day of December 2020, DONALD JOHN TRUMP** caused to be tweeted from the Twitter account @ RealDonaldTrump, "Wow! Blockbuster testimony taking place right now in Georgia. Ballot stuffing by Dems when Republicans were forced to leave the large counting room. Plenty more coming, but this alone leads to an easy win of the State!"* This was an overt act in furtherance of the conspiracy.

---

* Twitter (now X) has entered the charges. Here, the indictment alleges that Trump, an inveterate tweeter, used the social media platform to promote his claims of election fraud. Following the January 6, 2021, raid on the Capitol, the platform barred Trump. Elon Musk, after he purchased Twitter and rebranded it, reinstated him,

Act 27.

On or about the **3rd day of December 2020, DONALD JOHN TRUMP** caused to be tweeted from the Twitter account @ RealDonaldTrump, "People in Georgia got caught cold bringing in massive numbers of ballots and putting them in 'voting' machines. Great job @BrianKempGA!" This was an overt act in furtherance of the conspiracy.

Act 28.

On or about the **3rd day of December 2020, DONALD JOHN TRUMP** met with Speaker of the Pennsylvania House of Representatives Bryan Cutler in the Oval Office at the White House and discussed holding a special session of the Pennsylvania General Assembly. This was an overt act in furtherance of the conspiracy.

Act 29.

On or between the **3rd day of December 2020** and the **26th day of December 2020, RUDOLPH WILLIAM LOUIS GIULIANI** placed a telephone call to President Pro Tempore of the Georgia Senate Cecil Terrell "Butch" Miller for the purpose of making false statements concerning fraud in the November 3, 2020, presidential election in Georgia. This was an overt act in furtherance of the conspiracy.

Act 30.

On or between the **3rd day of December 2020** and the **26th day of December 2020, DONALD JOHN TRUMP** placed a telephone call to President Pro Tempore of the Georgia Senate Butch Miller. This was an overt act in furtherance of the conspiracy.

---

though Trump has only tweeted once since—to post his mugshot (and raise money) after surrendering to authorities in Georgia in this case.

Act 31.

On or about the **5th day of December 2020, DONALD JOHN TRUMP** placed a telephone call to Georgia Governor Brian Kemp and solicited, requested, and importuned Kemp to call a special session of the Georgia General Assembly. This was an overt act in furtherance of the conspiracy.

Act 32.

On or about the **6th day of December 2020, DONALD JOHN TRUMP** caused to be tweeted from the Twitter account @ RealDonaldTrump, "Gee, what a surprise. Has anyone informed the so-called (says he has no power to do anything!) Governor @BrianKempGA & his puppet Lt. Governor @GeoffDuncanGA, that they could easily solve this mess, & WIN. Signature verification & call a Special Session. So easy! https://t.co/5cb4QdYzpU." This was an overt act in furtherance of the conspiracy.*

Act 33.†

On or about the **6th day of December 2020, SIDNEY KATHERINE POWELL** entered into a written engagement agreement with SullivanStrickler LLC, a forensic data firm located in Fulton County, Georgia, for the performance of computer forensic collections and analytics on Dominion Voting Systems equipment in Michigan and elsewhere. The unlawful breach of election equipment in Coffee County, Georgia, was subsequently performed

---

* Citing a lack of authority to do so, Georgia governor Brian Kemp refused to intervene to invalidate the election results, prompting Trump to berate him on Twitter. The indictment alleges that this was an overt act in furtherance of the conspiracy on the view that Trump was urging Kemp and Lieutenant Governor Geoff Duncan to "solve this mess" by calling a special session of the legislature despite there being no evidence of any outcome-determinative fraud or other support for Trump's claims.

† The indictment alleges that Sidney Powell hired SullivanStrickler, a forensic data firm, to obtain access to private voting systems in Georgia and other states to scour for evidence of fraud or miscounts. A law firm hired by SullivanStrickler would later release a statement, saying of that company, "Knowing everything they know now, they would not take on any further work of this kind."

under this agreement. This was an overt act in furtherance of the conspiracy.*

Act 34.

On or about the **6th day of December 2020, ROBERT DAVID CHEELEY** sent an e-mail to **JOHN CHARLES EASTMAN,**† unindicted co-conspirator Individual 8, whose identity is known to the Grand Jury, and Georgia Senator Brandon Beach that stated, "I am working on setting up a call for you with the Speaker and the President Pro Tempore tomorrow. I am also making the leadership aware of the importance for Trump electors to meet on December 14. Please provide the citation to the requirements of the duties which they must comply with." This was an overt act in furtherance of the conspiracy.

Act 35.

On or about the **6th day of December 2020, JOHN CHARLES EASTMAN** sent an e-mail to **ROBERT DAVID CHEELEY,** unindicted co-conspirator Individual 8, whose iden-

---

* The indictment alleges that Sidney Powell sought a forensics analysis of voting machines made by Dominion Voting Systems. Media reporting notes that Powell claimed that the machines were programmed to register fraudulent votes. Dominion has sued Giuliani and Powell, among others, for defamation. (Remarkably, Powell has defended that civil case by saying that no one could have believed she was making statements of fact.) Dominion also sued Fox in a suit that settled for hundreds of millions of dollars. In that civil case, the court ruled that there was no evidence that Dominion had perpetrated election fraud. In *Trump v. Kemp*—Trump's effort to contest the Georgia election results—a judge found that Trump failed to establish likelihood of success on the merits, citing the multiple Georgia recounts and audits. Notably, despite privately dismissing Powell's allegations about Dominion and election fraud more generally as "unsupported" and "crazy," Trump repeated these allegations, including during his speech at the Ellipse on the morning of January 6.

† The indictment offers a more detailed account of Eastman's efforts on behalf of the Trump campaign than did the DC January 6 indictment, where Eastman was not charged. Eastman's lawyer has, however, confirmed that Eastman is "unindicted co-conspirator 2" in that indictment. The Georgia indictment alleges that Eastman pressured state legislators to overturn the election and create slates of fake electors in states where Trump lost.

tity is known to the Grand Jury, and Georgia Senator Brandon Beach that stated that the Trump presidential elector nominees in Georgia needed to meet on December 14, 2020, sign six sets of certificates of vote, and mail them "to the President of the Senate and to other officials." This was an overt act in furtherance of the conspiracy.

Act 36.

On or about the **6th day of December 2020, ROBERT DAVID CHEELEY** sent an e-mail to unindicted co-conspirator Individual 2, whose identity is known to the Grand Jury, that stated he had been speaking with **JOHN CHARLES EASTMAN** and was attempting to set up a call with Speaker of the Georgia House of Representatives David Ralston and President Pro Tempore of the Georgia Senate Butch Miller to encourage them to call a special session of the Georgia General Assembly. In the e-mail, **ROBERT DAVID CHEELEY** stated, "Professor Eastman told me tonight that it is *critical* that the 16 Electors for President Trump meet next Monday and vote in accordance with 3 U.S.C. § 7." In the e-mail, **ROBERT DAVID CHEELEY** further stated, "I assume you can make sure this happens." This was an overt act in furtherance of the conspiracy.

Act 37.

On or about the **7th day of December 2020**, unindicted co-conspirator Individual 2, whose identity is known to the Grand Jury, sent an e-mail to **ROBERT DAVID CHEELEY** and **DAVID JAMES SHAFER** that stated, "Bob, can u get on a call with David Shafer, state GOP chair and I later this morning to discuss. David has been on top of a lot of efforts in the state. I get off of a board call around 10:30." This was an overt act in furtherance of the conspiracy.

Act 38.

On or about the **7th day of December 2020, RUDOLPH WIL-LIAM LOUIS GIULIANI** caused to be tweeted from the Twitter account @RudyGiuliani a retweet of unindicted co-conspirator Individual 8, whose identity is known to the Grand Jury, that stated, "Georgia Patriot Call to Action: today is the day we need you to call your state Senate & House Reps & ask them to sign the petition for a special session. We must have free & fair elections in GA & a this is our only path to ensuring every legal vote is counted. @realDonaldTrump." This was an overt act in furtherance of the conspiracy.

Act 39.

On or about the **7th day of December 2020, JOHN CHARLES EASTMAN** sent an e-mail to **RUDOLPH WILLIAM LOUIS GIULIANI** with an attached memorandum titled "The Real Deadline for Settling a State's Electoral Votes." The body of the e-mail stated, "Here's the memo we discussed." The memorandum was written by **KENNETH JOHN CHESEBRO** to James R. Troupis, an attorney associated with the Trump Campaign, and advocates for the position that Trump presidential elector nominees in Wisconsin should meet and cast electoral votes for **DONALD JOHN TRUMP** on December 14, 2020, despite the fact that **DONALD JOHN TRUMP** lost the November 3, 2020, presidential election in Wisconsin. This e-mail was an overt act in furtherance of the conspiracy.

Act 40.

On or about the **7th day of December 2020, DONALD JOHN TRUMP** requested that Bill White, an individual associated with the Trump Campaign then residing in Fulton County, Georgia, provide him with certain information, including contact information for Majority Leader of the Georgia Senate Mike Dugan and President Pro Tempore of the Georgia Senate Butch Miller. The following day, White sent an e-mail containing the requested information to **RUDOLPH WILLIAM LOUIS GIULIANI,** unindicted co-conspirator Individual 5, whose identity is known to the Grand Jury, and others. This request was an overt act in furtherance of the conspiracy.

Act 41.

On or about the **7th day of December 2020, RUDOLPH WILLIAM LOUIS GIULIANI** placed a telephone call to Speaker of the Georgia House of Representatives David Ralston and discussed holding a special session of the Georgia General Assembly. This was an overt act in furtherance of the conspiracy.*

Act 42.

On or about the **7th day of December 2020, DONALD JOHN TRUMP** committed the felony offense of **SOLICITATION OF VIOLATION OF OATH BY PUBLIC OFFICER,** in violation of **O.C.G.A. §§ 16-4-7 & 16-10-1,** in Fulton County, Georgia, by unlawfully soliciting, requesting, and importuning Speaker of the Georgia House of Representatives David Ralston, a public officer, to engage in conduct constituting the felony offense of Violation of Oath by Public Officer, O.C.G.A. § 16-10-1, by calling a special session of the Georgia General Assembly for the purpose of unlawfully appointing presidential electors from Georgia, in willful and intentional violation of the terms of the oath of said person as prescribed by law, with intent that said person engage in said conduct. This was an overt act in furtherance of the conspiracy.

Act 43.

On or about the **8th day of December 2020, DONALD JOHN TRUMP** placed a telephone call to Georgia Attorney General Chris Carr for the purpose of making false statements concerning fraud in the November 3, 2020, presidential election in Georgia and elsewhere. During the telephone call, **DONALD JOHN TRUMP** asked Carr not to discourage other state attorneys general from joining a federal lawsuit filed by the State of Texas contesting the administration of the November 3, 2020, presidential election in Georgia,

---

* This series of allegations places Giuliani at the center of the alleged conspiracy. These three overt acts recount Giuliani's sustained efforts to overturn the election in two states—Georgia and Wisconsin.

Michigan, Pennsylvania, and Wisconsin. This was an overt act in furtherance of the conspiracy.

Act 44.

On or about the **8th day of December 2020, DONALD JOHN TRUMP** and **JOHN CHARLES EASTMAN** placed a telephone call to Republican National Committee Chairwoman Ronna McDaniel to request her assistance gathering certain individuals to meet and cast electoral votes for **DONALD JOHN TRUMP** on December 14, 2020, in certain states despite the fact that **DONALD JOHN TRUMP** lost the November 3, 2020, presidential election in those states.* This was an overt act in furtherance of the conspiracy.

Act 45.

On or about the **8th day of December 2020, MICHAEL A. ROMAN** sent a text message to unindicted co-conspirator Individual 4, whose identity is known to the Grand Jury, stated that he had spoken to **MISTY HAMPTON,** and asked unindicted co-conspirator Individual 4 to "get" **MISTY HAMPTON** to attend the hearing before the Georgia House of Representatives Governmental Affairs Committee on December 10, 2020. This was an overt act in furtherance of the conspiracy.

---

* This detail about Eastman's efforts to enlist Republican National Committee chairwoman Ronna McDaniel in the scheme to create fake slates of electors was first revealed by the January 6 committee. But while this is not a new revelation, it is nonetheless significant in this indictment, indicating that the Republican establishment was approached to help with the plan to falsify electors to the Electoral College. Notably, McDaniel, like many of the fake electors (for instance, those in Pennsylvania), may have been lied to by the conspirators to get her to go along with the scheme. Specifically, the conspirators are alleged to have told the fake electors that they would be substituted as electors if and only if a state court determined that Trump had won the state vote. The alleged scheme, however, was to put forth the slates of fake electors, regardless of the outcome of state court litigation, in order to upend the actual electoral college vote.

Act 46.

On or about the **9th day of December 2020, KENNETH JOHN CHESEBRO** wrote a memorandum titled "Statutory Requirements for December 14 Electoral Votes" to James R. Troupis, an attorney associated with the Trump Campaign. The memorandum provides detailed, state-specific instructions for how Trump presidential elector nominees in Georgia, Arizona, Michigan, Nevada, Pennsylvania, and Wisconsin would meet and cast electoral votes for **DONALD JOHN TRUMP** on December 14, 2020, despite the fact that **DONALD JOHN TRUMP** lost the November 3, 2020, presidential election in those states. This was an overt act in furtherance of the conspiracy.*

Act 47.

On or about the **10th day of December 2020, KENNETH JOHN CHESEBRO** sent an e-mail to Georgia Republican Party Chairman **DAVID JAMES SHAFER** and unindicted coconspirator Individual 9, whose identity is known to the Grand Jury. **KENNETH JOHN CHESEBRO** stated in the e-mail that certain individuals associated with the Trump Campaign asked him "to help coordinate with the other 5 contested States, to help with logistics

---

* The Chesebro memorandum detailing how fake electors could be enlisted to cast electoral votes for Trump was also referenced in the DC January 6 indictment. The DC January 6 indictment alleged that Chesebro wrote a series of memoranda that, in concert with his communications with state electors, made plain that the fake elector scheme was to enlist electors regardless of whether the state was legally called for Trump or whether the legal requirements for being an elector were otherwise met, and if necessary, to misrepresent their intent to electors who raised qualms about signing up for the job. (See, e.g., Act 58 below, regarding Chesebro's alleged intent in this scheme.) Notably, these memoranda may have played a pivotal role in Chesebro's decision to plead guilty. In advance of his October 23, 2023, trial start date, Chesebro sought to exclude these memoranda from evidence on the ground that they were privileged attorney-client work product. On October 18, 2023, Fulton County Superior Court Judge Scott McAfee rejected this request, concluding that, even assuming they had been protected as attorney-client communications that had not been waived, the attorney-client privilege was inapplicable because the state had established that the memoranda were in furtherance of the commission of a crime. Two days later, on October 20, 2023, Chesebro entered his guilty plea.

of the electors in other States hopefully joining in casting their votes on Monday." This was an overt act in furtherance of the conspiracy.

Act 48.

On or about the **10th day of December 2020, KENNETH JOHN CHESEBRO** sent an e-mail with attached documents to **DAVID JAMES SHAFER** and unindicted co-conspirators Individual 9, Individual 10, and Individual 11, whose identities are known to the Grand Jury. The documents were to be used by Trump presidential elector nominees in Georgia for the purpose of casting electoral votes for **DONALD JOHN TRUMP** on December 14, 2020, despite the fact that **DONALD JOHN TRUMP** lost the November 3, 2020, presidential election in Georgia. This was an overt act in furtherance of the conspiracy.

Act 49.

On or about the **10th day of December 2020, KENNETH JOHN CHESEBRO** sent an e-mail with attached documents to Arizona Republican Party Executive Director Greg Safsten and others. The documents were to be used by Trump presidential elector nominees in Arizona for the purpose of casting electoral votes for **DONALD JOHN TRUMP** on December 14,2020, despite the fact that **DONALD JOHN TRUMP** lost the November 3, 2020, presidential election in Arizona. This was an overt act in furtherance of the conspiracy.

Act 50.

On or about the **10th day of December 2020, KENNETH JOHN CHESEBRO*** sent an e-mail to Republican Party of Wiscon-

---

* After this indictment was brought, Chesebro demanded a speedy trial, which, under Georgia law, requires his case to be tried within two court terms. Co-defendant Sidney Powell also demanded a speedy trial. Both demands were granted, as required under Georgia law, with Judge Scott McAfee calendaring both to be tried together beginning on October 23, 2023. Chesebro also moved to sever his trial from Powell's, which would have resulted in at least three separate trials in this one case. Finding that

sin Chairman Brian Schimming with proposed language for documents to be used by Trump presidential elector nominees in Wisconsin for the purpose of casting electoral votes for **DONALD JOHN TRUMP** on December 14, 2020, despite the fact that **DONALD JOHN TRUMP** lost the November 3, 2020, presidential election in Wisconsin. This was an overt act in furtherance of the conspiracy.

Act 51.

On or about the **10th day of December 2020, KENNETH JOHN CHESEBRO** sent an e-mail to Nevada Republican Party Vice Chairman Jim DeGraffenreid. **KENNETH JOHN CHESEBRO** stated in the e-mail that **RUDOLPH WILLIAM LOUIS GIULIANI** and other individuals associated with the Trump Campaign asked him "to reach out to you and the other Nevada electors to run point on the plan to have all Trump-Pence electors in all six contested States meet and transmit their votes to Congress on Monday, Dec. 14." This was an overt act in furtherance of the conspiracy.

Act 52.

On or about the **10th day of December 2020, KENNETH JOHN CHESEBRO** sent an e-mail with attached documents to Jim DeGraffenreid. The documents were to be used by Trump presidential elector nominees in Nevada for the purpose of casting electoral votes for **DONALD JOHN TRUMP** on December 14, 2020,

---

a severance was unnecessary to achieve a fair trial for both defendants (a ruling fully in keeping with the law), Judge McAfee denied the motion on September 6, 2023. Both Powell and Chesebro have since pleaded guilty. As of this writing, it remains to be seen whether any of the other defendants will later seek a speedy trial or seek to have their cases severed and how Judge McAfee would rule on these motions so as to avoid a cascade of trials. One consideration in severance motions is whether separate trials would advantage those defendants whose trials are later. Because the evidence will be the same for most of the defendants, defendants with later trial dates will have the advantage of being able to watch the earlier trials and plan their defenses accordingly.

INSIDER NOTE: Some of the defendants who used to hold federal office (e.g., Meadows and Clark) as well as some who sought to serve as "electors," are seeking to remove their cases to federal court, and thus the number of defendants before Judge McAfee may be further reduced if removal is granted by a federal appellate court.

despite the fact that **DONALD JOHN TRUMP** lost the November 3, 2020, presidential election in Nevada. This was an overt act in furtherance of the conspiracy.

Act 52.*

On or about the **10th day of December 2020, KENNETH JOHN CHESEBRO** sent an e-mail with attached documents to Republican Party of Pennsylvania General Counsel Thomas W. King III. The documents were to be used by Trump presidential elector nominees in Pennsylvania for the purpose of casting electoral votes for **DONALD JOHN TRUMP** on December 14, 2020, despite the fact that **DONALD JOHN TRUMP** lost the November 3, 2020, presidential election in Pennsylvania. This was an overt act in furtherance of the conspiracy.

Act 54.

On or between the **10th day of December 2020 and the 14th day of December 2020, DAVID JAMES SHAFER** contacted unindicted co-conspirator Individual 2, whose identity is known to the Grand Jury, by telephone and discussed unindicted co-conspirator Individual 2's attendance at the December 14, 2020, meeting of Trump presidential elector nominees in Fulton County, Georgia. This was an overt act in furtherance of the conspiracy.

Act 55.

On or about the **10th day of December 2020, RUDOLPH WILLIAM LOUIS GIULIANI** and **RAY STALLINGS SMITH III** committed the felony offense of **SOLICITATION OF VIOLATION OF OATH BY PUBLIC OFFICER**, in violation of **O.C.G.A. §§ 16-4-7 & 16-10-1**, in Fulton County, Georgia, by unlawfully soliciting, requesting, and importuning certain public officers then serving as elected members of the Georgia House of Representatives and present at a House Governmental Affairs Com-

---

* Misnumbering as per original text.

mittee meeting, including Representatives Shaw Blackmon, Jon Burns, Barry Fleming, Todd Jones, Bee Nguyen, Mary Margaret Oliver, Alan Powell, Renitta Shannon, Robert Trammell, Scot Turner, and Bruce Williamson, to engage in conduct constituting the felony offense of Violation of Oath by Public Officer, O.C.G.A. § 16-10-1, by unlawfully appointing presidential electors from Georgia, in willful and intentional violation of the terms of the oath of said persons as prescribed by law, with intent that said persons engage in said conduct. This was an overt act in furtherance of the conspiracy.

Act 56.

On or about the **10th day of December 2020, RUDOLPH WILLIAM LOUIS GIULIANI** committed the felony offense of **FALSE STATEMENTS AND WRITINGS,** in violation of **O.C.G.A. § 16-10-20,** in Fulton County, Georgia, by knowingly, willfully, and unlawfully making at least one of the following false statements and representations to members of the Georgia House of Representatives present at a House Governmental Affairs Committee meeting:

1. That it is quite clear from the State Farm Arena video from November 3, 2020, that Fulton County election workers were stealing votes and that Georgia officials were covering up a crime in plain sight;

2. That at State Farm Arena on November 3, 2020, Democratic officials "got rid of all of the reporters, all the observers, anyone that couldn't be trusted," used the excuse of a watermain break, cleared out the voting area and then "went about their dirty, crooked business";

3. That between 12,000 and 24,000 ballots were illegally counted by Fulton County election workers at State Farm Arena on November 3, 2020;

4. That in Michigan, there were 700,000 more ballots counted than were sent out to voters in the November 3, 2020, presidential election, which was accounted for by quadruple counting ballots;

5.   That Ruby Freeman, Shaye Moss, and an unidentified man were "quite obviously surreptitiously passing around USB ports as if they're vials of heroin or cocaine" at State Farm Arena to be used to "infiltrate the crooked Dominion voting machines";*

6.   That 96,600 mail-in ballots were counted in the November 3, 2020, presidential election in Georgia, despite there being no record of those ballots having been returned to a county elections office;

said statements being within the jurisdiction of the Office of the Georgia Secretary of State and the Georgia Bureau of Investigation, departments and agencies of state government, and county and city law enforcement agencies. This was an act of racketeering activity under O.C.G.A. § 16-14-3(5)(A)(xxii) and an overt act in furtherance of the conspiracy.

Act 57.

On or about the **11th day of December 2020, DAVID JAMES SHAFER** reserved Room 216 at the Georgia State Capitol in Fulton County, Georgia, for the December 14, 2020, meeting of Trump presidential elector nominees in Fulton County, Georgia. This was an overt act in furtherance of the conspiracy.

Act 58.

On or about the **11th day of December 2020, KENNETH JOHN CHESEBRO** sent an e-mail to Jim DeGraffenreid and stated that "the purpose of having the electoral votes sent in to Congress is to provide the opportunity to debate the election irregulari-

---

* Based on these false claims, Freeman and Moss sued Giuliani civilly for defamation. On August 30, 2023, DC District Judge Beryl Howell granted Freeman and Moss's motion for summary judgment as to liability, and also sanctioned Giuliani monetarily for repeated discovery violations. A trial is set for a jury to determine the extent of damages, with the jury being instructed to make presumptions against Giuliani if he continues to withhold relevant documents from the plaintiffs. Notably, Giuliani has admitted that he intentionally lied about Freeman and Moss. This admission may be used against him in this criminal prosecution.

ties in Congress, and to keep alive the possibility that the votes could be flipped to Trump." This was an overt act in furtherance of the conspiracy.

Act 59.

On or about the **11th day of December 2020, KENNETH JOHN CHESEBRO** sent an e-mail with attached documents to Greg Safsten and others. The documents were to be used by Trump presidential elector nominees in Arizona for the purpose of casting electoral votes for **DONALD JOHN TRUMP** on December 14, 2020, despite the fact that **DONALD JOHN TRUMP** lost the November 3, 2020, presidential election in Arizona. This was an overt act in furtherance of the conspiracy.

Act 60.

On or about the **11th day of December 2020, KENNETH JOHN CHESEBRO** sent an e-mail with attached documents to **MICHAEL A. ROMAN** and other individuals associated with the Trump Campaign. The documents were to be used by Trump presidential elector nominees in Nevada for the purpose of casting electoral votes for **DONALD JOHN TRUMP** on December 14, 2020, despite the fact that **DONALD JOHN TRUMP** lost the November 3, 2020, presidential election in Nevada. This was an overt act in furtherance of the conspiracy.

Act 61.

On or about the **11th day of December 2020, KENNETH JOHN CHESEBRO** sent an e-mail with attached documents to **MICHAEL A. ROMAN,** unindicted co-conspirator Individual 5, whose identity is known to the Grand Jury, and others. The documents were to be used by Trump presidential elector nominees in Georgia for the purpose of casting electoral votes for **DONALD JOHN TRUMP** on December 14, 2020, despite the fact that **DONALD JOHN TRUMP** lost the November 3, 2020, presidential election in Georgia. This was an overt act in furtherance of the conspiracy.

Act 62.

On or about the **12th day of December 2020, DAVID JAMES SHAFER** contacted unindicted co-conspirator Individual 12, whose identity is known to the Grand Jury, and discussed unindicted co-conspirator Individual 12's attendance at the December 14, 2020, meeting of Trump presidential elector nominees in Fulton County, Georgia. This was an overt act in furtherance of the conspiracy.

Act 63.

On or about the **12th day of December 2020, MICHAEL A. ROMAN** sent an e-mail to unindicted co-conspirators Individual 4 and Individual 7, whose identities are known to the Grand Jury, and other individuals associated with the Trump Campaign. In the e-mail, **MICHAEL A. ROMAN** stated, "I need a tracker for the electors," and instructed individuals associated with the Trump Campaign to populate entries on a shared spreadsheet listing Trump presidential elector nominees in Georgia, Arizona, Michigan, Nevada, Pennsylvania, and Wisconsin. The entries on the spreadsheet included contact information for the Trump presidential elector nominees, whether the Trump presidential elector nominees had been contacted, and whether the Trump presidential elector nominees had confirmed that they would attend the December 14, 2020, meetings of Trump presidential elector nominees in their respective states, despite the fact that **DONALD JOHN TRUMP** lost the November 3, 2020, presidential election in those states. This was an overt act in furtherance of the conspiracy.

Act 64.

On or about the **12th day of December 2020, KENNETH JOHN CHESEBRO** met with Brian Schimming and discussed the December 14, 2020, meeting of Trump presidential elector nominees in Wisconsin. **RUDOLPH WILLIAM LOUIS GIULIANI** joined the meeting by telephone and stated that the media should not be notified of the December 14, 2020, meeting of Trump presidential elector nominees in Wisconsin. These were overt acts in furtherance of the conspiracy.

Act 65.

On or about the **12th day of December 2020, MICHAEL A. ROMAN** instructed an individual associated with the Trump Campaign to distribute certain information related to the December 14, 2020, meetings of Trump presidential elector nominees in Georgia, Arizona, Michigan, Nevada, New Mexico, Pennsylvania, and Wisconsin to unindicted co-conspirator Individual 4, whose identity is known to the Grand Jury, and to other individuals associated with the Trump Campaign. This was an overt act in furtherance of the conspiracy.

Act 66.

On or about the **12th day of December 2020,** unindicted co-conspirator Individual 4, whose identity is known to the Grand Jury, sent an e-mail to **MICHAEL A. ROMAN** and **DAVID JAMES SHAFER** with updates on the progress of organizing the December 14, 2020, meeting of Trump presidential elector nominees in Fulton County, Georgia. The e-mail stated which elector nominees had confirmed they would attend the meeting, that other individuals had been secured in case some of the elector nominees refused to participate in the meeting, that Georgia legislators had been contacted to ensure access to the Georgia Capitol, and that **DAVID JAMES SHAFER** had reserved Room 216 for the meeting. This was an overt act in furtherance of the conspiracy.

Act 67.

On or about the **12th day of December 2020, DAVID JAMES SHAFER** sent an e-mail to unindicted co-conspirator

Individual 4, whose identity is known to the Grand Jury, advising them to "touch base" with each of the Trump presidential elector nominees in Georgia in advance of the December 14, 2020, meeting to confirm their attendance. This was an overt act in furtherance of the conspiracy.

Act 68.

On or about the **12th day of December 2020,** unindicted co-conspirator Individual 4, whose identity is known to the Grand Jury, sent a text message with contact information for unindicted co-conspirator Individual 8, whose identity is known to the Grand Jury, and Georgia Senator Brandon Beach to **MICHAEL A. ROMAN** for the purpose of providing the contact information to **RUDOLPH WILLIAM LOUIS GIULIANI.** This was an overt act in furtherance of the conspiracy.

Act 69.

On or about the **13th day of December 2020, KENNETH JOHN CHESEBRO** sent an e-mail with attached documents to **MICHAEL A. ROMAN.** The documents were to be used by Trump presidential elector nominees in New Mexico for the purpose of casting electoral votes for **DONALD JOHN TRUMP** on December 14, 2020, despite the fact that **DONALD JOHN TRUMP** lost the November 3, 2020, presidential election in New Mexico. This was an overt act in furtherance of the conspiracy.*

Act 70.

On or about the **13th day of December 2020, KENNETH JOHN CHESEBRO** sent an e-mail to **RUDOLPH WILLIAM LOUIS GIULIANI** with the subject "PRIVILEGED AND CONFIDENTIAL – Brief notes on 'President of the Senate' strat-

---

* These allegations maintain that the scheme to create slates of false electors in various battleground states was coordinated by the Trump campaign and various lawyers affiliated with the campaign, as opposed to a grassroots effort arising organically in each state.

egy." In the e-mail, **KENNETH JOHN CHESEBRO** outlined multiple strategies for disrupting and delaying the joint session of Congress on January 6, 2021, the day prescribed by law for counting votes cast by the duly elected and qualified presidential electors from Georgia and the other states. In the e-mail, **KENNETH JOHN CHESEBRO** stated that the strategies outlined by him were "preferable to allowing the Electoral Count Act to operate by its terms." This was an overt act in furtherance of the conspiracy.[*]

Act 71.

On or about the **13th day of December 2020, KENNETH JOHN CHESEBRO** sent an e-mail with attached documents to **MICHAEL A. ROMAN** and unindicted co-conspirator Individual 4, whose identity is known to the Grand Jury. The documents were to be used by Trump presidential elector nominees in Georgia for the purpose of casting electoral votes for **DONALD JOHN TRUMP** on December 14, 2020, despite the fact that **DONALD JOHN TRUMP** lost the November 3, 2020, presidential election in Georgia. This was an overt act in furtherance of the conspiracy.

Act 72.

On or about the **13th day of December 2020, KENNETH JOHN CHESEBRO** sent an e-mail to **MICHAEL A. ROMAN**

---

[*] Prior to pleading guilty on October 20, 2023, Chesebro signaled that he would defend himself by insisting that his actions were those of an aggressive lawyer, and not the actions of a co-conspirator. Other defendants, like Eastman, may attempt a similar defense. If this was raised as a defense, it invariably would have to contend with, among other things, the defendants' alleged willingness to mislead electors to get them to sign on as fake electors and certain lawyers' unwillingness to participate when they learned the nature of the proposed scheme.

INSIDER NOTE: Media reporting and video evidence show that Chesebro was at the Capitol on January 6, along with InfoWars talk show host Alex Jones. Although Chesebro is not alleged to have illegally entered the Capitol, and there is nothing illegal about peacefully protesting, his decision to protest with Jones that day could be used by prosecutors to show his interest in obstructing the counting of the electoral votes—a goal consonant with his various memoranda and communications with state officials, and with his guilty plea to count 15.

and unindicted co-conspirator Individual 4, whose identity is known to the Grand Jury, and stated that **RUDOLPH WILLIAM LOUIS GIULIANI** "wants to keep this quiet until after all the voting is done," in reference to the December 14, 2020, meeting of Trump presidential elector nominees in Fulton County, Georgia. This was an overt act in furtherance of the conspiracy.*

Act 73.

On or about the **13th day of December 2020, DAVID JAMES SHAFER** sent a text message to unindicted co-conspirator Individual 4, whose identity is known to the Grand Jury, and stated that unindicted co-conspirator Individual 8, whose identity is known to the Grand Jury, would attend the December 14, 2020, meeting of Trump presidential elector nominees in Fulton County, Georgia, in the place of a Trump presidential elector nominee who refused to participate in the meeting. This was an overt act in furtherance of the conspiracy.

Act 74.

On or about the **13th day of December 2020,** unindicted co-conspirator Individual 9, whose identity is known to the Grand Jury, sent a text message to **DAVID JAMES SHAFER** and confirmed that he and unindicted co-conspirator Individual 13, whose identity is known to the Grand Jury, would attend the December 14, 2020, meeting of Trump presidential elector nominees in Fulton County, Georgia. This was an overt act in furtherance of the conspiracy.

---

* The surreptitious nature of the fake electors scheme is a key allegation. Prosecutors allege that Giuliani did not want the fact that slates of false electors had been assembled for Trump to be publicly known. But critically, Giuliani, Roman, and Chesebro told the assembled electors that their participation as electors was entirely legitimate, as they would only be advanced as electors in the event that state courts determined that Trump actually won the election in the challenged states. Allegations that Giuliani, Roman, and Chesebro insisted on secrecy, even as they assured the false electors of their legitimacy, can be used to suggest to a jury that the trio recognized the wrongfulness of their efforts. (See also Act 76, below, for additional allegations regarding secrecy.)

Act 75.

On or about the **14th day of December 2020, DONALD JOHN TRUMP** caused to be tweeted from the Twitter account @RealDonaldTrump, "What a fool Governor @BrianKempGA of Georgia is. Could have been so easy, but now we have to do it the hard way. Demand this clown call a Special Session and open up signature verification, NOW. Otherwise, could be a bad day for two GREAT Senators on January 5th." This was an overt act in furtherance of the conspiracy.

Act 76.

On or about the **14th day of December 2020, DAVID JAMES SHAFER** sent a text message to unindicted co-conspirator Individual 4, whose identity is known to the Grand Jury that stated, "Listen. Tell them to go straight to Room 216 to avoid drawing attention to what we are doing," in reference to the December 14, 2020, meeting of Trump presidential elector nominees in Fulton County, Georgia. This was an overt act in furtherance of the conspiracy.

Act 77.

On or about the **14th day of December 2020, MICHAEL A. ROMAN** sent an e-mail to unindicted co-conspirators Individual 4 and Individual 7, whose identities are known to the Grand Jury, and stated, "Please send me an update as soon as the State Electoral College has adjourned and all paperwork is secured." This was an overt act in furtherance of the conspiracy.

Act 78.

On or about the **14th day of December 2020, RAY STALLINGS SMITH III** and **DAVID JAMES SHAFER** encouraged certain individuals present at the December 14, 2020, meeting of Trump presidential elector nominees in Fulton County, Georgia, to sign the document titled "CERTIFICATE OF THE VOTES OF THE 2020 ELECTORS FROM GEORGIA." This was an overt act in furtherance of the conspiracy.

Act 79.*

On or about the **14th day of December 2020, DAVID JAMES SHAFER, SHAWN MICAH TRESHER STILL, CATHLEEN ALSTON LATHAM,** and unindicted coconspirators Individual 2, Individual 8, Individual 9, Individual 10, Individual 11, Individual 12, Individual 13, Individual 14, Individual 15, Individual 16, Individual 17, Individual 18, and Individual 19, whose identities are known to the Grand Jury, committed the felony offense of **IMPERSONATING A PUBLIC OFFICER,** in violation of **O.C.G.A. § 16-10-23,** in Fulton County, Georgia, by unlawfully falsely holding themselves out as the duly elected and qualified presidential electors from the State of Georgia, public officers, with intent to mislead the President of the United States Senate, the Archivist of the United States, the Georgia Secretary of State, and the Chief Judge of the United States District Court for the Northern District of Georgia into believing that they actually were such officers by placing in the United States mail to said persons a document titled "CERTIFICATE OF THE VOTES OF THE 2020 ELECTORS FROM GEORGIA." This was an act of racketeering activity under O.C.G.A. § 16-14-3 (5)(A)(xxiii) and an overt act in furtherance of the conspiracy.

Act 80.

On or about the **14th day of December 2020, DAVID JAMES SHAFER, SHAWN MICAH TRESHER STILL, CATHLEEN ALSTON LATHAM,** and unindicted coconspirators Individual 2, Individual 8, Individual 9, Individual 10, Individual 11, Individual 12, Individual 13, Individual 14, Individual 15, Individual 16, Individual 17, Individual 18, and Individual 19, whose identities are known to the Grand Jury, committed the fel-

---

* These allegations in Acts 79–86 are, in contrast to certain of the other acts we discuss above, independent crimes, and constitute the various ways that the fake electors are alleged to have violated Georgia criminal law by presenting themselves as electors, when they were not.

ony offense of **FORGERY IN THE FIRST DEGREE,** in violation of **O.C.G.A. § 16-9-1(b),** in Fulton County, Georgia, by, with the intent to defraud, knowingly making a document titled "CERTIFICATE OF THE VOTES OF THE 2020 ELECTORS FROM GEORGIA," a writing other than a check, in such manner that the writing as made purports to have been made by authority of the duly elected and qualified presidential electors from the State of Georgia, who did not give such authority, and uttered and delivered said document to the Archivist of the United States. This was an act of racketeering activity under O.C.G.A. § 16-14-3(5)(A)(xvi) and an overt act in furtherance of the conspiracy.

Act 81.

On or about the **14th day of December 2020, DAVID JAMES SHAFER, SHAWN MICAH TRESHER STILL, CATHLEEN ALSTON LATHAM,** and unindicted coconspirators Individual 2, Individual 8, Individual 9, Individual 10, Individual 11, Individual 12, Individual 13, Individual 14, Individual 15, Individual 16, Individual 17, Individual 18, and Individual 19, whose identities are known to the Grand Jury, committed the felony offense of **FALSE STATEMENTS AND WRITINGS,** in violation of **O.C.G.A. § 16-10-20,** in Fulton County, Georgia, by knowingly, willfully, and unlawfully making and using a false document titled "CERTIFICATE OF THE VOTES OF THE 2020 ELECTORS FROM GEORGIA," with knowledge that said document contained the false statement, "WE, THE UNDERSIGNED, being the duly elected and qualified Electors for President and Vice President of the United States of America from the State of Georgia, do hereby certify the following," said document being within the jurisdiction of the Office of the Georgia Secretary of State and the Office of the Governor of Georgia, departments and agencies of state government. This was an act of racketeering activity under O.C.G.A. § 16-14-3 (5)(A)(xxii) and an overt act in furtherance of the conspiracy.

Act 82.

On or about the **14th day of December 2020, DAVID JAMES SHAFER, SHAWN MICAH TRESHER STILL, CATHLEEN ALSTON LATHAM,** and unindicted coconspirators Individual 2, Individual 8, Individual 9, Individual 10, Individual 11, Individual 12, Individual 13, Individual 14, Individual 15, Individual 16, Individual 17, Individual 18, and Individual 19, whose identities are known to the Grand Jury, attempted to commit the felony offense of **FILING FALSE DOCUMENTS,** in violation of **O.C.G.A. § 16-10-20.1(b)(1),** in Fulton County, Georgia, by placing in the United States mail a document titled "CERTIFICATE OF THE VOTES OF THE 2020 ELECTORS FROM GEORGIA," addressed to Chief Judge, U.S. District Court, Northern District of Georgia, 2188 Richard D. Russell Federal Office Building and U.S. Courthouse, 75 Ted Turner Drive, SW, Atlanta, GA 30303, with intent to knowingly file, enter, and record said document in a court of the United States, having reason to know that said document contained the materially false statement, "WE, THE UNDERSIGNED, being the duly elected and qualified Electors for President and Vice President of the United States of America from the State of Georgia, do hereby certify the following." This was an act of racketeering activity under O.C.G.A. § 16-14-3(5)(A)(xxii) and an overt act in furtherance of the conspiracy.

Act 83.

On or about the **14th day of December 2020, DAVID JAMES SHAFER** and **SHAWN MICAH TRESHER STILL** committed the felony offense of **FORGERY IN THE FIRST DEGREE,** in violation of **O.C.G.A. § 16-9-1(b),** in Fulton County, Georgia, by, with the intent to defraud, knowingly making a document titled "RE: Notice of Filling of Electoral College Vacancy," a writing other than a check, in such manner that the writing as made purports to have been made by the authority of the duly elected and qualified presidential electors from the State of Georgia, who did not give such authority, and uttered and delivered said document to the Archivist of the United States. This was an act of racketeering activity under O.C.G.A. § 16-14-3(5)(A)(xvi) and an overt act in furtherance of the conspiracy.

Act 84.

On or about the **14th day of December 2020, DAVID JAMES SHAFER** and **SHAWN MICAH TRESHER STILL** committed the felony offense of **FALSE STATEMENTS AND WRITINGS,** in violation of **O.C.G.A. § 16-10-20,** in Fulton County, Georgia, by knowingly, willfully, and unlawfully making and using a false document titled "RE: Notice of Filling of Electoral College Vacancy," with knowledge that said document contained the false statements that **DAVID JAMES SHAFER** was Chairman of the 2020 Georgia Electoral College Meeting and **SHAWN MICAH TRESHER STILL** was Secretary of the 2020 Georgia Electoral College Meeting, said document being within the jurisdiction of the Office of the Georgia Secretary of State and the Office of the Governor of Georgia, departments and agencies of state government. This was an act of racketeering activity under O.C.G.A. § 16-14-3 (5)(A)(xxii) and an overt act in furtherance of the conspiracy.

Act 85.

On or about the **14th day of December 2020, DAVID JAMES SHAFER** instructed unindicted co-conspirator Individual 15, whose identity is known to the Grand Jury, to deliver to the Office of the Governor of Georgia a document signed by **DAVID JAMES SHAFER** and **SHAWN MICAH TRESHER STILL** titled "RE: Notice of Filling of Electoral College Vacancy." The document contained multiple false statements. This was an overt act in furtherance of the conspiracy.

Act 86.

On or about the **14th day of December 2020,** unindicted co-conspirator Individual 4, whose identity is known to the Grand

Jury, sent an e-mail to **MICHAEL A. ROMAN,** unindicted co-conspirator Individual 7, whose identity is known to the Grand Jury, and others that stated, "All votes cast, paperwork complete, being mailed now. Ran pretty smoothly," in reference to the December 14, 2020, meeting of Trump presidential elector nominees in Fulton County, Georgia. This was an overt act in furtherance of the conspiracy.

Act 87.

On or about the **14th day of December 2020, STEPHEN CLIFFGARD LEE** attempted to commit the felony offense of **INFLUENCING WITNESSES,** in violation of **O.C.G.A. § 16-10-93(b)(1)(A),** in Fulton County, Georgia, by traveling to the home of Ruby Freeman, a Fulton County, Georgia, election worker, and speaking to her neighbor, with intent to knowingly engage in misleading conduct toward Ruby Freeman, by purporting to offer her help, and with intent to influence her testimony in an official proceeding in Fulton County, Georgia, concerning events at State Farm Arena in the November 3, 2020, presidential election in Georgia. This was an act of racketeering activity pursuant to O.C.G.A. § 16-14-3(5)(A)(xxvii) and an overt act in furtherance of the conspiracy.

Act 88.*

On or about the **15th day of December 2020, STEPHEN CLIFFGARD LEE** attempted to commit the felony offense of **INFLUENCING WITNESSES,** in violation of **O.C.G.A. § 16-10-93(b)(1)(A),** in Fulton County, Georgia, by traveling to the

---

* These allegations are truly shocking—and speak to the dangers of disinformation and online radicalization. A minister and staunch supporter of candidate Trump, Lee was especially concerned when he heard the Trump campaign's claims of rampant voter fraud in Georgia. Indeed, according to media reports, Lee traveled from his home in Illinois to Georgia in order to help prove Trump's unsubstantiated claims of voter fraud. He is alleged to have gone to Ruby Freeman's home to meet with her. Lee allegedly tried to induce Freeman to admit to participating in the election-fraud scheme. (To be very clear, these claims of election fraud were entirely unsubstantiated and false.)

home of Ruby Freeman, a Fulton County, Georgia, election worker, and knocking on her door, with intent to knowingly engage in misleading conduct toward Ruby Freeman, by purporting to offer her help, and with intent to influence her testimony in an official proceeding in Fulton County, Georgia, concerning events at State Farm Arena in the November 3, 2020, presidential election in Georgia. This was an act of racketeering activity pursuant to O.C.G.A. § 16-14-3(5)(A)(xxvii) and an overt act in furtherance of the conspiracy.

Act 89.

On or between the **15th day of December 2020 and the 4th day of January 2021, STEPHEN CLIFFGARD LEE** solicited **HARRISON WILLIAM PRESCOTT FLOYD,** an individual associated with the organization Black Voices for Trump, to assist with his effort to speak to Ruby Freeman, a Fulton County, Georgia, election worker. **STEPHEN CLIFFGARD LEE** stated to **HARRISON WILLIAM PRESCOTT FLOYD** that Freeman was afraid to talk to **STEPHEN CLIFFGARD LEE** because he was a white man. These were overt acts in furtherance of the conspiracy.

Act 90.

On or about the **18th day of December 2020, DONALD JOHN TRUMP** met with **RUDOLPH WILLIAM LOUIS GIULIANI, SIDNEY KATHERINE POWELL**, unindicted co-conspirator Individual 20, whose identity is known to the Grand Jury, and others at the White House. The individuals present at the meeting discussed certain strategies and theories intended to influence the outcome of the November 3, 2020, presidential election, including seizing voting equipment and appointing **SIDNEY KATHERINE POWELL** as special counsel with broad authority to investigate allegations of voter fraud in Georgia and elsewhere. This was an overt act in furtherance of the conspiracy.*

---

* This detail is extraordinary—it alleges that not only were Trump and his allies contemplating seizing voting machines in various battleground states, but they were

Act 91.

On or about the **21st day of December 2020, SIDNEY KATHERINE POWELL** sent an e-mail to the Chief Operations Officer of SullivanStrickler LLC and instructed him that she and unindicted co-conspirators Individual 6, Individual 21, and Individual 22, whose identities are known to the Grand Jury, were to immediately "receive a copy of all data" obtained by SullivanStrickler LLC from Dominion Voting Systems equipment in Michigan. This was an overt act in furtherance of the conspiracy.

Act 92.

On or about the **22nd day of December 2020, MARK RANDALL MEADOWS** traveled to the Cobb County Civic Center in Cobb County, Georgia, and attempted to observe the signature match audit being performed there by law enforcement officers from the Georgia Bureau of Investigation and the Office of the Georgia Secretary of State, despite the fact that the audit process was not open to the public. While present at the center, **MARK RANDALL MEADOWS** spoke to Georgia Deputy Secretary of State Jordan Fuchs, Office of the Georgia Secretary of State Chief Investigator Frances Watson, Georgia Bureau of Investigation Special Agent in Charge Bahan Rich, and others, who prevented **MARK RANDALL MEADOWS** from entering into the space where the audit was being conducted. This was an overt act in furtherance of the conspiracy.

---

also considering appointing Sidney Powell, whose election fraud claims Trump once dismissed as "crazy," as special counsel in order to investigate electoral fraud. Powell's guilty plea to intentionally conspiring to illegally access Coffee County voting machines makes the allegation even more alarming.

INSIDER NOTE: This meeting is not referenced in the DC January 6 indictment, although it nonetheless can be the subject of trial testimony in that case since indictments do not and are not intended to set out all the proof that will be adduced at trial.

Act 93.

On or about the **23rd day of December 2020, DONALD JOHN TRUMP** placed a telephone call to Office of the Georgia Secretary of State Chief Investigator Frances Watson that had been previously arranged by **MARK RANDALL MEADOWS.** During the phone call, **DONALD JOHN TRUMP** falsely stated that he had won the November 3, 2020, presidential election in Georgia "by hundreds of thousands of votes" and stated to Watson that "when the right answer comes out you'll be praised." This was an overt act in furtherance of the conspiracy.

Act 94.

On or about the **23rd day of December 2020, JOHN CHARLES EASTMAN** sent an e-mail to **KENNETH JOHN CHESEBRO** and unindicted co-conspirator Individual 3, whose identity is known to the Grand Jury, with the subject "FW: Draft 2, with edits." In the e-mail, **JOHN CHARLES EASTMAN** attached a memorandum titled "PRIVILEGED AND CONFI-DENTIAL -- Dec 23 memo on Jan 6 scenario.docx" and stated, "As for hearings, I think both are unnecessary. The fact that we have multiple slates of electors demonstrates the uncertainty of either.* That should be enough. And I agree with Ken that Judiciary Committee hearings on the constitutionality of the Electoral Count Act could invite counter views that we do not believe should constrain Pence (or Grassley) in the exercise of power they have under the 12th Amendment. Better for them just to act boldly and be challenged, since the challenge would likely lead to the Court denying review on nonjusticiable political question grounds." This was an overt act in furtherance of the conspiracy.

---

* The corrupt use of the fake electors as alleged in the indictment is made explicit here: the fake electors were put in place not as a backup in case the state vote was determined to be for Trump; instead, they were put in place as a tool to create the false impression of uncertainty about the election outcome.

Act 95.

On or about the **25th day of December 2020, DONALD JOHN TRUMP** placed a telephone call to Speaker of the Arizona House of Representatives Rusty Bowers[*] for the purpose of soliciting, requesting, and importuning Bowers to unlawfully appoint presidential electors from Arizona. During the call, Bowers stated to Trump, "I voted for you. I worked for you. I campaigned for you. I just won't do anything illegal for you." This telephone call was an overt act in furtherance of the conspiracy.

Act 96.

On or about the **27th day of December 2020, MARK RANDALL MEADOWS** sent a text message to Office of the Georgia Secretary of State Chief Investigator Frances Watson that stated in part, "Is there a way to speed up Fulton county signature verification in order to have results before Jan 6 if the trump campaign assist financially." This was an overt act in furtherance of the conspiracy.

Act 97.

On or about the **27th day of December 2020, DONALD JOHN TRUMP** solicited Acting United States Attorney General Jeffrey Rosen and Acting United States Deputy Attorney General Richard Donoghue to make a false statement by stating, "Just say that the election was corrupt, and leave the rest to me and the Republican congressmen." This was an overt act in furtherance of the conspiracy.

---

[*] Bowers testified before the January 6 committee that Trump and Giuliani pressured him to flip the outcome of the Arizona election for Trump. He refused to do so, citing his oath of office to defend the Constitution. He further testified that his refusal to intervene on behalf of Trump came with consequences. He and his family, including his gravely ill daughter, were harassed for several weeks. As he recounted, his office was flooded with 20,000 emails and tens of thousands of voicemails and text messages from Trump supporters, all of which made it impossible for Bowers and his legislative staff to work.

Act 98.

On or about the **28th day of December 2020, JEFFREY BOSSERT CLARK** attempted to commit the felony offense of **FALSE STATEMENTS AND WRITINGS,** in violation of **O.C.G.A. § 16-10-20,** in Fulton County, Georgia, by knowingly and willfully making a false writing and document knowing the same to contain the false statement that the United States Department of Justice had "identified significant concerns that may have impacted the outcome of the election in multiple States, including the State of Georgia," said statement being within the jurisdiction of the Office of the Georgia Secretary of State and the Georgia Bureau of Investigation, departments and agencies of state government, and county and city law enforcement agencies;

And on or about the **28th day of December 2020, JEFFREY BOSSERT CLARK** sent an e-mail to Acting United States Attorney General Jeffrey Rosen and Acting United States Deputy Attorney General Richard Donoghue and requested authorization to send said false writing and document to Georgia Governor Brian Kemp, Speaker of the Georgia House of Representatives David Ralston, and President Pro Tempore of the Georgia Senate Butch Miller, which constitutes a substantial step toward the commission of False Statements and Writings, O.C.G.A. § 16-10-20. This was an act of racketeering activity under O.C.G.A. § 16-14-3(5)(A)(xxii) and an overt act in furtherance of the conspiracy.

Act 99.

On or about the **28th day of December 2020, JEFFREY BOSSERT CLARK*** solicited Acting United States Attorney Gen-

---

* Jeffrey Clark, who served as the acting head of the DOJ's Civil Division, was not named in the DC January 6 indictment, but, based on media reporting and extant evidence, he is believed to be "co-conspirator 4." Here, he is specifically named and charged with attempting to issue false statements and writings, in violation of Georgia law.

INSIDER NOTE: The allegations here with respect to Clark could also constitute federal crimes. For that reason, and given the gravity of the alleged actions and the fact that both Rosen and Donohue have testified before the January 6 committee

eral Jeffrey Rosen and Acting United States Deputy Attorney General Richard Donoghue to sign and send a document that falsely stated that the United States Department of Justice had "identified significant concerns that may have impacted the outcome of the election in multiple States, including the State of Georgia," to Georgia Governor Brian Kemp, Speaker of the Georgia House of Representatives David Ralston, and President Pro Tempore of the Georgia Senate Butch Miller. This was an overt act in furtherance of the conspiracy.

Act 100.

On or about the **30th day of December 2020, DONALD JOHN TRUMP** caused to be tweeted from the Twitter account @ RealDonaldTrump, "Hearings from Atlanta on the Georgia Election overturn now being broadcast. Check it out. @OANN @newsmax and many more. @BrianKempGA should resign from office. He is an obstructionist who refuses to admit that we won Georgia, BIG! Also won the other Swing States." This was an overt act in furtherance of the conspiracy.

Act 101.

On or about the **30th day of December 2020, DONALD JOHN TRUMP** caused to be tweeted from the Twitter account @RealDonaldTrump, "Hearings from Atlanta on the Georgia Election overturn now being broadcast LIVE via @RSBNetwork! https://t.co/ogBvLbKfqG." This was an overt act in furtherance of the conspiracy.

Act 102.

On or about the **30th day of December 2020, RUDOLPH WILLIAM LOUIS GIULIANI, RAY STALLINGS SMITH III,** and **ROBERT DAVID CHEELEY** committed the felony

---

about Clark's activities already, it is entirely likely that Special Counsel Jack Smith may, in the future, charge Clark.

offense of **SOLICITATION OF VIOLATION OF OATH BY PUBLIC OFFICER,** in violation of **O.C.G.A. §§ 16-4-7 & 16-10-1,** in Fulton County, Georgia, by soliciting, requesting, and importuning certain public officers then serving as elected members of the Georgia Senate and present at a Senate Judiciary Subcommittee meeting, including unindicted co-conspirator Individual 8, whose identity is known to the Grand Jury, Senators Brandon Beach, Bill Heath, William Ligon, Michael Rhett, and Blake Tillery, to engage in conduct constituting the felony offense of Violation of Oath by Public Officer, O.C.G.A. § 16-10-1, by unlawfully appointing presidential electors from the State of Georgia, in willful and intentional violation of the terms of the oath of said persons as prescribed by law, with intent that said persons engage in said conduct. This was an overt act in furtherance of the conspiracy.

Act 103.

On or about the **30th day of December 2020, RUDOLPH WILLIAM LOUIS GIULIANI** committed the felony offense of **FALSE STATEMENTS AND WRITINGS,** in violation of **O.C.G.A. § 16-10-20,** in Fulton County, Georgia, by knowingly, willfully, and unlawfully making at least one of the following false statements and representations to members of the Georgia Senate present at a Senate Judiciary Subcommittee meeting:

1. That Fulton County election workers fraudulently counted certain ballots as many as five times at State Farm Arena on November 3, 2020;

2. That 2,560 felons voted illegally in the November 3, 2020, presidential election in Georgia;

3. That 10,315 dead people voted in the November 3, 2020, presidential election in Georgia;

said statements being within the jurisdiction of the Office of the Georgia Secretary of State and the Georgia Bureau of Investigation, departments and agencies of state government, and county and city law enforcement agencies. This was an act of racketeering activity under O.C.G.A. § 16-14-3(5)(A)(xxii) and an overt act in furtherance of the conspiracy.

Act 104.

On or about the **30th day of December 2020, RAY STALL-INGS SMITH III** committed the felony offense of **FALSE STATEMENTS AND WRITINGS,** in violation of **O.C.G.A. § 16-10-20,** in Fulton County, Georgia, by knowingly, willfully, and unlawfully making at least one of the following false statements and representations to members of the Georgia Senate present at a Senate Judiciary Subcommittee meeting:

1.   That Georgia Secretary of State General Counsel Ryan Germany stated that his office had sent letters to 8,000 people who voted illegally in the November 3, 2020, presidential election and told them not to vote in the January 5, 2021, runoff election;

2.   That the Georgia Secretary of State admitted "that they had a 90% accuracy rate" in the November 3, 2020, presidential election and that "there's still a 10% margin that's not accurate";

said statements being within the jurisdiction of the Office of the Georgia Secretary of State and the Georgia Bureau of Investigation, departments and agencies of state government, and county and city law enforcement agencies. This was an act of racketeering activity under O.C.G.A. § 16-14-3(5)(A)(xxii) and an overt act in furtherance of the conspiracy.

Act 105.

On or about the **30th day of December 2020, ROBERT DAVID CHEELEY** committed the felony offense of **FALSE STATEMENTS AND WRITINGS,** in violation of **O.C.G.A. § 16-10-20,** in Fulton County, Georgia, by knowingly, willfully, and unlawfully making at least one of the following false statements and representations to members of the Georgia Senate present at a Senate Judiciary Subcommittee meeting:

1.   That poll watchers and media at State Farm Arena were told late in the evening of November 3, 2020, that the vote count was being suspended until the next morning and to go home because of "a major watermain break";

2.   That Fulton County election workers at State Farm Arena "voted" the same ballots "over and over again" on November 3, 2020;

said statements being within the jurisdiction of the Office of the Georgia Secretary of State and the Georgia Bureau of Investigation, departments and agencies of state government, and county and city law enforcement agencies. This was an act of racketeering activity under O.C.G.A. § 16-14-3(5)(A)(xxii) and an overt act in furtherance of the conspiracy.

Act 106.

On or about the **30th day of December 2020, DONALD JOHN TRUMP** caused to be tweeted from the Twitter account @ RealDonaldTrump, "We now have far more votes than needed to flip Georgia in the Presidential race. Massive VOTER FRAUD took place. Thank you to the Georgia Legislature for today's revealing meeting!" This was an overt act in furtherance of the conspiracy.

Act 107.

On or about the **31st day of December 2020, JENNA LYNN ELLIS** wrote a memorandum titled "Memorandum Re: Constitutional Analysis of Vice President Authority for January 6, 2021 Electoral College Vote Count" to **DONALD JOHN TRUMP.** The memorandum outlined a strategy for disrupting and delaying the joint session of Congress on January 6, 2021, the day prescribed by law for counting votes cast by the duly elected and qualified presidential electors from Georgia and the other states, and stated, "the Vice President should therefore not open any of the votes" from six states, including Georgia, that were falsely characterized as having "electoral delegates in dispute." This was an overt act in furtherance of the conspiracy.

Act 108.

On or about the **31st day of December 2020, DONALD JOHN TRUMP** and **JOHN CHARLES EASTMAN** committed the felony offense of **FILING FALSE DOCUMENTS,**[*] in violation of **O.C.G.A. § 16-10-20.1(b)(1),** in Fulton County, Georgia, by knowingly filing a document titled "VERIFIED COMPLAINT FOR EMERGENCY INJUNCTIVE AND DECLARATORY RELIEF" in the matter of Trump v. Kemp, Case 1:20-cv-05310-MHC, in the United States District Court for the Northern District of Georgia, a court of the United States having reason to know that said document contained at least one of the following materially false statements:

1. That "as many as 2,506 felons with an uncompleted sentence" voted illegally in the November 3, 2020, presidential election in Georgia;

2. That "at least 66,247 underage" people voted illegally in the November 3, 2020, presidential election in Georgia;

3. That "at least 2,423 individuals" voted illegally in the November 3, 2020, presidential election in Georgia "who were not listed in the State's records as having been registered to vote";

4. That "at least 1,043 individuals" voted illegally in the November 3, 2020, presidential election "who had illegally registered to vote using a postal office box as their habitation";

5. That "as many as 10,315 or more" dead people voted in the November 3, 2020, presidential election in Georgia;

6. That "[d]eliberate misinformation was used to instruct Republican poll watchers and members of the press to leave the premises for the night at approximately 10:00 p.m. on

---

[*] It is alleged that Trump and Eastman filed false statements, in violation of Georgia law, when they filed a lawsuit, *Trump v. Kemp*, challenging the results of Georgia's presidential election. Specifically, it is alleged that they signed statements alleging a series of claims about voter fraud, even though lawyers advised them that these claims were false or could not be substantiated.

November 3, 2020" at State Farm Arena in Fulton County, Georgia;

Earlier on the same day, **JOHN CHARLES EASTMAN** sent an e-mail to attorneys associated with the Trump Campaign admitting his knowledge that at least some of the allegations in the verified complaint were not accurate. This filing was an act of racketeering activity under O.C.G.A. § 16-14-3(5)(A)(xxii) and an overt act in furtherance of the conspiracy.

Act 109.

On or about the **1st day of January 2021, KENNETH JOHN CHESEBRO** sent an e-mail to **JOHN CHARLES EAST-MAN** and unindicted co-conspirator Individual 3, whose identity is known to the Grand Jury. In the e-mail, **KENNETH JOHN CHESEBRO** outlined a strategy for disrupting and delaying the joint session of Congress on January 6, 2021, the day prescribed by law for counting votes cast by the duly elected and qualified presidential electors from Georgia and the other states. This was an overt act in furtherance of the conspiracy.

Act 110.

On or about the **2nd day of January 2021, SCOTT GRA-HAM HALL,** a Georgia bail bondsman, placed a telephone call to **JEFFREY BOSSERT CLARK** and discussed the November 3, 2020, presidential election in Georgia. The telephone call was 63 minutes in duration. This was an overt act in furtherance of the conspiracy.

Act 111.

On or about the **2nd day of January 2021, JEFFREY BOSSERT CLARK** solicited Acting United States Attorney General Jeffrey Rosen and Acting United States Deputy Attorney General Richard Donoghue to sign and send a document that falsely stated that the United States Department of Justice had "identified significant concerns that may have impacted the outcome of the election in multiple States, including the State of Georgia," to Georgia Governor Brian Kemp, Speaker of the Georgia House of Representatives David Ralston, and President Pro Tempore of the Georgia Senate Butch Miller. This was an overt act in furtherance of the conspiracy.

Act 112.

On or about the **2nd day of January 2021, DONALD JOHN TRUMP** and **MARK RANDALL MEADOWS** committed the felony offense of **SOLICITATION OF VIOLATION OF OATH BY PUBLIC OFFICER,** in violation of **O.C.G.A. §§ 16-4-7 & 16-10-1,** in Fulton County, Georgia, by unlawfully soliciting, requesting, and importuning Georgia Secretary of State Brad Raffensperger, a public officer, to engage in conduct constituting the felony offense of Violation of Oath by Public Officer, O.C.G.A. § 16-10-1, by unlawfully altering, unlawfully adjusting, and otherwise unlawfully influencing the certified returns for presidential electors for the November 3, 2020, presidential election in Georgia, in willful and intentional violation of the terms of the oath of said person as prescribed by law, with intent that said person engage in said conduct. This was an overt act in furtherance of the conspiracy.*

---

* Acts 112 and 113 refer to the now infamous January 2, 2021, phone call in which Trump entreated Raffensperger, Georgia's secretary of state, to "find" the 11,780 votes that Trump needed to win the election in Georgia. Mark Meadows, the White House chief of staff, was also on the call and made false representations about alleged voter fraud. Trump threatened Raffensperger with potential criminal exposure if he did not capitulate.

INSIDER NOTE: Raffensperger must have taped this call because he knew that he might need it to be able to refute later claims as to what transpired. Trump claims it was a "perfect" call, a claim that recalls his call with Ukrainian president Volodymyr Zelenskyy, on which Trump allegedly used vital congressionally appropriated military aid (rather than criminal prosecution) as leverage to pressure Zelenskyy to initiate an investigation into Joe and Hunter Biden. The Zelenskyy phone call—and the alleged "quid pro quo"—was the subject of Trump's first impeachment.

Act 113.

On or about the **2nd day of January 2021, DONALD JOHN TRUMP** committed the felony offense of **FALSE STATEMENTS AND WRITINGS,** in violation of **O.C.G.A. § 16-10-20,** in Fulton County, Georgia, by knowingly, willfully, and unlawfully making at least one of the following false statements and representations to Georgia Secretary of State Brad Raffensperger, Georgia Deputy Secretary of State Jordan Fuchs, and Georgia Secretary of State General Counsel Ryan Germany:

1. That anywhere from 250,000 to 300,000 ballots were dropped mysteriously into the rolls in the November 3, 2020, presidential election in Georgia;

2. That thousands of people attempted to vote in the November 3, 2020, presidential election in Georgia and were told they could not because a ballot had already been cast in their name;

3. That 4,502 people voted in the November 3, 2020, presidential election in Georgia who were not on the voter registration list;

4. That 904 people voted in the November 3, 2020, presidential election in Georgia who were registered at an address that was a post office box;

5. That Ruby Freeman was a professional vote scammer and a known political operative;

6. That Ruby Freeman, her daughter, and others were responsible for fraudulently awarding at least 18,000 ballots to Joseph R. Biden at State Farm Arena in the November 3, 2020, presidential election in Georgia;*

---

* The claim that Freeman and Moss were engaged in election fraud at the State Farm Arena polling site was fueled by a video promoted by a conservative super PAC operating under the auspices of Restoration of America, a conservative interest group. The video showed Moss, Freeman, and other poll workers removing ballots from what were wrongly characterized as suspicious-looking "suitcases." In fact, the "suitcases" were merely the bags in which the ballots had been stored overnight and sealed before election officials instructed poll workers to scan the ballots again.

7. That close to 5,000 dead people voted in the November 3, 2020, presidential election in Georgia;

8. That 139% of people voted in the November 3, 2020, presidential election in Detroit;*

9. That 200,000 more votes were recorded than the number of people who voted in the November 3, 2020, presidential election in Pennsylvania;

10. That thousands of dead people voted in the November 3, 2020, presidential election in Michigan;

11. That Ruby Freeman stuffed the ballot boxes;†

12. That hundreds of thousands of ballots had been "dumped" into Fulton County and another county adjacent to Fulton

---

The video footage went viral, with various Trump lawyers, including Giuliani, citing it at Georgia House of Representatives hearings to promote the fraudulent election conspiracy theory. Giuliani stated that Freeman and Moss were "quite obviously surreptitiously passing around USB ports as if they're vials of heroin or cocaine." He also made similar allegations on Twitter, although he has since conceded, in a defamation suit brought by Moss and Freeman, that these allegations were "actionable" and "false." These rumors were disproven in multiple news outlets and the Trump DOJ investigated and confirmed that the allegations were false. Nevertheless, Trump continued to parrot claims of voter fraud, telling Raffensperger that "what looked to be suitcases or trunks" were "stuffed with votes" that contained at least "18,000 ballots, all for Biden." Trump also referenced Freeman by name, calling her "a professional vote scammer."

INSIDER NOTE: The Restoration PAC has made similar unfounded post-election allegations about other polling places around the country. Operating under the umbrella group, Restoration of America, the Restoration PAC is funded by billionaire and Uline Company CEO Richard Uihlein, who has contributed to conservative causes, including the effort to amend the Ohio Constitution to make it harder to use direct democracy initiatives to protect reproductive rights.

* These various allegations have all been refuted by those in charge of overseeing the elections; Trump was made aware that these claims were false at the time.

† When Freeman testified before the January 6 committee, she noted the impact that these allegations had on her life. "Do you know how it feels to have the president of the United States target you?" Freeman asked the committee. "The president of the United States made up lies about two ordinary Americans for his own personal gain." As she recounted to the committee, Freeman received death threats and for a time went into hiding. Moss was afraid to leave the house, and family members, including her teenage son, received racist threats by phone. Giuliani's reference to heroin or cocaine vials was a racist trope, one that clearly resonated among Trump's supporters.

County in the November 3, 2020, presidential election in Georgia;

13.   That he won the November 3, 2020, presidential election in Georgia by 400,000 votes;

said statements being within the jurisdiction of the Office of the Georgia Secretary of State and the Georgia Bureau of Investigation, departments and agencies of state government. This was an act of racketeering activity under O.C.G.A. § 16-14-3(5)(A)(xxii) and an overt act in furtherance of the conspiracy.

Act 114.

On or about the **3rd day of January 2021, DONALD JOHN TRUMP** caused to be tweeted from the Twitter account @Real-DonaldTrump, "I spoke to Secretary of State Brad Raffensperger yesterday about Fulton County and voter fraud in Georgia. He was unwilling, or unable, to answer questions such as the 'ballots under table' scam, ballot destruction, out of state 'voters', dead voters, and more. He has no clue!" This was an overt act in furtherance of the conspiracy.

Act 115.

On or about the **3rd day of January 2021, STEPHEN CLIFFGARD LEE, HARRISON WILLIAM PRESCOTT FLOYD, and TREVIAN C. KUTTI** placed multiple telephone calls and sent text messages to each other and to other individuals involved in the conspiracy. They include the following:

1.   At 7:48 p.m., **HARRISON WILLIAM PRESCOTT FLOYD**[*] placed a telephone call to Ruby Freeman, a Fulton County, Georgia, election worker, that was unsuccessful.

---

[*] Harrison Floyd once led a group called Black Voices for Trump. After turning himself in August 24, 2023, Floyd spent a number of days in jail—the only one of the nineteen defendants to do so. In the sections that follow, he is alleged to have worked with Trevian Kutti to pressure Ruby Freeman into acquiescing to claims of voter fraud.

2. At 7:49 p.m., **HARRISON WILLIAM PRESCOTT FLOYD** placed a telephone call to Ruby Freeman that was unsuccessful.

3. At 7:49 p.m., **HARRISON WILLIAM PRESCOTT FLOYD** placed a telephone call to **TREVIAN C. KUTTI**.

4. At 7:53 p.m., **HARRISON WILLIAM PRESCOTT FLOYD** sent a text message to Ruby Freeman.

5. At 8:03 p.m., **TREVIAN C. KUTTI*** placed a telephone call to **HARRISON WILLIAM PRESCOTT FLOYD**.

6. At 8:11 p.m., **HARRISON WILLIAM PRESCOTT FLOYD** placed a telephone call to unindicted co-conspirator Individual 23, whose identity is known to the Grand Jury.

7. At 8:18 p.m., **HARRISON WILLIAM PRESCOTT FLOYD** placed a telephone call to **STEPHEN CLIFF-GARD LEE**.

8. At 8:48 p.m., **HARRISON WILLIAM PRESCOTT FLOYD** placed a telephone call to **TREVIAN C. KUTTI**.

9. At 9:16 p.m., **HARRISON WILLIAM PRESCOTT FLOYD** placed a telephone call to **TREVIAN C. KUTTI**.

10. At 9:33 p.m., **HARRISON WILLIAM PRESCOTT FLOYD** placed a telephone call to **TREVIAN C. KUTTI**.

11. At 9:50 p.m., **HARRISON WILLIAM PRESCOTT FLOYD** placed a telephone call to **STEPHEN CLIFF-GARD LEE**.

These were overt acts in furtherance of the conspiracy.

Act 116.

On or about the **4th day of January 2021, TREVIAN C. KUTTI,** having been recruited by **HARRISON WILLIAM PRESCOTT FLOYD,** traveled from Chicago, Illinois, to Atlanta,

---

* According to the indictment, Floyd recruited Kutti, a former publicist to R. Kelly and Kanye West, who traveled from Chicago to Atlanta in order to participate in the events detailed.

Georgia, and caused a certain individual, whose identity is known to the Grand Jury, to pick her up from a train station in Fulton County, Georgia, for the purpose of attempting to contact Ruby Freeman, a Fulton County, Georgia, election worker. This was an overt act in furtherance of the conspiracy.

Act 117.

On or about the **4th day of January 2021, TREVIAN C. KUTTI** traveled to Ruby Freeman's home in Cobb County, Georgia, and attempted to contact her but was unsuccessful. **TREVIAN C. KUTTI** spoke with Freeman's neighbor and falsely stated that she was a crisis manager attempting to "help" Freeman before leaving Freeman's home. This was an overt act in furtherance of the conspiracy.

Act 118.

On or about the **4th day of January 2021, TREVIAN C. KUTTI,** while in Fulton County, Georgia, placed a telephone call to Ruby Freeman and stated that Freeman was in danger. **TREVIAN C. KUTTI** stated that she could "help" Freeman and requested that Freeman meet with and speak to her that night at a Cobb County Police Department precinct in Cobb County, Georgia. This was an overt act in furtherance of the conspiracy.

Act 119.

On or about the **4th day of January 2021, TREVIAN C. KUTTI** traveled to a Cobb County Police Department precinct in Cobb County, Georgia, and met with and spoke to Ruby Freeman for approximately one hour. **HARRISON WILLIAM PRESCOTT FLOYD** joined the meeting by telephone. **TREVIAN C. KUTTI** and **HARRISON WILLIAM PRESCOTT FLOYD** stated to Freeman that she needed protection and purported to offer her help. This was an overt act in furtherance of the conspiracy.

Act 120.

On or about the **4th day of January 2021 STEPHEN CLIFFGARD LEE, HARRISON WILLIAM PRESCOTT FLOYD,** and **TREVIAN C. KUTTI** committed the felony offense of **SOLICITATION OF FALSE STATEMENTS AND WRITINGS,*** in violation of **O.C.G.A. §§ 16-4-7 & 16-10-20,** in Cobb County, Georgia, by soliciting, requesting, and importuning Ruby Freeman, a Fulton County, Georgia, election worker, to engage in conduct constituting the felony offense of False Statements and Writings, O.C.G.A. § 16-10-20, by knowingly and willfully making a false statement and representation concerning events at State Farm Arena in the November 3, 2020, presidential election in Georgia, said statement and representation being within the jurisdiction of the Office of the Georgia Secretary of State and the Georgia Bureau of Investigation, departments and agencies of state government, and county and city law enforcement agencies, with intent that said person engage in said conduct. This was an act of racketeering activity under O.C.G.A. § 16-14-3(5)(A)(xxii) and an overt act in furtherance of the conspiracy.

Act 121.

On or about the **4th day of January 2021 STEPHEN CLIFFGARD LEE, HARRISON WILLIAM PRESCOTT FLOYD,** and **TREVIAN C. KUTTI** committed the felony offense of **INFLUENCING WITNESSES,** in violation of **O.C.G.A. § 16-10-93(b)(1)(A),** in Fulton County, Georgia, by knowingly and unlawfully engaging in misleading conduct toward Ruby Freeman, a Fulton County, Georgia, election worker, by stating that she needed protection and by purporting to offer her help, with intent to influence her testimony in an official proceeding in Fulton County, Georgia, concerning events at State Farm Arena in the November 3,

---

* It is notable that Floyd and Kutti, both of whom are Black, were enlisted, presumably because of their race, to take on the task of persuading Freeman, who is also Black.

2020, presidential election in Georgia. This was an act of racketeering activity under O.C.G.A. § 16-14-3(5)(A)(xxvii) and an overt act in furtherance of the conspiracy.

Act 122.

On or about the **4th day of January 2021, STEPHEN CLIFFGARD LEE, HARRISON WILLIAM PRESCOTT FLOYD, and TREVIAN C. KUTTI** placed multiple telephone calls and sent text messages to each other and to other individuals involved in the conspiracy. They include the following:

1. At 9:41 a.m., **STEPHEN CLIFFGARD LEE** placed a telephone call to **HARRISON WILLIAM PRESCOTT FLOYD.**

2. At 11:24 a.m., **HARRISON WILLIAM PRESCOTT FLOYD** placed a telephone call to **DAVID JAMES SHAFER.**

3. At 12:25 p.m., **STEPHEN CLIFFGARD LEE**[*] placed a telephone call to **HARRISON WILLIAM PRESCOTT FLOYD.**

4. At 12:32 p.m., **STEPHEN CLIFFGARD LEE** sent a text message to **HARRISON WILLIAM PRESCOTT FLOYD.**

5. At 8:10 p.m., **HARRISON WILLIAM PRESCOTT FLOYD** placed a telephone call to **DAVID JAMES SHAFER.**

---

[*] Lee is unusual among the nineteen defendants. Unlike the other defendants, many of whom are politicians and political operatives who worked with the Trump campaign, Lee is a seventy-year-old Lutheran pastor. Lee came to the ministry after serving as a sheriff's deputy in California in the 1980s. After being ordained a minister in 1992, he served as a police chaplain. In 1999, after moving to Colorado Springs, he was the head chaplain for the Bureau of Alcohol, Tobacco, Firearms and Explosives. Lee's decision to travel to Georgia to confront Ruby Freeman appears to have been influenced by a deceptively edited video depicting apparent electoral fraud at the State Farm Arena.

6. At 10:00 p.m., **HARRISON WILLIAM PRESCOTT FLOYD** placed a telephone call to **STEPHEN CLIFF-GARD LEE.**

7. At 10:19 p.m., **HARRISON WILLIAM PRESCOTT FLOYD** placed a telephone call to **TREVIAN C. KUTTI**.

8. At 10:43 p.m., **TREVIAN C. KUTTI** placed a telephone call to **HARRISON WILLIAM PRESCOTT FLOYD.**

9. At 11:10 p.m., **TREVIAN C. KUTTI** placed a telephone call to **HARRISON WILLIAM PRESCOTT FLOYD.**

10. At 12:12 a.m. on January 5, 2021, **TREVIAN C. KUTTI** placed a telephone call to **HARRISON WILLIAM PRESCOTT FLOYD.**

These were overt acts in furtherance of the conspiracy.[*]

Act 123.

On or about the **4th day of January 2020, JOHN CHARLES EASTMAN** placed a telephone call to Speaker of the Arizona House of Representatives Rusty Bowers and solicited, requested, and importuned Bowers to unlawfully appoint presidential electors from Arizona. During the telephone call, Bowers declined to comply with Eastman's request and stated that he would not risk violating his oath of office. The request was an overt act in furtherance of the conspiracy.

Act 124.

On or about the **4th day of January 2021, KENNETH JOHN CHESEBRO** sent an e-mail to **JOHN CHARLES EASTMAN** with the subject "Fwd: Draft 2, with edits" and included within the body of the e-mail another e-mail that **KENNETH JOHN**

---

[*] The indictment focuses on the scheme, circulated in memoranda and emails, to have Vice President Pence, in his capacity as President of the Senate, stop the certification of the electoral college votes. This scheme is a core focus of the DC January 6 indictment. Pence himself testified before the federal grand jury that brought that indictment.

CHESEBRO previously sent to **RUDOLPH WILLIAM LOUIS GIULIANI** with the subject "PRIVILEGED AND CONFIDENTIAL – Brief notes on 'President of the Senate' strategy." In the e-mail, **KENNETH JOHN CHESEBRO** outlined multiple strategies for disrupting and delaying the joint session of Congress on January 6, 2021, the day prescribed by law for counting votes cast by the duly elected and qualified presidential electors from Georgia and the other states, and stated that the outcomes of any of these strategies were "preferable to allowing the Electoral Count Act to operate by its terms." This was an overt act in furtherance of the conspiracy.

Act 123.*

On or about the **4th day of January 2021, DONALD JOHN TRUMP** and **JOHN CHARLES EASTMAN** met with Vice President Mike Pence, Chief of Staff to the Vice President Marc Short, and Counsel to the Vice President Greg Jacob in the Oval Office at the White House. During the meeting, **DONALD JOHN TRUMP** and **JOHN CHARLES EASTMAN** argued to Pence that he could either reject electoral votes from certain states or delay the joint session of Congress on January 6, 2021, the day prescribed by law for counting votes cast by the duly elected and qualified presidential electors from Georgia and the other states, for the purpose of allowing certain state legislatures to unlawfully appoint presidential electors in favor of **DONALD JOHN TRUMP**. During the meeting, **JOHN CHARLES EASTMAN** admitted both options violated the Electoral Count Act. This was an overt act in furtherance of the conspiracy.

Act 126.

On or about the **5th day of January 2021, JENNA LYNN ELLIS** wrote a memorandum titled "Re: Vice President Authority in Counting Electors pursuant to U.S. Constitution and 3 U.S. Code §§ 5 and 15" to an attorney associated with **DONALD JOHN**

---

* Misnumbering here as per original text.

TRUMP. The memorandum outlined a strategy for disrupting and delaying the joint session of Congress on January 6, 2021, the day prescribed by law for counting votes cast by the duly elected and qualified presidential electors from Georgia and the other states, and stated, "the Vice President should begin alphabetically in order of the states, and coming first to Arizona, not open the purported certification, but simply stop the count at that juncture." This was an overt act in furtherance of the conspiracy.*

Act 127.

On or about the **5th day of January 2021, ROBERT DAVID CHEELEY, STEPHEN CLIFFGARD LEE, HARRISON WILLIAM PRESCOTT FLOYD, TREVIAN C. KUTTI, and SCOTT GRAHAM HALL** placed multiple telephone calls to each other and to other individuals involved in the conspiracy. They include the following:

1. At 11:32 a.m., **STEPHEN CLIFFGARD LEE** placed a telephone call to **TREVIAN C. KUTTI.**

2. At 12:14 p.m., **HARRISON WILLIAM PRESCOTT FLOYD, TREVIAN C. KUTTI, STEPHEN CLIFFGARD LEE,** and unindicted co-conspirator Individual 23, whose identity is known to the Grand Jury, participated in a four-way telephone call.

3. At 12:19 p.m., **SCOTT GRAHAM HALL** placed a telephone call to **ROBERT DAVID CHEELEY.**

4. At 12:34 p.m., **SCOTT GRAHAM HALL** placed a telephone call to **ROBERT DAVID CHEELEY.**

5. At 1:07 p.m., **ROBERT DAVID CHEELEY** placed a telephone call to **SCOTT GRAHAM HALL.**

---

* The indictment details Jenna Ellis's draft memorandum discussing having the vice president disrupt the counting of the electoral college votes. On October 24, 2023, Ellis entered a guilty plea to one felony count of aiding and abetting false statements and writings.

6.   At 1:09 p.m., **ROBERT DAVID CHEELEY** placed a telephone call to **SCOTT GRAHAM HALL.**

7.   At 2:30 p.m., **ROBERT DAVID CHEELEY** placed a telephone call to **HARRISON WILLIAM PRESCOTT FLOYD.**

8.   At 2:45 p.m., **HARRISON WILLIAM PRESCOTT FLOYD** placed a telephone call to **ROBERT DAVID CHEELEY.**

9.   At 3:59 p.m., **ROBERT DAVID CHEELEY** placed a telephone call to **SCOTT GRAHAM HALL.**

10.   At 4:42 p.m., **STEPHEN CLIFFGARD LEE** placed a telephone call to **ROBERT DAVID CHEELEY.**

11.   At 4:50 p.m., **STEPHEN CLIFFGARD LEE** placed a telephone call to **HARRISON WILLIAM PRESCOTT FLOYD.**

12.   At 5:05 p.m., **STEPHEN CLIFFGARD LEE** placed a telephone call to **HARRISON WILLIAM PRESCOTT FLOYD.**

13.   At 7:19 p.m., **TREVIAN C. KUTTI** placed a telephone call to **ROBERT DAVID CHEELEY.**

14.   At 7:48 p.m., **ROBERT DAVID CHEELEY** placed a telephone call to **TREVIAN C. KUTTI.**

15.   At 8:27 p.m., **ROBERT DAVID CHEELEY** placed a telephone call to **TREVIAN C. KUTTI.**

16.   At 8:49 p.m., **ROBERT DAVID CHEELEY** placed a telephone call to **STEPHEN CLIFFGARD LEE.**

17.   At 9:18 p.m., **SCOTT GRAHAM HALL** placed a telephone call to **ROBERT DAVID CHEELEY.**

18.   At 9:31 p.m., **TREVIAN C. KUTTI** placed a telephone call to **ROBERT DAVID CHEELEY.**

19.   At 10:14 p.m., **ROBERT DAVID CHEELEY** placed a telephone call to **STEPHEN CLIFFGARD LEE.**

20.   At 11:16 p.m., **ROBERT DAVID CHEELEY** placed a telephone call to **TREVIAN C. KUTTI**.

21.   At 11:25 p.m., **SCOTT GRAHAM HALL** placed a telephone call to **ROBERT DAVID CHEELEY**.

22.   At 11:35 p.m., **ROBERT DAVID CHEELEY, TREVIAN C. KUTTI,** and **SCOTT GRAHAM HALL** participated in a three-way telephone call.

23.   At 12:09 a.m. on January 6, 2021, **TREVIAN C. KUTTI** placed a telephone call to **ROBERT DAVID CHEELEY**.

These were overt acts in furtherance of the conspiracy.

Act 128.

On or about the **5th day of January 2021, DONALD JOHN TRUMP** caused to be tweeted from the Twitter account @RealDonaldTrump, "The Vice President has the power to reject fraudulently chosen electors."* This was an overt act in furtherance of the conspiracy.

---

* The indictment notes Donald Trump's January 5, 2021, tweet in which Trump claimed that Vice President Pence had the authority to reject electors, even though Pence had told the president that he did not agree. On January 5, 2021, Pence's chief of staff Marc Short was so alarmed by Trump's inflammatory rhetoric that he alerted the Secret Service to his concerns of violence. Recent reporting shows that Senator Mitt Romney alerted Senate Majority leader Mitch McConnell to the same concerns of violence on January 6—and notably linked these concerns to the president's rhetoric and behavior, which he had learned about from sources at the Pentagon. That day, the assembled crowd would chant "Hang Mike Pence."

INSIDER NOTE: In spite of multiple credible sources reporting concerns of violence in advance of or on January 6—and the additional concerns that the unique colocation of political leaders at the Capitol presented—federal law enforcement agencies such as the DOJ, the FBI, the Department of Homeland Security, and the US Marshals Service all failed to act. This was in striking contrast to the Trump administration's law enforcement response to Black Lives Matter protests during the summer of 2020, when numerous protesters were arrested on the spot.

Act 129.

On or about the **5th day of January 2021, JOHN CHARLES EASTMAN** met with Chief of Staff to the Vice President Marc Short and Counsel to the Vice President Greg Jacob for the purpose of requesting that Vice President Mike Pence reject slates of presidential electors from Georgia and certain other states during the joint session of Congress on January 6, 2021, the day prescribed by law for counting votes cast by the duly elected and qualified presidential electors from Georgia and the other states. This was an overt act in furtherance of the conspiracy.

Act 130.

On or about the **5th day of January 2021, DONALD JOHN TRUMP** met with Vice President Mike Pence in the Oval Office at the White House. During the meeting, **DONALD JOHN TRUMP** stated that Pence had the power to decertify the November 3, 2020, presidential election results, that people cheated, and that Pence wanted to "play by Marquess of Queensberry rules."* When Pence stated that it was his duty to support and defend the Constitution and that only Congress had the power to decide to reject slates of presidential electors, **DONALD JOHN TRUMP** stated that Pence was naive, implied that he lacked courage, and stated that Pence was doing "a great disservice." This was an overt act in furtherance of the conspiracy.

---

* This is another version of Pence's reported statement that Trump told Pence that Pence was "too honest." If the jury credits this statement, it could be fatal to Trump, as it would demonstrate his criminal intent. It is hard to see what plausible motive Pence would have to lie here, given that he was on the same electoral ticket as Trump, and had been a loyal vice president to him—although, his loyalty to Trump did not overtake his adherence to the law and the Constitution. That is why Pence is not on "the other side of the v"—a phrase used by prosecutors to mean the "v" in "United States v. Defendant."

Act 131.

On or about the **5th day of January 2021, DONALD JOHN TRUMP** placed a telephone call to Vice President Mike Pence.* During the telephone call, **DONALD JOHN TRUMP** and **JOHN CHARLES EASTMAN** attempted to persuade Pence to reject slates of presidential electors or return the slates of presidential electors to state legislatures. This was an overt act in furtherance of the conspiracy.

Act 132.

On or about the **5th day of January 2021, DONALD JOHN TRUMP** placed a second telephone call to Vice President Mike Pence. During the telephone call, **DONALD JOHN TRUMP** asked Pence if he had received a copy of a letter from a group of Pennsylvania legislators urging Congress to return the state's electoral college votes and stated to Pence, "You gotta be tough tomorrow." This was an overt act in furtherance of the conspiracy.

Act 133.

On or about the **5th day of January 2021, DONALD JOHN TRUMP** issued a statement through the Trump Campaign that falsely stated, "The Vice President and I are in total agreement that the Vice President has the power to act. . . . Our Vice President has several options under the U.S. Constitution. He can decertify the results or send them back to the states for change and certification. He can also decertify the illegal and corrupt results and send them to the House of Representatives for the one vote for one state tabulation." This was an overt act in furtherance of the conspiracy.†

---

* The indictment details another infamous phone call, and another infamous conversation with Pence, in which Trump went even further than during the in-person meeting on January 5, 2021, now pressuring his vice president to disrupt the certification of the Electoral College votes by rejecting electors.

† Under this theory, in 2000 Vice President Al Gore could have declared himself the victor over George W. Bush, or in 1960, Nixon could have similarly declared victory over Kennedy, rather than submit to a peaceful transfer of power and the acceptance

Act 134.

On or about the **6th day of January 2021, CATHLEEN ALSTON LATHAM** placed a telephone call to **SCOTT GRAHAM HALL**. Several hours later, **SCOTT GRAHAM HALL** placed a telephone call to **CATHLEEN ALSTON LATHAM**. During at least one of the phone calls, they discussed **SCOTT GRAHAM HALL**'s request to assist with the unlawful breach of election equipment at the Coffee County Board of Elections & Registration Office in Coffee County, Georgia. These were overt acts in furtherance of the conspiracy.

Act 135.

On or about the **6th day of January 2021, DONALD JOHN TRUMP** appeared and spoke at a rally at the Ellipse in Washington, D.C. During the rally, **DONALD JOHN TRUMP** made false statements concerning fraud in the November 3, 2020, presidential election in Georgia and elsewhere, solicited Vice President Mike Pence to disrupt and delay the joint session of Congress on January 6, 2021, the day prescribed by law for counting votes cast by the duly elected and qualified presidential electors from Georgia and the other states, and encouraged those in attendance at the rally to march to the United States Capitol. This was an overt act in furtherance of the conspiracy.*

Act 136.

On or about the **6th day of January 2021, RUDOLPH WILLIAM LOUIS GIULIANI** appeared and spoke at a rally at the Ellipse in Washington, D.C. During the rally, **RUDOLPH WIL-**

---

of an electoral loss. That Nixon—who later resigned the presidency in disgrace and was pardoned for his obstruction crimes during the Watergate scandal—was a greater adherent to the rule of law than Trump is alleged to be, is a striking comment on both Trump and the arc of US history.

* Like the DC January 6 indictment, this indictment does not allege that Trump incited the assault on the Capitol, thereby avoiding at least one pitched battle concerning potential First Amendment defenses.

LIAM LOUIS GIULIANI made false statements concerning fraud in the November 3, 2020, presidential election in Georgia and elsewhere and solicited Vice President Mike Pence to disrupt and delay the joint session of Congress on January 6, 2021, the day prescribed by law for counting votes cast by the duly elected and qualified presidential electors from Georgia and the other states. This was an overt act in furtherance of the conspiracy.

Act 137.

On or about the **6th day of January 2021, JOHN CHARLES EASTMAN** appeared and spoke at a rally at the Ellipse in Washington, D.C. During the rally, **JOHN CHARLES EASTMAN** made false statements concerning fraud in the November 3, 2020, presidential election and solicited Vice President Mike Pence to disrupt and delay the joint session of Congress on January 6, 2021, the day prescribed by law for counting votes cast by the duly elected and qualified presidential electors from Georgia and the other states. This was an overt act in furtherance of the conspiracy.[*]

Act 138.

On or about the **6th day of January 2021, DONALD JOHN TRUMP** caused to be tweeted from the Twitter account @RealDonaldTrump, "If Vice President @Mike_Pence comes through for us, we will win the Presidency. Many States want to decertify the mistake they made in certifying incorrect & even fraudulent numbers in a process NOT approved by their State Legislatures (which

---

[*] The indictment here details John Eastman's speech at the Ellipse on the morning of January 6, in which Eastman reiterated false claims of voter fraud and called on Vice President Mike Pence to reject as fraudulent the duly elected electors from key battleground states. This is a good example of how an overt act can be entirely legal in and of itself, but if undertaken in furtherance of a crime, it could become illegal. An analogy is helpful here. Buying a sheet of paper is, by itself, an innocuous act— and surely not a crime. However, if the paper purchase is part of a broader scheme to hold up a bank by writing a note instructing a bank teller to give you all the money or you will shoot her, then the purchase of the paper is an overt act in furtherance of larceny or robbery.

it must be). Mike can send it back!" This was an overt act in further-ance of the conspiracy.

Act 139.

On or about the **6th day of January 2021, DONALD JOHN TRUMP** caused to be tweeted from the Twitter account @Real-DonaldTrump, "States want to correct their votes, which they now know were based on irregularities and fraud, plus corrupt process never received legislative approval. All Mike Pence has to do is send them back to the States, AND WE WIN. Do it Mike, this is a time for extreme courage!" This was an overt act in furtherance of the conspiracy.*

Act 140.

On or about the **6th day of January 2021, DONALD JOHN TRUMP** placed a telephone call to Vice President Mike Pence and solicited him to disrupt and delay the joint session of Congress on January 6, 2021, the day prescribed by law for counting votes cast by the duly elected and qualified presidential electors from Georgia and the other states. When Pence refused, **DONALD JOHN TRUMP** stated that Pence would "go down as a wimp" and that Pence was not protecting the United States. This was an overt act in further-ance of the conspiracy.†

---

* In these alleged pronouncements, Trump makes no mention of the litany of his own loyalists who told him that he lost and that there was no electoral fraud, including the current and former leadership of the DOJ, his campaign advisors, his pollsters, his election integrity senior official (who was fired after saying the 2020 election was the most secure in history), and numerous state election officials, among many oth-ers. Notably, all these individuals were Republicans. Acknowledging that truth could have prevented the assault on the Capitol and the death threats and actual deaths that ensued.

† This is remarkably detailed and presumably comes from Pence himself, whom Spe-cial Counsel Jack Smith subpoenaed to testify in the grand jury in DC. In yet another phone call intended to pressure Pence into participating in the plan to thwart the Electoral College vote, a frustrated Donald Trump responded to Pence's refusal to participate in the scheme by insisting that Pence would be remembered as a "wimp"

Act 141.

On or about the **6th day of January 2021, JOHN CHARLES EASTMAN** sent an e-mail to Counsel to the Vice President Greg Jacob that stated:

> "The Senate and House have both violated the Electoral Count Act this evening – they debated the Arizona objections for more than 2 hours. Violation of 3 USC 17. And the VP allowed further debate or statements by leadership after the question had been voted upon. Violation of 3 USC 17. And they had that debate upon motion approved by the VP, in violation of the requirement in 3 USC 15 that after the vote in the separate houses, 'they shall immediately again meet.'
>
> So now that the precedent has been set that the Electoral Count Act is not quite so sacrosanct as was previously claimed, I implore you to consider one more relatively minor violation* and adjourn for 10 days to allow the legislatures to finish their investigations, as well as to allow a full forensic audit of the massive amount of illegal activity that has occurred here. If none of that moves the needle, at least a good portion of the 75 million people who supported President Trump will have seen a process that allowed the illegality to be aired.
>
> John"

This was an overt act in furtherance of the conspiracy.

Act 142.

On or about the **7th day of January 2021, CATHLEEN ALSTON LATHAM** sent a text message to the Chief Operations Officer of SullivanStrickler LLC with the address for the Douglas Municipal Airport in Coffee County, Georgia, to coordinate picking up **SCOTT GRAHAM HALL** from the airport and driving him

---

for adhering to the law. Trump's own conduct since being indicted in four cases, on ninety-one felony counts, exemplifies the bravado that he wanted Pence to model.

* This allegation is striking, as it shows Eastman admitting in his own email to encouraging a violation of law—and notably, justifies the violation on the view that it is "relatively minor," an unusual standard for a lawyer to endorse (to say the least).

to the Coffee County Board of Elections & Registration Office for the purpose of assisting with the unlawful breach of election equipment at the Coffee County Board of Elections & Registration Office. This was an act of racketeering activity under O.C.G.A. § 16-14-3(5) (B) and an overt act in furtherance of the conspiracy.*

Act 143.

On or about the **7th day of January 2021, SCOTT GRA- HAM HALL** and unindicted co-conspirator Individual 24, whose identity is known to the Grand Jury, flew from DeKalb-Peachtree Airport in DeKalb County, Georgia, to Douglas Municipal Airport in Coffee County, Georgia, for the purpose of assisting with the unlawful breach of election equipment at the Coffee County Board of Elections & Registration Office. This was an act of racketeering activity under O.C.G.A. § 16-14-3(5)(B) and an overt act in furtherance of the conspiracy.

Act 144.

On or about the **7th day of January 2021, SIDNEY KATH- ERINE POWELL, CATHLEEN ALSTON LATHAM, SCOTT GRAHAM HALL,** and **MISTY HAMPTON** committed the felony offense of **INTERFERENCE WITH PRIMA- RIES AND ELECTIONS,** in violation of **O.C.G.A. § 21-2-566,** in Coffee County, Georgia, by willfully and unlawfully tampering with electronic ballot markers and tabulating machines in Cof-

---

* Here and in the following acts, the indictment focuses on the scheme to seize Dominion Voting Systems voting machines in Coffee County, Georgia, in order to access each machine's software code. Sidney Powell, and other Trump operatives, may have believed that the information would allow them to establish that the machines were used to flip votes from Trump to Biden or that the machines could be used or manipulated to make that claim. Powell has pled guilty to participating in this conspiracy.

INSIDER NOTE: Dominion Voting Systems sued Fox, Giuliani, and Powell for defamation related to claims of fraudulent operation and manipulation of voting machines in the 2020 election. So far, Dominion has settled its claims against Fox for $787 million; the judge overseeing the Fox suit found that it was "crystal clear" that none of the claims about Dominion and the 2020 election is true.

fee County, Georgia. This was an overt act in furtherance of the conspiracy.

Act 145.

On or about the **7th day of January 2021, SIDNEY KATH-ERINE POWELL, CATHLEEN ALSTON LATHAM, SCOTT GRAHAM HALL,** and **MISTY HAMPTON** committed the felony offense of **UNLAWFUL POSSESSION OF BAL-LOTS,** in violation of **O.C.G.A. § 21-2-574,** in Coffee County, Georgia, by causing certain members of the conspiracy, who were not officers charged by law with the care of ballots and who were not persons entrusted by any such officer with the care of ballots for a purpose required by law, to possess official ballots outside of the polling place in Coffee County, Georgia. This was an overt act in furtherance of the conspiracy.

Act 146.

On or about the **7th day of January 2021, SIDNEY KATH-ERINE POWELL, CATHLEEN ALSTON LATHAM, SCOTT GRAHAM HALL,** and **MISTY HAMPTON** committed the felony offense of **COMPUTER THEFT,** in violation of **O.C.G.A. § 16-9-93(a),** in Coffee County, Georgia, by using a computer with knowledge that such use was without authority and with the intention of taking and appropriating information, data, and software, the property of Dominion Voting Systems Corporation in Coffee County, Georgia. This was an act of racketeering activity under O.C.G.A. § 16-14-3(5)(A)(xix) and an overt act in furtherance of the conspiracy.

Act 147.

On or about the **7th day of January 2021, SIDNEY KATH-ERINE POWELL, CATHLEEN ALSTON LATHAM, SCOTT GRAHAM HALL,** and **MISTY HAMPTON** committed the felony offense of **COMPUTER TRESPASS,** in violation of **O.C.G.A. § 16-9-93(b),** in Coffee County, Georgia, by using a computer with knowledge that such use was without authority and with the intention of removing voter data and Dominion Voting Systems Corporation data from said computer in Coffee County, Georgia. This was an act of racketeering activity under O.C.G.A. § 16-14-3(5) (A)(xix) and an overt act in furtherance of the conspiracy.

Act 148.

On or about the **7th day of January 2021, SIDNEY KATH-ERINE POWELL, CATHLEEN ALSTON LATHAM, SCOTT GRAHAM HALL,** and **MISTY HAMPTON** committed the felony offense of **COMPUTER INVASION OF PRIVACY,** in violation of **O.C.G.A. § 16-9-93(c),** in Coffee County, Georgia, by using a computer with the intention of examining personal voter data with knowledge that such examination was without authority. This was an act of racketeering activity under O.C.G.A. § 16-14-3(5)(A)(xix) and an overt act in furtherance of the conspiracy.

Act 149.

On and between the **6th day of December 2020 and the 7th day of January 2021, SIDNEY KATHERINE POWELL, CATHLEEN ALSTON LATHAM, SCOTT GRAHAM HALL,** and **MISTY HAMPTON** committed the felony offense of **CONSPIRACY TO DEFRAUD THE STATE,** in violation of **O.C.G.A. § 16-10-21,** in Coffee County, Georgia, by unlawfully conspiring and agreeing to commit theft of voter data, property which was under the control of Georgia Secretary of State Brad Raffensperger, a state officer, in his official capacity. This was an act of racketeering activity under O.C.G.A. § 16-14-3(5)(B) and an overt act in furtherance of the conspiracy.

Act 150.

On or about the **9th day of January 2021, the 10th day of January 2021, the 11th day of January 2021, and the 13th day of January 2021,** unindicted co-conspirator Individual 25, whose identity is known to the Grand Jury, unlawfully accessed certain data copied from Dominion Voting Systems equipment at the Coffee County Board of Elections & Registration Office in Coffee County, Georgia, by downloading said data from a server maintained by SullivanStrickler LLC. This was an act of racketeering activity under O.C.G.A. § 16-14-3(5)(B) and an overt act in furtherance of the conspiracy.

Act 151.

On or about the **9th day of January 2021, the 10th day of January 2021, the 11th day of January 2021, the 18th day of January 2021, and the 19th day of January 2021,** unindicted co-conspirator Individual 26, whose identity is unknown to the Grand Jury, unlawfully accessed certain data copied from Dominion Voting Systems equipment at the Coffee County Board of Elections & Registration Office in Coffee County, Georgia, by downloading said data from a server maintained by SullivanStrickler LLC. This was an act of racketeering activity under O.C.G.A. § 16-14-3(5)(B) and an overt act in furtherance of the conspiracy.

Act 152.

On or about the **10th day of January 2021, the 12th day of January 2021, the 13th day of January 2021, the 25th day of February 2021, and the 26th day of February 2021,** unindicted co-conspirator Individual 27, whose identity is unknown to the Grand Jury, unlawfully accessed certain data copied from Dominion Voting Systems equipment at the Coffee County Board of Elections & Registration Office in Coffee County, Georgia, by downloading said data from a server maintained by SullivanStrickler LLC. This was an act of racketeering activity under O.C.G.A. § 16-14-3(5)(B) and an overt act in furtherance of the conspiracy.

Act 153.

On or about the **13th day of January 2021,** unindicted co-conspirator Individual 28, whose identity is known to the Grand Jury, unlawfully accessed certain data copied from Dominion Voting Systems equipment at the Coffee County Board of Elections & Registration Office in Coffee County, Georgia, by downloading said data from a server maintained by SullivanStrickler LLC. This was an act of racketeering activity under O.C.G.A. § 16-14-3(5)(B) and an overt act in furtherance of the conspiracy.

Act 154.

On or about the **18th day of January 2021, MISTY HAMP-TON** allowed unindicted co-conspirators Individual 25 and Individual 29, whose identities are known to the Grand Jury, to access non-public areas of the Coffee County Board of Elections & Registration Office in Coffee County, Georgia, and facilitated their access to Dominion Voting Systems equipment. This was an overt act in furtherance of the conspiracy.

Act 155.

On or about the **22nd day of April 2021,** unindicted co-conspirator Individual 28, whose identity is known to the Grand Jury, sent an e-mail to the Chief Operations Officer of SullivanStrickler LLC directing him to transmit all data copied from Dominion Voting Systems equipment at the Coffee County Board of Elections & Registration Office in Coffee County, Georgia, to unindicted co-conspirator Individual 30, whose identity is known to the Grand Jury, an attorney associated with **SIDNEY KATHERINE POWELL** and the Trump Campaign. This was an act of racketeering activity under O.C.G.A. § 16-14-3(5)(B) and an overt act in furtherance of the conspiracy.

Act 156.

On or about the **17th day of September 2021, DONALD JOHN TRUMP** committed the felony offense of **SOLICITATION OF VIOLATION OF OATH BY PUBLIC OFFICER,** in violation of **O.C.G.A. §§ 16-4-7 and 16-10-1,** in Fulton County, Georgia, by unlawfully soliciting, requesting, and importuning Georgia Secretary of State Brad Raffensperger, a public officer, to engage in conduct constituting the felony offense of Violation of Oath by Public Officer, O.C.G.A. § 16-10-1, by unlawfully "decertifying the Election, or whatever the correct legal remedy is, and announce the true winner," in willful and intentional violation of the terms of the oath of said person as prescribed by law, with intent that said person engage in said conduct. This was an overt act in furtherance of the conspiracy.*

Act 157.

On or about the **17th day of September 2021, DONALD JOHN TRUMP** committed the felony offense of **FALSE STATEMENTS AND WRITINGS,** in violation of **O.C.G.A. § 16-10-20,** in Fulton County, Georgia, by knowingly, willfully, and unlawfully making the following false statement and representation to Georgia Secretary of State Brad Raffensperger:

1.   "As stated to you previously, the number of false and/or irregular votes is far greater than needed to change the Georgia election result";

said statement being within the jurisdiction of the Office of the Georgia Secretary of State and the Georgia Bureau of Investigation, departments and agencies of state government, and county and city law enforcement agencies. This was an act of racketeering activity under O.C.G.A. § 16-14-3(5)(A)(xxii) and an overt act in furtherance of the conspiracy.

Act 158.

On or about the **25th day of April 2022, DAVID JAMES SHAFER** committed the felony offense of **FALSE STATEMENTS AND WRITINGS,** in violation of **O.C.G.A. § 16-10-20,** in Fulton County, Georgia, by knowingly, willfully, and unlawfully making at least one of the following false statements and represen-

---

* The infamous Trump-Raffensperger phone call appears again—this time, as a felony charge against Donald Trump for solicitation of a violation of oath by a public officer.

tations in the presence of Fulton County District Attorney's Office investigators:

1.   That he "attended and convened" the December 14, 2020, meeting of Trump presidential elector nominees in Fulton County, Georgia, but that he did not "call each of the individual members and notify them of the meeting or make any of the other preparations necessary for the meeting";

2.   That a court reporter was not present at the December 14, 2020, meeting of Trump presidential elector nominees in Fulton County, Georgia;

said statements being within the jurisdiction of the Fulton County District Attorney's Office, a department and agency of the government of a county of this state. This was an act of racketeering activity under O.C.G.A. § 16-14-3(5)(A)(xxii) and an overt act in furtherance of the conspiracy.

Act 159.

On or about the **7th day of May 2022, SIDNEY KATHERINE POWELL** made at least one of the following false statements and representations in a sworn deposition with the United States House of Representatives Select Committee to Investigate the January 6th Attack on the United States Capitol:*

1.   That she "didn't have any role in really setting up" efforts to access voting machines in Coffee County, Georgia, or Antrim County, Michigan;

2.   That she was aware there was an "effort by some people" to get access to voting machines in Georgia but that she did not "know what happened with that" and did not "remember whether that was Rudy or other folks."

This was an overt act in furtherance of the conspiracy.

---

* The indictment alleges that Powell made false statements in a deposition conducted as part of the January 6 committee's investigation. If proof of these allegations is credited, they would show that Powell lied to the congressional committee, which is a separate *federal* crime.

Act 160.

On or about the **1st day of September 2022, CATHLEEN ALSTON LATHAM** committed the felony offense of **PERJURY,** in violation of **O.C.G.A. § 16-10-70(a),** in Houston County, Georgia, by knowingly, willfully, and unlawfully making at least one of the following false statements in a deposition in the matter of Curling v. Raffensperger, Case 1:17-cv-02989-AT in the United States District Court for the Northern District of Georgia, a judicial proceeding, after having been administered a lawful oath:*

1.   That she was only present at the Coffee County Board of Elections & Registration Office in Coffee County, Georgia, for "just a few minutes" on January 7, 2021;

2.   That she only "walked into the front part" of the Coffee County Board of Elections & Registration Office on January 7, 2021, and "didn't go into the office";

3.   That she had "no idea" if employees of SullivanStrickler met Eric Chaney at the Coffee County Board of Elections & Registration Office on January 7, 2021;

4.   That she did not see Misty Hampton at the Coffee County Board of Elections & Registration Office on January 7, 2021;

5.   That her only interaction with Scott Hall at the Coffee County Board of Elections & Registration Office on January 7, 2021, was meeting him, speaking to him outside of the office, and then leaving the office;

6.   That she did not see Scott Hall speak to anyone other than herself at the Coffee County Board of Elections & Registration Office on January 7, 2021;

---

* The indictment charges Cathleen Latham with perjury for allegedly lying under oath about her role in the Coffee County voting machines scheme.

INSIDER NOTE: Crimes such as perjury and obstruction are both separate crimes in and of themselves and highly probative of—that is, very likely to demonstrate—the defendant's intent with respect to the underlying crime. When trying to prove these charges, prosecutors will implore a jury to ask themselves why a person would lie about their underlying conduct if they thought it was entirely lawful.

said statements being material to the accused's own involvement in the January 7, 2021, unlawful breach of election equipment at the Coffee County Board of Elections & Registration Office and to the accused's communications with others involved, the issues in question. This was an act of racketeering activity under O.C.G.A. § 16-14-3(5)(A)(xxv) and an overt act in furtherance of the conspiracy.

Act 161.

On or about the **15th day of September 2022, ROBERT DAVID CHEELEY** committed the felony offense of **PERJURY,** in violation of **O.C.G.A. § 16-10-70(a),** in Fulton County, Georgia, by knowingly, willfully, and unlawfully making at least one of the following false statements before the Fulton County Special Purpose Grand Jury, a judicial proceeding, after having been administered a lawful oath:*

1. That he was unaware of the December 14, 2020, meeting of Trump presidential elector nominees in Fulton County, Georgia, until after the meeting had already taken place;

2. That he had no substantive conversations with anyone concerning the December 14, 2020, meeting of Trump presidential elector nominees in Fulton County, Georgia, until after the meeting had already taken place;

3. That he never suggested to anyone that the Trump presidential elector nominees in Georgia should meet on December 14, 2020;

4. That the only communication he had with John Eastman concerning the November 3, 2020, presidential election was for the purpose of connecting Eastman to Georgia Senator Brandon Beach and unindicted co-conspirator Individual 8, whose identity is known to the Grand Jury, for possible legal representation;

---

* Robert Cheeley is accused of lying under oath to the Fulton County special grand jury charged with investigating election interference in Georgia.

5.   That he never worked to connect John Eastman with any Georgia legislators other than Georgia Senator Brandon Beach and unindicted co-conspirator Individual 8, whose identity is known to the Grand Jury;

said statements being material to the accused's own involvement in the December 14, 2020, meeting of Trump presidential elector nominees in Fulton County, Georgia, and to the accused's communications with others involved in the meeting, the issues in question. This was an act of racketeering activity under O.C.G.A. § 16-14-3(5) (A)(xxv) and an overt act in furtherance of the conspiracy.

* * *

The acts set forth above were committed in furtherance of the conspiracy alleged above and had the same and similar intents, results, accomplices, victims, and methods of commission and otherwise were interrelated by distinguishing characteristics and were not isolated acts.[*]

COUNT 2 of 41

And the Grand Jurors aforesaid, in the name and behalf of the citizens of Georgia, do charge and accuse **RUDOLPH WILLIAM LOUIS GIULIANI, JOHN CHARLES EASTMAN, JENNA LYNN ELLIS,** and **RAY STALLINGS SMITH III** with the offense of **SOLICITATION OF VIOLATION OF OATH BY PUBLIC OFFICER, O.C.G.A. §§ 16-4-7 & 16-10-1,** for the said accused, individually and as persons concerned in the commission of a crime, and together with unindicted co-conspirators, in the County of Fulton and State of Georgia, on the **3rd day of December 2020,** unlawfully solicited, requested, and importuned certain public officers then serving as elected members of the Georgia Senate and present at a Senate Judiciary Subcommittee meeting, includ-

---

[*] All of the foregoing acts were allegedly undertaken in furtherance of the criminal conspiracy. As a general matter, all co-conspirators are liable, whether they specifically committed the act or not, for each and every act undertaken in furtherance of the conspiracy by any conspirator.

ing unindicted co-conspirator Individual 8, whose identity is known to the Grand Jury, Senators Lee Anderson, Brandon Beach, Matt Brass, Greg Dolezal, Steve Gooch, Tyler Harper, Bill Heath, Jen Jordan, John F. Kennedy, William Ligon, Elena Parent, Michael Rhett, Carden Summers, and Blake Tillery, to engage in conduct constituting the felony offense of Violation of Oath by Public Officer, O.C.G.A. § 16-10-1, by unlawfully appointing presidential electors from the State of Georgia, in willful and intentional violation of the terms of the oath of said persons as prescribed by law, with intent that said persons engage in said conduct, said date being a material element of the offense, contrary to the laws of said State, the good order, peace and dignity thereof;*

COUNT 3 of 41

And the Grand Jurors aforesaid, in the name and behalf of the citizens of Georgia, do charge and accuse **RUDOLPH WILLIAM LOUIS GIULIANI** with the offense of **FALSE STATEMENTS AND WRITINGS, O.C.G.A. § 16-10-20,**† for the said accused, in the County of Fulton and State of Georgia, on or about the **3rd day of December 2020,** knowingly, willfully, and unlawfully made at least one of the following false statements and representations to members of the Georgia Senate present at a Senate Judiciary Subcommittee meeting:

1. That at least 96,600 mail-in ballots were counted in the November 3, 2020, presidential election in Georgia, despite there being no record of those ballots having been returned to a county elections office;

---

* The indictment charges four Trump lawyers—Giuliani, Eastman, Ellis, and Smith—with soliciting public officers to violate their oaths. This charge relates to the quartet's alleged efforts to advance a slate of fake electors. Here, Ellis's plea deal could prove pivotal, as she is able to relate to prosecutors the nature of this group's discussions with regard to the fake electors scheme.

† Giuliani is also individually charged with another crime: making false statements. Here, the grand jury alleges that Giuliani made false claims about voter fraud in Georgia to a Georgia Senate subcommittee.

2. That a Dominion Voting Systems machine used in the November 3, 2020, presidential election in Antrim County, Michigan, mistakenly recorded 6,000 votes for Joseph R. Biden when the votes were actually cast for Donald Trump;

said statements being within the jurisdiction of the Office of the Georgia Secretary of State and the Georgia Bureau of Investigation, departments and agencies of state government, and county and city law enforcement agencies, contrary to the laws of said State, the good order, peace and dignity thereof;

COUNT 4 of 41

And the Grand Jurors aforesaid, in the name and behalf of the citizens of Georgia, do charge and accuse **RAY STALLINGS SMITH III** with the offense of **FALSE STATEMENTS AND WRITINGS, O.C.G.A. § 16-10-20,** for the said accused, in the County of Fulton and State of Georgia, on or about the **3rd day of December 2020,** knowingly, willfully, and unlawfully made at least one of the following false statements and representations to members of the Georgia Senate present at a Senate Judiciary Subcommittee meeting:[*]

1. That 2,506 felons voted illegally in the November 3, 2020, presidential election in Georgia;

2. That 66,248 underage people illegally registered to vote before their seventeenth birthday prior to the November 3, 2020, presidential election in Georgia;

3. That at least 2,423 people voted in the November 3, 2020, presidential election in Georgia who were not listed as registered to vote;

4. That 1,043 people voted in the November 3, 2020, presidential election in Georgia who had illegally registered to vote using a post office box;

---

[*] Smith is also charged with lying about voter fraud in Georgia to the Georgia Senate subcommittee.

5. That 10,315 or more dead people voted in the November 3, 2020, presidential election in Georgia;

6. That Fulton County election workers at State Farm Arena ordered poll watchers and members of the media to leave the tabulation area on the night of November 3, 2020, and continued to operate after ordering everyone to leave;

said statements being within the jurisdiction of the Office of the Georgia Secretary of State and the Georgia Bureau of Investigation, departments and agencies of state government, and county and city law enforcement agencies, contrary to the laws of said State, the good order, peace and dignity thereof;

COUNT 5 of 41[*]

And the Grand Jurors aforesaid, in the name and behalf of the citizens of Georgia, do charge and accuse **DONALD JOHN TRUMP** with the offense of **SOLICITATION OF VIOLATION OF OATH BY PUBLIC OFFICER, O.C.G.A. §§ 16-4-7 & 16-10-1,** for the said accused, in the County of Fulton and State of Georgia, on or about the **7th day of December 2020,** unlawfully solicited, requested, and importuned Speaker of the Georgia House of Representatives David Ralston, a public officer, to engage in conduct constituting the felony offense of Violation of Oath by Public Officer, O.C.G.A. § 16-10-1, by calling for a special session of the Georgia General Assembly for the purpose of unlawfully appointing presidential electors from the State of Georgia, in willful and intentional violation of the terms of the oath of said person as pre-

---

[*] This count relates to Trump's December 7, 2020, phone call with then–Georgia House Speaker David Ralston.

INSIDER NOTE: In March 2023, Emily Kohrs, the foreperson of the Fulton County special grand jury that investigated claims of election interference and made recommendations for prosecution, confirmed that the special grand jury heard a recording of the phone call between Trump and Ralston. Kohrs recounted some of the substance of the recorded call. According to Kohrs, on the call, Trump asked Ralston who would stop him from holding a special session, to which Ralston responded, "A federal judge, that's who." Ralston served as Georgia House Speaker for more than a decade. He died in November 2022.

scribed by law, with intent that said person engage in said conduct, contrary to the laws of said State, the good order, peace and dignity thereof;

COUNT 6 of 41

And the Grand Jurors aforesaid, in the name and behalf of the citizens of Georgia, do charge and accuse **RUDOLPH WILLIAM LOUIS GIULIANI** and **RAY STALLINGS SMITH III** with the offense of **SOLICITATION OF VIOLATION OF OATH BY PUBLIC OFFICER, O.C.G.A. §§ 16-4-7 & 16-10-1,** for the said accused, individually and as persons concerned in the commission of a crime, and together with unindicted co-conspirators, in the County of Fulton and State of Georgia, on the **10th day of December 2020,** unlawfully solicited, requested, and importuned certain public officers then serving as elected members of the Georgia House of Representatives and present at a House Governmental Affairs Committee meeting, including Representatives Shaw Blackmon, Jon Burns, Barry Fleming, Todd Jones, Bee Nguyen, Mary Margaret Oliver, Alan Powell, Renitta Shannon, Robert Trammell, Scot Turner, and Bruce Williamson, to engage in conduct constituting the felony offense of Violation of Oath by Public Officer, O.C.G.A. § 16-10-1, by unlawfully appointing presidential electors from the State of Georgia, in willful and intentional violation of the terms of the oath of said persons as prescribed by law, with intent that said persons engage in said conduct, said date being a material element of the offense, contrary to the laws of said State, the good order, peace and dignity thereof;

COUNT 7 of 41[*]

And the Grand Jurors aforesaid, in the name and behalf of the citizens of Georgia, do charge and accuse **RUDOLPH WILLIAM**

---

[*] Giuliani is charged with the crime of making false statements about voter fraud, including the claim that Freeman and Moss, the Georgia poll workers, were passing around USB ports "like vials of heroin or cocaine."

LOUIS GIULIANI with the offense of **FALSE STATEMENTS AND WRITINGS, O.C.G.A.** § **16-10-20,** for the said accused, in the County of Fulton and State of Georgia, on or about the **10th day of December 2020,** knowingly, willfully, and unlawfully made at least one of the following false statements and representations to members of the Georgia House of Representatives present at a House Governmental Affairs Committee meeting:

1. That it is quite clear from the State Farm Arena video from November 3, 2020, that Fulton County election workers were stealing votes and that Georgia officials were covering up a crime in plain sight;

2. That at State Farm Arena on November 3, 2020, Democratic officials "got rid of all of the reporters, all the observers, anyone that couldn't be trusted," used the excuse of a watermain break, cleared out the voting area and then "went about their dirty, crooked business";

3. That between 12,000 and 24,000 ballots were illegally counted by Fulton County election workers at State Farm Arena on November 3, 2020;

4. That in Michigan, there were 700,000 more ballots counted than were sent out to voters in the November 3, 2020, presidential election, which was accounted for by quadruple counting ballots;

5. That Ruby Freeman, Shaye Moss, and an unidentified man were "quite obviously surreptitiously passing around USB ports as if they're vials of heroin or cocaine" at State Farm Arena to be used to "infiltrate the crooked Dominion voting machines";

6. That 96,600 mail-in ballots were counted in the November 3, 2020, presidential election in Georgia, despite there being no record of those ballots having been returned to a county elections office;

said statements being within the jurisdiction of the Office of the Georgia Secretary of State and the Georgia Bureau of Investigation, departments and agencies of state government, and county and city law enforcement agencies, contrary to the laws of said State, the good order, peace and dignity thereof;

COUNT 8 of 41*

And the Grand Jurors aforesaid, in the name and behalf of the citizens of Georgia, do charge and accuse **DAVID JAMES SHAFER, SHAWN MICAH TRESHER STILL,** and **CATHLEEN ALSTON LATHAM** with the offense of **IMPERSONATING A PUBLIC OFFICER, O.C.G.A. § 16-10-23,** for the said accused, individually and as persons concerned in the commission of a crime, and together with unindicted co-conspirators, in the County of Fulton and State of Georgia, on or about the **14th day of December 2020,** unlawfully falsely held themselves out as the duly elected and qualified presidential electors from the State of Georgia, public officers, with intent to mislead the President of the United States Senate, the Archivist of the United States, the Georgia Secretary of State, and the Chief Judge of the United States District Court for the Northern District of Georgia into believing that they actually were such officers by placing in the United States mail to said persons a document titled "CERTIFICATE OF THE VOTES OF THE 2020 ELECTORS FROM GEORGIA," contrary to the laws of said State, the good order, peace and dignity thereof;

COUNT 9 of 41†

And the Grand Jurors aforesaid, in the name and behalf of the citizens of Georgia, do charge and accuse **DONALD JOHN**

---

* This count pertains to the effort to substitute Georgia's electors with a slate of fake electors—here, some of the alleged fake electors are charged with impersonating a public officer, in violation of Georgia law. Also charged is David Shafer, the former chairman of the Georgia Republican Party, who allegedly presided over the meeting of the fake electors.

† This count charges Trump, Giuliani, Eastman, Chesebro, and others with coordinating to have the fake electors present themselves as legitimate electors. Here, Chesebro's cooperation with prosecutors could be pivotal, as he will be able to relate the precise nature of the group's discussions and plans regarding the fake electors scheme.

TRUMP, RUDOLPH WILLIAM LOUIS GIULIANI, JOHN CHARLES EASTMAN, KENNETH JOHN CHESEBRO, RAY STALLINGS SMITH III, ROBERT DAVID CHEE-LEY, and **MICHAEL A. ROMAN** with the offense of **CONSPIRACY TO COMMIT IMPERSONATING A PUBLIC OFFICER, O.C.G.A. §§ 16-4-8 & 16-10-23,** for the said accused, individually and as persons concerned in the commission of a crime, and together with indicted and unindicted co-conspirators, in the County of Fulton and State of Georgia, on and between the **6th day of December 2020 and the 14th day of December 2020,** unlawfully conspired to cause certain individuals to falsely hold themselves out as the duly elected and qualified presidential electors from the State of Georgia, public officers, with intent to mislead the President of the United States Senate, the Archivist of the United States, the Georgia Secretary of State, and the Chief Judge of the United States District Court for the Northern District of Georgia into believing that they actually were such officers;

And the Defendants named in Count 8, acting as co-conspirators, as described above and incorporated by reference as if fully set forth herein, falsely held themselves out as said public officers by placing in the United States mail to said persons a document titled "CERTIFICATE OF THE VOTES OF THE 2020 ELECTORS FROM GEORGIA" in Fulton County, Georgia, which was an overt act to effect the object of the conspiracy, contrary to the laws of said State, the good order, peace and dignity thereof;

COUNT 10 of 41[*]

And the Grand Jurors aforesaid, in the name and behalf of the citizens of Georgia, do charge and accuse **DAVID JAMES SHAFER, SHAWN MICAH TRESHER STILL,** and **CATHLEEN ALSTON LATHAM** with the offense of **FORGERY IN THE FIRST DEGREE, O.C.G.A. § 16-9-1(b),** for the said accused, individually and as persons concerned in the commission

---

[*] Those accused of impersonating a public officer are further charged with forgery—namely, creating a false certificate of the electors' votes.

of a crime, and together with unindicted co-conspirators, in the County of Fulton and State of Georgia, on or about the **14th day of December 2020,** unlawfully and with the intent to defraud, knowingly made a document titled "CERTIFICATE OF THE VOTES OF THE 2020 ELECTORS FROM GEORGIA," a writing other than a check, in such manner that the writing as made purports to have been made by authority of the duly elected and qualified presidential electors from the State of Georgia, who did not give such authority, and uttered and delivered said document to the Archivist of the United States, contrary to the laws of said State, the good order, peace and dignity thereof;

COUNT 11 of 41[*]

And the Grand Jurors aforesaid, in the name and behalf of the citizens of Georgia, do charge and accuse **DONALD JOHN TRUMP, RUDOLPH WILLIAM LOUIS GIULIANI, JOHN CHARLES EASTMAN, KENNETH JOHN CHESEBRO, RAY STALLINGS SMITH III, ROBERT DAVID CHEELEY,** and **MICHAEL A. ROMAN** with the offense of **CONSPIRACY TO COMMIT FORGERY IN THE FIRST DEGREE, O.C.G.A. §§ 16-4-8 & 16-9-1(b),** for the said accused, individually and as persons concerned in the commission of a crime, and together with indicted and unindicted co-conspirators, in the County of Fulton and State of Georgia, on and between the **6th day of December 2020 and the 14th day of December 2020,** unlawfully conspired, with the intent to defraud, to knowingly make a document titled "CERTIFICATE OF THE VOTES OF THE 2020 ELECTORS FROM GEORGIA," a writing other than a check, in such manner that the writing as made purports to have been made by authority of the duly elected and qualified presidential electors from the State of Georgia, who did not give such authority, and to utter and deliver said document to the Archivist of the United States;

---

[*] Trump and others are charged with conspiring to have these fake electors commit a forgery—the creation of the false certificate of votes.

And the Defendants named in Count 10, acting as co-conspirators, as described above and incorporated by reference as if fully set forth herein, made said document in Fulton County, Georgia, and uttered and delivered said document to the Archivist of the United States in Fulton County, Georgia, which were overt acts to effect the object of the conspiracy, contrary to the laws of said State, the good order, peace and dignity thereof;

COUNT 12 of 41

And the Grand Jurors aforesaid, in the name and behalf of the citizens of Georgia, do charge and accuse **DAVID JAMES SHAFER, SHAWN MICAH TRESHER STILL,** and **CATHLEEN ALSTON LATHAM** with the offense of **FALSE STATEMENTS AND WRITINGS, O.C.G.A. § 16-10-20,** for the said accused, individually and as persons concerned in the commission of a crime, and together with unindicted co-conspirators, in the County of Fulton and State of Georgia, on or about the **14th day of December 2020,** knowingly, willfully, and unlawfully made and used a false document titled "CERTIFICATE OF THE VOTES OF THE 2020 ELECTORS FROM GEORGIA," with knowledge that said document contained the false statement, "WE, THE UNDERSIGNED, being the duly elected and qualified Electors for President and Vice President of the United States of America from the State of Georgia, do hereby certify the following," said document being within the jurisdiction of the Office of the Georgia Secretary of State and the Office of the Governor of Georgia, departments and agencies of state government, contrary to the laws of said State, the good order, peace and dignity thereof;

COUNT 13 of 41

And the Grand Jurors aforesaid, in the name and behalf of the citizens of Georgia, do charge and accuse **DONALD JOHN TRUMP, RUDOLPH WILLIAM LOUIS GIULIANI, JOHN CHARLES EASTMAN, KENNETH JOHN CHESEBRO, RAY STALLINGS SMITH III, ROBERT DAVID CHEE-**

LEY, and **MICHAEL A. ROMAN** with the offense of **CONSPIRACY TO COMMIT FALSE STATEMENTS AND WRITINGS, O.C.G.A. §§ 16-4-8 & 16-10-20,** for the said accused, individually and as persons concerned in the commission of a crime, and together with indicted and unindicted co-conspirators, in the County of Fulton and State of Georgia, on and between the **6th day of December 2020 and the 14th day of December 2020,** unlawfully conspired to knowingly and willfully make and use a false document titled "CERTIFICATE OF THE VOTES OF THE 2020 ELECTORS FROM GEORGIA," with knowledge that said document contained the false statement, "WE, THE UNDERSIGNED, being the duly elected and qualified Electors for President and Vice President of the United States of America from the State of Georgia, do hereby certify the following," said document being within the jurisdiction of the Office of the Georgia Secretary of State and the Office of the Governor of Georgia, departments and agencies of state government;

And the Defendants named in Count 12, acting as co-conspirators, as described above and incorporated by reference as if fully set forth herein, made and used said document in Fulton County, Georgia, which were overt acts to effect the object of the conspiracy, contrary to the laws of said State, the good order, peace and dignity thereof;

COUNT 14 of 41

And the Grand Jurors aforesaid, in the name and behalf of the citizens of Georgia, do charge and accuse **DAVID JAMES SHAFER, SHAWN MICAH TRESHER STILL,** and **CATHLEEN ALSTON LATHAM** with the offense of **CRIMINAL ATTEMPT TO COMMIT FILING FALSE DOCUMENTS, O.C.G.A. §§ 16-4-1 & 16-10-20.1(b)(1),** for the said accused, individually and as persons concerned in the commission of a crime, and together with unindicted co-conspirators, in the County of Fulton and State of Georgia, on or about the **14th day of December 2020,** unlawfully, with intent to commit the crime of Filing False Documents, O.C.G.A. § 16-10-20.1(b)(1), placed in the United States mail a document titled "CERTIFICATE OF THE VOTES OF THE 2020 ELECTORS FROM GEORGIA," addressed to Chief Judge, U.S. District Court, Northern District of Georgia, 2188 Richard D. Russell Federal Office Building and U.S. Courthouse, 75 Ted Turner Drive, SW, Atlanta, GA 30303, a substantial step toward the commission of Filing False Documents, O.C.G.A. § 16-10-20.1(b)(1), with intent to knowingly file, enter, and record said document in a court of the United States, having reason to know that said document contained the materially false statement, "WE, THE UNDERSIGNED, being the duly elected and qualified Electors for President and Vice President of the United States of America from the State of Georgia, do hereby certify the following," contrary to the laws of said State, the good order, peace and dignity thereof;

COUNT 15 of 41*

And the Grand Jurors aforesaid, in the name and behalf of the citizens of Georgia, do charge and accuse **DONALD JOHN TRUMP, RUDOLPH WILLIAM LOUIS GIULIANI, JOHN CHARLES EASTMAN, KENNETH JOHN CHESEBRO, RAY STALLINGS SMITH III, ROBERT DAVID CHEELEY,** and **MICHAEL A. ROMAN** with the offense of **CONSPIRACY TO COMMIT FILING FALSE DOCUMENTS, O.C.G.A. §§ 16-4-8 & 16-10-20.1(b)(1),** for the said accused, individually and as persons concerned in the commission of a crime, and together with indicted and unindicted co-conspirators, in the County of Fulton and State of Georgia, on and between the **6th day of December 2020 and the 14th day of December 2020,** unlawfully conspired to knowingly file, enter, and record a document titled "CERTIFICATE OF THE VOTES OF THE 2020 ELECTORS FROM GEORGIA," in a court of the United States, having reason to know that said document contained the materially false statement,

---

* Chesebro pled guilty to this count on October 20, 2023, as part of a plea agreement with the Georgia prosecutors.

"WE, THE UNDERSIGNED, being the duly elected and qualified Electors for President and Vice President of the United States of America from the State of Georgia, do hereby certify the following";

And the Defendants named in Count 14, acting as co-conspirators, as described above and incorporated by reference as if fully set forth herein, placed in the United States mail said document, addressed to Chief Judge, U.S. District Court, Northern District of Georgia, 2188 Richard D. Russell Federal Office Building and U.S. Courthouse, 75 Ted Turner Drive, SW, Atlanta, GA 30303, in Fulton County, Georgia, which was an overt act to effect the object of the conspiracy, contrary to the laws of said State, the good order, peace and dignity thereof;

COUNT 16 of 41

And the Grand Jurors aforesaid, in the name and behalf of the citizens of Georgia, do charge and accuse **DAVID JAMES SHA-FER** and **SHAWN MICAH TRESHER STILL** with the offense of **FORGERY IN THE FIRST DEGREE, O.C.G.A. § 16-9-1(b),** for the said accused, individually and as persons concerned in the commission of a crime, and together with unindicted co-conspirators, in the County of Fulton and State of Georgia, on or about the **14th day of December 2020,** unlawfully and with the intent to defraud, knowingly made a document titled "RE: Notice of Filling of Electoral College Vacancy," a writing other than a check, in such manner that the writing as made purports to have been made by the authority of the duly elected and qualified presidential electors from the State of Georgia, who did not give such authority, and uttered and delivered said document to the Archivist of the United States and the Office of the Governor of Georgia, contrary to the laws of said State, the good order, peace and dignity thereof;

COUNT 17 of 41

And the Grand Jurors aforesaid, in the name and behalf of the citizens of Georgia, do charge and accuse **DONALD JOHN TRUMP, RUDOLPH WILLIAM LOUIS GIULIANI, JOHN CHARLES EASTMAN, KENNETH JOHN CHESEBRO,**

RAY STALLINGS SMITH III, ROBERT DAVID CHEELEY, and **MICHAEL A. ROMAN** with the offense of **CONSPIRACY TO COMMIT FORGERY IN THE FIRST DEGREE, O.C.G.A. §§ 16-4-8 & 16-9-1(b),** for the said accused, individually and as persons concerned in the commission of a crime, and together with indicted and unindicted co-conspirators, in the County of Fulton and State of Georgia, on and between the **6th day of December 2020 and the 14th day of December 2020,** unlawfully conspired, with the intent to defraud, to knowingly make a document titled "RE: Notice of Filling of Electoral College Vacancy," a writing other than a check, in such manner that the writing as made purports to have been made by the authority of the duly elected and qualified presidential electors from the State of Georgia, who did not give such authority, and to utter and deliver said document to the Archivist of the United States and the Office of the Governor of Georgia;

And the Defendants named in Count 16, acting as co-conspirators, as described above and incorporated by reference as if fully set forth herein, made said document in Fulton County, Georgia, and uttered and delivered said document to the Archivist of the United States and the Office of the Governor of Georgia in Fulton County, Georgia, which were overt acts to effect the object of the conspiracy, contrary to the laws of said State, the good order, peace and dignity thereof;

COUNT 18 of 41

And the Grand Jurors aforesaid, in the name and behalf of the citizens of Georgia, do charge and accuse **DAVID JAMES SHAFER** and **SHAWN MICAH TRESHER STILL** with the offense of **FALSE STATEMENTS AND WRITINGS, O.C.G.A. § 16-10-20,** for the said accused, individually and as persons concerned in the commission of a crime, and together with unindicted co-conspirators, in the County of Fulton and State of Georgia, on or about the **14th day of December 2020,** knowingly, willfully, and unlawfully made and used a false document titled "RE: Notice of Filling of Electoral College Vacancy," with knowledge that said document contained the false statements that **DAVID JAMES SHA-**

FER was Chairman of the 2020 Georgia Electoral College Meeting and **SHAWN MICAH TRESHER STILL** was Secretary of the 2020 Georgia Electoral College Meeting, said document being within the jurisdiction of the Office of the Georgia Secretary of State and the Office of the Governor of Georgia, departments and agencies of state government, contrary to the laws of said State, the good order, peace and dignity thereof;

COUNT 19 of 41

And the Grand Jurors aforesaid, in the name and behalf of the citizens of Georgia, do charge and accuse **DONALD JOHN TRUMP, RUDOLPH WILLIAM LOUIS GIULIANI, JOHN CHARLES EASTMAN, KENNETH JOHN CHESEBRO, RAY STALLINGS SMITH III, ROBERT DAVID CHEELEY** and **MICHAEL A. ROMAN** with the offense of **CONSPIRACY TO COMMIT FALSE STATEMENTS AND WRITINGS, O.C.G.A. §§ 16-4-8 & 16-10-20,** for the said accused, individually and as persons concerned in the commission of a crime, and together with indicted and unindicted co-conspirators, in the County of Fulton and State of Georgia, on and between the **6th day of December 2020 and the 14th day of December 2020,** unlawfully conspired to knowingly and willfully make and use a false document titled "RE: Notice of Filling of Electoral College Vacancy," with knowledge that said document contained the false statements that **DAVID JAMES SHAFER** was Chairman of the 2020 Georgia Electoral College Meeting and **SHAWN MICAH TRESHER STILL** was Secretary of the 2020 Georgia Electoral College Meeting, said document being within the jurisdiction of the Office of the Georgia Secretary of State and the Office of the Governor of Georgia, departments and agencies of state government;

And the Defendants named in Count 18, acting as co-conspirators, as described above and incorporated by reference as if fully set forth herein, made and used said document in Fulton County, Georgia, which were overt acts to effect the object of the conspiracy, contrary to the laws of said State, the good order, peace and dignity thereof;

COUNT 20 of 41

And the Grand Jurors aforesaid, in the name and behalf of the citizens of Georgia, do charge and accuse **STEPHEN CLIFF-GARD LEE** with the offense of **CRIMINAL ATTEMPT TO COMMIT INFLUENCING WITNESSES, O.C.G.A. §§ 16-4-1 & 16-10-93(b)(1)(A),** for the said accused, in the County of Fulton and State of Georgia, on the **14th day of December 2020,** unlawfully, with intent to commit the crime of Influencing Witnesses, O.C.G.A. § 16-10-93(b)(1)(A), traveled to the home of Ruby Freeman, a Fulton County, Georgia, election worker, and spoke to her neighbor, a substantial step toward the commission of Influencing Witnesses, O.C.G.A. § 16-10-93(b)(1)(A), with intent to knowingly engage in misleading conduct toward Ruby Freeman, by purporting to offer her help, and with intent to influence her testimony in an official proceeding in Fulton County, Georgia, concerning events at State Farm Arena in the November 3, 2020, presidential election in Georgia, said date being a material element of the offense, contrary to the laws of said State, the good order, peace and dignity thereof;

COUNT 21 of 41

And the Grand Jurors aforesaid, in the name and behalf of the citizens of Georgia, do charge and accuse **STEPHEN CLIFF-GARD LEE** with the offense of **CRIMINAL ATTEMPT TO COMMIT INFLUENCING WITNESSES, O.C.G.A. §§ 16-4-1 & 16-10-93(b)(1)(A),** for the said accused, in the County of Fulton and State of Georgia, on the **15th day of December 2020,** unlawfully, with intent to commit the crime of Influencing Witnesses, O.C.G.A. § 16-10-93(b)(1)(A), traveled to the home of Ruby Freeman, a Fulton County, Georgia, election worker, and knocked on her door, a substantial step toward the commission of Influencing Witnesses, O.C.G.A. § 16-10-93(b)(1)(A), with intent to knowingly engage in misleading conduct toward Ruby Freeman, by purporting to offer her help, and with intent to influence her testimony in an official proceeding in Fulton County, Georgia, concerning events at

State Farm Arena in the November 3, 2020, presidential election in Georgia, said date being a material element of the offense, contrary to the laws of said State, the good order, peace and dignity thereof;

COUNT 22 of 41[*]

And the Grand Jurors aforesaid, in the name and behalf of the citizens of Georgia, do charge and accuse **JEFFREY BOSSERT CLARK** with the offense of **CRIMINAL ATTEMPT TO COMMIT FALSE STATEMENTS AND WRITINGS, O.C.G.A. §§ 16-4-1 & 16-10-20,** for the said accused, individually and as a person concerned in the commission of a crime, and together with unindicted co-conspirators, in the County of Fulton and State of Georgia, on and between the **28th day of December 2020 and the 2nd day of January 2021,** unlawfully, with intent to commit the crime of False Statements and Writings, O.C.G.A. § 16-10-20, knowingly and willfully made a false writing and document knowing the same to contain the false statement that the United States Department of Justice had "identified significant concerns that may have impacted the outcome of the election in multiple States, including the State of Georgia," said statement being within the jurisdiction of the Office of the Georgia Secretary of State and the Georgia Bureau of Investigation, departments and agencies of state government, and county and city law enforcement agencies;

And, on or about the **28th day of December 2020,** the said accused sent an e-mail to Acting United States Attorney General Jeffrey Rosen and Acting United States Deputy Attorney General Richard Donoghue and requested authorization to send said false writing and document to Georgia Governor Brian Kemp, Speaker of the Georgia House of Rep-

---

[*] This charge focuses on Jeffrey Clark's efforts to bolster claims of voter fraud in Georgia. According to the indictment, Clark drafted a letter claiming that investigators had identified significant concerns regarding the Georgia election results. DOJ officials prevented Clark from sending the letter to the Georgia authorities because it was false. That is why Clark is charged with criminal *attempt* to commit false statements for drafting and trying to send the letter.

resentatives David Ralston, and President Pro Tempore of the Georgia Senate Butch Miller;

And, on or about the **2nd day of January 2021,** the said accused met with Acting United States Attorney General Jeffrey Rosen and Acting United States Deputy Attorney General Richard Donoghue and requested authorization to send said false writing and document to Georgia Governor Brian Kemp, Speaker of the Georgia House of Representatives David Ralston, and President Pro Tempore of the Georgia Senate Butch Miller;

And said acts constituted substantial steps toward the commission of False Statements and Writings, O.C.G.A. § 16-10-20, and said conduct committed outside the state of Georgia constituted an attempt to commit a crime within the state of Georgia, pursuant to O.C.G.A. § 17-2-1(b)(2), contrary to the laws of said State, the good order, peace and dignity thereof;

COUNT 23 of 41

And the Grand Jurors aforesaid, in the name and behalf of the citizens of Georgia, do charge and accuse **RUDOLPH WILLIAM LOUIS GIULIANI, RAY STALLINGS SMITH III,** and **ROBERT DAVID CHEELEY** with the offense of **SOLICITATION OF VIOLATION OF OATH BY PUBLIC OFFICER, O.C.G.A. §§ 16-4-7 & 16-10-1,** for the said accused, individually and as persons concerned in the commission of a crime, and together with unindicted co-conspirators, in the County of Fulton and State of Georgia, on the **30th day of December 2020,** unlawfully solicited, requested, and importuned certain public officers then serving as elected members of the Georgia Senate and present at a Senate Judiciary Subcommittee meeting, including unindicted co-conspirator Individual 8, whose identity is known to the Grand Jury, Senators Brandon Beach, Bill Heath, William Ligon, Michael Rhett, and Blake Tillery, to engage in conduct constituting the felony offense of Violation of Oath by Public Officer, O.C.G.A. § 16-10-1, by unlawfully appointing presidential electors from the State of Georgia, in willful and intentional violation of the terms of the oath of said persons as prescribed by law, with intent that said persons engage in said conduct, said date being a material element of the offense, contrary to the laws of said State, the good order, peace and dignity thereof;

COUNT 24 of 41

And the Grand Jurors aforesaid, in the name and behalf of the citizens of Georgia, do charge and accuse **RUDOLPH WILLIAM LOUIS GIULIANI** with the offense of **FALSE STATEMENTS AND WRITINGS, O.C.G.A. § 16-10-20,** for the said accused, in the County of Fulton and State of Georgia, on or about the **30th day of December 2020,** knowingly, willfully, and unlawfully made at least one of the following false statements and representations to members of the Georgia Senate present at a Senate Judiciary Subcommittee meeting:

1. That Fulton County election workers fraudulently counted certain ballots as many as five times at State Farm Arena on November 3, 2020;

2. That 2,560 felons voted illegally in the November 3, 2020, presidential election in Georgia;

3. That 10,315 dead people voted in the November 3, 2020, presidential election in Georgia;

said statements being within the jurisdiction of the Office of the Georgia Secretary of State and the Georgia Bureau of Investigation, departments and agencies of state government, and county and city law enforcement agencies, contrary to the laws of said State, the good order, peace and dignity thereof;

COUNT 25 of 41

And the Grand Jurors aforesaid, in the name and behalf of the citizens of Georgia, do charge and accuse **RAY STALLINGS SMITH III** with the offense of **FALSE STATEMENTS AND WRITINGS, O.C.G.A. § 16-10-20,** for the said accused, in the County of Fulton and State of Georgia, on or about the **30th day of December 2020,** knowingly, willfully, and unlawfully made at least one of the following false statements and representations to members of the Georgia Senate present at a Senate Judiciary Subcommittee meeting:

1. That Georgia Secretary of State General Counsel Ryan Germany stated that his office had sent letters to 8,000 people who voted illegally in the November 3, 2020, presidential election and told them not to vote in the January 5, 2021, runoff election;

2. That the Georgia Secretary of State admitted "that they had a 90% accuracy rate" in the November 3, 2020, presidential election and that "there's still a 10% margin that's not accurate";

said statements being within the jurisdiction of the Office of the Georgia Secretary of State and the Georgia Bureau of Investigation, departments and agencies of state government, and county and city law enforcement agencies, contrary to the laws of said State, the good order, peace and dignity thereof;

COUNT 26 of 41

And the Grand Jurors aforesaid, in the name and behalf of the citizens of Georgia, do charge and accuse **ROBERT DAVID CHEELEY** with the offense of **FALSE STATEMENTS AND WRITINGS, O.C.G.A. § 16-10-20,** for the said accused, in the County of Fulton and State of Georgia, on or about the **30th day of December 2020,** knowingly, willfully, and unlawfully made at least one of the following false statements and representations to members of the Georgia Senate present at a Senate Judiciary Subcommittee meeting:

1. That poll watchers and media at State Farm Arena were told late in the evening of November 3, 2020, that the vote count was being suspended until the next morning and to go home because of "a major watermain break";

2. That Fulton County election workers at State Farm Arena "voted" the same ballots "over and over again" on November 3, 2020;

said statements being within the jurisdiction of the Office of the Georgia Secretary of State and the Georgia Bureau of Investigation, departments and agencies of state government, and county and city law enforcement agencies, contrary to the laws of said State, the good order, peace and dignity thereof;

COUNT 27 of 41

And the Grand Jurors aforesaid, in the name and behalf of the citizens of Georgia, do charge and accuse **DONALD JOHN TRUMP** and **JOHN CHARLES EASTMAN** with the offense of **FILING FALSE DOCUMENTS, O.C.G.A. § 16-10-20.1(b) (1),** for the said accused, individually and as persons concerned in the commission of a crime, and together with unindicted co-conspirators, in the County of Fulton and State of Georgia, on or about the **31st day of December 2020,** knowingly and unlawfully filed a document titled "VERIFIED COMPLAINT FOR EMERGENCY INJUNCTIVE AND DECLARATORY RELIEF" in the matter of Trump v. Kemp, Case 1:20-cv-05310-MHC, in the United States District Court for the Northern District of Georgia, a court of the United States, having reason to know that said document contained at least one of the following materially false statements:[*]

1. That "as many as 2,506 felons with an uncompleted sentence" voted illegally in the November 3, 2020, presidential election in Georgia;

---

[*] The indictment recounts some of the most outlandish claims of voter fraud—any claims of material voter fraud have been roundly and repeatedly rejected by scores of judges, among others. For example, the Trump campaign's claim that more than 66,000 underage people voted in the election has been completely debunked. Raffensperger and his team rejected all of these claims and told Trump as much. The *New York Times* reported that roughly a dozen Georgia residents were recorded as being sixteen when they registered to vote in 2020, and those records appear to be data entry errors.

INSIDER NOTE: Trump widely publicized that he would hold a press conference in the late summer of 2023 to present "irrefutable" proof of election fraud. He canceled that press conference. As of this writing, it has not been rescheduled.

2.   That "at least 66,247 underage" people voted illegally in the November 3, 2020, presidential election in Georgia;

3.   That "at least 2,423 individuals" voted illegally in the November 3, 2020, presidential election in Georgia "who were not listed in the State's records as having been registered to vote";

4.   That "at least 1,043 individuals" voted illegally in the November 3, 2020, presidential election "who had illegally registered to vote using a postal office box as their habitation";

5.   That "as many as 10,315 or more" dead people voted in the November 3, 2020, presidential election in Georgia;

6.   That "[d]eliberate misinformation was used to instruct Republican poll watchers and members of the press to leave the premises for the night at approximately 10:00 p.m. on November 3, 2020" at State Farm Arena in Fulton County, Georgia;

contrary to the laws of said State, the good order, peace and dignity thereof;

COUNT 28 of 41[*]

And the Grand Jurors aforesaid, in the name and behalf of the citizens of Georgia, do charge and accuse **DONALD JOHN TRUMP** and **MARK RANDALL MEADOWS** with the offense of **SOLICITATION OF VIOLATION OF OATH BY PUBLIC OFFICER, O.C.G.A. §§ 16-4-7 & 16-10-1,** for the said accused, individually and as persons concerned in the commission of a crime, and together with unindicted co-conspirators, in the County of Fulton and State of Georgia, on or about the **2nd day of January 2021,** unlawfully solicited, requested, and importuned Georgia Secretary of State Brad Raffensperger, a public officer, to engage in conduct constituting the felony offense of Violation of Oath by Public Officer, O.C.G.A. § 16-10-1, by unlawfully altering, unlawfully adjust-

---

[*] Trump and his chief of staff, Mark Meadows, are charged with soliciting a public officer to violate his oath. This charge relates to the infamous January 2, 2021, phone call with Raffensperger.

ing, and otherwise unlawfully influencing the certified returns for presidential electors for the November 3, 2020, presidential election in Georgia, in willful and intentional violation of the terms of the oath of said person as prescribed by law, with intent that said person engage in said conduct, contrary to the laws of said State, the good order, peace and dignity thereof;

COUNT 29 of 41

And the Grand Jurors aforesaid, in the name and behalf of the citizens of Georgia, do charge and accuse **DONALD JOHN TRUMP** with the offense of **FALSE STATEMENTS AND WRITINGS, O.C.G.A. § 16-10-20,** for the said accused, in the County of Fulton and State of Georgia, on or about the **2nd day of January 2021,** knowingly, willfully, and unlawfully made at least one of the following false statements and representations to Georgia Secretary of State Brad Raffensperger, Georgia Deputy Secretary of State Jordan Fuchs, and Georgia Secretary of State General Counsel Ryan Germany:

1. That anywhere from 250,000 to 300,000 ballots were dropped mysteriously into the rolls in the November 3, 2020, presidential election in Georgia;

2. That thousands of people attempted to vote in the November 3, 2020, presidential election in Georgia and were told they could not because a ballot had already been cast in their name;

3. That 4,502 people voted in the November 3, 2020, presidential election in Georgia who were not on the voter registration list;

4. That 904 people voted in the November 3, 2020, presidential election in Georgia who were registered at an address that was a post office box;

5. That Ruby Freeman was a professional vote scammer and a known political operative;

6. That Ruby Freeman, her daughter, and others were responsible for fraudulently awarding at least 18,000 ballots to Joseph

R. Biden at State Farm Arena in the November 3, 2020, presidential election in Georgia;

7.   That close to 5,000 dead people voted in the November 3, 2020, presidential election in Georgia;

8.   That 139% of people voted in the November 3, 2020, presidential election in Detroit;

9.   That 200,000 more votes were recorded than the number of people who voted in the November 3, 2020, presidential election in Pennsylvania;

10.   That thousands of dead people voted in the November 3, 2020, presidential election in Michigan;

11.   That Ruby Freeman stuffed the ballot boxes;

12.   That hundreds of thousands of ballots had been "dumped" into Fulton County and another county adjacent to Fulton County in the November 3, 2020, presidential election in Georgia;

13.   That he won the November 3, 2020, presidential election in Georgia by 400,000 votes;

said statements being within the jurisdiction of the Office of the Georgia Secretary of State and the Georgia Bureau of Investigation, departments and agencies of state government, contrary to the laws of said State, the good order, peace and dignity thereof;

COUNT 30 of 41

And the Grand Jurors aforesaid, in the name and behalf of the citizens of Georgia, do charge and accuse **STEPHEN CLIFFGARD LEE, HARRISON WILLIAM PRESCOTT FLOYD,** and **TREVIAN C. KUTTI** with the offense of **CONSPIRACY TO COMMIT SOLICITATION OF FALSE STATEMENTS AND WRITINGS, O.C.G.A. §§ 16-4-8, 16-4-7, & 16-10-20,** for the said accused, individually and as persons concerned in the commission of a crime, and together with unindicted co-conspirators, in the County of Fulton and State of Georgia, on or about the **4th**

day of January 2021, unlawfully conspired to solicit, request, and importune Ruby Freeman, a Fulton County, Georgia, election worker, to engage in conduct constituting the felony offense of False Statements and Writings, O.C.G.A. § 16-10-20, by knowingly and willfully making a false statement and representation concerning events at State Farm Arena in the November 3, 2020, presidential election in Georgia, said statement and representation being within the jurisdiction of the Office of the Georgia Secretary of State and the Georgia Bureau of Investigation, departments and agencies of state government, and county and city law enforcement agencies, with intent that said person engage in said conduct; and **TREVIAN C. KUTTI** traveled to Fulton County, Georgia, and placed a telephone call to Ruby Freeman while in Fulton County, Georgia, which were overt acts to effect the object of the conspiracy, contrary to the laws of said State, the good order, peace and dignity thereof;

COUNT 31 of 41

And the Grand Jurors aforesaid, in the name and behalf of the citizens of Georgia, do charge and accuse **STEPHEN CLIFF-GARD LEE, HARRISON WILLIAM PRESCOTT FLOYD** and **TREVIAN C. KUTTI** with the offense of **INFLUENCING WITNESSES, O.C.G.A. § 16-10-93(b)(1)(A),** for the said accused, individually and as persons concerned in the commission of a crime, and together with unindicted co-conspirators, in the County of Fulton and State of Georgia, on or about the **4th day of January 2021,** knowingly and unlawfully engaged in misleading conduct toward Ruby Freeman, a Fulton County, Georgia, election worker, by stating that she needed protection and by purporting to offer her help, with intent to influence her testimony in an official proceeding in Fulton County, Georgia, concerning events at State Farm Arena in the November 3, 2020, presidential election in Georgia, contrary to the laws of said State, the good order, peace and dignity thereof;

COUNT 32 of 41*

And the Grand Jurors aforesaid, in the name and behalf of the citizens of Georgia, do charge and accuse **SIDNEY KATHER-INE POWELL, CATHLEEN ALSTON LATHAM, SCOTT GRAHAM HALL,** and **MISTY HAMPTON** with the offense of **CONSPIRACY TO COMMIT ELECTION FRAUD, O.C.G.A. §§ 21-2-603 & 21-2-566,** for the said accused, individually and as persons concerned in the commission of a crime, and together with unindicted co-conspirators, in the County of Fulton and State of Georgia, on and between the **1st day of December 2020 and the 7th day of January 2021,** unlawfully conspired and agreed to willfully tamper with electronic ballot markers and tabulating machines in the State of Georgia;

And **SIDNEY KATHERINE POWELL** entered into a contract with SullivanStrickler LLC in Fulton County, Georgia, delivered a payment to SullivanStrickler LLC in Fulton County, Georgia, and caused employees of SullivanStrickler LLC to travel from Fulton County, Georgia, to Coffee County, Georgia, for the purpose of willfully tampering with said electronic ballot markers and tabulating machines, which were overt acts to effect the object of the conspiracy;

And **CATHLEEN ALSTON LATHAM, SCOTT GRAHAM HALL,** and **MISTY HAMPTON** aided, abetted, and encouraged employees of SullivanStrickler LLC in willfully tampering with electronic ballot markers and tabulating machines while inside the Coffee County Elections & Registration Office in Coffee County, Georgia, which were overt acts to effect the object of the conspiracy, contrary to the laws of said State, the good order, peace and dignity thereof;

COUNT 33 of 41

And the Grand Jurors aforesaid, in the name and behalf of the citizens of Georgia, do charge and accuse **SIDNEY KATHER-INE POWELL, CATHLEEN ALSTON LATHAM, SCOTT GRAHAM HALL,** and **MISTY HAMPTON** with the offense

---

* This count pertains to Sidney Powell's alleged efforts to seize and scour Coffee County voting machines for evidence of voter fraud.

of **CONSPIRACY TO COMMIT ELECTION FRAUD, O.C.G.A. §§ 21-2-603 & 21-2-574,** for the said accused, individually and as persons concerned in the commission of a crime, and together with unindicted co-conspirators, in the County of Fulton and State of Georgia, on and between the **1st day of December 2020 and the 7th day of January 2021,** unlawfully conspired and agreed to cause certain members of the conspiracy, who were not officers charged by law with the care of ballots and who were not persons entrusted by any such officer with the care of ballots for a purpose required by law, to possess official ballots outside of the polling place in the State of Georgia;

And **SIDNEY KATHERINE POWELL** entered into a contract with SullivanStrickler LLC in Fulton County, Georgia, delivered a payment to SullivanStrickler LLC in Fulton County, Georgia, and caused employees of SullivanStrickler LLC to travel from Fulton County, Georgia, to Coffee County, Georgia, for the purpose of causing certain members of the conspiracy, who were not officers charged by law with the care of ballots and who were not persons entrusted by any such officer with the care of ballots for a purpose required by law, to possess official ballots outside of the polling place, which were overt acts to effect the object of the conspiracy;

And **CATHLEEN ALSTON LATHAM, SCOTT GRAHAM HALL,** and **MISTY HAMPTON** aided, abetted, and encouraged employees of SullivanStrickler LLC in accessing election equipment while inside the Coffee County Elections & Registration Office in Coffee County, Georgia, for the purpose of causing certain members of the conspiracy, who were not officers charged by law with the care of ballots and who were not persons entrusted by any such officer with the care of ballots for a purpose required by law, to possess official ballots outside of the polling place, which were overt acts to effect the object of the conspiracy, contrary to the laws of said State, the good order, peace and dignity thereof;

COUNT 34 of 41

And the Grand Jurors aforesaid, in the name and behalf of the citizens of Georgia, do charge and accuse **SIDNEY KATHERINE POWELL, CATHLEEN ALSTON LATHAM, SCOTT**

GRAHAM HALL, and **MISTY HAMPTON** with the offense of **CONSPIRACY TO COMMIT COMPUTER THEFT, O.C.G.A. §§ 16-4-8 & 16-9-93(a),** for the said accused, individually and as persons concerned in the commission of a crime, and together with unindicted co-conspirators, in the County of Fulton and State of Georgia, on and between the **1st day of December 2020 and the 7th day of January 2021,** unlawfully conspired to use a computer with knowledge that such use was without authority and with the intention of taking and appropriating information, data, and software, the property of Dominion Voting Systems Corporation,

And **SIDNEY KATHERINE POWELL** entered into a contract with SullivanStrickler LLC in Fulton County, Georgia, delivered a payment to SullivanStrickler LLC in Fulton County, Georgia, and caused employees of SullivanStrickler LLC to travel from Fulton County, Georgia, to Coffee County, Georgia, for the purpose of using a computer with knowledge that such use was without authority and with the intention of taking and appropriating information, data, and software, the property of Dominion Voting Systems Corporation, which were overt acts to effect the object of the conspiracy;

And **CATHLEEN ALSTON LATHAM, SCOTT GRAHAM HALL,** and **MISTY HAMPTON** aided, abetted, and encouraged employees of SullivanStrickler LLC in using a computer with knowledge that such use was without authority and with the intention of taking and appropriating information, data, and software, the property of Dominion Voting Systems Corporation, while inside the Coffee County Elections & Registration Office in Coffee County, Georgia, which were overt acts to effect the object of the conspiracy, contrary to the laws of said State, the good order, peace and dignity thereof;

COUNT 35 of 41

And the Grand Jurors aforesaid, in the name and behalf of the citizens of Georgia, do charge and accuse **SIDNEY KATHERINE POWELL, CATHLEEN ALSTON LATHAM, SCOTT GRAHAM HALL,** and **MISTY HAMPTON** with the offense of **CONSPIRACY TO COMMIT COMPUTER TRESPASS, O.C.G.A. §§ 16-4-8 & 16-9-93(b),** for the said accused, individually and as persons concerned in the commission of a crime, and together with unindicted co-conspirators, in the County of Fulton and State of Georgia, on and between the **1st day of December 2020 and the 7th day of January 2021,** unlawfully conspired to use a computer with knowledge that such use was without authority and with the intention of removing voter data and Dominion Voting Systems Corporation data from said computer;

And **SIDNEY KATHERINE POWELL** entered into a contract with SullivanStrickler LLC in Fulton County, Georgia, delivered a payment to SullivanStrickler LLC in Fulton County, Georgia, and caused employees of SullivanStrickler LLC to travel from Fulton County, Georgia, to Coffee County, Georgia, for the purpose of using a computer with knowledge that such use was without authority and with the intention of removing voter data and Dominion Voting Systems Corporation data from said computer, which were overt acts to effect the object of the conspiracy;

And **CATHLEEN ALSTON LATHAM, SCOTT GRAHAM HALL,** and **MISTY HAMPTON** aided, abetted, and encouraged employees of SullivanStrickler LLC in using a computer with knowledge that such use was without authority and with the intention of removing voter data and Dominion Voting Systems Corporation data from said computer, while inside the Coffee County Elections & Registration Office in Coffee County, Georgia, which were overt acts to effect the object of the conspiracy, contrary to the laws of said State, the good order, peace and dignity thereof;

COUNT 36 of 41

And the Grand Jurors aforesaid, in the name and behalf of the citizens of Georgia, do charge and accuse **SIDNEY KATHERINE POWELL, CATHLEEN ALSTON LATHAM, SCOTT GRAHAM HALL,** and **MISTY HAMPTON** with the offense of **CONSPIRACY TO COMMIT COMPUTER INVASION OF PRIVACY, O.C.G.A. §§ 16-4-8 & 16-9-93(c),** for the said accused, individually and as persons concerned in the commission of a crime, and together with unindicted co-conspirators, in the County of Fulton and State of Georgia, on and between the **1st day of December**

2020 and the 7th day of January 2021, unlawfully conspired to use a computer with the intention of examining personal voter data with knowledge that such examination was without authority;

And **SIDNEY KATHERINE POWELL** entered into a contract with SullivanStrickler LLC in Fulton County, Georgia, delivered a payment to SullivanStrickler LLC in Fulton County, Georgia, and caused employees of SullivanStrickler LLC to travel from Fulton County, Georgia, to Coffee County, Georgia, for the purpose of using a computer with the intention of examining personal voter data with knowledge that such examination was without authority, which were overt acts to effect the object of the conspiracy;

And **CATHLEEN ALSTON LATHAM, SCOTT GRAHAM HALL,** and **MISTY HAMPTON** aided, abetted, and encouraged employees of SullivanStrickler LLC in using a computer with the intention of examining personal voter data with knowledge that such examination was without authority, while inside the Coffee County Elections & Registration Office in Coffee County, Georgia, which were overt acts to effect the object of the conspiracy, contrary to the laws of said State, the good order, peace and dignity thereof;

COUNT 37 of 41

And the Grand Jurors aforesaid, in the name and behalf of the citizens of Georgia, do charge and accuse **SIDNEY KATHERINE POWELL, CATHLEEN ALSTON LATHAM, SCOTT GRAHAM HALL,** and **MISTY HAMPTON** with the offense of **CONSPIRACY TO DEFRAUD THE STATE, O.C.G.A. § 16-10-21,** for the said accused, individually and as persons concerned in the commission of a crime, and together with unindicted co-conspirators, in the County of Fulton and State of Georgia, on and between the **1st day of December 2020 and the 7th day of January 2021,** unlawfully conspired and agreed to commit theft of voter data, property which was under the control of Georgia Secretary of State Brad Raffensperger, a state officer, in his official capacity;

And **SIDNEY KATHERINE POWELL** entered into a contract with SullivanStrickler LLC in Fulton County, Georgia, delivered a payment to SullivanStrickler LLC in Fulton County, Georgia, and caused employees of SullivanStrickler LLC to travel from Fulton County, Georgia, to Coffee County, Georgia, for the purpose of committing theft of voter data, property which was under the control of Georgia Secretary of State Brad Raffensperger, a state officer, in his official capacity, which were overt acts to effect the object of the conspiracy;

And **CATHLEEN ALSTON LATHAM, SCOTT GRAHAM HALL,** and **MISTY HAMPTON** aided, abetted, and encouraged employees of SullivanStrickler LLC in accessing election equipment while inside the Coffee County Elections & Registration Office in Douglas, Georgia, for the purpose of committing theft of voter data, property which was under the control of Georgia Secretary of State Brad Raffensperger, a state officer, in his official capacity, which were overt acts to effect the object of the conspiracy, contrary to the laws of said State, the good order, peace and dignity thereof;

COUNT 38 of 41

And the Grand Jurors aforesaid, in the name and behalf of the citizens of Georgia, do charge and accuse **DONALD JOHN TRUMP** with the offense of **SOLICITATION OF VIOLATION OF OATH BY PUBLIC OFFICER, O.C.G.A. §§ 16-4-7 and 16-10-1,** for the said accused, in the County of Fulton and State of Georgia, on or about the **17th day of September 2021,** unlawfully solicited, requested, and importuned Georgia Secretary of State Brad Raffensperger, a public officer, to engage in conduct constituting the felony offense of Violation of Oath by Public Officer, O.C.G.A. § 16-10-1, by unlawfully "decertifying the Election, or whatever the correct legal remedy is, and announce the true winner," in willful and intentional violation of the terms of the oath of said person as prescribed by law, with intent that said person engage in said conduct, contrary to the laws of said State, the good order, peace and dignity thereof;

COUNT 39 of 41

And the Grand Jurors aforesaid, in the name and behalf of the citizens of Georgia, do charge and accuse **DONALD JOHN TRUMP** with the offense of **FALSE STATEMENTS AND**

WRITINGS, O.C.G.A. § 16-10-20, for the said accused, in the County of Fulton and State of Georgia, on or about the **17th day of September 2021,** knowingly, willfully, and unlawfully made the following false statement and representation to Georgia Secretary of State Brad Raffensperger:

1. "As stated to you previously, the number of false and/or irregular votes is far greater than needed to change the Georgia election result";

said statement being within the jurisdiction of the Office of the Georgia Secretary of State and the Georgia Bureau of Investigation, departments and agencies of state government, and county and city law enforcement agencies, contrary to the laws of said State, the good order, peace and dignity thereof;

COUNT 40 of 41

And the Grand Jurors aforesaid, in the name and behalf of the citizens of Georgia, do charge and accuse **DAVID JAMES SHA-FER** with the offense of **FALSE STATEMENTS AND WRITINGS, O.C.G.A. § 16-10-20,** for the said accused, in the County of Fulton and State of Georgia, on or about the **25th day of April 2022,** knowingly, willfully, and unlawfully made at least one of the following false statements and representations in the presence of Fulton County District Attorney's Office investigators:

1. That he "attended and convened" the December 14, 2020, meeting of Trump presidential elector nominees in Fulton County, Georgia, but that he did not "call each of the individual members and notify them of the meeting or make any of the other preparations necessary for the meeting";

2. That a court reporter was not present at the December 14, 2020, meeting of Trump presidential elector nominees in Fulton County, Georgia;

said statements being within the jurisdiction of the Fulton County District Attorney's Office, a department and agency of the government of a county of this state, contrary to the laws of said State, the good order, peace and dignity thereof;

COUNT 41 of 41*

And the Grand Jurors aforesaid, in the name and behalf of the citizens of Georgia, do charge and accuse **ROBERT DAVID CHEELEY** with the offense of **PERJURY, O.C.G.A. § 16-10-70(a),** for the said accused, in the County of Fulton and State of Georgia, on or about the **15th day of September 2022,** knowingly, willfully, and unlawfully made at least one of the following false statements before the Fulton County Special Purpose Grand Jury, a judicial proceeding, after having been administered a lawful oath:

1. That he was unaware of the December 14, 2020, meeting of Trump presidential elector nominees in Fulton County, Georgia, until after the meeting had already taken place;

2. That he had no substantive conversations with anyone concerning the December 14, 2020, meeting of Trump presidential elector nominees in Fulton County, Georgia, until after the meeting had already taken place;

3. That he never suggested to anyone that the Trump presidential elector nominees in Georgia should meet on December 14, 2020;

4. That the only communication he had with John Eastman concerning the November 3, 2020, presidential election was for the purpose of connecting Eastman to Georgia Senator Brandon Beach and unindicted co-conspirator Individual 8, whose identity is known to the Grand Jury, for possible legal representation;

5. That he never worked to connect John Eastman with any Georgia legislators other than Georgia Senator Brandon

---

* Robert Cheeley is accused of lying to the Fulton County special grand jury. Although a special grand jury cannot bring indictments, they hear sworn testimony, thereby making it a crime to lie to a special grand jury. The use of sworn testimony— and the threat of perjury for providing false testimony—provides strong incentives to enable the grand jury to obtain the truth in its investigations.

Beach and unindicted co-conspirator Individual 8, whose identity is known to the Grand Jury;

said statements being material to the accused's own involvement in the December 14, 2020, meeting of Trump presidential elector nominees in Fulton County, Georgia, and to the accused's communications with others involved in said meeting, the issues in question, contrary to the laws of said State, the good order, peace and dignity thereof.

FANI T. WILLIS, District Attorney

WITNESS LIST

Asst. Chief Inv. M. Hill – FCDA DA14
Sr. Inv. T. Swanson-Lucas – FCDA DA72

UNITED STATES OF AMERICA V. DONALD J. TRUMP, ET AL.

(SOUTHERN DISTRICT OF FLORIDA INDICTMENT)

INTRODUCTION

THE WORLD LEARNED IN AUGUST 2022 THAT THE Department of Justice had conducted a court-authorized search of Mar-a-Lago, Donald Trump's beach club/residence in Palm Beach, Florida. No president or former president has ever been the subject of a law enforcement search. But little did we know that what prompted the DOJ to take this unprecedented step was a profound matter of national security. As we would later learn, the search was intended to locate and recover thousands of government documents—some of them at the very highest classification level—that the former president had retained upon leaving office in January 2021. The history of what transpired is ugly: the indictment alleges that Trump cavalierly disregarded not just the law, but the nation's security—something that is particularly shocking for those in the Intelligence Community who understand the sensitivity of the information that is key to keeping our people safe from all manner of grave threats.

Keeping the nation's secrets secure is an important function of the executive branch, which the president leads. And presidents, no less than rank-and-file members of the Intelligence Community, must observe stringent rules that prescribe protocols for retaining, accessing, and storing various classified documents. It should go without saying that all classified documents that the Intelligence Community and the White House produce are government records; they do not belong to the president, but to the nation. To assure that this obligation is taken seriously, Congress has criminalized the mishandling of such records, making it a crime, for instance, to intentionally retain, without proper security clearance, documents that are "national defense information" (a term that is largely but not entirely synonymous with "classified documents").

It was revealed in the wake of the Mar-a-Lago search that, upon leaving office, Trump took and thereafter kept thousands of government documents, many hundreds of which were classified. Critically, when he retained these documents, he lacked the security clearance that would permit him to possess or access these sensitive materials. These documents were supposed to be turned over to the National Archives under a congressional statute that was passed after Watergate to ensure that presidents left their government records for safekeeping with the Archives.

For about a year, the National Archives negotiated with Trump and his legal team for the return of the government documents, with little success. In early 2022, Trump finally returned fifteen boxes of documents to the Archives. Upon reviewing the recovered boxes, the Archives discovered that they contained highly classified information.

The National Archives referred the matter to the DOJ, prompting the DOJ to take further action to assure that it had recovered all classified documents in Trump's possession. To do this, prosecutors served Trump with a grand jury subpoena requiring him to produce all documents taken from the White House that bore classified markings. The wording of the directive was purposeful—it meant that the documents had to be produced, regardless of whether: (1) Trump had later declassified them "with his mind" (as he has later claimed, without further proof); or (2) the documents were Trump's personal property (subpoenas routinely require people to produce personal documents). In short, anything responsive that bore classified markings was required to be produced.

As the indictment alleges, Trump did not produce all the remaining responsive documents and, indeed, obstructed efforts to comply with the subpoena. He sought to have his attorneys and others tell the government that the documents already had been returned (when he knew they were still in his possession). And, when his lawyers balked, Trump misled them into believing that only a handful of documents were responsive to the subpoena, when in fact, he was hiding a cache of documents in his private residence, including his office.

The government had information that not all the documents had in fact been returned and that the Trump lawyers' representations that they had been returned were false. The government established evidence sufficient to obtain a federal court-approved search warrant to retrieve the documents. As it turns out, there was good reason for the prosecutors to take this dramatic step. The search revealed that Trump possessed very highly classified documents—the kind of classified information that members of the Intelligence Community would guard with their lives. The photographs from that search and the inventory of what was seized were remarkable. They revealed highly classified documents in highly insecure locations, including in Trump's personal office and desk, as well as a ballroom and bathroom. This was all extremely concerning. Not only were these areas highly insecure, Mar-a-Lago itself was a known target of foreign adversaries. In other words, the risk of improper access was real and ongoing.

It is worth noting the description of the thirty-two documents that form the basis for the illegal retention charges. The documents include many top secret documents concerning US nuclear capabilities and that of foreign countries. Prosecutors typically must obtain permission from Intelligence Community agencies to use such documents at trial. It is thus remarkable that permission was granted in this case. And because the thirty-two documents are a subset of the voluminous cache of classified documents that was found, one can be fairly sure that even more sensitive documents were deemed too secret for use in a public trial.

After the initial indictment, there was even more to come. In August 2023 the government brought a superseding indictment, charging another obstruction scheme and another defendant. The government obtained evidence of Trump's alleged scheme to destroy the video surveillance footage from Mar-a-Lago's security cameras—the very footage that enabled prosecutors to discern Trump's alleged scheme to obstruct compliance with the subpoena. That scheme failed when the IT employee who was allegedly directed to destroy the surveillance footage refused to do so. The indictment makes clear the incriminating nature of that video footage.

In all, Trump kept an extraordinary array of classified documents.

The fifteen boxes he eventually returned to the National Archives contained 184 unique documents bearing classification markings:

- 67 documents marked as Confidential
- 92 documents marked as Secret
- 25 documents marked as Top Secret

In June 2022, Trump's attorneys returned thirty-seven additional unique documents bearing classification markings:

- 5 documents marked as Confidential
- 16 documents marked as Secret
- 17 documents marked as Top Secret

The August 2022 search uncovered another cache of classified documents.

- 103 unique documents bearing classification markings

The search of Trump's office revealed:

- 27 documents bearing classification markings
  - 3 documents marked as Confidential
  - 17 documents marked as Secret
  - 7 documents marked as Top Secret
- 43 empty folders with classified banners
- 28 empty folders labeled "return to staff secretary/military aide"
- Several documents had colored cover sheets showing their classification status
- 3 classified documents were located "in the desks in the '45 Office'"

The search of the Mar-a-Lago storage room produced:

- 76 documents bearing classification markings
  - 28 documents marked as Confidential
  - 37 documents marked as Secret
  - 11 documents marked as Top Secret, including Sensitive Compartmented Information ("SCI")

WHY DID TRUMP FAIL to return all of the documents as requested? The charges in the Florida case seem so avoidable: the documents could have—and should have—been returned upon demand. One need only look to the example of Trump's own vice president, Mike Pence, who, upon discovering documents inadvertently in his possession, avoided a criminal charge by simply alerting the authorities and returning the documents. It is not a crime to take or retain the documents by mistake.

Trump took a decidedly different course. Did he do so because he believed the law did not apply to him—another iteration of his now-infamous claim that he could shoot someone with no consequence? Was it to have "kompromat" on people, like the president of France, to whom some documents are reported to relate? Was it to be able to use the documents in deals with prospective foreign business partners (e.g., the Saudis) or even possibly to sell them? We do not know, and we may never know. It could be for all these reasons, with different motives for each document, or multiple motives for the same document.

None of this matters legally. The government need not prove why Trump did what he did—Trump's motive is not an element of the thirty-two illegal retention charges that the government is obliged to prove beyond a reasonable doubt. Although a jury, like us, may ask why, the fact of the matter is that intent is irrelevant. What is relevant are the actions taken to obstruct the documents' recovery and return.. And on this front, the evidence of guilt seems abundantly clear. And every day of the week, defendants are convicted for a lot less.

CAST OF CHARACTERS

Many of the indictments reference unnamed individuals by descriptions such as "Employee 1," "Woman 2," and "Co-Conspirator 3." To be clear, these unnamed individuals have not been charged with any crime. They are referenced because they play some role in the events alleged. Relying on media reports identifying these individuals, we have named them here in order to facilitate the reader's comprehension of these documents and the alleged conduct they describe. That said, it must be remembered that none of these individuals has been charged with any wrongdoing.

O = defendant (To charge a defendant, a grand jury has to determine that there is probable cause that the person committed the crime. At trial, the government needs to establish guilt beyond a reasonable doubt and the defendant is presumed innocent unless and until such time.)

▲ = involved in multiple cases

Christina Bobb ("Trump attorney 3")[*]—A Trump attorney who signed an erroneous June 2022 certification provided to the DOJ claiming that, to her knowledge, all of Trump's responsive documents had been returned to the DOJ after a diligent search.

Judge Aileen Cannon—The Florida-based federal judge presiding over the DOJ's classified documents case. Cannon, a Trump appointee, became a judge in 2020.

Alex Cannon ("Trump Representative 1")[†]—A former Trump lawyer who reportedly tried to effectuate Trump's compliance with the National

---

[*] Identity reported here: Caroline Anders, "These Are the Key Players in the Latest Trump Indictment," *Washinton Post*, June 10, 2023.
[†] Identity reported here: Katherine Faulders, John Santucci, and Alexander Mallin, "Top Trump Campaign Aide Identified as Key Individual in Classified Docs Indictment: Sources," ABC News, June 28, 2023.

Archives' request that Trump return records. Apparently, Cannon, uneasy about the possibility that Trump might be withholding documents, declined Trump's request to tell the Archives that all materials had been returned. Cannon is not related to Judge Aileen Cannon.

Evan Corcoran▲ ("Trump attorney 1")*—Trump's lawyer who participated in the response to the DOJ's 2022 grand jury subpoena for documents bearing classified markings. According to prosecutors, Corcoran informed Trump that he would search the Mar-a-Lago storage room for responsive documents. Before Corcoran could do so, Trump allegedly had aides remove boxes from the storage room and bring them to Trump's personal residence. Corcoran searched the storage room and found only thirty-eight classified documents, all of which he turned over to the FBI. Corcoran— apparently unaware of the removal of the boxes—asked Christina Bobb to sign a certification stating that all responsive documents had been returned. Corcoran's personal meeting notes feature prominently in the DOJ's Florida indictment and record that Trump repeatedly intimated that Corcoran should destroy or hide the documents that the DOJ requested. Corcoran recused himself as Trump's lawyer in the Florida documents case but apparently continues to represent Trump in other cases, including the DOJ's January 6 case.†

Carlos De Oliveira○—Mar-a-Lago property manager and Trump's co-defendant. The DOJ indictment alleges that De Oliveira—at Trump's direction—attempted to delete security footage of a Mar-a-Lago storage room ultimately sought by a DOJ subpoena. De Oliveira allegedly worked with Walt Nauta to locate the footage and unsuccessfully pressured Mar-a-Lago's IT director to delete it.

Liz Harrington ("Staffer") ‡—A Trump staffer who was present at a July 2021 Bedminster, New Jersey, meeting that was captured on tape. According to prosecutors, the tape shows Trump displaying a US plan related to attack-

---

* Identity reported here: Jacqueline Alemany, Josh Dawsey, and Spencer S. Hsu, "A Top Trump Lawyer Has Recused Himself from Mar-a-Lago Documents Case," *Washington Post*, April 15, 2023.

† Alemany, Dawsey, and Hsu, "A Top Trump Lawyer Has Recused Himself from Mar-a-Lago Documents Case."

‡ Jacqueline Alemany, Josh Dawsey, and Spencer S. Hsu, "It's Not Just Mar-a-Lago: Trump Charges Highlight His New Jersey Life," *Washington Post*, June 27, 2023; Alan Feuer, Maggie Haberman, and Jonathan Swan, "The Attention Was All on Mar-a-Lago. Some of the Action Was at Bedminster," *New York Times*, June 27, 2023.

ing Iran—described by Trump as "highly confidential" and "secret"—to a writer, a publisher, and others who lacked security clearances.

Hayley Harrison ("Trump Employee 1")[*]—Melania Trump's chief of staff and a former Trump White House aide, Harrison allegedly helped move Trump's boxes between different rooms at Mar-a-Lago.

Jennifer Little▲ ("Trump attorney 2")[†]—An attorney for Trump who, along with Corcoran, met with Trump at Mar-a-Lago to plan Trump's response to the DOJ's grand jury documents subpoena. Trump allegedly told Little that she need not be present during Corcoran's search for responsive documents, and she did not do so. Little remains a member of Trump's legal team in the Fulton County case.[‡]

Margo Martin ("Staffer")[§]—A Trump staffer present at the July 2021 Bedminster meeting at which Trump showed what prosecutors allege is a classified plan relating to Iran to a writer, a publisher, and others.

Molly Michael ("Trump Employee 2")[¶]—A former Trump staffer who allegedly helped Walt Nauta handle the return of documents to the National Archives.

Mark Milley ("Senior Military Official")[**]—The Chairman of the Joint Chiefs of Staff who Trump has publicly disparaged. As alleged by prosecutors, Trump appears to have shown the Iran classified material to the writer and publisher at Bedminster in order to rebut claims that Milley made.

Waltine ("Walt") Nauta○—Trump's co-defendant and personal aide. Nauta, a Navy valet stationed in the White House during the Trump pres-

---

[*] Faulders, Santucci, and Mallin, "Top Trump Campaign Aide Identified as Key Individual in Classified Docs Indictment: Sources."

[†] Scott R. Anderson, Anna Bower, Hyemin Han, Tyler McBrien, Roger Parloff, Stephanie Pell, Katherine Pompilio, Alan Z. Rozenshtein, and Benjamin Wittes, "United States of America v. Donald J. Trump and Waltine Nauta," Lawfare, June 9, 2023; Alan Feuer, Maggie Haberman, and Glenn Thrush, "They Are Trump's Aides and Lawyers. Now They Could Be Trial Witnesses," *New York Times,* June 14, 2023.

[‡] Richard Fausset, Maggie Haberman, and Danny Hakim, "Trump Shakes Up His Georgia Legal Team Ahead of Atlanta Booking," *New York Times,* August 24, 2023.

[§] Paula Reid and Jeremy Herb, "Exclusive: Donald Trump Admits on Tape He Didn't Declassify 'Secret Information,'" CNN Politics, June 9, 2023.

[¶] Faulders, Santucci, and Mallin, "Top Trump Campaign Aide Identified as Key Individual in Classified Docs Indictment: Sources."

[**] Shane Harris, "Trump's Disdain for Intelligence Rules Foretold His Indictment," *Washington Post,* June 10, 2023.

idency, became Trump's post-presidency personal aide and "body man." According to the DOJ indictment, Nauta helped oversee the handling of Trump's boxes of classified documents at Mar-a-Lago. Nauta—acting at Trump's direction—allegedly moved boxes containing classified documents from a Mar-a-Lago storage room to Trump's personal residence so that Trump could inspect them and conceal the fact of their existence—first from the National Archives, and later from Trump's own lawyers and the DOJ. The indictment alleges that Nauta lied to the FBI about his role in delivering the boxes of classified documents to Trump, and that Nauta and co-defendant Carlos De Oliveira worked unsuccessfully to delete security footage of a Mar-a-Lago storage room sought by the DOJ.

Yuscil Taveras ("Trump Employee 4")[*]—The Mar-a-Lago IT director. According to the indictment, Walt Nauta and Carlos De Oliveira pressured Taveras to delete security footage sought by the DOJ. Tavares is cooperating with the DOJ.

Susie Wiles ("PAC representative")[†]—A Florida political consultant and Trump campaign advisor with whom Trump allegedly shared a classified map related to a foreign military operation. Trump allegedly told Wiles, who lacked a security clearance, that he should not show her the map. The DOJ indictment also alleges that Wiles was a member of an encrypted messaging chat group with Walt Nauta and an unnamed Trump employee in which the unnamed employee assured the group that Carlos De Oliveira remained loyal to Trump.

PROSECUTORS

Jay Bratt—The Chief of the Justice Department's Counterintelligence and Export Control Section. Bratt was one of the DOJ attorneys who traveled to Mar-a-Lago in June 2022 to discuss missing documents with Trump's lawyers. Bratt, who has helped oversee numerous classified documents prosecutions at the DOJ, has appeared in court on behalf of the federal government following the Florida indictment.

Julie Edelstein—The Deputy Chief of the Justice Department's Counterintelligence and Export Control Section under Jay Bratt. Edelstein has been

---

[*] Kaitlan Collins and Katelyn Polantz, " 'Trump Employee 4' in Superseding Indictment Identified as Yuscil Traveras," CNN Politics, July 28, 2023.

[†] Faulders, Santucci, and Mallin, "Top Trump Campaign Aide Identified as Key Individual in Classified Docs Indictment: Sources"; Kaitlan Collins, Kristen Holmes, Paula Reid, and Sara Murray, "Top Trump Campaign Aide Susie Wiles Met Numerous Times with Special Counsel Investigators in Documents Probe," CNN Politics, June 29, 2023.

a lead prosecutor in multiple high-profile cases involving government leaks. She too has appeared in the Florida criminal case.

Karen Gilbert—A longtime federal prosecutor based in Miami. Gilbert formerly led the Narcotics Division of the US Attorney's Office for the Southern District of Florida, but she voluntarily stepped down from her leadership post in 2009 after she and her office were formally reprimanded for secretly recording witness interviews with defense attorneys as part of an investigation into potential witness tampering. Gilbert has remained an Assistant US Attorney.

David Harbach—A veteran DOJ public corruption prosecutor who has worked closely with Jack Smith in the past and left private practice to join the Special Counsel's team. As a federal prosecutor, Harbach tried high-profile corruption cases against former US senator John Edwards and former Virginia governor Bob McDonnell. Edwards was acquitted on one count and the jury deadlocked on the five remaining counts, which the government declined to retry; McDonnell was convicted at trial, but the United States Supreme Court later overturned his conviction. Harbach successfully prosecuted Rick Renzi, a former congressman from Arizona, on charges of corruption and money laundering.

David Raskin—David Raskin is a longtime federal prosecutor in Kansas City and New York and has extensive national security experience, including investigating and successfully prosecuting cases involving the illegal mishandling of classified documents.

Brett Reynolds—A trial attorney in the Justice Department's National Security Division.

Jack Smith▲—The Special Counsel overseeing the DOJ's investigation of Donald Trump. Smith, who was appointed by Attorney General Merrick Garland in November 2022, is heading both federal prosecutions of Trump—the classified documents case and the January 6 case. Smith is a longtime federal and state prosecutor whose former roles include serving as the Chief of the DOJ's Public Integrity Section, the Acting US Attorney for the Middle District of Tennessee, an Assistant US Attorney in the Eastern District of New York, and an Assistant District Attorney in the Manhattan District Attorney's Office. Smith left his post as the chief prosecutor in the Kosovo Specialist Prosecutor's Office to become DOJ Special Counsel.

Michael Thakur—An Assistant US Attorney for the Southern District of Florida. Thakur has appeared in court on behalf of the federal government post-indictment.

DEFENSE ATTORNEYS

Todd Blanche▲—A white-collar criminal defense lawyer and former federal prosecutor. Blanche, previously a partner at a well-known New York law firm, launched his own firm in 2023 to represent Trump in three criminal investigations: the New York case and both federal cases. Blanche successfully represented Trump's former presidential campaign manager Paul Manafort in the Manhattan District Attorney's prosecution that was ultimately dismissed on state double-jeopardy grounds.

Lindsey Halligan—A Florida-based lawyer who was present at Mar-a-Lago during the FBI's search for classified documents in August 2022 and has remained a member of Trump's defense team.

Christopher Kise—A veteran defense lawyer and the former Solicitor General of Florida. Kise, who recently joined a small Florida-based law firm, has successfully argued several cases before the Supreme Court. He joined Trump's legal team in 2022 and is defense counsel in various Trump criminal and civil cases.

Stephen Weiss—A junior lawyer at Blanche Law, the small law firm that Todd Blanche, one of Trump's lead defense attorneys, established after agreeing to represent Trump.

UNITED STATES DISTRICT COURT
SOUTHERN DISTRICT OF FLORIDA*

Case No. 23-CR-80101-CANNON(s)

18 U.S.C. § 793(e)

18 U.S.C. § 1512(k)

18 U.S.C. § 1512(b)(2)(A)

18 U.S.C. § 1512(b)(2)(B)

18 U.S.C. § 1512(c)(1)

18 U.S.C. § 1519

18 U.S.C. § 1001(a)(1)

18 U.S.C. § 1001(a)(2)

18 U.S.C. § 2

FILED BY _____ mdc _____ D.C.

Jul 27, 2023

ANGELA E. NOBLE
CLERK U.S. DIST. CT.
S. D. OF FLA. – West Palm Beach, Fl

UNITED STATES OF AMERICA

v.

DONALD J. TRUMP,
WALTINE NAUTA, and
CARLOS DE OLIVEIRA,
Defendants.

_____/

SUPERSEDING INDICTMENT†

The Grand Jury charges that:

---

* The US Constitution requires a charge to be brought where the crime occurred; that typically gives the prosecution considerable discretion as crimes often occur in multiple jurisdictions. Here, however, it was not clear that venue existed elsewhere for all of the charges; moreover, bringing the case in any other venue might have appeared to be "forum shopping," since the main locus of the crimes was Florida.

† This is the second indictment in this case; after the first indictment issued, prosecutors, likely responding to new evidence, issued this superseding indictment containing additional charges and charging one additional defendant, Carlos De Oliveira.

GENERAL ALLEGATIONS

At times material to this Superseding Indictment, on or about the dates and approximate times stated below:

Introduction

1.   Defendant **DONALD J. TRUMP** was the forty-fifth President of the United States of America. He held office from January 20, 2017, until January 20, 2021. As president, **TRUMP** had lawful access to the most sensitive classified documents and national defense information gathered and owned by the United States government, including information from the agencies that comprise the United States Intelligence Community and the United States Department of Defense.

2.   Over the course of his presidency, **TRUMP** gathered newspapers, press clippings, letters, notes, cards, photographs, official documents, and other materials in cardboard boxes that he kept in the White House. Among the materials **TRUMP** stored in his boxes were hundreds of classified documents.*

3.   The classified documents **TRUMP** stored in his boxes included information regarding defense and weapons capabilities of both the United States and foreign countries; United States nuclear programs; potential vulnerabilities of the United States and its allies to military attack; and plans for possible retaliation in response to a foreign attack. The unauthorized disclosure of these classified documents could put at risk the national security of the United States, foreign relations, the safety of the United States military, and human sources and the continued viability of sensitive intelligence collection methods.

---

* This paragraph sets out a theme reprised repeatedly, that Trump appeared to be obsessive and possessive about these classified documents. The theme culminates in two underlings referring to Trump by nodding to *A Beautiful Mind*, a movie about John Nash, the brilliant but schizophrenic Princeton economist plagued by obsessive fits and delusions.

4.   At 12:00 p.m. on January 20, 2021, **TRUMP** ceased[*] to be president. As he departed the White House, **TRUMP** caused scores of boxes, many of which contained classified documents, to be transported to The Mar-a-Lago Club in Palm Beach, Florida, where he maintained his residence. **TRUMP** was not authorized to possess or retain those classified documents.

5.   The Mar-a-Lago Club was an active social club, which, between January 2021 and August 2022, hosted events for tens of thousands of members and guests. After **TRUMP**'s presidency, The Mar-a-Lago Club was not an authorized location for the storage, possession, review, display, or discussion of classified documents. Nevertheless, **TRUMP** stored his boxes containing classified[†] documents in various locations at The Mar-a-Lago Club—including in a ballroom, a bathroom and shower, an office space, his bedroom, and a storage room.[‡]

6.   On two occasions in 2021, **TRUMP** showed classified documents to others, as follows:

a.   In July 2021, at Trump National Golf Club in Bedminster, New Jersey ("The Bedminster Club"), during an audio-recorded meeting with a writer, a publisher, and two members of his staff, none of whom possessed a security clearance, **TRUMP** showed and described a "plan of attack" that **TRUMP** said was prepared for him by the Department of Defense and a senior military official. **TRUMP** told the individuals that the plan was "highly confidential" and "secret."

---

[*] Like the other criminal cases, this one gives no quarter to the idea that the election was stolen.

[†] The government directly alleges that the documents remained classified, which is at odds with Trump's public statement that he declassified documents that he moved to the White House residence pursuant to a standing order. Notably, Trump has not made that claim in court, and there is reason to believe that his lawyers are unwilling to make that representation in court (making knowingly false statements to a court can be a crime and can lead to disbarment proceedings).

[‡] The indictment simply could have said the club was not an authorized location for classified information, but the additional allegations drive home the point that this location, in particular, was insecure and risked our nation's secrets falling into the wrong hands. Indeed, the club was a known target of foreign intelligence services.

TRUMP also said, "as president I could have declassified it," and, "Now I can't, you know, but this is still a secret."

b.   In August or September 2021, at The Bedminster Club, **TRUMP** showed a representative of his political action committee who did not possess a security clearance a classified map related to a military operation and told the representative that he should not be showing it to the representative and that the representative should not get too close.*

7.   On March 30, 2022, the Federal Bureau of Investigation ("FBI") opened a criminal investigation into the unlawful retention of classified documents at The Mar-a-Lago Club. A federal grand jury investigation began the next month. The grand jury issued a subpoena requiring **TRUMP** to turn over all documents with classification markings. **TRUMP** endeavored to obstruct the FBI and grand jury investigations and conceal his continued retention of classified documents by, among other things:

a.   suggesting that his attorney falsely represent to the FBI and grand jury that **TRUMP** did not have documents called for by the grand jury subpoena;

b.   directing defendant **WALTINE NAUTA** to move boxes of documents to conceal them from **TRUMP**'s attorney, the FBI, and the grand jury;

c.   suggesting that his attorney hide or destroy documents called for by the grand jury subpoena;

d.   providing to the FBI and grand jury just some of the documents called for by the grand jury subpoena, while claiming that he was cooperating fully;

e.   causing a certification to be submitted to the FBI and grand jury falsely representing that all documents called for by the

---

* This paragraph is important as it includes an allegation that classified information was actually shared with people without clearance to see them. That makes the alleged actions more serious. The unlawful retention of the documents, by itself, posed the risk of improper dissemination. But as the indictment maintains, in fact, this risk actually came to fruition. Such dissemination, if proved, can be relied on by a court to enhance any sentence imposed.

grand jury subpoena had been produced—while knowing that, in fact, not all such documents had been produced; and

f.   attempting to delete security camera footage at The Mar-a-Lago Club to conceal information from the FBI and grand jury.[*]

8.   As a result of **TRUMP**'s retention of classified documents after his presidency and refusal to return them, hundreds of classified documents were not recovered by the United States government until 2022, as follows:

a.   On January 17, nearly one year after **TRUMP** left office, and after months of demands by the National Archives and Records Administration for **TRUMP** to provide all missing presidential records, **TRUMP** provided only 15 boxes, which contained 197 documents with classification markings.

b.   On June 3, in response to a grand jury subpoena demanding the production of all documents with classification markings, **TRUMP**'s attorney provided to the FBI 38 more documents with classification markings.

c.   On August 8, pursuant to a court-authorized search warrant, the FBI recovered from **TRUMP**'s office and a storage room at The Mar-a-Lago Club 102 more documents with classification markings.[†]

TRUMP's Co-Conspirators

9.   Defendant **NAUTA** was a member of the United States Navy stationed as a valet in the White House during **TRUMP**'s pres-

---

[*] This overview of the obstruction charges is followed by more detailed allegations about each of these matters that support the various criminal charges, which are specified at the conclusion of the indictment. Obstruction is, by itself, a crime. Here, however, the charges of obstruction also help prove the underlying illegal retention charges, as the government will argue that if you did nothing wrong, there is no need to obstruct the investigation.

[†] This is a helpful timeline. It does two things. It helps explain why the FBI needed to conduct a court-authorized search. It is also evidence of Trump's intentional retention of the documents, as the government will contend that he had many months to return the documents, and eventually and belatedly returned some, but not all, of them.

idency. Beginning in August 2021, **NAUTA** became an executive assistant in The Office of Donald J. Trump and served as **TRUMP**'s personal aide or "body man." **NAUTA** reported to **TRUMP**, worked closely with **TRUMP**, and traveled with **TRUMP**.*

10. Beginning in January 2022, Defendant **CARLOS DE OLIVEIRA** was employed as the property manager at The Mar-a-Lago Club. Prior to holding the position of property manager. **DE OLIVEIRA** was employed as a valet at The Mar-a-Lago Club.†

The Mar-a-Lago Club

11. The Mar-a-Lago Club was located on South Ocean Boulevard in Palm Beach, Florida, and included **TRUMP**'s residence, more than 25 guest rooms, two ballrooms, a spa, a gift store, exercise facilities, office space, and an outdoor pool and patio. As of January 2021. The Mar-a-Lago Club had hundreds of members and

---

* Reports that the government sought to "flip" Nauta (i.e., obtain his cooperation) are entirely understandable. Nauta was in close proximity to Trump both in the White House and after his presidency. Accordingly, he could provide firsthand information pertinent to this indictment, as well as to the DC indictment. Nauta, who is represented by counsel whom a Trump PAC pays for, and who also represents various other Trump loyalists, has declined to cooperate with the government as is his right.
† De Oliveira was not charged in the original indictment, which was issued on June 8, 2023. The grand jury investigation continued thereafter, and the government obtained the cooperation of Yuscil Taveras, a junior worker at Mar-a-Lago. Taveras was represented by the same lawyer as Nauta, but changed lawyers (with the approval of the Chief Judge of the District Court for the District of Columbia) and decided to cooperate shortly thereafter. This new evidence no doubt led to the superseding indictment charging additional crimes and a new defendant—De Oliveira—on July 27, 2023.

INSIDER NOTE: This change of counsel is reminiscent of what happened with Cassidy Hutchinson, a close aide to former chief of staff Mark Meadows. Hutchinson testified that her initial lawyer did not tell her who was paying for his services and, while instructing her not to lie, also told her to "downplay" her role in the events surrounding January 6 when testifying before the January 6 congressional committee. Further, Hutchinson claims she was advised that if she testified that she did not recall something, the committee would not be able to discern whether she did or did not in fact recall it. Shortly after obtaining new counsel, Hutchinson began cooperating with the committee and, subsequently, the government. Her prior lawyer, who is facing a bar complaint in the District of Columbia, has denied that he did anything untoward.

was staffed by more than 150 full-time, part-time, and temporary employees.

12.   Between January 2021 and August 2022, The Mar-a-Lago Club hosted more than 150 social events, including weddings, movie premieres, and fundraisers that together drew tens of thousands of guests.

13.   The United States Secret Service (the "Secret Service") provided protection services to **TRUMP** and his family after he left office, including at The Mar-a-Lago Club, but it was not responsible for the protection of **TRUMP**'s boxes or their contents. **TRUMP** did not inform the Secret Service that he was storing boxes containing classified documents at The Mar-a-Lago Club.[*]

Classified Information[†]

14.   National security information was information owned by, produced by, produced for, and under the control of the United States government. Pursuant to Executive Order 12958, signed on April 17, 1995, as amended by Executive Order 13292 on March 25, 2003, and Executive Order 13526 on December 29, 2009, national security information was classified as "TOP SECRET," "SECRET," or "CONFIDENTIAL," as follows:

a.   Information was classified as TOP SECRET if the unauthorized disclosure of that information reasonably could be expected to cause exceptionally grave damage to the national security that the original classification authority was able to identify or describe.

---

[*] These allegations about the Secret Service serve to prebut a possible Trump argument: that the documents, although not stored in a designated area for classified information, were nevertheless safe because the Secret Service knew about their existence and was protecting them from disclosure.

[†] This section provides a crash course on the government's classification process and the nomenclature used for various levels of classified information. This section is especially detailed because of the extraordinary sensitivity of the array of classified information at Mar-a-Lago and Bedminster. The cache of documents included Top Secret information that was within special compartmented programs within that TS level (which require being "read into" the program only if you have a need to know the information).

b.   Information was classified as SECRET if the unauthorized disclosure of that information reasonably could be expected to cause serious damage to the national security that the original classification authority was able to identify or describe.

c.   Information was classified as CONFIDENTIAL if the unauthorized disclosure of that information reasonably could be expected to cause damage to the national security that the original classification authority was able to identify or describe.

15.   The classification marking "**NOFORN**" stood for "Not Releasable to Foreign Nationals" and denoted that dissemination of that information was limited to United States persons.

16.   Classified information related to intelligence sources, methods, and analytical processes was designated as Sensitive Compartmented Information ("SCI"). SCI was to be processed, stored, used, or discussed in an accredited Sensitive Compartmented Information Facility ("SCIF"),* and only individuals with the appropriate security clearance and additional SCI permissions were authorized to have access to such national security information.

17.   When the vulnerability of, or threat to, specific classified information was exceptional, and the normal criteria for determining eligibility for access to classified information were insufficient to protect the information from unauthorized disclosure, the United States could establish Special Access Programs ("SAPs") to further protect the classified information. The number of these programs was to be kept to an absolute minimum and limited to programs in which the number of persons who ordinarily would have access would be reasonably small and commensurate with the objective of providing enhanced protection for the information involved. Only

---

* Government employees who handle classified information are well acquainted with SCIFs, as they are the only locations in which one can access classified material. SCIFs are highly secure. For instance, in a SCIF, electronic devices—phones, laptops, watches, Fitbits, iPads, etc.—are prohibited in order to prevent them from being used to record or remotely see or hear what is occurring in the SCIF. Windows in a SCIF, to the extent there are any, are covered so one cannot see inside. (For instance, venetian blinds are required to be at certain angles that prevent anyone seeing inside.) And a log is kept of anyone entering or leaving a SCIF.

individuals with the appropriate security clearance and additional SAP permissions were authorized to have access to such national security information, which was subject to enhanced handling and storage requirements.

18.   Pursuant to Executive Order 13526, information classified at any level could be lawfully accessed only by persons determined by an appropriate United States government official to be eligible for access to classified information and who had signed an approved non-disclosure agreement, who received a security clearance, and who had a "need-to-know" the classified information.* After his presidency, **TRUMP** was not authorized to possess or retain classified documents.†

19.   Executive Order 13526 provided that a former president could obtain a waiver of the "need-to-know" requirement, if the agency head or senior agency official of the agency that originated the classified information: (1) determined in writing that access was consistent with the interest of national security and (2) took appropriate steps to protect classified information from unauthorized disclosure or compromise and ensured that the information was safeguarded in a manner consistent with the order. **TRUMP** did not obtain any such waiver after his presidency.‡

---

* Normally, one has to be approved by the government to be granted access to classified information. Defense counsel and prosecutors must receive clearance, but certain people are given clearance automatically: sitting presidents and vice presidents, members of Congress, federal judges, and trial jurors all may be able to see classified material without going through a formal clearance process.

† This is an important fact, as it is what made it illegal for Trump to retain classified information. Given the allegations here and in the other indictments, President Biden's decision not to extend Trump's security clearance post-presidency appears wise.

‡ This paragraph makes clear that Trump had a legal alternative he could have pursued, if he believed he should be able to access classified information. However, as this paragraph notes, he did not avail himself of this process.

The Executive Branch Departments and Agencies Whose Classified Documents TRUMP Retained After His Presidency

20.   As part of his official duties as president, **TRUMP** received intelligence briefings from high-level United States government officials, including briefings from the Director of the Central Intelligence Agency, the Chairman of the Joint Chiefs of Staff, senior White House officials, and a designated briefer. He regularly received a collection of classified intelligence from the United States Intelligence Community ("USIC") known as the "President's Daily Brief."

21.   The USIC's mission was to collect, analyze, and deliver foreign intelligence and counterintelligence information to America's leaders, including the president, policymakers, law enforcement, and the military, so they could make sound decisions to protect the United States. The USIC consisted of United States executive branch departments and agencies responsible for the conduct of foreign relations and the protection of national security.

22.   After his presidency, **TRUMP** retained classified documents originated by, or implicating the equities of, multiple USIC members and other executive branch departments and agencies, including the following:*

a.   **The Central Intelligence Agency ("CIA").** CIA was responsible for providing intelligence on foreign countries and global issues to the president and other policymakers to help them make national security decisions.

b.   **The Department of Defense ("DoD").** DoD was responsible for providing the military forces needed to deter war and

---

* Welcome to the world of DC acronyms. The indictment gives the reader another crash course, this time on the many government agencies that comprise what is referred to by the umbrella term "the Intelligence Community" (referred to in the indictment as the "USIC").

ensure national security. Some of the executive branch agencies comprising the USIC were within DoD.

c.   **The National Security Agency.** The National Security Agency was a combat support agency within DoD and a member of the USIC responsible for foreign signals intelligence and cybersecurity. This included collecting, processing, and disseminating to United States policymakers and military leaders foreign intelligence derived from communications and information systems; protecting national security systems; and enabling computer network operations.

d.   **The National Geospatial Intelligence Agency.** The National Geospatial Intelligence Agency was a combat support agency within DoD responsible for the exploitation and analysis of imagery, imagery intelligence, and geospatial information in support of the national security objectives of the United States and the geospatial intelligence requirements of DoD, the Department of State, and other federal agencies.

e.   **The National Reconnaissance Office.** The National Reconnaissance Office was an agency within DoD responsible for developing, acquiring, launching, and operating space-based surveillance and reconnaissance systems that collected and delivered intelligence to enhance national security.

f.   **The Department of Energy.** The Department of Energy was responsible for maintaining a safe, secure, and effective nuclear deterrent to protect national security, including ensuring the effectiveness of the United States nuclear weapons stockpile without nuclear explosive testing.

g.   **The Department of State and Bureau of Intelligence and Research.** The Department of State was responsible for protecting and promoting United States security, prosperity, and democratic values. Within the Department of State, the Bureau of Intelligence and Research was a member of the USIC and responsible for providing intelligence to inform diplomacy and support United States diplomats.

TRUMP's Public Statements on Classified Information

23.   As a candidate for President of the United States, **TRUMP** made the following public statements, among others, about classified information:

    a.   On August 18, 2016, **TRUMP** stated, "In my administration I'm going to enforce all laws concerning the protection of classified information. No one will be above the law."

    b.   On September 6, 2016. **TRUMP** stated, "We also need to fight this battle by collecting intelligence and then protecting, protecting our classified secrets. . . . We can't have someone in the Oval Office who doesn't understand the meaning of the word confidential or classified."

    c.   On September 7, 2016, **TRUMP** stated, "[O]ne of the first things we must do is to enforce all classification rules and to enforce all laws relating to the handling of classified information."

    d.   On September 19, 2016, **TRUMP** stated, "We also need the best protection of classified information."

    e.   On November 3, 2016, **TRUMP** stated, "Service members here in North Carolina have risked their lives to acquire classified intelligence to protect our country."*

---

* Why does the indictment make these allegations about what Trump said about classified information? Because the government must show that Trump knew the material he had in his possession was national defense information (which is almost synonymous with the document being classified) and that he was aware of the rules concerning how such information must be handled (i.e., if you do not have a security clearance, you cannot possess these documents). It is not a crime for Trump merely to negligently or unknowingly retain documents that were national defense information. To convict on the illegal retention charges, the prosecution must show that Trump *knew* that he possessed the documents that contained national defense information. The indictment makes skillful use of Trump's own statements (made in the context of attacking his presidential rival Hillary Clinton over State Department emails kept on a home server) about the importance of keeping classified information secure. Each of these statements is admissible under the Federal Rules of Evidence against Trump as his own admissions. The admissions will have the added benefit of underscoring the defendant's own awareness of why keeping such documents under lock and key is vital to the nation's security.

24. As President of the United States, on July 26, 2018, **TRUMP** issued the following statement about classified information:

> As the head of the executive branch and Commander in Chief, I have a unique, Constitutional responsibility to protect the Nation's classified information, including by controlling access to it.... More broadly, the issue of [a former executive branch official's] security clearance raises larger questions about the practice of former officials maintaining access to our Nation's most sensitive secrets long after their time in Government has ended. Such access is particularly inappropriate when former officials have transitioned into highly partisan positions and seek to use real or perceived access to sensitive information to validate their political attacks. Any access granted to our Nation's secrets should be in furtherance of national, not personal, interests.*

TRUMP's Retention of Classified Documents After His Presidency†

25. In January 2021, as he was preparing to leave the White House, **TRUMP** and his White House staff, including **NAUTA**, packed items, including some of **TRUMP**'s boxes. **TRUMP** was

---

INSIDER NOTE: During his presidency, Trump signed into law increased criminal penalties for improper handling of classified information. That is not just ironic; it potentially could be used as additional proof of his awareness of the rules he is alleged to have knowingly violated.

* This Trump statement is particularly apt given that he is charged with illegal retention of classified documents after he was no longer in office. The admission also has Trump suggesting one reason why a former official might retain such documents. But, meaningfully, the indictment does not allege why Trump retained these documents. Motive need not be alleged: the crimes are the unlawful retention of documents and obstruction of the investigation. Trump's motive as to why he retained the documents need not be proved; indeed, he may have had various motives, and mixed motives, for different sets of the many documents he is alleged to have retained.

† Trump is not charged with improper retention of such documents while he was president, as he was authorized at that time to have such material; the charges focus on the period after he no longer was president and lacked the requisite security clearance.

INSIDER NOTE: Because the charges relate to his post-presidency time period, Trump cannot make a claim that he enjoys presidential immunity for his conduct (a claim he is litigating in the DC indictment case).

personally involved in this process. **TRUMP** caused his boxes, containing hundreds of classified documents, to be transported from the White House to The Mar-a-Lago Club.*

26.   From January through March 15, 2021, some of **TRUMP**'s boxes were stored in The Mar-a-Lago Club's White and Gold Ballroom, in which events and gatherings took place. **TRUMP**'s boxes were for a time stacked on the ballroom's stage, as depicted in the photograph below (redacted to obscure an individual's identity).†

27.   In March 2021, **NAUTA** and others moved some of **TRUMP**'s boxes from the White and Gold Ballroom to the business center at The Mar-a-Lago Club.

---

* Here, the indictment specifies that Trump himself was involved in the process, which is an important allegation. CEOs and other people in charge of large operations often assert that they were unaware of what underlings were doing. The government in a criminal case must be able to show that this is not true; here the indictment notes Trump's personal involvement in packing the boxes; other allegations make the same point about Trump's alleged personal involvement with the handling of the boxes once they arrived at Mar-a-Lago.

† It is unusual to include a photograph in an indictment, but here the photograph shows the cavalier manner in which the documents were placed in the club, in striking contrast to Trump's public statements about the need to keep such documents secure. The photo helped explain why the FBI was required to conduct a court-authorized search and to undercut Trump's initial claims that the FBI planted the documents at Mar-a-Lago—a claim that, as of this writing, has not been made in court.

28. On April 5, 2021, an employee of The Office of Donald J. Trump* ("Trump Employee 1") texted another employee of that office ("Trump Employee 2") to ask whether **TRUMP**'s boxes could be moved out of the business center to make room for staff to use it as an office. Trump Employee 2 replied, "Woah!! Ok so potus specifically asked Walt for those boxes to be in the business center because they are his 'papers.'" Later that day, Trump Employee 1 and Trump Employee 2 exchanged the following text messages:

Trump Employee 2:

We can definitely make it work if we move his papers into the lake room?

Trump Employee 1:

There is still a little room in the shower where his other stuff is. Is it only his papers he cares about? Theres some other stuff in there that are not papers. Could that go to storage? Or does he want everything in there on property

Trump Employee 2:

Yes - anything that's not the beautiful mind† paper boxes can definitely go to storage. Want to take a look at the space and start moving tomorrow AM?

29. After the text exchange between Trump Employee 1 and Trump Employee 2, in April 2021, some of **TRUMP**'s boxes were moved from the business center to a bathroom and shower in The Mar-a-Lago Club's Lake Room, as depicted in the photograph below.

---

* The Office of Donald J. Trump is Trump's post-presidential office. Most former presidents establish a post-presidential office. Indeed, the Former Presidents Act authorizes and appropriates funds for post-presidential office staff for such purposes.
† The contemporaneous discussion among Trump employees evinces Trump's knowledge and hands-on approach to the boxes taken from the White House. It also plainly belies any claim that these boxes were planted, since the FBI did not conduct the search until well over a year later.

INSIDER NOTE: Trump will surely litigate the admissibility of the texts and any related testimony under the Federal Rules of Evidence hearsay rules; however, it seems unlikely, under a correct application of those rules, that the entirety of this conversation would be inadmissible.

30.   In May 2021, **TRUMP** directed that a storage room on the ground floor of The Mar-a-Lago Club (the "Storage Room") be cleaned out so that it could be used to store his boxes. The hallway leading to the Storage Room could be reached from multiple outside entrances, including one accessible from The Mar-a-Lago Club pool patio through a doorway that was often kept open. The Storage Room was near the liquor supply closet, linen room, lock shop, and various other rooms.*

31.   On June 24, 2021, **TRUMP**'s boxes that were in the Lake Room were moved to the Storage Room. After the move, there were more than 80 boxes in the Storage Room, as depicted in the photographs below.†

---

* The indictment continues to prebut, in words and photos, any defense claim that the documents were securely stored under lock and key, and inaccessible to people at the club. The photograph of the boxes stored cavalierly in a garish club bathroom— adjacent to unobstructed windows, a shower, a toilet, and a sink—drives the point home. Note, although any such defense claim likely would be unavailing as a legal defense, it could prompt a jury to nullify the charges against the defendant. Moreover, such a defense could gain traction in the court of public opinion by continuing to make the case that the charges lack seriousness.

† It is meaningful that the prosecution specifically notes that number of boxes in the storage room. This information, in tandem with specific dates and times, indicates that in addition to testimonial evidence, the government has video footage with time stamps from which it can ascertain with precision when items were moved. Such video footage is thus surely going to be used by the government at trial to prove its case. Indeed, it is notable that in this superseding indictment, the prosecution filed

32. On December 7, 2021, **NAUTA** found several of **TRUMP**'s boxes fallen and their contents spilled onto the floor of the Storage Room, including a document marked "SECRET// REL TO USA, FVEY," which denoted that the information in the document was releasable only to the Five Eyes intelligence alliance consisting of Australia, Canada, New Zealand, the United Kingdom, and the United States. **NAUTA** texted Trump Employee 2, "I opened the door and found this . . ." **NAUTA** also attached two photographs he took of the spill. Trump Employee 2 replied, "Oh no oh no," and "I'm sorry potus had my phone." One of the photographs **NAUTA** texted to Trump Employee 2 is depicted below with the visible classified information redacted. **TRUMP**'s unlawful retention of this document is charged in Count 8 of this Superseding Indictment.*

---

additional charges against the three defendants alleging their efforts to delete this incriminating video footage.

* This is a particularly damning photograph, as it was taken by Nauta, a co-defendant, not by the FBI. The photograph (see page 248) depicts a classified document in a pile of other materials in disarray. The photograph and texts make any claim that the FBI planted the classified document untenable.

INSIDER NOTE: The text exchange between Nauta and "Trump Employee 2" in which Employee 2 says Trump had his phone is tantalizing: it suggests that Trump, despite his vaunted aversion to email, was able to communicate by commandeering other people's devices. The fact of the text exchange also indicates that the government was able to access the information on one or both of the phones involved, which can be done pursuant to a search warrant based on probable cause or with the consent of the phone's owner.

TRUMP's Disclosures of Classified Information in Private Meetings

33. In May 2021, **TRUMP** caused some of his boxes to be brought to his summer residence at The Bedminster Club. Like The Mar-a-Lago Club, after **TRUMP**'s presidency, The Bedminster Club was not an authorized location for the storage, possession, review, display, or discussion of classified documents.

34. On July 21, 2021, when he was no longer president, **TRUMP** gave an interview in his office at The Bedminster Club to a writer and a publisher in connection with a then-forthcoming book. Two members of **TRUMP**'s staff also attended the interview, which was recorded with **TRUMP**'s knowledge and consent. Before the interview, the media had published reports that, at the end of **TRUMP**'s term as president, a senior military official (the "Senior Military Official") purportedly feared that **TRUMP** might order an attack on Country A and that the Senior Military Official advised **TRUMP** against doing so.

35. Upon greeting the writer, publisher, and his two staff members, **TRUMP** stated, "Look what I found, this was [the Senior Military Official's] plan of attack, read it and just show . . . it's interesting." Later in the interview, **TRUMP** engaged in the following exchange:

TRUMP: Well, with [the Senior Military Official]—uh, let me see
            that, I'll show you an example. He said that I wanted to
            attack [Country A]. Isn't it amazing? I have a big pile of
            papers, this thing just came up. Look. This was him.
            They presented me this—this is off the record, but—
            they presented me this. This was him. This was the
            Defense Department and him.

WRITER: Wow.

TRUMP: We looked at some. This was him. This wasn't done by
            me, this was him. All sorts of stuff—pages long, look.

STAFFER: Mm.

TRUMP: Wait a minute, let's see here.

STAFFER: *[Laughter]* Yeah.

TRUMP: I just found, isn't that amazing? This totally wins my
            case, you know.

STAFFER: Mm-hm.

TRUMP: Except it is like, highly confidential.

STAFFER: Yeah. *[Laughter]*

TRUMP: Secret. This is secret information. Look, look at this.
            You attack, and—

                              * * *

TRUMP: By the way. Isn't that incredible?

STAFFER: Yeah.

TRUMP: I was just thinking, because we were talking about it.
            And you know, he said, "he wanted to attack [Country
            A], and what . . ."

STAFFER: You did.

TRUMP: This was done by the military and given to me. Uh, I
            think we can probably, right?

STAFFER: I don't know, we'll, we'll have to see. Yeah, we'll have to
            try to—

TRUMP: Declassify it.

STAFFER: —figure out a—yeah.

TRUMP: See as president I could have declassified it.

STAFFER: Yeah. *[Laughter]*

TRUMP: Now I can't, you know, but this is still a secret.

STAFFER: Yeah. *[Laughter]* Now we have a problem.

TRUMP: Isn't that interesting?

At the time of this exchange, the writer, the publisher, and **TRUMP**'s two staff members did not have security clearances or any need-to-know any classified information about a plan of attack on Country A. The document that **TRUMP** possessed and showed on July 21, 2021, is charged as Count 32 in this Superseding Indictment.*

36.   In August or September 2021, when he was no longer president, **TRUMP** met in his office at The Bedminster Club with a representative of his political action committee (the "PAC Representative"). During the meeting, **TRUMP** commented that an ongoing military operation in Country B was not going well. **TRUMP** showed the PAC Representative a classified map of Country B and told the PAC Representative that he should not be showing the map

---

* These allegations were made in the initial indictment, but the conduct was not charged as a stand-alone crime. If it had not been charged in the superseding indictment, the defense could seek to exclude this evidence at trial on the ground that, because it was not direct proof of a charged crime, it was unduly prejudicial. However, by charging this alleged conduct as a crime in count 38, the superseding indictment remedies this issue by making it legally impossible to exclude this evidence on that ground. The government will now be able to contend this is evidence of the defendant on tape confessing to one of the charged crimes. And, of course, there are witnesses who were present for the conversation as well.

INSIDER NOTE: Why was this conduct not initially charged? We don't know, but it is notable that in the first indictment all of the thirty-one illegal document retention charges related to documents found in the FBI search in August 2022. This new charge relates to a different time period: it is for a document that Trump returned to the National Archives in January 2022. This new timeline opens the trial up to a more complicated factual front. The government may have also obtained more evidence about the facts underlying count 32, resulting in a decision that the count could be proved beyond a reasonable doubt.

to the PAC Representative and to not get too close. The PAC Representative did not have a security clearance or any need-to-know classified information about the military operation.

37.   On February 16, 2017, four years before **TRUMP**'s disclosures of classified information set forth above, **TRUMP** said at a press conference:

> The first thing I thought of when I heard about it is, how does the press get this information that's classified? How do they do it? You know why? Because it's an illegal process, and the press should be ashamed of themselves. But more importantly, the people that gave out the information to the press should be ashamed of themselves. Really ashamed.*

TRUMP's Production of 15 Cardboard Boxes to the National Archives and Records Administration

38.   Beginning in May 2021, the National Archives and Records Administration ("NARA"), which was responsible for archiving presidential records, repeatedly demanded that **TRUMP** turn over presidential records that he had kept after his presidency. On multiple occasions, beginning in June, NARA warned **TRUMP** through his representatives that if he did not comply, it would refer the matter of the missing records to the Department of Justice.

39.   Between November 2021 and January 2022, **NAUTA** and Trump Employee 2—at **TRUMP**'s direction—brought boxes from the Storage Room to **TRUMP**'s residence for **TRUMP** to review.†

40.   On November 12, 2021, Trump Employee 2 provided **TRUMP** a photograph of his boxes in the Storage Room by taping it

---

* This is another skillful use of Trump's own statements to show his awareness of the rules regarding handling of such information.

† The factual allegations here are so important to show Trump's knowledge of the existence of the classified documents, and that Trump was not simply relying on junior people to comply with the National Archives' and DOJ's demands for the documents' return.

to one of the boxes that Trump Employee 2 had placed in **TRUMP**'s residence. Trump Employee 2 provided **TRUMP** the photograph so that **TRUMP** could see how many of his boxes were stored in the Storage Room. The photograph, shown below, depicted a wall of the Storage Room against which dozens of **TRUMP**'s boxes were stacked.

41. On November 17, 2021, **NAUTA** texted Trump Employee 2 about the photograph Trump Employee 2 had provided to **TRUMP**, stating, "He mentioned about a picture of the 'boxes' he wants me to see it?" Trump Employee 2 replied, "Calling you shortly."

42. On November 25, 2021, Trump Employee 2 texted **NAUTA** about **TRUMP**'s review of the contents of his boxes, asking, "Has he mentioned boxes to you? I delivered some, but I think he may need more. Could you ask if he'd like more in pine hall?" Pine Hall was an entry room in **TRUMP**'s residence. **NAUTA** replied in three successive text messages:

> Nothing about boxes yet
>
> He has one he's working on in pine hall
>
> Knocked out 2 boxes yesterday

43. On November 29, 2021, Trump Employee 2 texted **NAUTA**, asking, "Next you are on property (no rush) could you help me bring 4 more boxes up?" **NAUTA** replied, "Yes!! Of course."

44. On December 29, 2021. Trump Employee 2 texted a **TRUMP** representative who was in contact with NARA ("Trump Representative 1"), "box answer will be wrenched out of him today, promise!" The next day, Trump Representative 1 replied in two successive text messages:

> Hey - Just checking on Boxes . . .
>
> would love to have a number to them today

Trump Employee 2 spoke to **TRUMP*** and then responded a few hours later in two successive text messages:

> 12
>
> Is his number

45. On January 13, 2022, **NAUTA** texted Trump Employee 2 about **TRUMP**'s "tracking" of boxes, stating, "He's tracking the boxes, more to follow today on whether he wants to go through more today or tomorrow." Trump Employee 2 replied. "Thank you!"†

46. On January 15, 2022, **NAUTA** sent Trump Employee 2 four successive text messages:

> One thing he asked
>
> Was for new covers for the boxes, for Monday m.
>
> Morning
>
> *can we get new box covers before giving these to them on Monday? They have too much writing on them. I marked too much

Trump Employee 2 replied, "Yes, I will get that!"

---

* Indictments typically do not set out what witnesses are expected to say at trial. While this indictment generally follows that practice, here it makes clear that "Trump Employee 2" had a direct conversation with Trump, and we should expect that the employee will be a trial witness.

† The contemporaneous exchange between Nauta and "Trump Employee 2" will be an important piece of evidence for the government to prove Trump's awareness of what was in the boxes.

254 THE TRUMP INDICTMENTS

47.   On January 17, 2022, Trump Employee 2 and **NAUTA** gathered 15 boxes from **TRUMP**'s residence, loaded the boxes in **NAUTA**'s car, and took them to a commercial truck for delivery to NARA.

48.   When interviewed by the FBI in May 2022 regarding the location and movement of boxes before the production to NARA, **NAUTA** made false and misleading statements as set forth in Count 38 of this Superseding Indictment, including:

a.   falsely stating that he was not aware of **TRUMP**'s boxes being brought to **TRUMP**'s residence for his review before **TRUMP** provided 15 boxes to NARA in January 2022;

b.   falsely stating that he did not know how the boxes that he and Trump Employee 2 brought from **TRUMP**'s residence to the commercial truck for delivery to NARA on January 17, 2022, had gotten to the residence; and

c.   when asked whether he knew where **TRUMP**'s boxes had been stored before they were in **TRUMP**'s residence and whether they had been in a secure or locked location, **NAUTA** falsely responded, "I wish, I wish I could tell you. I don't know. I don't—I honestly just don't know."*

49.   When the 15 boxes that **TRUMP** had provided reached NARA in January 2022, NARA reviewed the contents and determined that 14 of the boxes contained documents with classification markings. Specifically, as the FBI later determined, the boxes contained 197 documents with classification markings, of which 98 were marked "SECRET," 30 were marked "TOP SECRET," and the remainder were marked "CONFIDENTIAL." Some of those documents also contained SCI and SAP markings.

---

* The government taped the interview with Nauta and will be able to prove the falsity of his claims to the FBI using Nauta's own texts. As a defense, Nauta might argue that by May 2022, he forgot that he had done this earlier. However, such a defense may be a hard sell given the recency of the events, his categorical and repeated denials of having knowledge of the boxes, and the seriousness of an FBI interview for which he undoubtedly prepared with his counsel.

50.   On February 9, 2022, NARA referred the discovery of classified documents in **TRUMP**'s boxes to the Department of Justice for investigation.

The FBI and Grand Jury Investigations

51.   On March 30, 2022, the FBI opened a criminal investigation.

52.   On April 26, 2022, a federal grand jury opened an investigation.*

The Defendants' Concealment of Boxes

53.   On May 11, 2022, the grand jury issued a subpoena (the "May 11 Subpoena") to The Office of Donald J. Trump requiring the production of all documents with classification markings in the possession, custody, or control of **TRUMP** or The Office of Donald J. Trump. Two attorneys representing **TRUMP** ("Trump Attorney 1" and "Trump Attorney 2") informed **TRUMP** of the May 11 Subpoena, and he authorized Trump Attorney 1 to accept service.†

---

* The timeline will be the government's friend at trial; it will help establish Trump's intent to retain the documents and the efforts to hide them from the government.

INSIDER NOTE: The timeline also serves to differentiate the case, in the court of public opinion, from Pence's and Biden's possession of classified documents, as there is no evidence that they hid the inadvertently retained documents from the government.

† The subpoena calling for the production of all the documents bearing classified markings poses serious difficulties for the defense. It makes irrelevant whether the documents were declassified or not, since the subpoena called for the production of documents bearing classified markings (regardless of whether they had previously been declassified by Trump, as to which there is to date scant evidence, in any event). Further, Trump's public statements that he could take and keep whatever he wanted from the White House, and that these were his personal documents, in addition to being legally and factually not true, is not a defense to not complying with a subpoena. Subpoenas routinely call for a person to produce both personal and business records. Trump's own significant history with civil litigation would make him well acquainted with this truism, but the indictment makes plain that lawyers advised Trump of this as well.

54. On May 22, 2022, **NAUTA** entered the Storage Room at 3:47 p.m. and left approximately 34 minutes later, carrying one of **TRUMP**'s boxes.

55. On May 23, 2022. **TRUMP** met with Trump Attorney 1 and Trump Attorney 2 at The Mar-a-Lago Club to discuss the response to the May 11 Subpoena. Trump Attorney 1 and Trump Attorney 2 told **TRUMP** that they needed to search for documents that would be responsive to the subpoena and provide a certification that there had been compliance with the subpoena. **TRUMP**, in sum and substance, made the following statements, among others, as memorialized by Trump Attorney 1:

 a. I don't want anybody looking. I don't want anybody looking through my boxes, I really don't, I don't want you looking through my boxes.

 b. Well what if we, what happens if we just don't respond at all or don't play ball with them?

 c. Wouldn't it be better if we just told them we don't have anything here?*

 d. Well look isn't it better if there are no documents?

56. While meeting with Trump Attorney 1 and Trump Attorney 2 on May 23, **TRUMP**, in sum and substance, told the following story, as memorialized by Trump Attorney 1:

> [Attorney], he was great, he did a great job. You know what? He said, he said that it – that it was him. That he was the one who deleted all of her emails, the 30,000 emails, because they basically dealt with her scheduling and her going to the gym and her having beauty appointments. And he was great. And

---

* The indictment alleges that the former president of the United States raised the question of whether it would be better to lie to the government in response to the subpoena. When his lawyers did not go along with this idea, Trump is alleged to have misled them into thinking they were turning over all documents responsive to the subpoena, which forms the basis of the first obstruction scheme charged in the indictment.

he, so she didn't get in any trouble because he said that he was the one who deleted them.

TRUMP related the story more than once that day.*

57.   On May 23, **TRUMP** also confirmed his understanding with Trump Attorney 1 that Trump Attorney 1 would return to The Mar-a-Lago Club on June 2 to search for any documents with classification markings to produce in response to the May 11 Subpoena. Trump Attorney 1 made it clear to **TRUMP** that Trump Attorney 1 would conduct the search for responsive documents by looking through **TRUMP**'s boxes that had been transported from the White House and remained in storage at The Mar-a-Lago Club. **TRUMP** indicated that he wanted to be at The Mar-a-Lago Club when Trump Attorney 1 returned to review his boxes on June 2, and that **TRUMP** would change his summer travel plans to do so. **TRUMP** told Trump Attorney 2 that Trump Attorney 2 did not need to be present for the review of boxes.

58.   After meeting with Trump Attorney 1 and Trump Attorney 2 on May 23, **TRUMP** delayed his departure from The Mar-a-Lago Club to The Bedminster Club for the summer so that he would be present at The Mar-a-Lago Club on June 2, when Trump Attorney 1 returned to review the boxes.

59.   Between **TRUMP**'s May 23 meeting with Trump Attorney 1 and Trump Attorney 2 to discuss the May 11 Subpoena, and June 2, when Trump Attorney 1 returned to The Mar-a-Lago Club to review the boxes in the Storage Room, **NAUTA** removed—at **TRUMP**'s direction—a total of approximately 64 boxes from the

---

* This is a reference to Trump's beliefs as to how Hillary Clinton and her lawyer responded to a subpoena; it is an unsubtle suggestion that Trump's lawyers obstruct justice for him, as he believes Hillary's lawyers did for her.

INSIDER NOTE: This allegation is eerily reminiscent of Trump's conversation with Don McGahn when McGahn was Trump's White House counsel. McGahn reported that Trump asked him to make a false statement about whether Trump had sought to fire Special Counsel Robert Mueller, and McGahn refused. The McGahn incident may be admissible under Federal Rule of Evidence 404(b), permitting "other crime" evidence against a defendant under certain circumstances and for certain purposes.

Storage Room and brought them to **TRUMP**'s residence, as set forth below:

a.   On May 24, 2022, between 5:30 p.m. and 5:38 p.m., **NAUTA** removed three boxes from the Storage Room.*

b.   On May 30, 2022, at 9:08 a.m., **TRUMP** and **NAUTA** spoke by phone for approximately 30 seconds. Between 10:02 a.m. and 11:51 a.m., **NAUTA** removed a total of approximately 50 boxes from the Storage Room.

c.   On May 30, 2022, at 12:33 p.m., a Trump family member texted **NAUTA**:

> Good afternoon Walt,
> Happy Memorial Day!
>
> I saw you put boxes to Potus room. Just FYI and I will tell him as well:
> Not sure how many he wants to take on Friday on the plane. We will NOT have a room for them. Plane will be full with luggage.
> Thank you!

NAUTA replied:

> Good Afternoon Ma'am [Smiley Face Emoji]
>
> Thank you so much.

---

* The precise time noted here again makes plain that the government's allegations are supported by time-stamped video surveillance evidence—likely the same video surveillance evidence that is the basis for the second obstruction scheme alleged in the superseding indictment. According to the superseding indictment, the defendants sought to destroy this evidence.

INSIDER NOTE: We can expect the government, after it introduces the video evidence, to tell the jury that this is the inculpatory evidence that the defendants did not want the jury to see. The defendants, by contrast, likely will say that the fact that the evidence still exists (and is in the government's possession) is proof that the defendants did not intend to destroy the evidence (an argument that is often made when a conspiracy to commit a crime is unsuccessful in achieving its goal).

I think he wanted to pick from them. I don't imagine him wanting to take the boxes.

He told me to put them in the room and that he was going to talk to you about them.

d.   On June 1, 2022, beginning at 12:52 p.m., **NAUTA** removed approximately 11 boxes from the Storage Room.

60.   On June 1, 2022, **TRUMP** spoke with Trump Attorney 1 by phone and asked whether Trump Attorney 1 was coming to The Mar-a-Lago Club the next day and for exactly what purpose. Trump Attorney 1 reminded **TRUMP** that Trump Attorney 1 was going to review the boxes that had been transported from the White House and remained in storage at The Mar-a-Lago Club so that Trump Attorney 1 could have a custodian of records certify that the May 11 subpoena had been complied with fully.

61.   On June 2, 2022, the day that Trump Attorney 1 was scheduled to review **TRUMP**'s boxes in the Storage Room, **TRUMP** spoke with **NAUTA** on the phone at 9:29 a.m. for approximately 24 seconds.

62.   Later that day, between 12:33 p.m. and 12:52 p.m., **NAUTA** and **DE OLIVEIRA** moved approximately 30 boxes from **TRUMP**'s residence to the Storage Room.*

63.   In sum, between May 23, 2022, and June 2, 2022, before Trump Attorney 1's review of **TRUMP**'s boxes in the Storage Room, **NAUTA**—at **TRUMP**'s direction—moved approximately 64 boxes from the Storage Room to **TRUMP**'s residence, and **NAUTA** and **DE OLIVEIRA** brought to the Storage Room only approximately 30 boxes. Neither **TRUMP** nor **NAUTA** informed Trump Attorney 1 of this information.

---

* It's a bit of a math exercise, but the gist of the allegations is that Trump had various boxes brought to him so that he could remove the material he did not want to produce to the government. He then returned to the storage room fewer boxes than had been taken to his private residence so that his attorney would not see the removed material, and would thus not know that he was not complying with the subpoena.

The False Certification to the FBI and the Grand Jury

64.   On the afternoon of June 2, 2022, as **TRUMP** had been informed, Trump Attorney 1 arrived at The Mar-a-Lago Club to review **TRUMP**'s boxes to look for documents with classification markings in response to the May 11 Subpoena. **TRUMP** met with Trump Attorney 1 before Trump Attorney 1 conducted the review. **NAUTA** escorted Trump Attorney 1 to the Storage Room.

65.   Between 3:53 p.m. and 6:23 p.m., Trump Attorney 1 reviewed the contents of **TRUMP**'s boxes in the Storage Room. Trump Attorney 1 located 38 documents with classification markings inside the boxes, which Trump Attorney 1 removed and placed in a Redweld folder. Trump Attorney 1 contacted **NAUTA** and asked him to bring clear duct tape to the Storage Room, which **NAUTA** did. Trump Attorney 1 used the clear duct tape to seal the Redweld folder with the documents with classification markings inside.*

66.   After Trump Attorney 1 finished sealing the Redweld folder containing the documents with classification markings that he had found inside **TRUMP**'s boxes, **NAUTA** took Trump Attorney 1 to a dining room in The Mar-a-Lago Club to meet with **TRUMP**. After Trump Attorney 1 confirmed that he was finished with his search of the Storage Room, **TRUMP** asked, "Did you find anything? . . . Is it bad? Good?"

67.   **TRUMP** and Trump Attorney 1 then discussed what to do with the Redweld folder containing documents with classification markings and whether Trump Attorney 1 should bring them to his hotel room and put them in a safe there. During that conversation, **TRUMP** made a plucking motion, as memorialized by Trump Attorney 1:

---

* Why the references to how this material was packaged? According to the government's logic, it shows that Trump's own lawyers understood that these documents were classified and needed to be kept secure until they could be returned to the government. If the lawyers were not aware of the documents' classified status, there would be no reason to take such precautions.

He made a funny motion as though – well okay why don't you take them with you to your hotel room and if there's anything really bad in there, like, you know, pluck it out. And that was the motion that he made. He didn't say that.*

68.   That evening, Trump Attorney 1 contacted the Department of Justice and requested that an FBI agent meet him at The Mar-a-Lago Club the next day, June 3, so that he could turn over the documents responsive to the May 11 Subpoena.

69.   Also that evening, Trump Attorney 1 contacted another **TRUMP** attorney ("Trump Attorney 3") and asked her if she would come to The Mar-a-Lago Club the next morning to act as a custodian of records and sign a certification regarding the search for documents with classification markings in response to the May 11 Subpoena. Trump Attorney 3, who had no role in the review of **TRUMP**'s boxes in the Storage Room, agreed.

70.   The next day, on June 3, 2022, at Trump Attorney 1's request, Trump Attorney 3 signed a certification as the custodian of records for The Office of Donald J. Trump and took it to The Mar-a-Lago Club to provide it to the Department of Justice and FBI. In the certification, Trump Attorney 3—who performed no search of **TRUMP**'s boxes, had not reviewed the May 11 Subpoena, and had not reviewed the contents of the Redweld folder—stated, among other things, that "[b]ased upon the information that [had] been provided to" her:

a.   "A diligent search was conducted of the boxes that were moved from the White House to Florida";

b.   "This search was conducted after receipt of the subpoena, in order to locate any and all documents that are responsive to the subpoena"; and

---

* The indictment alleges that Trump's efforts to thwart the production of documents pursuant to the subpoena was unrelenting, even after his attorneys found responsive material. Notably, these allegations come from Trump's own counsel, not the FBI.

c.   "Any and all responsive documents accompany this certification."*

71.   These statements were false because, among other reasons, **TRUMP** had directed **NAUTA** to move boxes before Trump Attorney 1's June 2 review, so that many boxes were not searched and many documents responsive to the May 11 Subpoena could not be found—and in fact were not found—by Trump Attorney 1.

72.   Shortly after Trump Attorney 3 executed the false certification, on June 3, 2022, Trump Attorney 1 and Trump Attorney 3 met at The Mar-a-Lago Club with personnel from the Department of Justice and FBI. Trump Attorney 1 and Trump Attorney 3 turned over the Redweld folder containing documents with classification markings, as well as the false certification signed by Trump Attorney 3 as custodian of records. **TRUMP**, who had delayed his departure from The Mar-a-Lago Club, joined Trump Attorney 1 and Trump Attorney 3 for some of the meeting. **TRUMP** claimed to the Department of Justice and FBI that he was "an open book."

73.   Earlier that same day, **NAUTA, DE OLIVEIRA**, and others loaded several of **TRUMP**'s boxes along with other items on aircraft that flew **TRUMP** and his family north for the summer.

The Attempt to Delete Security Camera Footage†

74.   On June 3, 2022, when FBI agents were at The Mar-a-Lago Club to collect the documents with classification markings

---

* It is widely reported that "Trump Attorney 1" is Evan Corcoran. He will be a witness at the trial. It remains to be seen how Corcoran will fare as a witness, although the indictment makes clear that the government believes that Trump duped him into believing that the certification that Corcoran drafted was truthful.

INSIDER NOTE: Remarkably, as of this writing, Corcoran remains an attorney for Trump in other matters, even though he will be an important witness in the Florida case. Perhaps Trump is adhering to the old adage, "Keep your friends close and your enemies closer."

† This section is entirely new in the superseding indictment, and relates to a scheme to delete incriminating video surveillance at Mar-a-Lago. It is not uncommon for prosecutors to seek a superseding indictment announcing new charges as its investigation continues.

from Trump Attorney 1 and Trump Attorney 3, the agents observed that there were surveillance cameras located near the Storage Room.

75. On June 22, 2022. the Department of Justice emailed an attorney for **TRUMP**'s business organization a draft grand jury subpoena requiring the production of certain security camera footage from The Mar-a-Lago Club, including footage from cameras "on ground floor (basement)," where the Storage Room was located.

76. On June 23, 2022, at 8:46 p.m., **TRUMP** called **DE OLIVEIRA** and they spoke for approximately 24 minutes.

77. On Friday, June 24, 2022, the Department of Justice emailed the attorney for **TRUMP**'s business organization the final grand jury subpoena, which required the production of "[a]ny and all surveillance records, videos, images, photographs and/or CCTV from internal cameras" at certain locations at The Mar-a-Lago Club, including "on ground floor (basement)." from January 10, 2022, to June 24, 2022.

78. That same day, June 24, 2022, at 1:25 p.m., Trump Attorney 1 spoke with **TRUMP** by phone regarding the subpoena for security camera footage. At 3:44 p.m., **NAUTA** received a text message from a co-worker, Trump Employee 3, indicating that **TRUMP** wanted to see **NAUTA**. Less than two hours later, **NAUTA**—who was scheduled to travel with **TRUMP** to Illinois the next day—changed his travel schedule and began to make arrangements to go to Palm Beach, Florida, instead.

79. **NAUTA** provided inconsistent explanations to colleagues for his sudden travel to Florida. At 7:14 p.m. on June 24, he texted one person that he would not be traveling with **TRUMP** the next day because he had a family emergency and used "shushing" emojis; at 9:48 p.m. that night, he texted a Secret Service agent that he had to check on a family member in Florida; and after he arrived in Florida on June 25, he texted the same Secret Service agent that he was in Florida working.

INSIDER NOTE: A grand jury cannot be used to prepare for trial, but can be used to investigate new crimes and new defendants.

80. Around the same time on June 24 that **NAUTA** was making his travel plans to go to Florida, **NAUTA** and **DE OLIVEIRA** contacted Trump Employee 4, who was the Director of Information Technology ("IT") at The Mar-a-Lago Club,* as follows:

    a.   At 5:02 p.m., **NAUTA** sent text messages to Trump Employee 4 asking, "Hey bro You around this weekend."

    b.   At 5:05 p.m., **NAUTA** texted **DE OLIVEIRA**, asking, "Hey brother You working today?" **DE OLIVEIRA** responded, "Yes I just left." **NAUTA** then called **DE OLIVEIRA** and they spoke for approximately two minutes.

    c.   At 5:09 p.m., Trump Employee 4 texted a response to **NAUTA**, "I am local. Entertaining some family that came to visit. What's up?" **NAUTA** responded to Trump Employee 4, "Ok, cool. No biggie just wanted to see if you where around. Enjoy bro!"

    d.   At 6:56 p.m., **DE OLIVEIRA** texted Trump Employee 4, "Hey buddy how are you . . . Walter call me early said it was trying to get in touch with you I guess he's coming down tomorrow I guess needs you for something." Trump Employee 4 responded, "He reached out but he didn't say what he wanted. I told him I was local but entertaining some family that came from NYC this weekend. He told me to no worries."

    e.   At 6:58 p.m., Trump Employee 4 texted **NAUTA**, "Bro, if you need me I can get away for a few. Just let me know." **NAUTA** responded, "Sounds good!! Thank you."

81. On Saturday, June 25, 2022, **NAUTA** traveled from Bedminster, New Jersey, to Palm Beach, Florida. Prior to **NAUTA**'s trip, **DE OLIVEIRA** told a valet at The Mar-a-Lago Club ("Trump

---

* This is a reference to Yuscil Taveras. In their filings, the prosecutors allege that Taveras initially lied to the government, but then with court oversight, spoke with independent counsel, changed lawyers from one paid for by a Trump PAC, and began cooperating with the government.

INSIDER NOTE: Cassidy Hutchinson followed a somewhat similar trajectory with regard to her counsel. It is an all-too-common phenomenon in organized crime cases where "house counsel" paid for by senior members of a group are used to have underlings protect their bosses.

Employee 5") that **NAUTA** was coming down. **DE OLIVEIRA** asked Trump Employee 5 not to tell anyone that **NAUTA** was coming down because **NAUTA** wanted the trip to remain secret. **DE OLIVEIRA** also told Trump Employee 5 that **NAUTA** wanted **DE OLIVEIRA** to talk to Trump Employee 4 to see how long camera footage was stored.

82. Shortly after arriving in Palm Beach on the evening of June 25, **NAUTA** went to The Mar-a-Lago Club and met with **DE OLIVEIRA** at 5:46 p.m. At The Mar-a-Lago Club, **NAUTA** and **DE OLIVEIRA** went to the security guard booth where surveillance video is displayed on monitors, walked with a flashlight through the tunnel where the Storage Room was located, and observed and pointed out surveillance cameras.

83. On Monday, June 27, 2022, at 9:48 a.m., **DE OLIVEIRA** walked to the IT office where Trump Employee 4 was working with another employee in the IT department. **DE OLIVEIRA** requested that Trump Employee 4 step away from the office so that **DE OLIVEIRA** and Trump Employee 4 could talk.

84. At 9:49 a.m., Trump Employee 4 and **DE OLIVEIRA** left the area of the IT office together and walked through a basement tunnel. **DE OLIVEIRA** took Trump Employee 4 to a small room known as an "audio closet" near the White and Gold Ballroom. Once inside the audio closet, **DE OLIVEIRA** and Trump Employee 4 had the following exchange:

a. **DE OLIVEIRA** told Trump Employee 4 that their conversation should remain between the two of them.

b. **DE OLIVEIRA** asked Trump Employee 4 how many days the server retained footage. Trump Employee 4 responded that he believed it was approximately 45 days.

c. **DE OLIVEIRA** told Trump Employee 4 that "the boss" wanted the server deleted. Trump Employee 4 responded that he would not know how to do that, and that he did not believe that he would have the rights to do that. Trump Employee 4 told **DE OLIVEIRA** that **DE OLIVEIRA** would have to reach out to another employee who was a supervisor of security for **TRUMP**'s business organization. **DE OLIVEIRA** then insisted to **TRUMP** Employee 4 that "the boss" wanted the server deleted and asked, "what are we going to do?"*

85.   At 10:14 a.m., **DE OLIVEIRA** texted **NAUTA**, who was still in Florida, "Hey buddy are you working today?" **DE OLIVEIRA** then called **NAUTA** at 10:15 a.m., and they spoke for approximately one minute.

86.   Later that day, at 1:06 p.m., **NAUTA** texted **DE OLIVEIRA**, who was at The Mar-a-Lago Club, "On my way to you." Between 1:31 p.m. and 1:50 p.m., **DE OLIVEIRA** walked through the bushes on the northern edge of The Mar-a-Lago Club property to meet with **NAUTA** on the adjacent property; then walked back to the IT office that he had visited that morning; and then walked again through the bushes on the northern edge of The Mar-a-Lago Club property to meet with **NAUTA** on the adjacent property.

87.   At 3:55 p.m., **TRUMP** called **DE OLIVEIRA** and they spoke for approximately three and a half minutes.

The Court-Authorized Search of The Mar-a-Lago Club

88.   In July 2022, the FBI and grand jury obtained and reviewed surveillance video from The Mar-a-Lago Club showing the movement of boxes set forth above.

89.   August 8, 2022, the FBI executed a court-authorized search warrant at The Mar-a-Lago Club. The search warrant authorized the FBI to search for and seize, among other things, all documents with classification markings.

---

* This is the most incriminating statement against Trump in this particular obstruction scheme.

INSIDER NOTE: This statement should be admissible as a co-conspirator statement under the Federal Rules of Evidence. But even if it is admitted into evidence at trial, Trump will argue that this statement is unreliable because it comes from Trump Employee 4 (Taveras, who initially lied to the FBI), who in turn is relating De Oliveira's account of what he heard Trump say.

90. During the execution of the warrant at The Mar-a-Lago Club, the FBI seized 102 documents with classification markings in **TRUMP**'s office and the Storage Room, as follows:

LOCATION	NUMBER OF DOCUMENTS	CLASSIFICATION MARKINGS
TRUMP's Office	27	Top Secret (6) Secret (18) Confidential (3)
Storage Room	75	Top Secret (11) Secret (36) Confidential (28)

91. Just over two weeks after the FBI discovered classified documents in the Storage Room and **TRUMP**'s office, on August 26, 2022, **NAUTA** called Trump Employee 5 and said words to the effect of, "someone just wants to make sure Carlos is good." In response, Trump Employee 5 told **NAUTA** that **DE OLIVEIRA** was loyal and that **DE OLIVEIRA** would not do anything to affect his relationship with **TRUMP**. That same day, at **NAUTA**'s request, Trump Employee 5 confirmed in a Signal chat group* with **NAUTA** and the PAC Representative that **DE OLIVEIRA** was loyal. That same day, **TRUMP** called **DE OLIVEIRA** and told **DE OLIVEIRA** that **TRUMP** would get **DE OLIVEIRA** an attorney.

---

* The indictment alleges an obvious effort to make sure employees were not cooperating with the government.

INSIDER NOTE: The indictment's reference to "Signal" is notable. Signal is a secure, encrypted messaging system. This reference demonstrates that the government has been able to secure access to the chat group on Signal, perhaps through obtaining phone devices that have the Signal application or accessing the messages with consent of a member of the Signal chat group, among other things.

COUNTS 1-32*

Willful Retention of National Defense Information
(18 U.S.C. § 793(e))

92.   The General Allegations of this Superseding Indictment are re-alleged and fully incorporated here by reference.

93.   On or about the dates set forth in the table below, in Palm Beach County, in the Southern District of Florida, and elsewhere, the defendant,

DONALD J. TRUMP,

having unauthorized possession of, access to, and control over documents relating to the national defense, did willfully retain the documents and fail to deliver them to the officer and employee of the United States entitled to receive them; that is—**TRUMP**, without authorization, retained at The Mar-a-Lago Club documents relating to the national defense, including the following:

---

* Counts 1–31 relate to individual classified documents found at Mar-a-Lago; count 32 refers to a document that was at the Trump National Golf Club in Bedminster, New Jersey. The extraordinarily high security classification levels are notable. It explains why the DOJ would undertake an unprecedented search of a former president's residence to make sure these documents, so important to US security, were not at risk of becoming public or falling into our adversaries' hands. It is also remarkable that the Intelligence Community permitted these documents to be used at trial, since the jury will see them as part of the trial. This is the perennial conundrum the government faces when it prosecutes these types of cases: the enforcement of the criminal laws is intended to deter improper handling of sensitive materials, but the trial itself risks public exposure of sensitive documents. With that tension in mind, the government carefully chooses the documents that are the basis for criminal charges.

COUNT	DATE OF OFFENSE / CLASSIFICATION MARKING / DOCUMENT DESCRIPTION
1	January 20, 2021 – August 8, 2022
	TOP SECRET//NOFORN//SPECIAL HANDLING
	Document dated May 3, 2018, concerning White House intelligence briefing related to various foreign countries
2	January 20, 2021 – August 8, 2022
	TOP SECRET//SI//NOFORN//SPECIAL HANDLING
	Document dated May 9, 2018, concerning White House intelligence briefing related to various foreign countries
3	January 20, 2021 – August 8, 2022
	TOP SECRET//SI//NOFORN//FISA
	Undated document concerning military capabilities of a foreign country and the United States, with handwritten annotation in black marker
4	January 20, 2021 – August 8, 2022
	TOP SECRET//SPECIAL HANDLING
	Document dated May 6, 2019, concerning White House intelligence briefing related to foreign countries, including military activities and planning of foreign countries
5	January 20, 2021 – August 8, 2022
	TOP SECRET//[redacted]/[redacted]//ORCON/ NOFORN
	Document dated June 2020 concerning nuclear capabilities of a foreign country
6	January 20, 2021 – August 8, 2022
	TOP SECRET//SPECIAL HANDLING
	Document dated June 4, 2020, concerning White House intelligence briefing related to various foreign countries

COUNT	DATE OF OFFENSE / CLASSIFICATION MARKING / DOCUMENT DESCRIPTION
7	January 20, 2021 – August 8, 2022
	SECRET//NOFORN
	Document dated October 21, 2018, concerning communications with a leader of a foreign country
8	January 20, 2021 – August 8, 2022
	SECRET//REL TO USA, FVEY
	Document dated October 4, 2019, concerning military capabilities of a foreign country
9	January 20, 2021 – August 8, 2022
	TOP SECRET//[redacted]/[redacted]//ORCON/ NOFORN/FISA
	Undated document concerning military attacks by a foreign country
10	January 20, 2021 – August 8, 2022
	TOP SECRET//TK//NOFORN
	Document dated November 2017 concerning military capabilities of a foreign country
11	January 20, 2021 – August 8, 2022
	No marking
	Undated document concerning military contingency planning of the United States
12	January 20, 2021 – August 8, 2022
	SECRET//REL TO USA, FVEY
	Pages of undated document concerning projected regional military capabilities of a foreign country and the United States

COUNT	DATE OF OFFENSE / CLASSIFICATION MARKING / DOCUMENT DESCRIPTION
13	January 20, 2021 – August 8, 2022
	TOP SECRET//SI/TK//NOFORN
	Undated document concerning military capabilities of a foreign country and the United States
14	January 20, 2021 – August 8, 2022
	SECRET//ORCON/NOFORN
	Document dated January 2020 concerning military options of a foreign country and potential effects on United States interests
15	January 20, 2021 – August 8, 2022
	SECRET//ORCON/NOFORN
	Document dated February 2020 concerning policies in a foreign country
16	January 20, 2021 – August 8, 2022
	SECRET//ORCON/NOFORN
	Document dated December 2019 concerning foreign country support of terrorist acts against United States interests
17	January 20, 2021 – August 8, 2022
	TOP SECRET//[redacted]/TK//ORCON/IMCON/ NOFORN
	Document dated January 2020 concerning military capabilities of a foreign country
18	January 20, 2021 – August 8, 2022
	SECRET//NOFORN
	Document dated March 2020 concerning military operations against United States forces and others

COUNT	DATE OF OFFENSE / CLASSIFICATION MARKING / DOCUMENT DESCRIPTION
19	January 20, 2021 – August 8, 2022
	SECRET//FORMERLY RESTRICTED DATA
	Undated document concerning nuclear weaponry of the United States
20	January 20, 2021 – August 8, 2022
	TOP SECRET//[redacted]//ORCON/NOFORN
	Undated document concerning timeline and details of attack in a foreign country
21	January 20, 2021 – August 8, 2022
	SECRET//NOFORN
	Undated document concerning military capabilities of foreign countries
22	January 20, 2021 – June 3, 2022
	TOP SECRET//[redactcd]//RSEN/ORCON/NOFORN
	Document dated August 2019 concerning regional military activity of a foreign country
23	January 20, 2021 – June 3, 2022
	TOP SECRET//SPECIAL HANDLING
	Document dated August 30, 2019, concerning White House intelligence briefing related to various foreign countries, with handwritten annotation in black marker
24	January 20, 2021 – June 3, 2022
	TOP SECRET//HCS-P/SI//ORCON-USGOV/NOFORN
	Undated document concerning military activity of a foreign country

COUNT	DATE OF OFFENSE / CLASSIFICATION MARKING / DOCUMENT DESCRIPTION
25	January 20, 2021 – June 3, 2022
	TOP SECRET//HCS-P/SI//ORCON-USGOV/NOFORN
	Document dated October 24, 2019, concerning military activity of foreign countries and the United States
26	January 20, 2021 – June 3, 2022
	TOP SECRET//[redacted]//ORCON/NOFORN/F1SA
	Document dated November 7, 2019, concerning military activity of foreign countries and the United States
27	January 20, 2021 – June 3, 2022
	TOP SECRET//SI/TK//NOFORN
	Document dated November 2019 concerning military activity of foreign countries
28	January 20, 2021 – June 3, 2022
	TOP SECRET//SPECIAL HANDLING
	Document dated October 18, 2019, concerning White House intelligence briefing related to various foreign countries
29	January 20, 2021 – June 3, 2022
	TOP SECRET//[redacted]/SI/TK//ORCON/NOFORN
	Document dated October 18, 2019, concerning military capabilities of a foreign country
30	January 20, 2021 – June 3, 2022
	TOP SECRET//[redacted]//ORCON/NOFORN/FISA
	Document dated October 15, 2019, concerning military activity in a foreign country

COUNT	DATE OF OFFENSE / CLASSIFICATION MARKING / DOCUMENT DESCRIPTION
31	January 20, 2021 – June 3, 2022
	TOP SECRET//SI/TK//NOFORN
	Document dated February 2017 concerning military activity of a foreign country
32	January 20, 2021 – January 17, 2022
	TOP SECRET//NOFORN
	Presentation concerning military activity in a foreign country

All in violation of Title 18, United States Code, Section 793(e).[*]

COUNT 33

Conspiracy to Obstruct Justice
(18 U.S.C. § 1512(k))

94.   The General Allegations of this Superseding Indictment are re-alleged and fully incorporated here by reference.

The Conspiracy and its Objects

95.   From on or about May 11, 2022, through in or around August 2022, in Palm Beach County, in the Southern District of Florida, and elsewhere, the defendants,

DONALD J. TRUMP,
WALTINE NAUTA, and
CARLOS DE OLIVEIRA

---

[*] It is worth noting that the government uses this charge frequently in cases that are far less egregious than what is alleged to have occurred here. Just Security has created an index of all known recent cases, with the goal of showing how Trump is not being singled out for harsher treatment and that the failure to prosecute Trump would have been showing a leniency that others do not receive in similar (or even less serious) circumstances. (See Model Prosecution Memo for Trump Classified Documents, Appendix A.)

did knowingly combine, conspire, confederate, and agree with each other and with others known and unknown to the grand jury, to engage in misleading conduct toward another person and corruptly persuade another person to withhold a record, document, and other object from an official proceeding, in violation of 18 U.S.C. § 1512(b)(2)(A); to corruptly persuade another person, with intent to cause and induce any person to alter, destroy, mutilate, and conceal an object with intent to impair the object's integrity and availability for use in an official proceeding, in violation of 18 U.S.C. § 1512(b)(2)(B); and to corruptly alter, destroy, mutilate, and conceal a record, document, and other object from an official proceeding, in violation of 18 U.S.C. § 1512(c)(1).

The Purpose of the Conspiracy

96.   The purpose of the conspiracy was for **TRUMP** to keep classified documents he had taken with him from the White House and to hide and conceal them from a federal grand jury.

The Manner and Means of the Conspiracy

97.   The manner and means by which the defendants sought to accomplish the objects and purpose of the conspiracy included, among other things, the following:

a.   Suggesting that Trump Attorney 1 falsely represent to the FBI and grand jury that **TRUMP** did not have documents called for by the May 11 Subpoena;

b.   moving boxes of documents to conceal them from Trump Attorney 1, the FBI, and the grand jury;

c.   suggesting that Trump Attorney 1 hide or destroy documents called for by the May 11 Subpoena;

d.   providing to the FBI and grand jury just some of the documents called for by the May 11 Subpoena, while **TRUMP** claimed he was cooperating fully;

e.   causing a false certification to be submitted to the FBI and grand jury representing that all documents with classification markings had been produced, when in fact they had not;

f.   making false and misleading statements to the FBI; and

g.   attempting to delete security camera footage from The Mar-a-Lago Club to conceal the footage from the FBI and grand jury.

All in violation of Title 18, United States Code, Section 1512(k).

COUNT 34
Withholding a Document or Record
(18 U.S.C. §§ 1512(b)(2)(A), 2)

98.   The General Allegations of this Superseding Indictment are re-alleged and fully incorporated here by reference.

99.   From on or about May 11, 2022, through in or around August 2022, in Palm Beach County, in the Southern District of Florida, and elsewhere, the defendants,

DONALD J. TRUMP and
WALTINE NAUTA,

did knowingly engage in misleading conduct toward another person, and knowingly corruptly persuade and attempt to persuade another person, with intent to cause and induce any person to withhold a record, document, and other object from an official proceeding; that is—(1) **TRUMP** attempted to persuade Trump Attorney 1 to hide and conceal documents from a federal grand jury; and (2) **TRUMP** and **NAUTA** misled Trump Attorney 1 by moving boxes that contained documents with classification markings so that Trump Attorney 1 would not find the documents and produce them to a federal grand jury.

All in violation of Title 18, United States Code,
Sections 1512(b)(2)(A) and 2.

COUNT 35
Corruptly Concealing a Document or Record
(18 U.S.C. §§ 1512(c)(1), 2)

100.   The General Allegations of this Superseding Indictment are re-alleged and fully incorporated here by reference.

101. From on or about May 11, 2022, through in or around August 2022, in Palm Beach County, in the Southern District of Florida, and elsewhere, the defendants,

DONALD J. TRUMP and
WALTINE NAUTA,

did corruptly conceal a record, document, and other object, and attempted to do so, with the intent to impair the object's integrity and availability for use in an official proceeding; that is—**TRUMP** and **NAUTA** hid and concealed boxes that contained documents with classification markings from Trump Attorney 1 so that Trump Attorney 1 would not find the documents and produce them to a federal grand jury.

All in violation of Title 18, United States Code,
Sections 1512(c)(1) and 2.

COUNT 36

Concealing a Document in a Federal Investigation
(18 U.S.C. §§ 1519, 2)

102. The General Allegations of this Superseding Indictment are re-alleged and fully incorporated here by reference.

103. From on or about May 11, 2022, through in or around August 2022, in Palm Beach County, in the Southern District of Florida, and elsewhere, the defendants,

DONALD J. TRUMP and
WALTINE NAUTA,

did knowingly conceal, cover up, falsify, and make a false entry in any record, document, and tangible object with the intent to impede, obstruct, and influence the investigation and proper administration of any matter within the jurisdiction of a department and agency of the United States, and in relation to and contemplation of any such matter; that is—during a federal criminal investigation being conducted by the FBI, (1) **TRUMP** and **NAUTA** hid, concealed, and covered up from the FBI **TRUMP**'s continued possession of documents with classification markings at The Mar-a-Lago Club; and (2) **TRUMP** caused a false certification to be submitted to the FBI.

All in violation of Title 18, United States Code,
Sections 1519 and 2.

COUNT 37

Scheme to Conceal
(18 U.S.C. §§ 1001(a)(1), 2)

104. The General Allegations of this Superseding Indictment are re-alleged and fully incorporated here by reference.

105. From on or about May 11, 2022, through in or around August 2022, in Palm Beach County, in the Southern District of Florida, and elsewhere, the defendants,

**DONALD J. TRUMP and
WALTINE NAUTA,**

in a matter within the jurisdiction of the judicial branch and executive branch of the United States government, did knowingly and willfully falsify, conceal, and cover up by any trick, scheme, and device a material fact; that is—during a federal grand jury investigation and a federal criminal investigation being conducted by the FBI, **TRUMP** and **NAUTA** hid and concealed from the grand jury and the FBI **TRUMP**'s continued possession of documents with classification markings.

All in violation of Title 18, United States Code,
Sections 1001(a)(1) and 2.

COUNT 38

False Statements and Representations
(18 U.S.C. §§ 1001(a)(2), 2)

106. The General Allegations of this Superseding Indictment are re-alleged and fully incorporated here by reference.

107. On or about June 3, 2022, in Palm Beach County, in the Southern District of Florida, and elsewhere, the defendant,

DONALD J. TRUMP,

in a matter within the jurisdiction of the judicial branch and executive branch of the United States government, did knowingly and willfully make and cause to be made a materially false, fictitious, and fraudulent statement and representation; that is -during a federal grand jury investigation and a federal criminal investigation being conducted by the FBI. **TRUMP** caused the following false statements and representations to be made to the grand jury and the FBI in a sworn certification executed by Trump Attorney 3:

    a.   "A diligent search was conducted of the boxes that were moved from the White House to Florida";

    b.   "This search was conducted after receipt of the subpoena, in order to locate any and all documents that are responsive to the subpoena"; and

    c.   "Any and all responsive documents accompany this certification."

108. The statements and representations set forth above were false, as **TRUMP** knew, because **TRUMP** had directed that boxes be removed from the Storage Room before Trump Attorney 1 conducted the June 2, 2022 search for documents with classification markings, so that Trump Attorney 1's search would not and did not include all of **TRUMP**'s boxes that were removed from the White House; Trump Attorney 1's search would not and did not locate all documents responsive to the May 11 Subpoena; and all responsive documents were not provided to the FBI and the grand jury with the certification. In fact, after June 3, 2022, more than 100 documents with classification markings remained at The Mar-a-Lago Club until the FBI search on August 8, 2022.

All in violation of Title 18, United States Code,
Sections 1001(a)(2) and 2.

COUNT 39

False Statements and Representations
(18 U.S.C. § 1001(a)(2))

109. The General Allegations of this Superseding Indictment are re-alleged and fully incorporated here by reference.

110. On May 26, 2022, **NAUTA** participated in a voluntary interview with the FBI. During the interview, the FBI explained to **NAUTA** that the FBI was investigating how classified documents had been kept at The Mar-a-Lago Club, and the FBI asked **NAUTA** questions about the location and movement of **TRUMP**'s boxes before **TRUMP** provided 15 boxes to NARA on January 17, 2022. **NAUTA** was represented by counsel, and the FBI advised **NAUTA** that the interview was voluntary and that he could leave at any time. The FBI also advised **NAUTA** that it was a criminal offense to lie to the FBI. The interview was recorded.

111. On or about May 26, 2022, in Palm Beach County, in the Southern District of Florida, and elsewhere, the defendant,

WALTINE NAUTA,

in a matter within the jurisdiction of the executive branch of the United States government, did knowingly and willfully make a materially false, fictitious, and fraudulent statement and representation; that is—in a voluntary interview during a federal criminal investigation being conducted by the FBI, **NAUTA** was asked the following questions and gave the following false answers:

Question: Does any – are you aware of any boxes being brought to his home – his suite?

Answer: **No.**

* * *

Question: All right. So, so to the best of your knowledge, you're saying that those boxes that you brought onto the truck, first time you ever laid eyes on them was just the day of when [Trump Employee 2] needed you to—

Answer:	**Correct.**
Question:	—to take them. Okay.

* * *

Question:	In knowing that we're trying to track the life of these boxes and where they could have been kept and stored and all that kind of stuff—
Answer:	Mm-hm.
Question:	—do you have any information that could—that would—that could help us understand, like, where they were kept, how they were kept, were they secured, were they locked? Something that makes the intelligence community feel better about these things, you know?
Answer:	**I wish, I wish I could tell you. I don't know. I don't—I honestly just don't know.**

* * *

Question:	And what—so, so you only saw the 15 boxes, 15, 17 boxes—
Answer:	Mm-hm.
Question:	—the day of the move? Even—they just showed up that day?
Answer:	They were in Pine Hall. [Trump Employee 2] just asked me, hey, can we move some boxes?
Question:	Okay.
Answer:	And I was like, okay.
Question:	So, you didn't know—had no idea how they got there before?
Answer:	**No.**

112. The underscored statements and representations above were false, as **NAUTA** knew, because (1) **NAUTA** did in fact know that the boxes in Pine Hall had come from the Storage Room, as **NAUTA** himself, with the assistance of Trump Employee 2, had

moved the boxes from the Storage Room to Pine Hall; and (2) **NAUTA** had observed the boxes in and moved them to various locations at The Mar-a-Lago Club.

All in violation of Title 18, United States Code, Section 1001(a)(2).

COUNT 40

Altering, Destroying, Mutilating, or Concealing an Object
(18 U.S.C. §§ 1512(b)(2)(B), 2)

113. The General Allegations of this Superseding Indictment are re-alleged and fully incorporated here by reference.

114. From on or about June 22, 2022, through in or around August 2022, in Palm Beach County, in the Southern District of Florida, and elsewhere, the defendants,

DONALD J. TRUMP,
WALTINE NAUTA, and
CARLOS DE OLIVEIRA

did knowingly corruptly persuade and attempt to persuade another person, with intent to cause and induce any person to alter, destroy, mutilate, and conceal an object with intent to impair the object's integrity and availability for use in an official proceeding; that is— **TRUMP, NAUTA,** and **DE OLIVEIRA** requested that Trump Employee 4 delete security camera footage at The Mar-a-Lago Club to prevent the footage from being provided to a federal grand jury.

All in violation of Title 18, United States Code,
Sections 1512(b)(2)(B) and 2.

COUNT 41

Corruptly Altering, Destroying, Mutilating or
Concealing a Document, Record, or Other Object
(18 U.S.C. §§ 1512(c)(1), 2)

115. The General Allegations of this Superseding Indictment are re-alleged and fully incorporated here by reference.

116. From on or about June 22, 2022, through in or around August 2022, in Palm Beach County, in the Southern District of Florida, and elsewhere, the defendants,

DONALD J. TRUMP,
WALTINE NAUTA, and
CARLOS DE OLIVEIRA

did corruptly alter, destroy, mutilate, and conceal a record, document and other object and attempted to do so, with the intent to impair the object's integrity and availability for use in an official proceeding; that is—**TRUMP, NAUTA,** and **DE OLIVEIRA** requested that Trump Employee 4 delete security camera footage at The Mar-a-Lago Club to prevent the footage from being provided to a federal grand jury.

All in violation of Title 18, United States Code,
Sections 1512(c)(1) and 2.

COUNT 42

False Statements and Representations
(18 U.S.C. § 1001(a)(2))

117. The General Allegations of this Superseding Indictment are re-alleged and fully incorporated here by reference.

118. On January 13, 2023, **DE OLIVEIRA** participated in a voluntary interview with the FBI at **DE OLIVEIRA**'s residence. During the interview, the FBI explained to **DE OLIVEIRA** that the FBI was investigating how classified documents had been kept at The Mar-a-Lago Club, and the FBI asked **DE OLIVEIRA** questions about the location and movement of **TRUMP**'s boxes and other items. **DE OLIVEIRA** was advised by the FBI that the interview was voluntary and that he could tell the agents to leave at any time. The FBI also advised **DE OLIVEIRA** that it was a criminal offense to lie to the FBI. The interview was recorded.*

---

* The FBI recorded this interview, so De Oliveira will not be able to contest what he said; he thus will likely have to argue that he did not recall the underlying facts at the

119. On or about January 13, 2023, in Palm Beach County, in the Southern District of Florida, and elsewhere, the defendant,

CARLOS DE OLIVEIRA,

in a matter within the jurisdiction of the executive branch of the United States government, did knowingly and willfully make a materially false, fictitious, and fraudulent statement and representation; that is—in a voluntary interview during a federal criminal investigation being conducted by the FBI, **DE OLIVEIRA** was asked the following questions and gave the following false answers:

Question: When -- after the end of the presidency, boxes arrived to Mar-a-Lago. Were you part of any group to help –

Answer: **No.**

Question: -- unload them and move them?

Answer: **No.**

* * *

Question: Do you -- were you -- do you even know, like, or were you even there or aware that boxes were –

Answer: **No.**

Question: -- like, all this stuff was being moved in?

Answer: **Never saw anything.**

Question: Okay.

Answer: Yeah. And then –

Question: Even his personal stuff, like, his clothes –

Answer: **Never.**

Question: -- and furniture, nothing?

Answer: **Never saw nothing.**

---

time, and thus did not intentionally lie to the FBI. That may be a difficult argument, given other evidence in the case and the circumstances of the interview.

Question: Okay. So you don't know where items would have been stored, as soon as he moved back to Mar-aLago?

Answer: **No.**

120. The underscored statements and representations above were false, as **DE OLIVEIRA** knew, because **DE OLIVEIRA** had personally observed and helped move **TRUMP**'s boxes when they arrived at The Mar-a-Lago Club in January 2021.

All in violation of Title 18, United States Code, Section 1001(a)(2).

A TRUE BILL*

FOREPERSON

JACK SMITH
SPECIAL COUNSEL
UNITED STATES DEPARTMENT OF JUSTICE

---

* Normally, the names of grand jurors are not redacted, but given the volume of significant threats to jurors, prosecutors, judges, election workers, elected officials, and their families, this redaction is a wise precaution.

UNITED STATES DISTRICT COURT
SOUTHERN DISTRICT OF FLORIDA

UNITED STATES OF AMERICA

v.

Donald J. Trump,
Waltine Nauta, and
Carlos De Oliveira,_____/

Defendants.

Court Division (select one)
☐ Miami ☐ Key West ☐ FTP
☐ FTL ☒ WPB

CASE NO.: 23-CR-80101-AMC(s)_____

CERTIFICATE OF
TRIAL ATTORNEY
Superseding Case Information:
New Defendant(s) (Yes or No) Yes
Number of New Defendants 1
Total number of counts 42

I do hereby certify that:

1. I have carefully considered the allegations of the indictment, the number of defendants, the number of probable witnesses and the legal complexities of the Indictment/Information attached hereto.

2. I am aware that the information supplied on this statement will be relied upon by the Judges of this Court in setting their calendars and scheduling criminal trials under the mandate of the Speedy Trial Act, Title 28 U.S.C. §3161.

3. Interpreter: (Yes or No) No
   List language and/or dialect: _____

4. This case will take 21 days for the parties to try.

5. Please check appropriate category and type of offense listed below:
   (Check only one)   (Check only one)
   I   ☐ 0 to 5 days   ☐ Petty
   II   ☐ 6 to 10 days   ☐ Minor
   III ☐ 11 to 20 days   ☐ Misdemeanor
   IV   ☒ 21 to 60 days   ☒ Felony
   V   ☐ 61 days and over

6. Has this case been previously filed in this District Court? (Yes or No) Yes
   If yes, Judge Cannon   Case No. 23-cr-80101

7. Has a complaint been filed in this matter? (Yes or No) No
   If yes, Magistrate Case No. _____

8. Does this case relate to a previously filed matter in this District Court?
   (Yes or No) No
   If yes, Judge _____   Case No. _____

9. Defendant(s) in federal custody as of N/A_____

10. Defendant(s) in state custody as of _____

11. Rule 20 from the _____ District of _____

12. Is this a potential death penalty case? (Yes or No) No

13. Does this case originate from a matter pending in the Northern Region of the U.S. Attorney's Office prior to August 8, 2014 (Mag. Judge Shaniek Maynard? (Yes or No) No

14. Does this case originate from a matter pending in the Central Region of the U.S. Attorney's Office prior to October 3, 2019 (Mag. Judge Jared Strauss? (Yes or No) No

15. Did this matter involve the participation of or consultation with now Magistrate Judge Eduardo I. Sanchez during his tenure at the U.S. Attorney's Office, which concluded on January 22, 2023? No

By: _____

JAY I. BRATT
Counselor to the Special Counsel
Court ID No.   A5502946

UNITED STATES DISTRICT COURT
SOUTHERN DISTRICT OF FLORIDA

PENALTY SHEET

Defendant's Name: ___Donald J. Trump___

Case No: ___23-CR-80101-AMC(s)___

Counts#: 1-32

Willful Retention of National Defense Information, 18 U.S.C. § 793(e)

---

* Max. Term of Imprisonment: 10 years
* Mandatory Min. Term of Imprisonment (if applicable): N/A
* Max. Supervised Release: 3 years
* Max. Fine: $250,000

Count #: 33

Conspiracy to Obstruct Justice, 18 U.S.C. § 1512(k)

---

* Max. Term of Imprisonment: 20 years
* Mandatory Min. Term of Imprisonment (if applicable): N/A
* Max. Supervised Release: 3 years
* Max. Fine: $250,000

Count #: 34

Withholding a Document or Record, 18 U.S.C. §§ 1512(b)(2)(A), 2

---

* Max. Term of Imprisonment: 20 years
* Mandatory Min. Term of Imprisonment (if applicable): N/A
* Max. Supervised Release: 3 years
* Max. Fine: $250,000

***Refers only to possible term of incarceration, supervised release and fines.
It does not include restitution, special assessments, parole terms,
or forfeitures that may be applicable.**

Count #: 35

Corruptly Concealing a Document or Record, 18 U.S.C. §§ 1512(c)(1), 2

---

* **Max. Term of Imprisonment: 20 years**
* **Mandatory Min. Term of Imprisonment (if applicable): N/A**
* **Max. Supervised Release: 3 years**
* **Max. Fine: $250,000**

Count #: 36

Concealing a Document in a Federal Investigation, 18 U.S.C. §§ 1519, 2

---

* **Max. Term of Imprisonment: 20 years**
* **Mandatory Min. Term of Imprisonment (if applicable): N/A**
* **Max. Supervised Release: 3 years**
* **Max. Fine: $250,000**

Count #: 37

Scheme to Conceal, 18 U.S.C. §§ 1001(a)(1), 2

---

* **Max. Term of Imprisonment: 5 years**
* **Mandatory Min. Term of Imprisonment (if applicable): N/A**
* **Max. Supervised Release: 3 years**
* **Max. Fine: $250,000**

Count #: 38

False Statements and Representations, 18 U.S.C. §§ 1001(a)(2), 2

---

* **Max. Term of Imprisonment: 5 years**
* **Mandatory Min. Term of Imprisonment (if applicable): N/A**
* **Max. Supervised Release: 3 years**
* **Max. Fine: $250,000**

***Refers only to possible term of incarceration, supervised release and fines.
It does not include restitution, special assessments, parole terms,
or forfeitures that may be applicable.**

Count #: 40

Altering, Destroying, Mutilating, or Concealing an Object, 18 U.S.C. §§ 1512(b)(2)(B), 2

---

* Max. Term of Imprisonment: 20 years
* Mandatory Min. Term of Imprisonment (if applicable): N/A
* Max. Supervised Release: 3 years
* Max. Fine: $250,000

Count #: 41

Corruptly Altering, Destroying, Mutilating, or Concealing a Document, Record, or Other Object, 18 U.S.C. §§ 1512(c)(1), 2

---

* Max. Term of Imprisonment: 20 years
* Mandatory Min. Term of Imprisonment (if applicable): N/A
* Max. Supervised Release: 3 years
* Max. Fine: $250,000

---

* Refers only to possible term of incarceration, supervised release and fines.
It does not include restitution, special assessments, parole terms,
or forfeitures that may be applicable.

UNITED STATES DISTRICT COURT
SOUTHERN DISTRICT OF FLORIDA

PENALTY SHEET

Defendant's Name: ___Waltine Nauta___

Case No: ___23-CR-80101-AMC(s)___

Count #: 33

Conspiracy to Obstruct Justice, 18 U.S.C. § 1512(k)

---

* **Max. Term of Imprisonment: 20 years**
* **Mandatory Min. Term of Imprisonment (if applicable): N/A**
* **Max. Supervised Release: 3 years**
* **Max. Fine: $250,000**

Count #: 34

Withholding a Document or Record, 18 U.S.C. §§ 1512(b)(2)(A), 2

---

* **Max. Term of Imprisonment: 20 years**
* **Mandatory Min. Term of Imprisonment (if applicable): N/A**
* **Max. Supervised Release: 3 years**
* **Max. Fine: $250,000**

Count #: 35

Corruptly Concealing a Document or Record, 18 U.S.C. §§ 1512(c)(1), 2

---

* **Max. Term of Imprisonment: 20 years**
* **Mandatory Min. Term of Imprisonment (if applicable): N/A**
* **Max. Supervised Release: 3 years**
* **Max. Fine: $250,000**

Count #: 36

Concealing a Document in a Federal Investigation, 18 U.S.C. §§ 1519, 2

---

* **Max. Term of Imprisonment: 20 years**
* **Mandatory Min. Term of Imprisonment (if applicable): N/A**
* **Max. Supervised Release: 3 years**
* **Max. Fine: $250,000**

***Refers only to possible term of incarceration, supervised release and fines.
It does not include restitution, special assessments, parole terms,
or forfeitures that may be applicable.**

Count #: 37

Scheme to Conceal, 18 U.S.C. §§ 1001(a)(1), 2

* Max. Term of Imprisonment: 5 years
* Mandatory Min. Term of Imprisonment (if applicable): N/A
* Max. Supervised Release: 3 years
* Max. Fine: $250,000

Count #: 39

False Statements and Representations, 18 U.S.C. § 1001(a)(2)

* Max. Term of Imprisonment: 5 years
* Mandatory Min. Term of Imprisonment (if applicable): N/A
* Max. Supervised Release: 3 years
* Max. Fine: $250,000

Count #: 40

Altering, Destroying, Mutilating, or Concealing an Object, 18 U.S.C. §§ 1512(b)(2)(B), 2

* Max. Term of Imprisonment: 20 years
* Mandatory Min. Term of Imprisonment (if applicable): N/A
* Max. Supervised Release: 3 years
* Max. Fine: $250,000

Count #: 41

Corruptly Altering, Destroying, Mutilating, or Concealing a Document, Record, or Other Object, 18 U.S.C. §§ 1512(c)(1), 2

* Max. Term of Imprisonment: 20 years
* Mandatory Min. Term of Imprisonment (if applicable): N/A
* Max. Supervised Release: 3 years
* Max. Fine: $250,000

*Refers only to possible term of incarceration, supervised release and fines. It does not include restitution, special assessments, parole terms, or forfeitures that may be applicable.

UNITED STATES DISTRICT COURT
SOUTHERN DISTRICT OF FLORIDA

PENALTY SHEET

Defendant's Name: ___Carlos De Oliveira___

Case No: ___23-CR-80101-AMC(s)___

Count #: 33

Conspiracy to Obstruct Justice, 18 U.S.C. § 1512(k)

* **Max. Term of Imprisonment: 20 years**
* **Mandatory Min. Term of Imprisonment (if applicable): N/A**
* **Max. Supervised Release: 3 years**
* **Max. Fine: $250,000**

Count #: 40

Altering, Destroying, Mutilating, or Concealing an Object, 18 U.S.C. §§ 1512(b)(2)(B), 2

* **Max. Term of Imprisonment: 20 years**
* **Mandatory Min. Term of Imprisonment (if applicable): N/A**
* **Max. Supervised Release: 3 years**
* **Max. Fine: $250,000**

Count #: 41

Corruptly Altering, Destroying, Mutilating, or Concealing a Document, Record, or Other Object, 18 U.S.C. §§ 1512(c)(1), 2

* **Max. Term of Imprisonment: 20 years**
* **Mandatory Min. Term of Imprisonment (if applicable): N/A**
* **Max. Supervised Release: 3 years**
* **Max. Fine: $250,000**

Count #: 42

False Statements and Representations, 18 U.S.C. § 1001(a)(2)

* **Max. Term of Imprisonment: 5 years**
* **Mandatory Min. Term of Imprisonment (if applicable): N/A**
* **Max. Supervised Release: 3 years**
* **Max. Fine: $250,000**

* **Refers only to possible term of incarceration, supervised release and fines.
It does not include restitution, special assessments, parole terms,
or forfeitures that may be applicable.**

THE PEOPLE OF THE STATE OF NEW YORK V. DONALD J. TRUMP

(NEW YORK INDICTMENT)

INTRODUCTION

HANKS TO TELEVISION SHOWS LIKE *CAGNEY & LACEY*, *Blue Bloods*, and Dick Wolf's many *Law & Order* franchises, the Manhattan District Attorney's Office is perhaps the most celebrated local prosecutor's office in the country—if not the world. But even if you haven't watched any of these shows, you've probably heard plenty about the Manhattan DA's office. The office has been at the center of some of the most closely watched criminal cases in recent decades, from the famously flawed prosecution of the Central Park Five—now known as the Exonerated Five—to the successful rape and assault prosecution of film producer Harvey Weinstein.

But the Manhattan DA's office gained an even higher profile on April 4, 2023, when Alvin Bragg, the first African American to serve as Manhattan DA, secured a criminal indictment charging former US president Donald Trump with crimes related to a "hush money" scheme orchestrated in advance of the 2020 presidential election and continuing into the early days of his presidency. This was the first time in the history of the United States that a former president had been charged with a crime.

Because of its unprecedented nature, the indictment of a former president, by itself, was likely to be controversial. But the nature of the charges that the district attorney filed also raised eyebrows. The indictment charged Trump thirty-four times with falsifying business records *in the first degree*, which is a class E felony, the lowest-level felony in New York's penal code. Simply falsifying business records is chargeable only as a class A misdemeanor in New York, and is criminalized as falsifying business records *in the second degree*. However, if the falsification of the records is undertaken with the intent to commit another crime or to aid or conceal the commission of another crime—whether that other crime is a felony or a misdemeanor—then the legislature considers the falsification offense more serious and permits the conduct to be charged as a "first-degree" felony. Accordingly, to render this a felony, the DA had to tie the falsification of business records to some other contemplated offense. That is, charging falsifying business records as a felony requires the DA to prove beyond a reasonable doubt that the falsification of business records was undertaken as part of a broader effort to commit another crime or to conceal the commission of another crime. "Bootstrapping" the crimes in order to charge a felony struck some commentators as an aggressive move—one of the reasons why this indictment has been controversial.

In order to link the falsification of business records to another predicate crime, the indictment details an elaborate plan involving Trump's lawyer Michael Cohen and the CEO of a major tabloid to funnel tens of thousands of dollars to certain individuals as "hush money" in order to prevent the public from discovering then-candidate Trump's alleged sexual indiscretions during the crucial final days of the 2016 presidential campaign. The state crimes are alleged to have occurred in order to cover up that scheme: the "hush money" payments were disbursed to Cohen from Trump as legal fees, when, as alleged, they were actually reimbursements to Cohen for the hush money payments he paid to women to prevent them from publicly disclosing past interactions with Trump.

Remarkable, too, is that Trump is alleged to have committed the alleged crimes even after he was sworn in as president, allegedly signing checks to Cohen in the Oval Office.

CAST OF CHARACTERS

M ANY OF THE INDICTMENTS REFERENCE UNNAMED individuals by descriptions such as "Employee 1," "Woman 2," and "Co-Conspirator 3." To be clear, these unnamed individuals have not been charged with any crime. They are referenced because they play some role in the events alleged. Relying on media reports identifying these individuals, we have named them here in order to facilitate the reader's comprehension of these documents and the alleged conduct they describe. That said, it must be remembered that none of these individuals has been charged with any wrongdoing.

▲ = involved in multiple cases

Alvin Bragg—The Manhattan District Attorney. Bragg was elected in 2021 and previously served as a federal prosecutor and as Chief Deputy Attorney General of New York. Bragg inherited the Trump investigation from his predecessor, Cyrus Vance, when he took office.

Stephanie Clifford (aka Stormy Daniels) ("Woman 2")—An adult film actor who claims to have had an affair with Donald Trump. Michael Cohen told prosecutors that he submitted false invoices for legal services to the Trump Organization for the purpose of concealing "hush money" payments to Clifford to prevent her from disclosing her relationship with Trump.

Michael Cohen ("Lawyer A")—Trump's longtime lawyer and "fixer," Cohen provided key evidence to the Manhattan District Attorney as to a scheme to create false invoices for legal services that would be used to disguise "hush money" payments to adult film actor Stormy Daniels.

Robert Costello ("Lawyer C")*—A New York City lawyer and Trump grand jury defense witness. According to the New York State prosecutor's State-

---

* Identities of every character in the Manhattan DA's indictment, as reported by the *Wall Street Journal*, are listed here: "Here's the Trump Indictment with Actual Names Added," *Wall Street Journal*, updated April 5, 2023.

ment of Facts filed alongside the New York indictment, following the FBI's search of Michael Cohen's home and office, Costello discouraged Cohen from cooperating with the prosecution and offered to represent him in order to maintain a "back channel" to Trump. In the days preceding Trump's New York indictment, Costello, acting as a witness for Trump, testified before the Manhattan grand jury.

Keith Davidson ("Lawyer B")—Stormy Daniels's lawyer who negotiated the $130,000 sale of Daniels's story to American Media, Inc. ("AMI").

Dylan Howard ("AMI Editor-in-Chief")—The former Chief Content Officer of AMI, who, according to the New York Statement of Facts, helped AMI's CEO, David Pecker carry out the "catch and kill" scheme to suppress damaging stories about then-candidate Trump during the 2016 election. Howard allegedly notified Michael Cohen about the existence of the Karen McDougal and Stormy Daniels stories and connected Cohen with Daniels's lawyer.

Jeffrey McConney ("TO Controller")—The Trump Organization employee who, according to prosecutors, received Michael Cohen's false invoices for legal services and instructed the Trump Organization's accounts payable supervisor to fulfill them and record the payments as legal expenses. Prosecutors allege that, in reality, the payments reimbursed Cohen for the "hush money" payments that Cohen made to Stormy Daniels.

Karen McDougal ("Woman 1")—A former *Playboy* model who claims to have had a ten-month affair with Donald Trump. AMI, the then-owner of the *National Enquirer*, according to the New York Statement of Facts, paid McDougal $150,000 for the rights to her story in order to hide the alleged affair from the public until after the 2016 election. In a non-prosecution agreement with the US Attorney for the Southern District of New York, AMI stipulated that it made the payment to McDougal at the Trump campaign's request.

Justice Juan Merchan—The New York trial judge presiding over the Manhattan District Attorney's case against Donald Trump. (In the New York State system, the Supreme Court of New York is a trial court and its trial judges are called justices.) Merchan, who has served in his current role since 2009, began his legal career as a prosecutor in the Manhattan DA's Office. Merchan oversaw the 2022 trial of two Trump organizations, which resulted in their conviction on all seventeen charged counts.

David Pecker ("AMI CEO")—According to the prosecution, the former Chairman and CEO of AMI, was integral to the scheme to suppress negative stories about then-candidate Trump during the 2016 presidential election.

Shortly after Trump launched his 2016 campaign, Pecker allegedly met with Trump and Michael Cohen in Trump Tower and agreed to help Trump's campaign by devising a "catch and kill" scheme: Pecker would alert Trump to the existence of stories that could damage Trump's electoral prospects so that Trump could buy the rights to those stories to prevent their publication. Pecker approved AMI's purchases of three salacious and potentially damaging stories about Trump.

Dino Sajudin ("Doorman")—A former Trump Tower doorman who, in 2015, claimed to know about a child that Trump fathered out of wedlock. AMI paid Sajudin $30,000 for the rights to his story in order to suppress it. As New York prosecutors allege, AMI made the payments as part of the "catch and kill" scheme with Trump and Cohen. Prosecutors allege that when AMI later concluded that the story was false, Cohen told AMI's CEO not to release Sajudin from his confidentiality agreement until after the presidential election.

Deborah Tarasoff ("TO Accounts Payable Supervisor")—The Trump Organization accounts payable supervisor who, according to the New York Statement of Facts, fulfilled the "hush money" reimbursement payments to Michael Cohen and recorded the payments as legal expenses.

Allen Weisselberg ("TO CFO")—The former longtime Chief Financial Officer of the Trump Organization. According to the prosecution, Trump instructed Weisselberg to work with Cohen to arrange the $130,000 "hush money" payment to Stormy Daniels. Cohen paid Daniels's lawyer with his personal funds, and the prosecution alleges that Weisselberg devised a scheme to reimburse Cohen with checks—drawn from the Trump Organization's assets and Trump's personal bank account—that were falsely characterized as payments for legal services. In 2022, Weisselberg pleaded guilty to fifteen felony charges—each unrelated to the hush money payments to Daniels—that resulted from the Manhattan DA's investigation into the Trump Organization. Weisselberg served a five-month prison sentence under a plea deal with the New York prosecutors. He testified at the successful Trump organizations criminal trial in New York in 2022.

PROSECUTORS

Matthew Colangelo—Senior Counsel to the Manhattan District Attorney. Colangelo previously served alongside Alvin Bragg at the New York Attorney General's Office, where he worked with Bragg to investigate the Trump Foundation's misuse of charitable funds. Colangelo recently held a senior role at the DOJ and served as a law clerk to United States Supreme Court

Justice Sonia Sotomayor when she was a judge on the United States Court of Appeals for the Second Circuit.

Christopher Conroy—Senior Advisor in the Investigation Division of the Manhattan District Attorney's Office. Conroy, a twenty-seven-year veteran of that office and the former chief of its Major Economic Crimes Bureau and Investigation Division, has overseen several high-profile prosecutions of financial institutions on charges of falsifying business records.

Katherine Ellis—An Assistant District Attorney in the Manhattan District Attorney's Major Economic Crimes Bureau.

Susan Hoffinger—The Chief of the Investigation Division of the Manhattan District Attorney's Office. Hoffinger led the successful 2022 prosecution of two Trump organizations.

Rebecca Mangold—An Assistant District Attorney in the Manhattan District Attorney's Major Economic Crimes Bureau. Mangold, formerly a partner at a prominent New York law firm, joined the office in 2022.

Catherine McCaw—Counsel to the Investigation Division of the Manhattan District Attorney's Office. McCaw is known for her role as a lead lawyer in that office's successful prosecution of fake heiress Anna Sorokin (aka Anna Delvey), memorialized in the Netflix series *Inventing Anna*.

DEFENSE ATTORNEYS

Todd Blanche▲—A white-collar criminal defense lawyer and former federal prosecutor. Blanche, previously a partner at a well-known New York law firm, launched his own firm in 2023 to represent Trump in three criminal investigations: the New York case and both federal cases. Blanche successfully represented Trump's former presidential campaign manager Paul Manafort in the Manhattan District Attorney's prosecution that was ultimately dismissed on state double-jeopardy grounds.

Susan Necheles—A longtime New York criminal defense attorney. Necheles was a member of the 2022 trial team that unsuccessfully defended the Trump organizations against criminal charges brought by the Manhattan District Attorney's Office.

Joseph Tacopina—A New York criminal defense attorney. Tacopina represented Trump in the civil lawsuit brought by E. Jean Carroll—a case that resulted in a 2023 civil jury verdict in New York federal court that Trump had sexually abused and defamed Carroll and owed her $5 million in damages.

SUPREME COURT OF THE STATE OF NEW YORK COUNTY OF NEW YORK

THE PEOPLE OF THE STATE OF NEW YORK*

-against-

DONALD J. TRUMP,

Defendant.

THE GRAND JURY OF THE COUNTY OF NEW YORK,† by this indictment, accuses the defendant of the crime of **FALSIFYING BUSINESS RECORDS IN THE FIRST DEGREE**, in violation of Penal Law §175.10,‡ committed as follows:

---

* In the State of New York, as in other jurisdictions, criminal charges are brought on behalf of the government—and those it serves.

INSIDER NOTE: In the State of New York, the case is brought on behalf of "the people." In the federal system, charges are brought on behalf of "the United States."

† In the US legal system, a grand jury typically makes the decision to charge an individual with a felony. A grand jury, like a trial jury (also known as a petit jury), is a panel of individuals who reside in the jurisdiction. Unlike a trial jury, which hears evidence at trial and determines whether a conviction is warranted, members of the grand jury are impaneled for a period of time for the purpose of determining whether the evidence presented meets the legal standard of "probable cause" that a crime was committed. If a majority of the grand jury votes that there is probable cause to indict, the individual is criminally charged. Based on the evidence presented to them, the grand jurors, on March 30, 2023, voted to issue an indictment charging Trump with thirty-four counts of falsifying business records.

INSIDER NOTE: Despite the word "probable," the probable cause standard is less onerous than a "preponderance of the evidence" standard (which requires that a showing be made by anything over 50 percent) or the "beyond a reasonable doubt" standard required to convict. "Probable cause" generally means when, based on the totality of the circumstances, there is a reasonable basis to believe that a crime may have been committed.

‡ This is the crime with which Trump was charged thirty-four times in this indictment. It is a class E felony, the lowest-level felony in New York's penal code. To successfully convict, the Manhattan DA must prove beyond a reasonable doubt that Donald Trump committed the crime of falsifying business records in the second degree as part of a broader effort to commit another crime or to aid or conceal the commission of another crime. Falsifying business records in the second degree is a

The defendant, in the County of New York and elsewhere, on or about February 14, 2017, with intent to defraud and intent to commit another crime and aid and conceal the commission thereof, made and caused a false entry in the business records of an enterprise, to wit, an invoice from Michael Cohen* dated February 14, 2017, marked as a record of the Donald J. Trump Revocable Trust, and kept and maintained by the Trump Organization. †

---

class A *misdemeanor*. However, when this crime is committed in tandem with the commission of another crime, it is a felony. Thus, to convict on this felony, DA Bragg must convince a jury beyond a reasonable doubt that Trump falsified business records *and* did so as part of the commission of another crime.

INSIDER Note: Under the doctrine of "lesser included" offenses, if the DA is able to convince a jury only that Trump committed the misdemeanor offense of falsifying a business record, but not in tandem with another crime, then the jury can convict Trump of the misdemeanor. Because it is a "lesser included" crime, it need not be charged in the indictment specifically, because it is legally subsumed by the felony charge.

* Michael Cohen was Donald Trump's longtime lawyer and "fixer"—and a central participant in the charged scheme. Here, the prosecution alleges that Cohen created false invoices charging Trump for legal services as part of a broader scheme whereby Cohen paid Stephanie Clifford (aka Stormy Daniels), an adult film actor, "hush money" to prevent her from disclosing her sexual relationship with Donald Trump.

INSIDER NOTE: In 2018, Cohen pleaded guilty to two separate federal cases, encompassing an array of crimes, including perjury and tax offenses. Although federal prosecutors charged Cohen with crimes related to this "hush money" scheme, they did not pursue charges against Trump for the same scheme, even though he was plainly identified in the federal charges as a participant (he was identified in one of the Cohen indictments as "Individual 1").

In December 2018, Cohen was sentenced to three years in federal prison and ordered to pay a $50,000 fine. Of note, Cohen has since testified under oath that he lied to the court when he pled guilty to a tax charge. He now says he was not guilty of that offense.

† Here, we learn the facts underlying the thirty-four counts of falsifying business records in the third degree. According to the prosecution, on or around February 14, 2017, Trump directed his lawyer, Michael Cohen, to create the first of a series of fake invoices requesting Trump to remit payment to Cohen for "legal services" rendered. According to prosecutors, the payments were not for legal services, but rather "hush money" payments to Stephanie Clifford (aka Stormy Daniels), and the invoices were a way to mask those payments as being ostensibly for legal services. According to the DA's Statement of Facts, the scheme was intended to conceal damaging information about Daniels and Trump from voters during the 2016 election. The Statement of Facts further alleges that AMI, which publishes the tabloid the *National Enquirer*,

SECOND COUNT:*

AND THE GRAND JURY AFORESAID, by this indict-ment, further accuses the defendant of the crime of **FALSIFYING BUSINESS RECORDS IN THE FIRST DEGREE**, in viola-tion of Penal Law §175.10, committed as follows:

The defendant, in the County of New York and elsewhere, on or about February 14, 2017, with intent to defraud and intent to commit another crime and aid and conceal the commission thereof, made and caused a false entry in the business records of an enter-prise, to wit, an entry in the Detail General Ledger for the Donald J. Trump Revocable Trust, bearing voucher number 842457, and kept and maintained by the Trump Organization.

THIRD COUNT:

AND THE GRAND JURY AFORESAID, by this indict-ment, further accuses the defendant of the crime of **FALSIFYING BUSINESS RECORDS IN THE FIRST DEGREE**, in viola-tion of Penal Law §175.10, committed as follows:

The defendant, in the County of New York and elsewhere, on or about February 14, 2017, with intent to defraud and intent to commit another crime and aid and conceal the commission thereof,† made and

---

worked with Trump to "catch and kill" stories that were damaging to Trump and his candidacy.

* Eleven of the thirty-four counts concern the creation of false invoices for legal fees that Michael Cohen allegedly submitted to the Trump Organization. Another eleven counts concern checks that were used to reimburse Cohen for the alleged payments to Daniels. The remaining twelve counts are related to the accounting records made for the reimbursements in the Trump Organization's ledgers.

† This language points to the prosecution's effort to link a misdemeanor—falsifying business records in the second degree—to another crime in order to charge Trump with a felony—falsifying business records in the first degree. Accordingly, to secure a felony conviction, the DA must convince a jury that not only did Trump falsify business records, but also that he did so in furtherance of another crime or the con-cealment of another crime.

The indictment does not specify the second crime that is the necessary predicate for felony charge; however, the prosecution's "Statement of Facts" and subsequent filing in court specifying the other crimes clarifies that the DA will show that the false business records were created for the purpose of violating state and federal election

caused a false entry in the business records of an enterprise, to wit, an entry in the Detail General Ledger for the Donald J. Trump Revocable Trust, bearing voucher number 842460, and kept and maintained by the Trump Organization.

FOURTH COUNT:

AND THE GRAND JURY AFORESAID, by this indictment, further accuses the defendant of the crime of **FALSIFYING BUSINESS RECORDS IN THE FIRST DEGREE**, in violation of Penal Law §175.10, committed as follows:

The defendant, in the County of New York and elsewhere, on or about February 14, 2017, with intent to defraud and intent to commit another crime and aid and conceal the commission thereof, made and caused a false entry in the business records of an enterprise, to wit, a Donald J. Trump Revocable Trust Account check and check stub dated February 14, 2017, bearing check number 000138, and kept and maintained by the Trump Organization.

FIFTH COUNT:

AND THE GRAND JURY AFORESAID, by this indictment, further accuses the defendant of the crime of **FALSIFYING BUSINESS RECORDS IN THE FIRST DEGREE**, in violation of Penal Law §175.10, committed as follows:

The defendant, in the County of New York and elsewhere, on or about March 16, 2017 through March 17, 2017, with intent to defraud and intent to commit another crime and aid and conceal the commission thereof, made and caused a false entry in the business records of an enterprise, to wit, an invoice from Michael Cohen

---

laws, as well as state tax laws, and the prior false statement misdemeanors. It is unclear whether New York's false business record statute contemplated violations of federal election laws as a predicate for escalating a state misdemeanor charge to the level of a felony. It is likely that for this reason, the prosecution has offered multiple possibilities for a predicate crime that would make this a felony. Linking the felony charge to a violation of federal law might also present broader questions, as it is unclear if the alleged conduct violates the specified federal crime (which neither the government nor the defense challenged in the Cohen federal case).

dated February 16, 2017 and transmitted on or about March 16, 2017, marked as a record of the Donald J. Trump Revocable Trust, and kept and maintained by the Trump Organization.

SIXTH COUNT:

AND THE GRAND JURY AFORESAID, by this indictment, further accuses the defendant of the crime of **FALSIFYING BUSINESS RECORDS IN THE FIRST DEGREE**, in violation of Penal Law §175.10,* committed as follows:

The defendant, in the County of New York and elsewhere, on or about March 17, 2017, with intent to defraud and intent to commit another crime and aid and conceal the commission thereof, made and caused a false entry in the business records of an enterprise, to wit, an entry in the Detail General Ledger for the Donald J. Trump Revocable Trust, bearing voucher number 846907, and kept and maintained by the Trump Organization.

SEVENTH COUNT:

AND THE GRAND JURY AFORESAID, by this indictment, further accuses the defendant of the crime of **FALSIFYING BUSINESS RECORDS IN THE FIRST DEGREE**, in violation of Penal Law §175.10, committed as follows:

The defendant, in the County of New York and elsewhere, on or about March 17, 2017, with intent to defraud and intent to commit another crime and aid and conceal the commission thereof, made and caused a false entry in the business records of an enterprise, to wit, a Donald J. Trump Revocable Trust Account check and check stub dated

---

* A conviction under N.Y. Penal Law §175.10 can result in a sentence of up to four years' imprisonment. If Trump were to be convicted on more than one charge, it seems likely that a judge would direct his sentence for each charge to run concurrently, but it is possible that the number of crimes and the pattern of criminal activity could be factors that a sentencing court would consider in determining whether to run the sentences in part consecutively or whether and how much time to impose in prison.

Insider Note: Trump would serve any prison sentence resulting from this case in the State of New York's prison system.

March 17, 2017, bearing check number 000147, and kept and maintained by the Trump Organization.*

EIGHTH COUNT:

AND THE GRAND JURY AFORESAID, by this indictment, further accuses the defendant of the crime of **FALSIFYING BUSINESS RECORDS IN THE FIRST DEGREE**, in violation of Penal Law §175.10, committed as follows:

The defendant, in the County of New York and elsewhere, on or about April 13, 2017 through June 19, 2017, with intent to defraud and intent to commit another crime and aid and conceal the commission thereof, made and caused a false entry in the business records of an enterprise, to wit, an invoice from Michael Cohen dated April 13, 2017, marked as a record of Donald J. Trump, and kept and maintained by the Trump Organization.

NINTH COUNT:

AND THE GRAND JURY AFORESAID, by this indictment, further accuses the defendant of the crime of **FALSIFYING BUSINESS RECORDS IN THE FIRST DEGREE**, in violation of Penal Law §175.10, committed as follows:

The defendant, in the County of New York and elsewhere, on or about June 19, 2017, with intent to defraud and intent to commit another crime and aid and conceal the commission thereof, made and caused a false entry in the business records of an enterprise, to wit, an entry in the Detail General Ledger for Donald J. Trump, bearing voucher number 858770, and kept and maintained by the Trump Organization.

---

* Prosecutors allege here that, in response to Cohen's false invoices, Trump issued a series of check payments to Cohen from Trump Organization accounts. These checks, in addition to the invoices, were also alleged to be false business records. These check payments are the *second* type of false business that Trump is accused of creating, in violation of the law.

INSIDER NOTE: The indictment alleges that Trump signed these checks while he served as president of the United States. Cohen has said that the checks were signed in the Oval Office.

TENTH COUNT:

AND THE GRAND JURY AFORESAID, by this indictment, further accuses the defendant of the crime of **FALSIFYING BUSINESS RECORDS IN THE FIRST DEGREE**, in violation of Penal Law §175.10, committed as follows:

The defendant, in the County of New York and elsewhere, on or about June 19, 2017, with intent to defraud and intent to commit another crime and aid and conceal the commission thereof, made and caused a false entry in the business records of an enterprise, to wit, a Donald J. Trump account check and check stub dated June 19, 2017, bearing check number 002740, and kept and maintained by the Trump Organization.

ELEVENTH COUNT:

AND THE GRAND JURY AFORESAID, by this indictment, further accuses the defendant of the crime of **FALSIFYING BUSINESS RECORDS IN THE FIRST DEGREE**, in violation of Penal Law §175.10, committed as follows:

The defendant, in the County of New York and elsewhere, on or about May 22, 2017, with intent to defraud and intent to commit another crime and aid and conceal the commission thereof, made and caused a false entry in the business records of an enterprise, to wit, an invoice from Michael Cohen dated May 22, 2017, marked as a record of Donald J. Trump, and kept and maintained by the Trump Organization.

TWELFTH COUNT:

AND THE GRAND JURY AFORESAID, by this indictment, further accuses the defendant of the crime of **FALSIFYING BUSINESS RECORDS IN THE FIRST DEGREE**, in violation of Penal Law §175.10, committed as follows:

The defendant, in the County of New York and elsewhere, on or about May 22, 2017, with intent to defraud and intent to commit another crime and aid and conceal the commission thereof, made and caused a false entry in the business records of an enterprise, to wit, an entry in the Detail General Ledger for Donald J. Trump, bearing voucher number 855331,* and kept and maintained by the Trump Organization.

THIRTEENTH COUNT:

AND THE GRAND JURY AFORESAID, by this indictment, further accuses the defendant of the crime of **FALSIFYING BUSINESS RECORDS IN THE FIRST DEGREE**, in violation of Penal Law §175.10, committed as follows:

The defendant, in the County of New York and elsewhere, on or about May 23, 2017, with intent to defraud and intent to commit another crime and aid and conceal the commission thereof, made and caused a false entry in the business records of an enterprise, to wit, a Donald J. Trump account check and check stub dated May 23, 2017, bearing check number 002700, and kept and maintained by the Trump Organization.

FOURTEENTH COUNT:

AND THE GRAND JURY AFORESAID, by this indictment, further accuses the defendant of the crime of **FALSIFYING BUSINESS RECORDS IN THE FIRST DEGREE**, in violation of Penal Law §175.10, committed as follows:

The defendant, in the County of New York and elsewhere, on or about June 16, 2017 through June 19, 2017, with intent to defraud and intent to commit another crime and aid and conceal the commission thereof, made and caused a false entry in the business records of an enterprise, to wit, an invoice from Michael Cohen dated June 16, 2017, marked as a record of Donald J. Trump, and kept and maintained by the Trump Organization.

---

* Here, the prosecutors allege that Trump directed the creation of Trump Organization accounting records aimed at disguising the alleged hush money payments as legitimate business expenses (i.e., legal services). These accounting records are the *third* type of false business record that Trump is alleged to have created in violation of the law.

FIFTEENTH COUNT:

AND THE GRAND JURY AFORESAID, by this indictment, further accuses the defendant of the crime of **FALSIFYING BUSINESS RECORDS IN THE FIRST DEGREE**, in violation of Penal Law §175.10, committed as follows:

The defendant, in the County of New York and elsewhere, on or about June 19, 2017, with intent to defraud and intent to commit another crime and aid and conceal the commission thereof, made and caused a false entry in the business records of an enterprise, to wit, an entry in the Detail General Ledger for Donald J. Trump, bearing voucher number 858772, and kept and maintained by the Trump Organization.

SIXTEENTH COUNT:

AND THE GRAND JURY AFORESAID, by this indictment, further accuses the defendant of the crime of **FALSIFYING BUSINESS RECORDS IN THE FIRST DEGREE**, in violation of Penal Law §175.10, committed as follows:

The defendant, in the County of New York and elsewhere, on or about June 19, 2017, with intent to defraud and intent to commit another crime and aid and conceal the commission thereof, made and caused a false entry in the business records of an enterprise, to wit, a Donald J. Trump account check and check stub dated June 19, 2017, bearing check number 002741, and kept and maintained by the Trump Organization.

SEVENTEENTH COUNT:

AND THE GRAND JURY AFORESAID, by this indictment, further accuses the defendant of the crime of **FALSIFYING BUSINESS RECORDS IN THE FIRST DEGREE**, in violation of Penal Law §175.10, committed as follows:

The defendant, in the County of New York and elsewhere, on or about July 11, 2017, with intent to defraud and intent to commit another crime and aid and conceal the commission thereof, made and caused a false entry in the business records of an enterprise, to wit, an invoice from Michael Cohen dated July 11, 2017, marked as a record of Donald J. Trump, and kept and maintained by the Trump Organization.

EIGHTEENTH COUNT:

AND THE GRAND JURY AFORESAID, by this indictment, further accuses the defendant of the crime of **FALSIFYING BUSINESS RECORDS IN THE FIRST DEGREE**, in violation of Penal Law §175.10, committed as follows:

The defendant, in the County of New York and elsewhere, on or about July 11, 2017, with intent to defraud and intent to commit another crime and aid and conceal the commission thereof, made and caused a false entry in the business records of an enterprise, to wit, an entry in the Detail General Ledger for Donald J. Trump, bearing voucher number 861096, and kept and maintained by the Trump Organization.

NINETEENTH COUNT:

AND THE GRAND JURY AFORESAID, by this indictment, further accuses the defendant of the crime of **FALSIFYING BUSINESS RECORDS IN THE FIRST DEGREE**, in violation of Penal Law §175.10, committed as follows:

The defendant, in the County of New York and elsewhere, on or about July 11, 2017, with intent to defraud and intent to commit another crime and aid and conceal the commission thereof, made and caused a false entry in the business records of an enterprise, to wit, a Donald J. Trump account check and check stub dated July 11, 2017, bearing check number 002781, and kept and maintained by the Trump Organization.

TWENTIETH COUNT:

AND THE GRAND JURY AFORESAID, by this indictment, further accuses the defendant of the crime of **FALSIFYING BUSINESS RECORDS IN THE FIRST DEGREE**, in violation of Penal Law §175.10, committed as follows:

The defendant, in the County of New York and elsewhere, on or about August 1, 2017, with intent to defraud and intent to commit another crime and aid and conceal the commission thereof, made and caused a false entry in the business records of an enterprise, to wit, an invoice from Michael Cohen dated August 1, 2017, marked as a record of Donald J. Trump, and kept and maintained by the Trump Organization.

TWENTY-FIRST COUNT:

AND THE GRAND JURY AFORESAID, by this indictment, further accuses the defendant of the crime of **FALSIFYING BUSINESS RECORDS IN THE FIRST DEGREE**, in violation of Penal Law §175.10, committed as follows:

The defendant, in the County of New York and elsewhere, on or about August 1, 2017, with intent to defraud and intent to commit another crime and aid and conceal the commission thereof, made and caused a false entry in the business records of an enterprise, to wit, an entry in the Detail General Ledger for Donald J. Trump, bearing voucher number 863641, and kept and maintained by the Trump Organization.

TWENTY-SECOND COUNT:

AND THE GRAND JURY AFORESAID, by this indictment, further accuses the defendant of the crime of **FALSIFYING BUSINESS RECORDS IN THE FIRST DEGREE**, in violation of Penal Law §175.10, committed as follows:

The defendant, in the County of New York and elsewhere, on or about August 1, 2017, with intent to defraud and intent to commit another crime and aid and conceal the commission thereof, made and caused a false entry in the business records of an enterprise, to wit, a Donald J. Trump account check and check stub dated August 1, 2017, bearing check number 002821, and kept and maintained by the Trump Organization.[*]

---

[*] The Trump Organization, which includes an array of subsidiary companies, looms large in this indictment. According to prosecutors, false Trump Organization

TWENTY-THIRD COUNT:

AND THE GRAND JURY AFORESAID, by this indictment, further accuses the defendant of the crime of **FALSIFYING BUSINESS RECORDS IN THE FIRST DEGREE**, in violation of Penal Law §175.10, committed as follows:

The defendant, in the County of New York and elsewhere, on or about September 11, 2017, with intent to defraud and intent to commit another crime and aid and conceal the commission thereof, made and caused a false entry in the business records of an enterprise, to wit, an invoice from Michael Cohen dated September 11, 2017, marked as a record of Donald J. Trump, and kept and maintained by the Trump Organization.

TWENTY-FOURTH COUNT:

AND THE GRAND JURY AFORESAID, by this indictment, further accuses the defendant of the crime of **FALSIFYING BUSINESS RECORDS IN THE FIRST DEGREE**, in violation of Penal Law §175.10, committed as follows:

---

accounting records were created and maintained as part of the scheme to funnel payments to Daniels.

INSIDER NOTE: On December 2022, a Manhattan jury found two Trump companies—The Trump Corporation and the Trump Payroll Corporation—guilty on multiple charges of criminal tax fraud and falsifying business records connected to a fifteen-year scheme to defraud tax authorities by failing to report and pay taxes on compensation for top executives.

INSIDER NOTE: On September 21, 2022, after a years-long investigation, New York Attorney General Letitia James filed a civil suit against Donald Trump, his three oldest children, and the Trump Organization for fraud and other forms of misrepresentation, alleging the overvaluing of assets by billions of dollars. James described the alleged fraud as "staggering." The case was set for an autumn trial in New York City. On September 26, 2023, on the eve of the trial, a New York judge granted summary judgment for the state, holding that Donald J. Trump had committed fraud by inflating his assets. Having concluded that Trump committed fraud, the trial is focused on the resulting penalties. Attorney General James seeks $250 million in restitution and a prohibition barring Trump and the Trump Organization from entering into any New York State commercial real estate deals and applying for loans from any New York bank for the next five years. She also seeks to permanently bar Trump and his adult sons from running any New York companies. As of this writing, the trial has not concluded and penalties remain undetermined.

The defendant, in the County of New York and elsewhere, on or about September 11, 2017, with intent to defraud and intent to commit another crime and aid and conceal the commission thereof, made and caused a false entry in the business records of an enterprise, to wit, an entry in the Detail General Ledger for Donald J. Trump, bearing voucher number 868174, and kept and maintained by the Trump Organization.

TWENTY-FIFTH COUNT:

AND THE GRAND JURY AFORESAID, by this indictment, further accuses the defendant of the crime of **FALSIFYING BUSINESS RECORDS IN THE FIRST DEGREE**, in violation of Penal Law §175.10, committed as follows:

The defendant, in the County of New York and elsewhere, on or about September 12, 2017, with intent to defraud and intent to commit another crime and aid and conceal the commission thereof, made and caused a false entry in the business records of an enterprise, to wit, a Donald J. Trump account check and check stub dated September 12, 2017, bearing check number 002908, and kept and maintained by the Trump Organization.

TWENTY-SIXTH COUNT:

AND THE GRAND JURY AFORESAID, by this indictment, further accuses the defendant of the crime of **FALSIFYING BUSINESS RECORDS IN THE FIRST DEGREE**, in violation of Penal Law §175.10, committed as follows:

The defendant, in the County of New York and elsewhere, on or about October 18, 2017, with intent to defraud and intent to commit another crime and aid and conceal the commission thereof, made and caused a false entry in the business records of an enterprise, to wit, an invoice from Michael Cohen dated October 18, 2017, marked as a record of Donald J. Trump, and kept and maintained by the Trump Organization.

TWENTY-SEVENTH COUNT:

AND THE GRAND JURY AFORESAID, by this indictment, further accuses the defendant of the crime of **FALSIFYING BUSINESS RECORDS IN THE FIRST DEGREE**, in violation of Penal Law §175.10, committed as follows:

The defendant, in the County of New York and elsewhere, on or about October 18, 2017, with intent to defraud and intent to commit another crime and aid and conceal the commission thereof, made and caused a false entry in the business records of an enterprise, to wit, an entry in the Detail General Ledger for Donald J. Trump, bearing voucher number 872654, and kept and maintained by the Trump Organization.

TWENTY-EIGHTH COUNT:

AND THE GRAND JURY AFORESAID, by this indictment, further accuses the defendant of the crime of **FALSIFYING BUSINESS RECORDS IN THE FIRST DEGREE**, in violation of Penal Law §175.10, committed as follows:

The defendant, in the County of New York and elsewhere, on or about October 18, 2017, with intent to defraud and intent to commit another crime and aid and conceal the commission thereof, made and caused a false entry in the business records of an enterprise, to wit, a Donald J. Trump account check and check stub dated October 18, 2017, bearing check number 002944, and kept and maintained by the Trump Organization.

TWENTY-NINTH COUNT:

AND THE GRAND JURY AFORESAID, by this indictment, further accuses the defendant of the crime of **FALSIFYING BUSINESS RECORDS IN THE FIRST DEGREE**, in violation of Penal Law §175.10, committed as follows:

The defendant, in the County of New York and elsewhere, on or about November 20, 2017, with intent to defraud and intent to commit another crime and aid and conceal the commission thereof, made and caused a false entry in the business records of an enterprise, to wit, an invoice from Michael Cohen dated November 20, 2017, marked as a record of Donald J. Trump, and kept and maintained by the Trump Organization.

THIRTIETH COUNT:

AND THE GRAND JURY AFORESAID, by this indictment, further accuses the defendant of the crime of **FALSIFYING BUSINESS RECORDS IN THE FIRST DEGREE**, in violation of Penal Law §175.10, committed as follows:

The defendant, in the County of New York and elsewhere, on or about November 20, 2017, with intent to defraud and intent to commit another crime and aid and conceal the commission thereof, made and caused a false entry in the business records of an enterprise, to wit, an entry in the Detail General Ledger for Donald J. Trump, bearing voucher number 876511, and kept and maintained by the Trump Organization.

THIRTY-FIRST COUNT:

AND THE GRAND JURY AFORESAID, by this indictment, further accuses the defendant of the crime of **FALSIFYING BUSINESS RECORDS IN THE FIRST DEGREE**, in violation of Penal Law §175.10, committed as follows:

The defendant, in the County of New York and elsewhere, on or about November 21, 2017, with intent to defraud and intent to commit another crime and aid and conceal the commission thereof, made and caused a false entry in the business records of an enterprise, to wit, a Donald J. Trump account check and check stub dated November 21, 2017, bearing check number 002980, and kept and maintained by the Trump Organization.

THIRTY-SECOND COUNT:

AND THE GRAND JURY AFORESAID, by this indictment, further accuses the defendant of the crime of **FALSIFYING BUSINESS RECORDS IN THE FIRST DEGREE**, in violation of Penal Law §175.10, committed as follows:

The defendant, in the County of New York and elsewhere, on or about December 1, 2017, with intent to defraud and intent to commit another crime and aid and conceal the commission thereof, made and caused a false entry in the business records of an enterprise, to wit, an invoice from Michael Cohen dated December 1, 2017, marked as a record of Donald J. Trump, and kept and maintained by the Trump Organization.

THIRTY-THIRD COUNT:

AND THE GRAND JURY AFORESAID, by this indictment, further accuses the defendant of the crime of **FALSIFYING BUSINESS RECORDS IN THE FIRST DEGREE**, in violation of Penal Law §175.10, committed as follows:

The defendant, in the County of New York and elsewhere, on or about December 1, 2017, with intent to defraud and intent to commit another crime and aid and conceal the commission thereof, made and caused a false entry in the business records of an enterprise, to wit, an entry in the Detail General Ledger for Donald J. Trump, bearing voucher number 877785, and kept and maintained by the Trump Organization.

THIRTY-FOURTH COUNT:

AND THE GRAND JURY AFORESAID, by this indictment, further accuses the defendant of the crime of **FALSIFYING BUSINESS RECORDS IN THE FIRST DEGREE**, in violation of Penal Law §175.10, committed as follows:

The defendant, in the County of New York and elsewhere, on or about December 5, 2017, with intent to defraud and intent to commit another crime and aid and conceal the commission thereof, made and caused a false entry in the business records of an enterprise, to wit, a Donald J. Trump account check and check stub dated December 5, 2017, bearing check number 003006, and kept and maintained by the Trump Organization.

ALVIN L. BRAGG, JR.
District Attorney

GJ #8-5

Filed: NA

No

THE PEOPLE OF THE STATE OF NEW YORK

-against-

DONALD J. TRUMP,

Defendant.

INDICTMENT

FALSIFYING BUSINESS RECORDS IN THE FIRST DEGREE, P.L. §175.10, 34 Cts

---

ALVIN L. BRAGG JR., District Attorney[*]

A True Bill

Foreperson

ADJOURNED TO PART _____ ON _____

---

[*] Although the indictment was issued under Alvin Bragg's name, it is unlikely that the Manhattan DA will appear in court to try the case personally. Instead, as is typical, experienced assistant district attorneys—so-called "line" prosecutors—will do so.

SUPREME COURT OF THE STATE OF NEW YORK COUNTY OF NEW YORK

THE PEOPLE OF THE STATE OF NEW YORK

-against-

DONALD J. TRUMP,

Defendant.

STATEMENT
OF FACTS*
IND–71543–23

INTRODUCTION

1.   The defendant DONALD J. TRUMP repeatedly and fraudulently falsified New York business records to conceal criminal conduct that hid damaging information from the voting public during the 2016 presidential election.

2.   From August 2015 to December 2017, the Defendant orchestrated a scheme with others to influence the 2016 presidential election by identifying and purchasing negative information about him to suppress its publication and benefit the Defendant's electoral prospects. In order to execute the unlawful scheme, the participants violated election laws and made and caused false entries in the business records of various entities in New York.

---

* Although the New York indictment is relatively spare, outlining only the crimes charged, in this "Statement of Facts," DA Bragg gives a more comprehensive account of the alleged criminal scheme. An indictment need only enumerate the crimes charged and need not allege all or even some of the facts to support each charge. Here, DA Bragg has decided to include a separate Statement of Facts to give context and a detailed narrative of the crimes charged. In this regard, the Statement of Facts functions in the manner of a "Bill of Particulars"—that is, a prosecutor's written statement specifying factual information that is not recited in the indictment and that pertains to the offense charged and includes the substance of the defendant's conduct relating to each charge that the government intends to prove at trial.

INSIDER NOTE: Taken together, the indictment and the Statement of Facts operate like a federal "speaking indictment," which provides in one document detailed factual information related to each charge. The other three indictments against Trump are examples of "speaking indictments."

The participants also took steps that mischaracterized, for tax purposes, the true nature of the payments made in furtherance of the
scheme.*

    3.   One component of this scheme was that, at the Defen-
dant's request, a lawyer who then worked for the Trump Organization as Special Counsel to Defendant ("Lawyer A"),† covertly paid
$130,000 to an adult film actress shortly before the election to pre-
vent her from publicizing a sexual encounter with the Defendant.
Lawyer A made the $130,000 payment through a shell corporation
he set up and funded at a bank in Manhattan. This payment was illegal, and Lawyer A has since pleaded guilty to making an illegal campaign contribution and served time in prison. Further, false entries
were made in New York business records to effectuate this payment,
separate and apart from the New York business records used to conceal the payment.

    4.   After the election, the Defendant reimbursed Law-
yer A for the illegal payment through a series of monthly checks,
first from the Donald J. Trump Revocable Trust (the "Defendant's
Trust")—a Trust created under the laws of New York which held
the Trump Organization entity assets after the Defendant was
elected President—and then from the Defendant's bank account.
Each check was processed by the Trump Organization, and each
check was disguised as a payment for legal services rendered in a
given month of 2017 pursuant to a retainer agreement. The payment

---

* Here, Bragg elaborates the allegations supporting the indictment. As the Statement
of Facts explains, not only did Trump orchestrate the falsification of records to hide
hush money payments, he did so for the purpose of shielding his extramarital conduct
from the voting public during the 2016 presidential election.

    In addition to elaborating the details of the "hush-money" payments, the State-
ment of Facts also notes the alleged role of tabloid giant AMI in identifying—and
suppressing through payments to various individuals—stories that would be damaging to Trump's electoral prospects.

    The Statement of Facts alleges that Trump violated unspecified election and tax
laws. Notably, the indictment does not and need not charge those crimes; but the
indictment does claim that Trump used the false business filings to conceal these
crimes. DA Bragg delineated these specific crimes in a later filing with the court.

† "Lawyer A" is Michael Cohen, Trump's longtime lawyer and "fixer."

records, kept and maintained by the Trump Organization, were false New York business records. In truth, there was no retainer agreement, and Lawyer A was not being paid for legal services rendered in 2017. The Defendant caused his entities' business records to be falsified to disguise his and others' criminal conduct.

BACKGROUND

5.   The Defendant is the beneficial owner of a collection of business entities known by the trade name the Trump Organization. The Trump Organization comprises approximately 500 separate entities that, among other business activities, own and manage hotels, golf courses, commercial real estate, condominium developments, and other properties. The Trump Organization is headquartered at 725 Fifth Avenue in New York County.

6.   From approximately June 2015 to November 2016, the Defendant was a candidate for the office of President of the United States. On January 20, 2017, he became President of the United States.

THE SCHEME

I.   The Catch and Kill Scheme to Suppress Negative Information[*]

7.   During and in furtherance of his candidacy for President, the Defendant and others agreed to identify and suppress negative

---

[*] The term "catch and kill" refers to a media practice of suppressing news items that would be damaging to a third party. Catch and kill practices can work in the following way: publishers "catch" the story by purchasing from the source the exclusive rights to her story. Often, the terms of the sale require sources to sign a nondisclosure agreement, preventing them from publicly discussing the matter in the future. Then, for the benefit of a third party, the publisher "kills" the story by "burying" it and preventing its publication. The source often does not realize that the publisher intends to "bury" the story rather than publish it.

Perhaps the most significant allegation here is that the *National Enquirer* and its parent company, AMI, allegedly used the practice for political purposes: to benefit Trump and his election prospects.

stories about him. Two parties to this agreement have admitted to committing illegal conduct in connection with the scheme. In August 2018, Lawyer A pleaded guilty to two federal crimes involving illegal campaign contributions, and subsequently served time in prison. In addition, in August 2018, American Media, Inc. ("AMI"), a media company that owned and published magazines and supermarket tabloids including the *National Enquirer,* admitted in a non-prosecution agreement that it made a payment to a source of a story to ensure that the source "did not publicize damaging allegations" about the Defendant "before the 2016 presidential election and thereby influence that election."

A.   The 2015 Trump Tower Meeting

8.   In June 2015, the Defendant announced his candidacy for President of the United States.

9.   Soon after, in August 2015, the Defendant met with Lawyer A and AMI's Chairman and Chief Executive Officer (the "AMI CEO")* at Trump Tower in New York County. At the meeting, the AMI CEO agreed to help with the Defendant's campaign, saying that he would act as the "eyes and ears" for the campaign by looking out for negative stories about the Defendant and alerting Lawyer A before the stories were published. The AMI CEO also agreed to publish negative stories about the Defendant's competitors for the election.

B.   Suppressing the Doorman's Story

10.   A few months later, in or about October or November 2015, the AMI CEO learned that a former Trump Tower doorman (the "Doorman") was trying to sell information regarding a child that the Defendant had allegedly fathered out of wedlock. At the AMI CEO's direction, AMI negotiated and signed an agreement to pay the Doorman $30,000 to acquire exclusive rights to the story. AMI falsely characterized this payment in AMI's books and records,

---

* Although he is not specifically named in either the indictment or the Statement of Facts, the CEO of AMI during this time was David Pecker, a friend of Trump. Pecker testified before the Manhattan grand jury.

including in its general ledger. AMI purchased the information from the Doorman without fully investigating his claims, but the AMI CEO directed that the deal take place because of his agreement with the Defendant and Lawyer A.*

11.   When AMI later concluded that the story was not true, the AMI CEO wanted to release the Doorman from the agreement. However, Lawyer A instructed the AMI CEO not to release the Doorman until after the presidential election, and the AMI CEO complied with that instruction because of his agreement with the Defendant and Lawyer A.

C.   Suppressing Woman 1's Account

12.   About five months before the presidential election, in or about June 2016, the editor-in-chief of the *National Enquirer* and AMI's Chief Content Officer (the "AMI Editor-in-Chief") contacted Lawyer A about a woman ("Woman 1") who alleged she had a sexual relationship with the Defendant while he was married.† The AMI Editor-in-Chief updated Lawyer A regularly about the matter over text message and by telephone. The Defendant did not want this information to become public because he was concerned about the effect it could have on his candidacy. Thereafter, the Defendant, the AMI CEO, and Lawyer A had a series of discussions about who should pay off Woman 1 to secure her silence.

13.   AMI ultimately paid $150,000 to Woman 1 in exchange for her agreement not to speak out about the alleged sexual relationship, as well as for two magazine cover features of Woman 1

---

* This section details the first of three "hush money" payments that the prosecution alleges were paid as part of a larger scheme to influence the 2016 election by keeping Trump's alleged indiscretions out of the public eye. Here, AMI made a deal with Dino Sajudin, a former doorman at Trump Tower, to purchase Sajudin's story alleging that Trump had fathered a child out of wedlock. AMI purchased the rights to Sajudin's story, but never intended to publish it. The publisher later learned that Sajudin's story was false. Sajudin is not named in the Statement of Facts but has been identified in news reporting.

† "Woman 1" is Karen McDougal, a *Playboy* model, who alleges having an affair with Trump. Again, AMI allegedly deployed the "catch and kill" strategy, paying MacDougal $150,000 for her story without intending to publish it.

and a series of articles that would be published under her byline. AMI falsely characterized this payment in AMI's books and records, including in its general ledger. The AMI CEO agreed to the deal after discussing it with both the Defendant and Lawyer A, and on the understanding from Lawyer A that the Defendant or the Trump Organization would reimburse AMI.

14. In a conversation captured in an audio recording in approximately September 2016 concerning Woman 1's account, the Defendant and Lawyer A discussed how to obtain the rights to Woman 1's account from AMI and how to reimburse AMI for its payment.* Lawyer A told the Defendant he would open up a company for the transfer of Woman 1's account and other information, and stated that he had spoken to the Chief Financial Officer for the Trump Organization (the "TO CFO") about "how to set the whole thing up." The Defendant asked, "So what do we got to pay for this? One fifty?" and suggested paying by cash.† When Lawyer A disagreed, the Defendant then mentioned payment by check. After the conversation, Lawyer A created a shell company called Resolution Consultants, LLC on or about September 30, 2016.

15. Less than two months before the election, on or about September 30, 2016, the AMI CEO signed an agreement in which AMI agreed to transfer its rights to Woman 1's account to Lawyer A's shell company for $125,000. However, after the assignment agreement was signed but before the reimbursement took place, the AMI CEO consulted with AMI's general counsel and then told Lawyer A that the deal to transfer the rights to Lawyer A's shell company was off.

---

* According to Cohen, he and Trump discussed purchasing the rights to McDougal's story from AMI; however, this purchase was never executed.

† Trump is alleged to have made this statement on a September 2016 telephone call with Cohen that Cohen taped. (Cohen apparently taped other conversations with Trump as well.) FBI agents apparently seized the recordings in the April 2016 court-authorized search of Cohen's office and residences. Cohen's lawyer, Lanny Davis, later released the tape to CNN in order to rebut statements that Rudy Giuliani made about Cohen's role in the scheme. As Davis explained, "We were not going to let Michael become a punching bag."

D. Suppressing Woman 2's Account

16. About one month before the election, on or about October 7, 2016, news broke that the Defendant had been caught on tape saying to the host of *Access Hollywood:* "I just start kissing them [women]. It's like a magnet. Just kiss. I don't even wait. And when you're a star, they let you do it. You can do anything. . . . Grab 'em by the [genitals]. You can do anything."* The evidence shows that both the Defendant and his campaign staff were concerned that the tape would harm his viability as a candidate and reduce his standing with female voters in particular.

17. Shortly after the *Access Hollywood* tape became public, the AMI Editor-in-Chief contacted the AMI CEO about another woman ("Woman 2") who alleged she had a sexual encounter with the Defendant while he was married.† The AMI CEO told the AMI Editor-in-Chief to notify Lawyer A.

18. On or about October 10, 2016, the AMI Editor-in-Chief connected Lawyer A with Woman 2's lawyer ("Lawyer B").‡ Lawyer A then negotiated a deal with Lawyer B to secure Woman 2's silence and prevent disclosure of the damaging information in the final weeks before the presidential election. Under the deal that Lawyer B negotiated, Woman 2 would be paid $130,000 for the rights to her account.

---

* This is a reference to the infamous *Access Hollywood* interview between host Billy Bush and Trump that took place in September 2005. News of the taped interview broke on October 7, 2016, roughly a month before the presidential election.

INSIDER NOTE: Just hours after the *Access Hollywood* tape was reported, Russians who hacked into email accounts related to Hillary Clinton began releasing the hacked material in what appeared to be an effort to distract from the tape.

† "Woman 2" refers to Stormy Daniels, who claimed to have had a sexual encounter with Trump during his marriage.

‡ Daniels's lawyer was Michael Avenatti. No stranger to legal trouble, Avenatti was later sentenced to two and a half years in prison for trying to extort more than $20 million from Nike. And in June 2022, Avenatti was sentenced to four years in prison for defrauding Daniels of $300,000. And, again in December 2022, he was sentenced to fourteen years' imprisonment for stealing millions of dollars from his clients and obstructing efforts of the Internal Revenue Service to collect taxes from his coffee business, Global Baristas.

19.   The Defendant directed Lawyer A to delay making a payment to Woman 2 as long as possible. He instructed Lawyer A that if they could delay the payment until after the election, they could avoid paying altogether, because at that point it would not matter if the story became public. As reflected in emails and text messages between and among Lawyer A, Lawyer B, and the AMI Editor-in-Chief, Lawyer A attempted to delay making payment as long as possible.

20.   Ultimately, with pressure mounting and the election approaching, the Defendant agreed to the payoff and directed Lawyer A to proceed. Lawyer A discussed the deal with the Defendant and the TO CFO. The Defendant did not want to make the $130,000 payment himself, and asked Lawyer A and the TO CFO to find a way to make the payment. After discussing various payment options with the TO CFO, Lawyer A agreed he would make the payment. Before making the payment, Lawyer A confirmed with the Defendant that Defendant would pay him back.

21.   On or about October 26, shortly after speaking with the Defendant on the phone, Lawyer A opened a bank account in Manhattan in the name of Essential Consultants LLC, a new shell company he had created to effectuate the payment. He then transferred $131,000 from his personal home equity line of credit ("HELOC") into that account. On or about October 27, Lawyer A wired $130,000 from his Essential Consultants LLC account in New York to Lawyer B to suppress Woman 2's account.

E.   Post-Election Communications with AMI CEO

22.   On November 8, 2016, the Defendant won the presidential election and became the President-Elect. Thereafter, AMI released both the doorman and Woman 1 from their non-disclosure agreements.*

---

* The alleged Trump-McDougal affair was a poorly kept secret. Just four days before the 2016 election in which Trump was a presidential candidate, the *Wall Street Journal* published a story reporting that McDougal had discussed with a friend the alleged affair with Trump. It was also reported that AMI paid McDougal $150,000

23. The Defendant was inaugurated as President on January 20, 2017. Between Election Day and Inauguration Day, during the period of the Defendant's transition to his role as President, the Defendant met with the AMI CEO privately in Trump Tower in Manhattan. The Defendant thanked the AMI CEO for handling the stories of the Doorman and Woman 1, and invited the AMI CEO to the Inauguration. In the summer of 2017, the Defendant invited the AMI CEO to the White House for a dinner to thank him for his help during the campaign.

II.   The Defendant Falsified Business Records

24. Shortly after being elected President, the Defendant arranged to reimburse Lawyer A for the payoff he made on the Defendant's behalf. In or around January 2017, the TO CFO* and Lawyer A

---

for exclusive rights to her story, but never published it. Trump campaign spokeswoman Hope Hicks denied the existence of an affair between Trump and McDougal as "totally untrue."

In February 2018, while Trump was in office, *The New Yorker*'s Ronan Farrow wrote about the affair and AMI's purchase of the story, largely corroborating the 2016 *Wall Street Journal* report. On March 22, 2018, CNN's Anderson Cooper conducted an interview in which McDougal detailed the affair and apologized to Melania Trump. She said that Trump tried to give her money after they first had sex, that their relationship lasted ten months, and that she visited Trump "many dozens of times."

In March 2018, McDougal filed a lawsuit against AMI in Los Angeles Superior Court, aiming to invalidate the nondisclosure agreement. On April 19, 2018, AMI settled with McDougal, allowing her to speak about the alleged affair.

* The Trump Organization CFO referenced here is Allen Weisselberg. In July 2018, Weisselberg was subpoenaed to testify before a federal grand jury regarding the Cohen investigation. In exchange for this testimony, Weisselberg was granted immunity.

In July 2021, a New York State grand jury charged Weisselberg with fifteen felony charges related to evading $344,745 in taxes over fifteen years. Although Weisselberg initially pleaded not guilty, on August 18, 2022, he pleaded guilty to all fifteen counts of grand larceny, criminal tax fraud, and falsifying business records. As part of his plea deal, he was sentenced to five months in jail and agreed to testify truthfully if called as a witness at the Trump Organization's criminal trial and to pay roughly $2 million in back taxes and fees. As part of his state plea deal, Weisselberg waived any claim that the state charges were tainted by the use of his federal immunized testimony. Weisselberg ultimately served his sentence in the infirmary unit of Rikers Island. He was released on April 19, 2023.

met to discuss how Lawyer A would be reimbursed for the money he paid to ensure Woman 2's silence. The TO CFO asked Lawyer A to bring a copy of a bank statement for the Essential Consultants account showing the $130,000 payment.*

25. The TO CFO and Lawyer A agreed to a total repayment amount of $420,000. They reached that figure by adding the $130,000 payment to a $50,000 payment for another expense for which Lawyer A also claimed reimbursement, for a total of $180,000. The TO CFO then doubled that amount to $360,000 so that Lawyer A could characterize the payment as income on his tax returns, instead of a reimbursement, and Lawyer A would be left with $180,000 after paying approximately 50% in income taxes. Finally, the TO CFO added an additional $60,000 as a supplemental year-end bonus. Together, these amounts totaled $420,000. The TO CFO memorialized these calculations in handwritten notes on the copy of the bank statement that Lawyer A had provided.

26. The Defendant, the TO CFO, and Lawyer A then agreed that Lawyer A would be paid the $420,000 through twelve monthly payments of $35,000 over the course of 2017. Each month, Lawyer A was to send an invoice to the Defendant through Trump Organization employees, falsely requesting payment of $35,000 for legal services rendered in a given month of 2017 pursuant to a retainer agreement. At no point did Lawyer A have a retainer agreement with the Defendant or the Trump Organization.

27. In early February 2017, the Defendant and Lawyer A met in the Oval Office at the White House and confirmed this repayment arrangement.

28. On or about February 14, 2017, Lawyer A emailed the Controller of the Trump Organization (the "TO Controller") the first monthly invoice, which stated: "Pursuant to the retainer agree-

---

* These facts are critical. Here, DA Bragg explains how Trump reimbursed Cohen for payment to Daniels, forming the predicate for the false business filings charges in the indictment.

ment, kindly remit payment for services rendered for the months of January and February, 2017." The invoice requested payment in the amount of $35,000 for each of those two months. The TO CFO approved the payment, and, in turn, the TO Controller sent the invoice to the Trump Organization Accounts Payable Supervisor (the "TO Accounts Payable Supervisor") with the following instructions: "Post to legal expenses. Put 'retainer for the months of January and February 2017' in the description."

29. Lawyer A submitted ten similar monthly invoices by email to the Trump Organization for the remaining months in 2017. Each invoice falsely stated that it was being submitted "[p]ursuant to the retainer agreement," and falsely requested "payment for services rendered" for a month of 2017. In fact, there was no such retainer agreement and Lawyer A was not being paid for services rendered in any month of 2017.

30. The TO Controller forwarded each invoice to the TO Accounts Payable Supervisor. Consistent with the TO Controller's initial instructions, the TO Accounts Payable Supervisor printed out each invoice and marked it with an accounts payable stamp and the general ledger code "51505" for legal expenses. The Trump Organization maintained the invoices as records of expenses paid.

31. As instructed, the TO Accounts Payable Supervisor recorded each payment in the Trump Organization's electronic accounting system, falsely describing it as a "legal expense" pursuant to a retainer agreement for a month of 2017. The Trump Organization maintained a digital entry for each expense, called a "voucher," and these vouchers, like vouchers for other expenses, became part of the Trump Organization's general ledgers.

32. The TO Accounts Payable Supervisor then prepared checks with attached check stubs for approval and signature. The first check was paid from the Defendant's Trust and signed by the TO CFO and the Defendant's son, as trustees. The check stub falsely recorded the payment as "Retainer for 1/1-1/31/17" and "Retainer for 2/1-2/28/17." The second check, for March 2017, was also paid

from the Trust and signed by two trustees. The check stub falsely recorded the payment as "Retainer for 3/1-3/31/17."

33.   The remaining nine checks, corresponding to the months of April through December of 2017, were paid by the Defendant personally. Each of the checks was cut from the Defendant's bank account and sent, along with the corresponding invoices from Lawyer A, from the Trump Organization in New York County to the Defendant in Washington, D.C. The checks and stubs bearing the false statements were stapled to the invoices also bearing false statements. The Defendant signed each of the checks personally and had them sent back to the Trump Organization in New York County. There, the checks, the stubs, and the invoices were scanned and maintained in the Trump Organization's data system before the checks themselves were detached and mailed to Lawyer A for payment.

34.   The $35,000 payments stopped after the December 2017 payment.

III. The Investigation into Lawyer A and the Defendant's Pressure Campaign

35.   On or about April 9, 2018, the FBI executed a search warrant on Lawyer A's residences and office.* In the months that followed, the Defendant and others engaged in a public and private

---

* To obtain a search warrant, law enforcement must convince a judge that there is probable cause to believe that evidence of illegal activity is present. According to Cohen's lawyer, federal prosecutors obtained a warrant to search Cohen's office and residence after receiving a referral from the special counsel in the Russia investigation, Robert Mueller. The search did not appear to be directly related to the remit of Special Counsel Mueller's investigation, but rather emanated from information that the Mueller team referred to federal prosecutors in the Southern District of New York, who ultimately charged Cohen, alongside a separate charge that the special counsel brought against Cohen.

pressure campaign to ensure that Lawyer A did not cooperate with law enforcement in the federal investigation.*

36.   On the day of the FBI searches, Lawyer A called to speak with the Defendant to let him know what had occurred. In a return call, the Defendant told Lawyer A to "stay strong."

37.   On or about April 21, 2018, the Defendant publicly commented on Twitter encouraging Lawyer A not to "flip," stating, "Most people will flip if the Government lets them out of trouble, even if . . . it means lying or making up stories. Sorry, I don't see [Lawyer A] doing that. . . ."

38.   In mid-April 2018, Lawyer A was also approached by an attorney ("Lawyer C"), who offered to represent him in the interest of maintaining a "back channel of communication" to the Defendant. On or about April 21, 2018, Lawyer C emailed Lawyer A, highlighting that he had a close relationship with the Defendant's personal attorney ("Lawyer D") and stating, "[T]his could not be a better situation for the President or you." Later that day, Lawyer C emailed Lawyer A again, writing, "I spoke with [Lawyer D]. Very Very Positive. You are 'loved.' . . . [Lawyer D] said this communication channel must be maintained. . . . Sleep well tonight, you have friends in high places."†

39.   On or about June 14, 2018, Lawyer C emailed Lawyer A a news clip discussing the possibility of Lawyer A cooperating, and continued to urge him not to cooperate with law enforcement, writing, "The whole objective of this exercise by the [federal prosecutors] is to drain you, emotionally and financially, until you reach a point that you see them as your only means to salvation." In the same email, Lawyer C, wrote, "You are making a very big mistake if you believe the stories these 'journalists' are writing about you. They want you to cave. They want you to fail. They do not want you to persevere and succeed."

---

* This section details the federal investigation of Cohen—which resulted in his prosecution, guilty plea, and sentence. As this section alleges, Trump repeatedly pressured Cohen to refuse the federal prosecutors' requests for his cooperation.

† Based on context and evidence, "Lawyer C" is Robert Costello.

40. On August 21, 2018, Lawyer A pleaded guilty in the federal investigation. The next day, on or about August 22, 2018, the Defendant commented on Twitter, "If anyone is looking for a good lawyer, I would strongly suggest that you don't retain the services of [Lawyer A]!" Later that day, the Defendant posted to Twitter again, stating, "I feel very badly for" one of his former campaign managers who had been criminally charged, saying, "[U]nlike [Lawyer A], he refused to 'break' – make up stories in order to get a 'deal.'"

IV. Lawyer A and AMI Admit Guilt in Connection with Payoffs of Woman 1 and Woman 2

41. Ultimately, other participants in the scheme admitted that the payoffs were unlawful.

42. In or about September 2018, AMI entered into a non-prosecution agreement with the United States Attorney's Office for the Southern District of New York in connection with AMI's payoff of Woman 1, admitting that "[a]t no time during the negotiation or acquisition of [Woman 1's] story did AMI intend to publish the story or disseminate information about it publicly." Rather, AMI admitted that it made the payment to ensure that Woman 1 "did not publicize damaging allegations" about the Defendant "before the 2016 presidential election and thereby influence that election."*

43. In August 21, 2018, Lawyer A pleaded guilty to a felony in connection with his role in AMI's payoff to Woman 1, admitting in his guilty plea that he had done so at the Defendant's direction:

> [O]n or about the summer of 2016, **in coordination with, and at the direction of, a candidate for federal office,** I and the CEO of a media company at the request of the candidate worked together to keep an individual with information that would be harmful to the candidate and to the campaign from publicly disclosing this information. After a number of discussions, we eventually accomplished the goal by the media company entering into a contract with the individual under

---

* As this section explains, AMI eventually decided to cooperate with federal prosecutors, admitting its efforts to "catch and kill" Karen McDougal's story in order to bolster Trump's electoral prospects.

which she received compensation of $150,000. I participated in this conduct, which on my part took place in Manhattan, for the principal purpose of influencing the election.

(emphasis added).

44.   Lawyer A also pleaded guilty to a felony in connection with his payoff of Woman 2 to secure her silence, again at the Defendant's direction. Lawyer A admitted as part of his guilty plea:

> [O]n or about October of 2016, **in coordination with, and at the direction of, the same candidate,** I arranged to make a payment to a second individual with information that would be harmful to the candidate and to the campaign to keep the individual from disclosing the information. To accomplish this, I used a company that was under my control to make a payment in the sum of $130,000. The monies I advanced through my company were later repaid to me by the candidate. I participated in this conduct, which on my part took place in Manhattan, for the principal purpose of influencing the election.

(emphasis added).[1*]

DATED: New York, New York
         April 4, 2023

ALVIN L. BRAGG, JR.
District Attorney
New York County

---

[1] This Statement of Facts contains certain of the information that is relevant to the events described herein, and does not contain all facts relevant to the charged conduct.

---

[*] This footnote is not an annotation, but rather, appears in the Statement of Facts.

COMPLETE CAST
OF CHARACTERS

M ANY OF THE INDICTMENTS REFERENCE UNNAMED
individuals by descriptions such as "Employee 1," "Woman 2,"
and "Co-Conspirator 3." To be clear, these unnamed individuals have
not been charged with any crime. They are referenced because they play
some role in the events alleged. Relying on media reports identifying
these individuals, we have named them here in order to facilitate the
reader's comprehension of these documents and the alleged conduct
they describe. That said, it must be remembered that none of these individuals has been charged with any wrongdoing.

○ = defendant (To charge a defendant, a grand jury has to determine that
there is probable cause that the person committed the crime. At trial, the
government needs to establish guilt beyond a reasonable doubt and the
defendant is presumed innocent unless and until such time.)

▲ = involved in multiple cases

Bernick, Alex [GA]—An Assistant District Attorney in the Fulton County
DA's Office. Bernick became a Fulton County prosecutor in 2023 and previously worked in the Georgia Attorney General's Office.

Biggs, Joe [DC]—The former head of the Florida chapter of the Proud
Boys. Biggs, an army veteran, commanded a large group of Trump supporters in attacking the Capitol on January 6. Biggs was convicted of seditious conspiracy and sentenced to seventeen years in prison.

Blanche, Todd▲ [DC/FL/NY]—A white-collar criminal defense lawyer and former federal prosecutor. Blanche, previously a partner at a well-
known New York law firm, launched his own firm in 2023 to represent
Trump in three criminal investigations: the New York case and both federal
cases. Blanche successfully represented Trump's former presidential campaign manager Paul Manafort in the Manhattan District Attorney's prosecution that was ultimately dismissed on state double-jeopardy grounds.

Bobb, Christina [FL] ("Trump attorney 3")—A Trump attorney who
signed an erroneous June 2022 certification provided to the DOJ claim-

ing that, to her knowledge, all of Trump's responsive documents had been returned to the DOJ after a diligent search.

Bowers, Rusty [DC] ("Arizona House Speaker")—The former Speaker of the Arizona House of Representatives. According to Bowers's sworn testimony before the January 6 committee, Trump and his team repeatedly pressured Bowers, a Republican loyalist, not to recognize Arizona's legitimate electors. Bowers declined to comply with these entreaties and issued a public statement that his constitutional duty required him to honor the popular vote.

Bragg, Alvin [NY]—The Manhattan District Attorney. Bragg was elected in 2021 and previously served as a federal prosecutor and as Chief Deputy Attorney General of New York. Bragg inherited the Trump investigation from his predecessor, Cyrus Vance, when he took office.

Brannan, Joseph [GA] (Unindicted Co-Conspirator)—The former treasurer of the Georgia GOP and, according to prosecutors, one of Trump's sixteen fraudulent Georgia electors.

Bratt, Jay [FL]—The Chief of the Justice Department's Counterintelligence and Export Control Section. Bratt was one of the DOJ attorneys who traveled to Mar-a-Lago in June 2022 to discuss missing documents with Trump's lawyers. Bratt, who has helped oversee numerous classified documents prosecutions at the DOJ, has appeared in court on behalf of the federal government following the Florida indictment.

Cannon, Judge Aileen [FL]—The Florida-based federal judge presiding over the DOJ's classified documents case. Cannon, a Trump appointee, became a judge in 2020.

Cannon, Alex [FL] ("Trump Representative 1")—A former Trump lawyer who reportedly tried to effectuate Trump's compliance with the National Archives' request that Trump return records. Apparently, Cannon, uneasy about the possibility that Trump might be withholding documents, declined Trump's request to tell the Archives that all materials had been returned. Cannon is not related to Judge Aileen Cannon.

Chatfield, Lee [DC] ("Michigan House Speaker")—The former Speaker of the Michigan House of Representatives whom, according to the January 6 congressional report, Trump and Giuliani unsuccessfully pressured to reject Michigan's legitimate electors.

Cheeley, Robert○ [GA]—A Georgia-based lawyer who prosecutors say worked with Trump's attorneys to overturn Georgia's election results. Cheeley presented at a Georgia Senate subcommittee meeting and told lawmakers that election workers had double- and triple-counted votes. The Fulton County indictment alleges that Cheeley later committed perjury by lying to the Fulton County grand jury about his involvement in Trump's efforts to overturn Georgia's election results. Cheeley faces ten criminal charges in Fulton County.

Chesebro, Kenneth○▲ [DC/GA] ("Co-Conspirator 5")—Trump's co-defendant and former legal advisor. Chesebro, who was a defendant in the Fulton County indictment and referred to as "co-conspirator 5" in the DOJ's January 6 indictment, was charged with his role in devising a plan to appoint slates of fraudulent electors in seven states that Trump lost. According to the Georgia and the January 6 indictments, the plan called for slates of Trump electors—individuals who would have served as electors if Trump had won the popular vote in those states—to convene to mimic the actions of real electors by casting fraudulent "votes" and signing false certifications that they were the legitimate electors. The fraudulent certificates were then provided to the President of the Senate and others. The plan was supposed to culminate on January 6, 2021, with Vice President Pence opening the fraudulent certificates on the Senate floor and counting them as real votes, but Pence never complied. Chesebro faced seven criminal charges in Fulton County.On October 20, 2023, just days before his trial was scheduled to begin, Chesebro pleaded guilty to one felony count of conspiracy to commit filing false documents. As part of his Fulton County plea deal, Chesebro is sentenced to five years' probation and will pay $5,000 in restitution. He has also agreed to testify truthfully in all future proceedings.

Chutkan, Judge Tanya [DC]—The Washington, DC, federal judge presiding over the DOJ's January 6 case. Chutkan, a former public defender and law firm partner, was nominated by Barack Obama and began serving in 2014.

Cipollone, Pat [DC]—Trump's White House Counsel from 2018 to January 20, 2021. Cipollone allegedly pushed back on Trump's false claims about election fraud and threatened to resign if Trump fired Acting Attorney General Jeffrey Rosen. A few hours after Trump's supporters attacked the Capitol on January 6, Cipollone called Trump to ask him to withdraw his objection to the certification of the election—a request Trump declined. Cipollone defended Trump during his first impeachment trial.

Clark, Jeffrey○▲ [DC/GA] ("Co-Conspirator 4")—Trump's co-defendant and the former acting head of the DOJ's civil division. On January 3, 2021, Trump briefly appointed Clark Acting Attorney General so that he could lend the DOJ's backing to Trump's efforts to overturn the election. Trump

rescinded the appointment later that day when threatened with the prospect of mass resignations. According to the DOJ January 6 indictment,
Clark drafted a letter (never ultimately sent) to Georgia lawmakers stating
the DOJ had significant concerns about election fraud and viewed Trump's
fraudulent Georgia electors—the individuals who would have served as
electors if Trump had won the popular vote—as legitimate electors. Clark's
bosses at the DOJ, Acting Attorney General Jeffrey Rosen and Acting Deputy Attorney General Richard Donoghue, refused to sign the Georgia letter.

Clifford, Stephanie (aka Stormy Daniels) [NY] ("Woman 2")—An adult
film actor who claims to have had an affair with Donald Trump. Michael
Cohen told prosecutors that he submitted false invoices for legal services
to the Trump Organization for the purpose of concealing "hush money"
payments to Clifford to prevent her from disclosing her relationship with
Trump.

Cohen, Michael [NY] ("Lawyer A")—Trump's longtime lawyer and
"fixer," Cohen provided key evidence to the Manhattan District Attorney
as to a scheme to create false invoices for legal services that would be used
to disguise "hush money" payments to adult film actor Stormy Daniels.

Colangelo, Matthew [NY]—Senior Counsel to the Manhattan District
Attorney. Colangelo previously served alongside Alvin Bragg at the New
York Attorney General's Office, where he worked with Bragg to investigate
the Trump Foundation's misuse of charitable funds. Colangelo recently
held a senior role at the DOJ and served as a law clerk to United States
Supreme Court Justice Sonia Sotomayor when she was a judge on the
United States Court of Appeals for the Second Circuit.

Conroy, Christopher [NY]—Senior Advisor in the Investigation Division
of the Manhattan District Attorney's Office. Conroy, a twenty-seven-year
veteran of that office and the former chief of its Major Economic Crimes
Bureau and Investigation Division, has overseen several high-profile prosecutions of financial institutions on charges of falsifying business records.

Consiglio, Vikki Townsend [GA] (Unindicted Co-Conspirator 10 or
11)—One of Georgia's sixteen illegitimate Trump electors.

Cooney, J. P. [DC]—A veteran prosecutor who worked under Jack Smith
and Raymond Hulser in the DOJ's Public Integrity Section. Cooney, now
an Assistant United States Attorney for the District of Columbia, worked
on the unsuccessful prosecutions of Senator Bob Menendez and former
Obama White House Counsel Gregory Craig, and he worked on the successful prosecutions of Steve Bannon and Roger Stone. Cooney also played

a role in the DOJ's investigation of former FBI Acting Director Andrew McCabe, whom the grand jury reportedly declined to charge.

Corcoran, Evan▲ [DC/FL] ("Trump attorney 1")—Trump's lawyer who participated in the response to the DOJ's 2022 grand jury subpoena for documents bearing classified markings. According to prosecutors, Corcoran informed Trump that he would search the Mar-a-Lago storage room for responsive documents. Before Corcoran could do so, Trump allegedly had aides remove boxes from the storage room and bring them to Trump's personal residence. Corcoran searched the storage room and found only thirty-eight classified documents, all of which he turned over to the FBI. Corcoran—apparently unaware of the removal of the boxes—asked Christina Bobb to sign a certification stating that all responsive documents had been returned. Corcoran's personal meeting notes feature prominently in the DOJ's Florida indictment and record that Trump repeatedly intimated that Corcoran should destroy or hide the documents that the DOJ requested. Corcoran recused himself as Trump's lawyer in the Florida documents case but apparently continues to represent Trump in other cases, including the DOJ's January 6 case.[*]

Costello, Robert [NY] ("Lawyer C")—A New York City lawyer and Trump grand jury defense witness. According to the New York State prosecutor's Statement of Facts filed alongside the New York indictment, following the FBI's search of Michael Cohen's home and office, Costello discouraged Cohen from cooperating with the prosecution and offered to represent him in order to maintain a "back channel" to Trump. In the days preceding Trump's New York indictment, Costello, acting as a witness for Trump, testified before the Manhattan grand jury.

Cross, Anna Green [GA]—A private attorney and former prosecutor who Fani Willis brought on to the Trump investigation. Cross, who currently works at a firm she co-founded, spent twenty years as a Georgia prosecutor and has considerable appellate experience.

Cruce, Alex [GA] (Unindicted Co-Conspirator)—A Trump supporter who, according to the indictment, flew to Coffee County, Georgia, to assist with the illegal breach of voting machines.

Davidson, Keith [NY] ("Lawyer B")—Stormy Daniels's lawyer who negotiated the $130,000 sale of Daniels's story to AMI.

---

[*] Jacqueline Alemany, Josh Dawsey, and Spencer S. Hsu, "A Top Trump Lawyer Has Recused Himself from Mar-a-Lago Documents Case," *Washington Post*, April 15, 2023.

De Oliveira, Carlos○ [FL]—Mar-a-Lago property manager and Trump's co-defendant. The DOJ indictment alleges that De Oliveira—at Trump's direction—attempted to delete security footage of a Mar-a-Lago storage room ultimately sought by a DOJ subpoena. De Oliveira allegedly worked with Walt Nauta to locate the footage and unsuccessfully pressured Mar-a-Lago's IT director to delete it.

Dohrmann, Mary [DC]—An Assistant United States Attorney for the District of Columbia who prosecuted several Capitol rioters.

Donoghue, Richard [DC]—Former Acting Deputy Attorney General to Trump. Donoghue, along with Acting Attorney General Jeffrey Rosen, refused to lend the DOJ's support to Trump's efforts to overturn the election.

Eastman, John○▲ [DC/GA] ("Co-Conspirator 2")—Trump's co-defendant and former legal advisor. Eastman is a defendant in the Fulton County District Attorney's indictment and referred to as "co-conspirator 2" in the DOJ's January 6 indictment. Prosecutors allege that Eastman was an architect of the plan to have Mike Pence leverage his ceremonial role as President of the Senate to obstruct the certification of the 2020 election by rejecting the electoral votes of seven states that Biden won. Eastman later devised a second plan whereby Pence, instead of outright rejecting the seven "disputed" states' electoral votes, would send dueling slates of electors to those seven states' legislatures and ask the legislatures to determine which electors to count. Eastman and Trump met with Pence in the White House on January 4, 2021, and attempted to convince Pence to adopt either of the two plans, even though Eastman acknowledged in communications cited by prosecutors that the plans violated the Electoral Count Act and would be rejected by courts. Eastman spoke to the crowd of Trump supporters gathered in Washington, DC, on the morning of January 6, 2021, and, hours after the attack on the Capitol, emailed Pence's counsel to "implore" him to delay the count for another ten days. Eastman faces nine criminal charges in Fulton County.

Edelstein, Julie [FL]—The Deputy Chief of the Justice Department's Counterintelligence and Export Control Section under Jay Bratt. Edelstein has been a lead prosecutor in multiple high-profile cases involving government leaks. She too has appeared in the Florida criminal case.

Ellis, Jenna○ [GA]—A former Trump campaign attorney. Prosecutors claim that Ellis was among the lawyers who presented false claims about election fraud to Georgia lawmakers at a Georgia Senate subcommittee meeting. Ellis also met with legislators in Arizona, Pennsylvania, and Michigan to promote similarly baseless claims of election fraud. Ellis faced two criminal charges in Fulton County. On October 24, 2023, Ellis entered into a plea agreement with Fulton County prosecutors. Ellis pleaded guilty to a felony charge of aiding and abetting false statements and writings. As part of the agreement, Ellis will be sentenced to five years' probation, pay $5,000 in restitution, and perform 100 hours of community service. She agreed to cooperate fully with Fulton County prosecutors as the case progresses.

Ellis, Katherine [NY]—An Assistant District Attorney in the Manhattan District Attorney's Major Economic Crimes Bureau.

Epshteyn, Boris▲ [DC/GA] ("Co-Conspirator 6")—A political consultant who has publicly said he helped Trump implement the plan to submit slates of electors claiming that they were "alternate" electors, rather than fraudulent electors. The Fulton County indictment states that "Individual 3"—reportedly Epshteyn—made false statements about election fraud at a November 19, 2020, press conference at Republican National Committee ("RNC") headquarters.

Fisher, Carolyn [GA] (Unindicted Co-Conspirator 10 or 11)—One of Georgia's sixteen illegitimate Trump electors.

Fitton, Tom [GA] (Unindicted Co-Conspirator 1)—A conservative activist reported to be unindicted co-conspirator 1 in the Fulton County indictment. The indictment alleges that Trump spoke with Fitton four days before the 2020 presidential election and discussed a draft of a speech that falsely claimed voter fraud and declared a Trump electoral victory.

Floyd, Harrison○ [GA]—A Trump supporter who, according to Fulton County prosecutors, attempted to intimidate a Georgia election worker. The indictment asserts that Floyd, the former leader of a group called "Black Voices for Trump," arranged a meeting between election worker Ruby Freeman and former Kanye West publicist Trevian Kutti. At the meeting, which Floyd joined by telephone, Kutti and Floyd allegedly pressured Freeman to admit to election fraud. Floyd faces two criminal charges in Fulton County.

Floyd, John [GA]—An Atlanta-based lawyer tapped by Fani Willis to work on the Trump investigation. Floyd is viewed as an expert in Georgia's racketeering law.

Freeman, Ruby [GA]—A Georgia election worker whom Trump and Giuliani falsely accused of committing election fraud. Trump repeatedly targeted Freeman by name, and she was harassed and threatened by Trump supporters who attempted to pressure her to admit to fraud.

Gaston, Molly [DC]—An experienced federal prosecutor in the District of Columbia who worked alongside J. P. Cooney on the high-profile investigations of Gregory Craig, Andrew McCabe, Roger Stone, and Steve Bannon.

Gilbert, Karen [FL]—A longtime federal prosecutor based in Miami. Gilbert formerly led the Narcotics Division of the US Attorney's Office for the Southern District of Florida, but she voluntarily stepped down from her leadership post in 2009 after she and her office were formally reprimanded for secretly recording witness interviews with defense attorneys as part of an investigation into potential witness tampering. Gilbert has remained an Assistant US Attorney.

Giuliani, Rudy○▲ [DC/GA] ("Co-Conspirator 1")—Trump's co-defendant and former personal attorney. He is named as a defendant in the Fulton County District Attorney's indictment and referred to as "co-conspirator 1" in the DOJ's January 6 indictment. Prosecutors claim that Giuliani spearheaded the Trump legal team's efforts to overturn the results of the 2020 presidential election. Giuliani repeatedly spread bogus claims about fraud in the 2020 presidential election and personally met with lawmakers in several states that Biden won in an attempt to convince them to adopt his baseless theories. Giuliani arranged a presentation to Georgia lawmakers at which he and other Trump lawyers promoted debunked theories of voter fraud and asked the Georgia state legislature not to recognize Georgia's legitimate, Biden-chosen electors. After Giuliani failed to persuade state legislatures not to recognize the legitimate electors, he helped carry out a new scheme to have slates of fake electors meet to declare themselves the true electors and send fraudulent certifications to the President of the Senate. In addressing the crowd of Trump supporters gathered in Washington, DC, on January 6, 2021, Giuliani called for "trial by combat" and declared that Mike Pence had the power to unilaterally stop the certification of the election. That night, after rioters had violently stormed the Capitol, Giuliani reportedly called seven members of Congress to ask them to further delay the certification of the election. Giuliani faces thirteen criminal charges in Fulton County.

Hackett, Joseph [DC]—A former member of the Oath Keepers who stormed the Capitol on January 6. Hackett was convicted of seditious conspiracy and destruction of evidence and received a three-and-a-half-year prison sentence.

Hall, Scott Graham○ [GA]—A pro-Trump poll watcher who prosecutors claim participated in Trump attorney Sidney Powell's plan to illegally access and tamper with Georgia voting machines. Hall faced seven criminal charges in Fulton County. On September 29, 2023, Hall became the first of the nineteen defendants to enter a guilty plea in the Fulton County criminal case. Under the terms of his plea agreement with Fulton County prosecutors, Hall pleaded guilty to five misdemeanor charges and was sentenced to five years' probation. He also agreed to testify in related court hearings and trials.

Halligan, Lindsey [FL]—A Florida-based lawyer who was present at Mar-a-Lago during the FBI's search for classified documents in August 2022 and has remained a member of Trump's defense team.

Hampton, Misty○ [GA]—A former Georgia election supervisor who, the indictment alleges, breached Georgia voting machines and provided illegal access to those machines to forensic data analysts working for Sidney Powell.

Harbach, David [FL]—A veteran DOJ public corruption prosecutor who has worked closely with Jack Smith in the past and left private practice to join the Special Counsel's team. As a federal prosecutor, Harbach tried high-profile corruption cases against former US senator John Edwards and former Virginia governor Bob McDonnell. Edwards was acquitted on one count and the jury deadlocked on the five remaining counts, which the government declined to retry; McDonnell was convicted at trial, but the United States Supreme Court later overturned his conviction. Harbach successfully prosecuted Rick Renzi, a former congressman from Arizona, on charges of corruption and money laundering.

Harrelson, Kenneth [DC]—A ground leader of the Oath Keepers' January 6 attack on the Capitol. Harrelson was convicted of several felonies and sentenced to four years in prison.

Harrington, Liz [FL] ("Staffer")—A Trump staffer who was present at a July 2021 Bedminster, New Jersey, meeting that was captured on tape. According to prosecutors, the tape shows Trump displaying a US plan related to attacking Iran—described by Trump as "highly confidential" and "secret"—to a writer, a publisher, and others who lacked security clearances.

Harrison, Hayley [FL] ("Trump Employee 1")—Melania Trump's chief of staff and a former Trump White House aide, Harrison allegedly helped move Trump's boxes between different rooms at Mar-a-Lago.

Hayes, Conan [GA] (Unindicted Co-Conspirator)—A former professional surfer, according to media reports, who was involved in Sidney Powell's alleged efforts to infiltrate voting machines in Coffee County, Georgia; Hayes was designated to receive data obtained from Georgia voting machines.

344   *Complete Cast of Characters*

Herschmann, Eric [DC] ("Senior Advisor")—A senior White House attorney who challenged Trump's attorneys' legal theories for keeping Trump in power.

Hoffinger, Susan [NY]—The Chief of the Investigation Division of the Manhattan District Attorney's Office. Hoffinger led the successful 2022 prosecution of two Trump organizations.

Howard, Dylan [NY] ("AMI Editor-in-Chief")—The former Chief Content Officer of AMI, who, according to the New York Statement of Facts, helped AMI's CEO, David Pecker, carry out the "catch and kill" scheme to suppress damaging stories about then-candidate Trump during the 2016 election. Howard allegedly notified Michael Cohen about the existence of the Karen McDougal and Stormy Daniels stories and connected Cohen with Daniels's lawyer.

Hulser, Raymond [DC]—An experienced prosecutor from the Justice Department's Public Integrity Section. Hulser served as Jack Smith's deputy at the Public Integrity Section and later succeeded Smith as the section's chief. Hulser's notable cases include prosecutions of Senator Bob Menendez and Trump White House trade advisor Peter Navarro. Menendez's case ended with a hung jury and was not retried; Navarro was convicted of contempt of Congress.

Jacob, Greg [DC] ("Vice President's Counsel")—Former Counsel to Vice President Pence. According to the January 6 committee report, Jacob met with John Eastman on multiple occasions and was present at the meeting in which Trump and Eastman tried to convince Pence to reject the electoral votes of seven states. Jacob testified that Pence rejected their idea that as vice president he could reject the electoral votes.

Jones, Burt [GA] (Unindicted Co-Conspirator 8)—The Lieutenant Governor of Georgia and one of Georgia's sixteen illegitimate electors for Trump. On December 7, 2020, Jones sent a tweet telling Georgians to call their representatives and demand a special session of the General Assembly—a session he allegedly sought for the purpose of appointing fake electors.

Kemp, Brian [GA]—The Governor of Georgia. Trump repeatedly tried to enlist Kemp, a Republican, to help him overturn the results of the 2020 presidential election in Georgia. Kemp pushed back on Trump's claims of voter fraud and declined to interfere with the legitimate election results.

Kerik, Bernard [GA] (Unindicted Co-Conspirator 5)—The former Commissioner of the New York City Police Department under then-Mayor Rudy

Giuliani. Kerik, a Trump supporter and convicted felon, allegedly accompanied Giuliani to meetings with Arizona and Pennsylvania lawmakers in which Giuliani promoted false claims about election fraud.

Kise, Christopher [FL]—A veteran defense lawyer and the former Solicitor General of Florida. Kise, who recently joined a small Florida-based law firm, has successfully argued several cases before the Supreme Court. He joined Trump's legal team in 2022 and is defense counsel in various Trump criminal and civil cases.

Kutti, Trevian C.○ [GA]—A Chicago-based publicist and Trump supporter who prosecutors allege traveled to Georgia to pressure an election worker. Kutti, formerly the publicist to R. Kelly and Kanye West, traveled to election worker Ruby Freeman's Fulton County home and unsuccessfully attempted to speak with her. Kutti then called Freeman on the phone and warned her that she was in danger and offered to meet with her at a police department precinct. According to the Georgia indictment, Kutti met with Freeman at the precinct and pressured her to admit to election fraud. Kutti faces three criminal charges in Fulton County.

Lambert, Stefanie [GA] (Unindicted Co-Conspirator)—A Michigan lawyer who prosecutors allege worked with Sidney Powell to overturn the 2020 election. According to media reporting, Lambert was one of the individuals designated to receive data obtained from Georgia voting machines. A Michigan special prosecutor charged Lambert with four felonies, including one related to willfully damaging a Michigan voting machine.

Latham, Cathleen Alston○ [GA]—The former head of the Republican Party in Coffee County, Georgia. According to the Fulton County indictment, Latham was both a fake elector for Trump and a participant in Trump attorney Sidney Powell's alleged efforts to illegally access Georgia voting machines. The Fulton County indictment alleges that Latham also committed perjury by lying to the grand jury about her role in the scheme. Latham faces eleven criminal charges in Fulton County.

Lauro, John [DC]—A former federal prosecutor in the Eastern District of New York and longtime white-collar criminal defense attorney. Lauro appeared on several Sunday talk shows as the public face of Trump's defense. In those appearances, Lauro has argued that Trump believed he won the election and was exercising his First Amendment rights to protest the results. Lauro is known for his defense of Tim Donaghy, a former NBA referee who admitted to betting on games he officiated.

Lee, Stephen○ [GA]—A Lutheran pastor from Illinois who, according to prosecutors, traveled to Georgia for the purpose of addressing so-called election fraud. According to the Georgia indictment, Lee knocked on the front door of Ruby Freeman's home in an attempt to get the election worker, whom Trump allies had targeted, to admit to election fraud. Lee faces five criminal charges in Fulton County.

Lenberg, Jeffrey [GA] (Unindicted Co-Conspirator)—A former employee at a National Nuclear Security Administration laboratory in New Mexico who, according to media reports, entered nonpublic areas of the Coffee County, Georgia, elections office as part of an effort to gain access to voting machines.

Little, Jennifer▲ [FL/GA] ("Trump attorney 2")—A former Georgia prosecutor and current Trump defense lawyer. Little has been identified as "Trump Attorney 2" in the DOJ's classified documents indictment, which maintains that she, along with Evan Corcoran, met with Trump at Mar-a-Lago to plan Trump's response to the DOJ's subpoena for classified documents. Trump allegedly told Little that she need not be present during Corcoran's search for responsive documents, and she did not do so. Little runs her own law firm in Atlanta and has been a member of Trump's Fulton County defense team since the case's inception.

Logan, Doug [GA] (Unindicted Co-Conspirator)—The former head of cybersecurity firm Cyber Ninjas. Media reports allege that Logan entered nonpublic areas of a Georgia election office and downloaded election data. Logan's firm was later hired by Republican state lawmakers in Arizona to conduct an audit of the Arizona election.

Mangold, Rebecca [NY]—An Assistant District Attorney in the Manhattan District Attorney's Major Economic Crimes Bureau. Mangold, formerly a partner at a prominent New York law firm, joined the office in 2022.

Martin, Margo [FL] ("Staffer")—A Trump staffer present at the July 2021 Bedminster meeting at which Trump showed what prosecutors allege is a classified plan relating to Iran to a writer, a publisher, and others.

McAfee, Judge Scott [GA]—The Georgia trial judge presiding over the Fulton County case. Previously the Georgia inspector general and a state and federal prosecutor, McAfee became a state court judge in 2023. McAfee once worked under Fani Willis at the Fulton County District Attorney's Office.

McCaw, Catherine [NY]—Counsel to the Investigation Division of the Manhattan District Attorney's Office. McCaw is known for her role as a lead lawyer in that office's successful prosecution of fake heiress Anna Sorokin (aka Anna Delvey), memorialized in the Netflix series *Inventing Anna*.

McConney, Jeffrey [NY] ("TO Controller")—The Trump Organization employee who, according to prosecutors, received Michael Cohen's false invoices for legal services and instructed the Trump Organization's accounts payable supervisor to fulfill them and record the payments as legal expenses. Prosecutors allege that, in reality, the payments reimbursed Cohen for the "hush money" payments that Cohen made to Stormy Daniels.

McDaniel, Ronna [DC] ("RNC Chair")—The chairwoman of the Republican National Committee. As revealed during the January 6 committee hearings and the Georgia indictment, Trump and John Eastman called McDaniel to seek her help in arranging the gatherings of Trump electors. McDaniel testified in the congressional investigation that Eastman assured McDaniel that the "contingent" electors' votes would be used only if Trump's litigation succeeded. McDaniel agreed to help and later updated Trump with the news that his electors had successfully met and cast their "votes."

McDougal, Karen [NY] ("Woman 1")—A former *Playboy* model who claims to have had a ten-month affair with Donald Trump. AMI, the then-owner of the *National Enquirer*, according to the New York Statement of Facts, paid McDougal $150,000 for the rights to her story in order to hide the alleged affair from the public until after the 2016 election. In a non-prosecution agreement with the US Attorney for the Southern District of New York, AMI stipulated that it made the payment to McDougal at the Trump campaign's request.

Mark Meadows○▲ [DC/GA] ("Chief of Staff")—Trump's co-defendant and last Chief of Staff, from March 2020 until January 20, 2021. Prior to that, he served for seven years as a congressman from North Carolina and was a leading member of the Freedom Caucus. In connection with his effort to "remove" the State of Georgia criminal charges against him to federal court for trial, Meadows testified at a federal hearing that all the alleged acts in the state indictment were undertaken by him as part of his official position as Chief of Staff. News reports have also suggested that Meadows may have testified under a grant of immunity before a federal grand jury investigating the January 6 insurrection.

Meggs, Kelly [DC]—The former leader of the Florida chapter of the Oath Keepers. Meggs was convicted of seditious conspiracy for his role in the January 6 attack on the Capitol and received a twelve-year prison sentence.

Merchan, Justice Juan [NY]—The New York trial judge presiding over the Manhattan District Attorney's case against Donald Trump. (In the New York State system, the Supreme Court of New York is a trial court and its trial judges are called justices.) Merchan, who has served in his current role since 2009, began his legal career as a prosecutor in the Manhattan DA's Office. Merchan oversaw the 2022 trial of two Trump organizations, which resulted in their conviction on all seventeen charged counts.

Michael, Molly [FL] ("Trump Employee 2")—A former Trump staffer who allegedly helped Walt Nauta handle the return of documents to the National Archives.

Miller, Butch [GA]—The former President Pro Tempore of the Georgia Senate. Trump and Giuliani made phone calls to Miller, a Republican, to attempt to convince him to call a special session of the Georgia General Assembly to appoint Trump's fraudulent slate of Georgia electors. Miller rejected Trump and Giuliani's requests.

Miller, Jason [DC] ("Senior Campaign Advisor")—A senior campaign advisor to Trump who allegedly spoke with Trump frequently and repeatedly told him that the election fraud claims being promoted by Rudy Giuliani's legal team were untrue.

Milley, Mark [FL] ("Senior Military Official")—The Chairman of the Joint Chiefs of Staff who Trump has publicly disparaged. As alleged by prosecutors, Trump appears to have shown the Iran classified material to the writer and publisher at Bedminster in order to rebut claims that Milley made.

Minuta, Roberto [DC]—A member of the Oath Keepers who attacked the Capitol on January 6. Minuta was convicted of seditious conspiracy and other felonies and sentenced to four-and-a-half years in prison.

Moerschel, David [DC]—A former member of the Oath Keepers who acted as a "battering ram" in the Oath Keepers' military-style stack formation that attacked the Capitol on January 6. Moerschel was convicted of seditious conspiracy and sentenced to three years in prison.

Moss, Shaye [GA]—A former Georgia poll worker falsely accused of running an illegal ballot scheme by Trump and his team. Trump supporters repeatedly threatened and harassed Moss and her mother, fellow poll worker Ruby Freeman, after Trump publicly alleged that they were responsible for election fraud.

Nauta, Waltine ("Walt")○ [FL]—Trump's co-defendant and personal aide. Nauta, a Navy valet stationed in the White House during the Trump presidency, became Trump's post-presidency personal aide and "body man." According to the DOJ indictment, Nauta helped oversee the handling of Trump's boxes of classified documents at Mar-a-Lago. Nauta—

acting at Trump's direction—allegedly moved boxes containing classified documents from a Mar-a-Lago storage room to Trump's personal residence so that Trump could inspect them and conceal the fact of their existence—first from the National Archives, and later from Trump's own lawyers and the DOJ. The indictment alleges that Nauta lied to the FBI about his role in delivering the boxes of classified documents to Trump, and that Nauta and co-defendant Carlos De Oliveira worked unsuccessfully to delete security footage of a Mar-a-Lago storage room sought by the DOJ.

Necheles, Susan [NY]—A longtime New York criminal defense attorney. Necheles was a member of the 2022 trial team that unsuccessfully defended the Trump organizations against criminal charges brought by the Manhattan District Attorney's Office.

Ney, Adam [GA]—An Assistant District Attorney in the Fulton County DA's Office.

Nordean, Ethan [DC]—A former Proud Boys leader and commander in the January 6 attack on the Capitol. Nordean was convicted of multiple felonies, including seditious conspiracy, and sentenced to eighteen years in prison.

Pecker, David [NY] ("AMI CEO")—According to the prosecution, the former Chairman and CEO of AMI was integral to the scheme to suppress negative stories about then-candidate Trump during the 2016 presidential election. Shortly after Trump launched his 2016 campaign, Pecker allegedly met with Trump and Michael Cohen in Trump Tower and agreed to help Trump's campaign by devising a "catch and kill" scheme: Pecker would alert Trump to the existence of stories that could damage Trump's electoral prospects so that Trump could buy the rights to those stories to prevent their publication. Pecker approved AMI's purchases of three salacious and potentially damaging stories about Trump.

Penrose, Jim [GA] (Unindicted Co-Conspirator)—A former NSA officer and the current president of a cybersecurity company. Media reporting maintains that Penrose downloaded data from Georgia voting machines and instructed the Chief Operating Officer of SullivanStrickler, the company that collected the data, to send the data to Trump attorney Sidney Powell.

Pezzola, Dominic [DC]—A New York Proud Boy who attacked the Capitol on January 6. Pezzola, who helped ignite the breach of the Capitol by smashing a window with a stolen police riot shield, was convicted of multiple felonies and sentenced to ten years in prison.

Powell, Sidney○▲ [DC/GA] ("Co-Conspirator 3")—Trump's co-defendant and former attorney. Powell was a defendant in the Fulton County indictment and is referred to as "co-conspirator 3" in the DOJ's January 6 indictment. Powell is alleged to have concocted and promulgated several outlandish election fraud claims advanced by Trump and his team. Though Trump privately acknowledged that Powell sounded "crazy," he promoted her theories and considered appointing her special counsel with broad authority to investigate voter fraud. Powell claimed that a network of rigged voting machines—set up by former Venezuelan president Hugo Chávez, who died in 2013, and controlled by the likes of Democratic billionaire George Soros and Antifa—had switched Trump votes to Biden votes. Powell claimed without basis that the manufacturer of the voting machines, Dominion Voting Systems, had bribed the governor and secretary of state of Georgia, and she launched a failed lawsuit against the governor of Georgia that alleged "massive election fraud" accomplished through voting machine software and hardware. The Georgia indictment charged Powell with engaging a private forensic data company to access voting machines in Georgia and Michigan. Powell pleaded guilty in Georgia to misdemeanor criminal charges related to her participation in this scheme. She will serve six years' probation, pay a $6,000 fine, as well as $2,700 to the Georgia Secretary of State's Office, and is required to testify truthfully at future hearings and trials related to the Georgia criminal case.

Raffensperger, Brad [GA]—The Secretary of State of Georgia. Raffensperger repeatedly refused Trump's requests that he overturn Georgia's election results and declare Trump the rightful winner. Trump, in a phone call with Raffensperger and other Georgia officials, asked Raffensperger to "find" him 11,780 votes—enough to overturn Trump's loss in Georgia.

Ralston, David [GA]—The former Speaker of the Georgia House of Representatives. Ralston, who died in November 2022, received phone calls from Trump urging him to call a special session of the Georgia General Assembly to recognize Trump's fraudulent slate of Georgia electors.

Raskin, David [FL]—David Raskin is a longtime federal prosecutor in Kansas City and New York and has extensive national security experience, including investigating and successfully prosecuting cases involving the illegal mishandling of classified documents.

Rehl, Zachary [DC]—The former leader of the Philadelphia chapter of the Proud Boys and a commander in the January 6 attack on the Capitol. Rehl, an ex-Marine, was convicted of seditious conspiracy and received a fifteen-year prison sentence.

Reynolds, Brett [FL]—A trial attorney in the Justice Department's National Security Division.

Rhodes, Elmer Stewart [DC]—The founder of the far-right extremist group known as the Oath Keepers and a leader of the January 6 attack on the Capitol. Rhodes was convicted of seditious conspiracy and sentenced to eighteen years in prison.

Roman, Michael○ [GA]—Trump's co-defendant and former campaign staffer. Prosecutors allege that Roman helped coordinate Trump's attorneys' efforts to convene slates of illegitimate electors in seven states so that those electors could submit fraudulent votes for Trump. Roman faces seven criminal charges in Fulton County.

Root, Grant [GA]—A senior attorney in the Civil Forfeiture Unit of the Fulton County DA's Office.

Rosen, Jeffrey [DC] ("Acting Attorney General")—The former Acting Attorney General who repeatedly told Trump that his various claims about election fraud were untrue. Trump asked Rosen to announce that the DOJ was investigating fraud in the election and, when Rosen refused, threatened to replace him with Jeffrey Clark (which he did for part of January 3, 2021). Trump ultimately backed down when attorneys from the DOJ and White House Counsel's Office threatened to resign if Rosen was fired.

Sadow, Steven [GA]—A veteran criminal defense lawyer based in Atlanta. In August 2023, Trump overhauled his Fulton County defense team, hiring Sadow to replace his former lead counsel. Sadow rose to prominence defending several high-profile recording artists, including Usher, Rick Ross, and T.I. More recently, Sadow represented Atlanta rapper Gunna in a racketeering case brought by Willis's office. In that case, the rapper entered a negotiated deal, pleading guilty without admitting to criminal conduct, and was released from jail.

Sajudin, Dino [NY] ("Doorman")—A former Trump Tower doorman who, in 2015, claimed to know about a child that Trump fathered out of wedlock. AMI paid Sajudin $30,000 for the rights to his story in order to suppress it. As New York prosecutors allege, AMI made the payments as part of the "catch and kill" scheme with Trump and Cohen. Prosecutors allege that when AMI later concluded that the story was false, Cohen told AMI's CEO not to release Sajudin from his confidentiality agreement until after the presidential election.

Sanders, Todd [GA] (Unindicted Co-Conspirator)—A cybersecurity analyst. Media reports claim that Sidney Powell designated Sanders to receive data obtained from Georgia voting machines.

Shafer, David○ [GA]—The former chairman of the Republican Party in Georgia and a former Georgia State Senator. According to the Georgia indictment, Shafer falsely portrayed himself as the "chairman" of the electoral college in Georgia and convened a meeting of Georgia's sixteen fake electors at the Georgia State Capitol in which the fraudulent electors signed a certificate falsely representing that they were Georgia's legitimate electors. Prosecutors maintain that Shafer, who was himself one of the sixteen fake electors, subsequently helped transmit the fraudulent electoral votes to the Archivist of the United States and President of the United States Senate. Shafer faces eight criminal charges in Fulton County.

Shirkey, Mike [DC] ("Michigan Senate Majority Leader")—The former Michigan Senate Majority Leader whom Trump unsuccessfully pressured to reject Michigan's legitimate electors and instead appoint Trump's fraudulent slate of electors.

Short, Marc [DC] ("Vice President's Chief of Staff")—Former Chief of Staff to Vice President Pence. Short testified in the January 6 committee investigation that he was present at the meeting in which Trump and John Eastman tried to convince Pence to reject the electoral votes of seven states and declare Trump president. According to the January 6 indictment, on January 5, 2021, Short became so concerned about Pence's safety the following day that he alerted the head of Pence's Secret Service detail to his concerns.

Sinners, Robert [GA] (Unindicted Co-Conspirator 4)—A former Trump campaign staffer. Media reports indicate that Sinners, who is apparently identified as Individual 4 in the Georgia indictment, played a role in carrying out the fake elector scheme. Documents uncovered by the January 6 congressional committee show that Sinners instructed Georgia's fake electors to maintain "complete secrecy" about their work. Sinners is now a spokesman for Georgia Secretary of State Brad Raffensperger and has renounced his views about election fraud.

Smith, Jack▲ [DC/FL]—The Special Counsel overseeing the DOJ's investigation of Donald Trump. Smith, who was appointed by Attorney General Merrick Garland in November 2022, is heading both federal prosecutions of Trump—the classified documents case and the January 6 case. Smith is a longtime federal and state prosecutor whose former roles include serving as the Chief of the DOJ's Public Integrity Section, the Acting US Attorney for the Middle District of Tennessee, an Assistant US Attorney in the Eastern District of New York, and an Assistant District Attorney in the Manhattan District Attorney's Office. Smith left his post as the chief prosecutor in the Kosovo Specialist Prosecutor's Office to become DOJ Special Counsel.

Smith, Ray, III○ [GA]—A former Trump campaign attorney. Smith, along with several other Trump campaign lawyers, presented false claims about election fraud to a group of Georgia lawmakers who were present at a Georgia Senate subcommittee meeting. Smith's false statements included allegations that over 10,000 dead people and over 60,000 underaged people voted in Georgia during the 2020 presidential election. Smith faces twelve criminal charges in Fulton County.

Stepien, Bill [DC] ("Campaign Manager")—Trump's 2020 campaign manager. Stepien has testified that he told the Trump team that claims about thousands of noncitizens voting in Arizona were false and that when Trump was dissatisfied with what he was hearing from his legal team headed by Justin Clark, he replaced Clark with Giuliani.

Still, Shawn Micah Tresher○ [GA]—One of Georgia's sixteen fake electors and, since 2023, a Georgia State Senator. Prosecutors allege that Still signed a fraudulent certificate in which he represented himself to be a legitimate elector of Georgia. Still faces seven criminal charges in Fulton County.

Tacopina, Joe [NY]—A New York criminal defense attorney. Tacopina represented Trump in the civil lawsuit brought by E. Jean Carroll—a case that resulted in a 2023 civil jury verdict in New York federal court that Trump had sexually abused and defamed Carroll and owed her $5 million in damages.

Tarasoff, Deborah [NY] ("TO Accounts Payable Supervisor")—The Trump Organization accounts payable supervisor who, according to the New York Statement of Facts, fulfilled the "hush money" reimbursement payments to Michael Cohen and recorded the payments as legal expenses.

Tarrio, Enrique [DC]—The former national leader of the Proud Boys and a plotter of the January 6 attack on the Capitol. Tarrio was convicted of seditious conspiracy and received a twenty-two-year prison sentence.

Taveras, Yuscil [FL] ("Trump Employee 4")—The Mar-a-Lago IT director. According to the indictment, Walt Nauta and Carlos De Oliveira pressured Taveras to delete security footage sought by the DOJ. Tavares is cooperating with the DOJ.

Thakur, Michael [FL]—An Assistant US Attorney for the Southern District of Florida. Thakur has appeared in court on behalf of the federal government post-indictment.

Vallejo, Edward [DC]—A former member of the Oath Keepers who helped plot the January 6 attack on the Capitol. Vallejo did not enter the

Capitol on January 6 and instead remained on standby from a heavily armed Virginia hotel room. Vallejo was convicted of seditious conspiracy and sentenced to three years in prison.

Wade, Nathan [GA]—A private attorney and former prosecutor tapped by Fani Willis to lead the Trump investigation. Wade, who also serves as a municipal court judge in Cobb County, has been on Willis's team since early 2022.

Wakeford, Donald [GA]—A senior attorney in the Anti-Corruption Unit of the Fulton County DA's Office. Wakeford has been a prosecutor since 2016.

Waldron, Phil [GA] (Unindicted Co-Conspirator 6)—A former Army colonel trained in information warfare who, according to media reports, worked with Trump attorneys to spread false theories about election fraud. Waldron was present at a White House meeting between Rudy Giuliani and Pennsylvania legislators.

Watkins, Jessica [DC]—A former Oath Keepers leader and Army veteran who commanded an Ohio militia in the January 6 attack on the Capitol. Watkins was convicted of several felony charges and received an eight-and-a-half-year sentence.

Weiss, Stephen [FL]—A junior lawyer at Blanche Law, the small law firm that Todd Blanche, one of Trump's lead defense attorneys, established after agreeing to represent Trump.

Weisselberg, Allen [NY] ("TO CFO")—The former longtime Chief Financial Officer of the Trump Organization. According to the prosecution, Trump instructed Weisselberg to work with Cohen to arrange the $130,000 "hush money" payment to Stormy Daniels. Cohen paid Daniels's lawyer with his personal funds, and the prosecution alleges that Weisselberg devised a scheme to reimburse Cohen with checks—drawn from the Trump Organization's assets and Trump's personal bank account—that were falsely characterized as payments for legal services. In 2022, Weisselberg pleaded guilty to fifteen felony charges—each unrelated to the hush money payments to Daniels—that resulted from the Manhattan DA's investigation into the Trump Organization. Weisselberg served a five-month prison sentence under a plea deal with the New York prosecutors. He testified at the successful Trump organizations criminal trial in New York in 2022.

Whiting, Alex [DC]—A former Harvard Law School professor of practice and Jack Smith's successor as the acting specialist prosecutor at the Kosovo Specialist Prosecutor's Office. Whiting, who has also served as a federal prosecutor and as the Prosecutions Coordinator for the International Criminal Court, joined Smith's team in 2023.

Wiles, Susie [FL] ("PAC representative")—A Florida political consultant and Trump campaign advisor with whom Trump allegedly shared a classified map related to a foreign military operation. Trump allegedly told Wiles, who lacked a security clearance, that he should not show her the map. The DOJ indictment also alleges that Wiles was a member of an encrypted messaging chat group with Walt Nauta and an unnamed Trump employee in which the unnamed employee assured the group that Carlos De Oliveira remained loyal to Trump.

Willis, Fani [GA]—The Fulton County District Attorney. Willis, a longtime Fulton County prosecutor, was elected in 2020.

Windom, Thomas [DC]—A Maryland-based federal prosecutor who, since 2021, has been investigating Trump and his allies for election obstruction. Windom, whose investigation predated Smith's appointment as Special Counsel, was one of the first lawyers to join Smith's team.

Wooten, Will [GA]—A Deputy District Attorney in the White-Collar Crime Unit of the Fulton County DA's Office. Wooten, a former public defender, has worked in the Fulton County DA's Office since 2021.

Young, Daysha [GA]—An Executive District Attorney in the Special Victims Division of the Fulton County DA's Office. Young is a veteran prosecutor who has also worked in the DeKalb County DA's Office.